Emotive Language in Argumentation

This book analyzes the uses of emotive language and redefinitions from pragmatic, dialectical, epistemic, and rhetorical perspectives, investigating the relationship between emotions, persuasion, and meaning and focusing on the implicit dimension of the use of a word and its dialectical effects. It offers a method for evaluating the persuasive and manipulative uses of emotive language in ordinary and political discourse. Through the analysis of political speeches (including President Obama's Nobel Peace Prize address) and legal arguments, the book offers a systematic study of emotive language in argumentation, rhetoric, communication, political science, and public speaking.

Fabrizio Macagno is a Postdoctoral Researcher at the Universidade Nova de Lisboa, Portugal, where he teaches courses on argumentation theory and conducts research in the field of argumentation and communication. He is doing research in the field of argumentation and philosophy of language in cooperation with the University of Windsor, Ontario. His research interests are focused on the relationship between argumentation and semantics, which he investigates from epistemological, logical, and linguistic perspectives. He coauthored *Argumentation Schemes* (Cambridge, 2008). His articles have appeared in international peer-reviewed journals such as *Pragmatics and Cognition, Journal of Pragmatics, Argumentation, Ratio Juris, Philosophy & Rhetoric,* and *Informal Logic.*

Douglas Walton is a Professor of Philosophy, Assumption Chair in Argumentation Studies, and Distinguished Research Fellow of the Centre for Research in Reasoning, Argumentation and Rhetoric at the University of Windsor, Canada. His most recent book is *Argumentation Schemes*, coauthored with Chris Reed and Fabrizio Macagno (Cambridge, 2008). Walton's work has been used to better prepare legal arguments and to help develop artificial intelligence. His books have been translated worldwide, and he attracts students from many countries to study with him.

Emotive Language in Argumentation

FABRIZIO MACAGNO

Universidade Nova de Lisboa

DOUGLAS WALTON

University of Windsor

CAMBRIDGE
UNIVERSITY PRESS

CAMBRIDGE
UNIVERSITY PRESS

32 Avenue of the Americas, New York, NY 10013-2473, USA

Cambridge University Press is part of the University of Cambridge.

It furthers the University's mission by disseminating knowledge in the pursuit of education, learning, and research at the highest international levels of excellence.

www.cambridge.org
Information on this title: www.cambridge.org/9781107676657

© Fabrizio Macagno and Douglas Walton 2014

This publication is in copyright. Subject to statutory exception and to the provisions of relevant collective licensing agreements, no reproduction of any part may take place without the written permission of Cambridge University Press.

First published 2014

Printed in the United States of America

A catalog record for this publication is available from the British Library.

Library of Congress Cataloging in Publication data
Macagno, Fabrizio.
Emotive language in argumentation / Fabrizio Macagno, Universidade Nova de Lisboa, Douglas Walton, University of Windsor.
pages cm
Includes bibliographical references and index.
ISBN 978-1-107-03598-0 – ISBN 978-1-107-67665-7 (pbk.)
1. Reasoning. 2. Language and emotions. I. Title.
BC177.M227 2013
401′.4–dc23 2012050925

ISBN 978-1-107-03598-0 Hardback
ISBN 978-1-107-67665-7 Paperback

Cambridge University Press has no responsibility for the persistence or accuracy of URLs for external or third-party Internet Web sites referred to in this publication and does not guarantee that any content on such Web sites is, or will remain, accurate or appropriate.

For my family, with love. – F.M.
For Karen, with love. – D.W.

Contents

Acknowledgments   *page* xi

Introduction... 1

1 When Words Are Emotive 5
   1. Triggering Emotions by Defining Reality 5
      1.1. The Aristotelian Tradition 6
      1.2. Emotive Words and Definitions in the Latin Tradition. 8
   2. When Words Are Masks 15
      2.1. Omitting and Distorting 17
      2.2. Hiding Reality 19
   3. Modifying Meaning and Emotions: Persuasive Definitions 20
   4. Conclusion.. 28

2 The Emotions in Our Words 30
   1. The Force of Ethical Words 31
      1.1. The Dimensions of Emotive Meaning 31
      1.2. The Reasons behind Value Judgments. 33
      1.3. Reasons and Meanings 34
   2. The Structure of Emotive Words 36
      2.1. The Descriptive Meaning of Ethical Terms 36
      2.2. Emotive Meaning: Emotions Dependent and
           Independent of Reality 38
      2.3. Emotions Triggered by Words: Values in the Frames 41
   3. The Logical Dimension of Emotive Meaning: Reasoning
      from Values 45
      3.1. The Reasoning Process within Words 45
      3.2. The Prescriptive Meaning: Values as Principles of Action ... 47
   4. The Logic of Values. 50
      4.1. Argument from Values 51
      4.2. The Logical Components of Prescriptive Meaning. 54

    5. Hierarchies and Conflicts of Values 57
    6. The Reasonableness of Emotions 63
    7. Conclusion 67

3 When Words Are Reasoning: Definitions as Strategies of
    Classification 69
    1. Why Definitions Cannot Be Persuasive 70
    2. Definitions as Premises: Reasoning for Classifying 73
        2.1. The Logical Structure of Classification 74
        2.2. Reasoning from What Is Acceptable 78
        2.3. The Structure of Reasoning from Classification 80
    3. Definitions and Definitional Structure 84
    4. The Nature of Definition: The Tradition and the Theory of
       Predicables 88
    5. Strategies of Obscurity: The Correctness of Definitions 92
    6. Strategies of Circularity: The Logic of Prior Terms 96
    7. The Logical Force of Definition by Genus and Difference 102
        7.1. The Logic of the Genus 102
        7.2. Specifying the Genus 103
        7.3. The Logical Force of the Genus-Difference Definition 105
    8. Conclusion 107

4 The Acts of Defining 109
    1. How Definitions Can Change Reality 110
    2. The Acts of Defining 117
        2.1. Positive Acts of Defining 118
        2.2. Non-Negative Definitions 123
        2.3. Implicit Definitions 125
    3. Describing Speech Acts 128
    4. Speech Acts of Defining 131
        4.1. Defining for Informing 132
        4.2. Defining for Reminding 132
        4.3. Definitions as Standpoints 134
        4.4. Declaring a Definition 135
        4.5. Defining for Committing 137
    5. Acts of Non-Commitment 139
        5.1. Omitting Definitions 140
        5.2. Taking Redefinitions for Granted 142
    6. Strategies of Ambiguity 145
    7. Conclusion 152

5 What Our Words Hide: Presupposition and Dark-Side
    Commitments 154
    1. Presuppositions 155
    2. Presupposition Triggers 157
        2.1. Sentence Presuppositions: Semantic Presuppositions 158

2.2. Sentence Presuppositions: Syntactic Presuppositions...... 159
2.3. Inter-Sentence Presuppositions 160
2.4. Dialogical Presuppositions 162
2.5. Summary: Levels of Presupposition 166
3. How to Presuppose 166
  3.1. Sentence Presuppositions............................ 167
  3.2. Intra-Sentence Presuppositions 169
  3.3. Dialogical Presuppositions 170
4. The Dialectical and Rhetorical Force of Presupposition: The
  Act of Presupposing 171
  4.1. The Act of Presupposing............................. 171
  4.2. The Worlds Presupposed 174
5. The Limits of Presuppositions 175
  5.1. Accommodation 176
  5.2. The Conditions of Accommodation. 176
  5.3. The Conditions of Presupposing 178
6. Presuming Knowledge: Presupposition as Presumptive
  Reasoning 180
  6.1. Presumptive Reasoning.............................. 180
  6.2. Presumptions as Epistemic Bridges 182
  6.3. Assessing Presuppositions........................... 185
  6.4. Presuppositions as Presumptions 187
7. The Dialectics of Presupposition 187
  7.1. The Burdens of Presupposition 188
  7.2. Dialectical Uses of Presupposition 189
  7.3. Presupposing Redefinitions 192
  7.4. Redefining Values 194
8. Presuppositions as Rhetorical Strategies 196
  8.1. Presuppositions as Implicit Character Attacks. 197
  8.2. Presuppositions as Instruments to Alter the Weight of
    Evidence.. 199
  8.3. Presuppositions as Instruments for Fabricating
    Evidence.. 200
  8.4. Presuppositions as Instruments for Jumping to
    Conclusions 201
  8.5. The Rhetorical Power of Presuppositions 204
9. Conclusion... 204

6 Dialogues and Commitments.............................. 207
1. Persuasion Dialogues 208
  1.1. The Structure of Persuasion Dialogues 208
  1.2. Commitments and Persuasion Dialogues 210
2. Models of Persuasion Dialogues.......................... 213
  2.1. Persuasion Dialogue as a Type of Dialogue 213
  2.2. Persuasion Dialogue as a Critical Discussion............ 215

  3. Dark-Side Commitments. 217
     3.1. Dark-Side Moves 217
     3.2. Enthymemes and Common Knowledge. 219
  4. Use of Defeasible Reasoning in Persuasion Dialogues. 220
  5. Defeasible Reasoning in the Airbag Example. 223
  6. The Formal Dialogue System CK. 226
     6.1. Limits of the Existing Models. 226
     6.2. Developing Formal Dialogue Models. 227
     6.3. Rules of the CKP Dialogue System 229
     6.4. Argumentation in CKP 231
  7. Dialogues Containing Arguments about Definitions 232
     7.1. Persuasion Dialogues and Definitions 232
     7.2. Persuasion Dialogues and Persuasive Definitions 234
  8. Applying Argumentation Schemes to Persuasive
     Definitions in CKP 237
     8.1. Definitional Moves and Argumentation Schemes. 237
     8.2. Countermoves and Critical Questions 239
  9. Conclusions. 240

7 Metadialogues and Redefinitions 243
  1. Types of Definitions and Dialogue Moves 243
     1.1. Genus-Difference Definition 244
     1.2. Definite Description 245
     1.3. Definition by Etymology 246
     1.4. Definition by Essential Parts 247
     1.5. Definition by Material Parts 248
     1.6. Definition by Operation 248
     1.7. Definition by Negation 249
     1.8. Inductive Definition 250
     1.9. Definition by Example 251
    1.10. Definition by Metaphor 252
  2. Acts of Defining and Dialogue Commitment Structure. 253
     2.1. A. Advancing a Definition. 253
     2.2. B. Defining for Informing. 254
     2.3. C. Defining for Reminding. 255
     2.4. D. Declaring a Definition 256
     2.5. E. Defining for Committing 257
     2.6. F. Implicit Definition. 258
  3. Conclusion. 259

Conclusion 260

References   265
Index   281

Acknowledgments

We acknowledge support for the work in this book from the Portuguese Fundação para a Ciência ea Tecnologia (research grant on Argumentation, Communication and Context PTDC/FIL-FIL/110117/2009) and the Social Sciences and Humanities Research Council of Canada (Insight Grant 435-2012-0104).

For discussions on topics that related to chapters of the book, we thank Floris J. Bex, J. Anthony Blair, Thomas F. Gordon, Marcello Guarini, Hans V. Hansen, Cate Hundelby, Ralph Johnson, Erik C. W. Krabbe, Steven Patterson, Robert C. Pinto, Henry Prakken, Eddo Rigotti, and Andrea Rocci. We also thank Rita Campbell for composing the index, Lynn Fraser for helping us with the task of the final proofreading, and the international law firm of Martinez & Novebaci for providing materials and consulting on legal issues.

Fabrizio Macagno thanks in particular João Saagua, who made it possible to write this book and continue to develop his research in argumentation theory, for all his trust and enthusiasm. A special thought to Eddo Rigotti, from whom he learned what he knows about linguistics and argumentation, and from whom he received his love for these disciplines.

He special thanks to his family, who has always supported, helped, and encouraged him through the years.

Douglas Walton thanks Giovanni Sartor for his work with him at the European University Institute in Florence in 2012 on legal argumentation (funded by a Fernand Braudel Research Fellowship). Special thanks also go to Christopher W. Tindale who, as Director of the Centre for Research in Reasoning, Argumentation and Rhetoric (CRRAR), provided research facilities and a stimulating intellectual work environment.

Introduction

Words are often used to describe reality, to refer to objects, and to communicate feelings, desires, and emotions. Words can be powerful. They can move us, they can frighten us, and they can lead us to action. Words have been described as tools and weapons, as signs and masks. Words have been described as instruments having the force of creating and changing reality. They have been investigated with regard to their semantic structures, their co-occurrences, and their syntactic combinations. Even so, we rarely realize that words can be arguments. In this book we show how they can be moves that guide us toward judgment or action and function as speech acts that allow certain replies and prevent others. In everyday communications we hardly consider that complex forms of reasoning lie under their uses, and that these forms of reasoning are interwoven with meaning presumptions and dialogical games. In our words we can conceal an implicit change of our interlocutor's knowledge or a silent alteration of his system of values. These are powerful effects, but they typically go unnoticed.

When Chesterton claimed in one of his famous paradoxical quotes that "Impartiality is a pompous name for indifference, which is an elegant name for ignorance" (Chesterton, *The Speaker*, 15 December 1900), he did much more than simply describe impartiality. He condensed an attack on a commonly accepted and widely praised implication in a definition, an argument reversing the shared hierarchy of values. When politicians refuse to define 'terrorism' or 'torture,' or when they use words like 'peace' and 'hostilities' with new definitions, they cannot be accused of distorting reality or telling lies. They are simply performing a much more powerful action – changing the rules of the game of discourse. When science and knowledge are used "to provide long words to cover the errors of the rich" (Chesterton, *Heretics*, 88), they are employed to provide instruments for forcing the hearer to accept actions, thereby allowing the speaker to avoid commitment or justification of a kind that might normally be required. Words employed in this way are clever dialectical moves, implicit arguments

1

that not only escape the normal burden to provide reasons for a conclusion, but at the same time lead the hearer to a value judgment or a decision and implicitly modify his possible reactions.

The argumentative and dialectical structures of words emerge in so-called emotive words. Words like 'ignorance,' 'indifference,' 'peace,' or 'terrorism' are emotive in the sense that they are used to elicit emotions or change our evaluation of reality. In the *Brains Trust* program on BBC Radio, Bertrand Russell gave three examples of emotive conjugations:

> I am firm, you are obstinate, he is a pig-headed fool.
> I am righteously indignant, you are annoyed, he is making a fuss over nothing.
> I have reconsidered the matter, you have changed your mind, he has gone back on his word.

This format mimics the form of a grammatical conjugation of an irregular verb to illustrate the natural tendency to use emotive language to label one's own point of view on a controversial matter in a different way from views attributed to others, especially those who take opposing views. This way of using emotively loaded language is highly familiar to all of us. We use it all the time without reflecting very deeply on what we are doing.

These examples are meant to be humorous to make a point, but they dramatically reveal the power of a very common argumentation maneuver of using emotive language to subtly glide over the need to offer support for a claim you are making that implies that, on some issue being discussed, you are right and your opponents are wrong. One problem with the use of this kind of tactic, from a logical point of view, is that it covers up that an argument is being put forward that depends on using words in an argumentative way, words that are likely to be vague and undefined and whose meanings are very much at issue. This way of proceeding can be hard to combat, for its proponent has seemed to have established that she is in the right in only a few slick words, while the respondent has to struggle to question or counteract the argument by getting into difficult territory. He has to start talking about meanings of words and definitions and about emotive language, easily risking seeming to be picky or even incoherent.

The seriousness of this kind of tactic when it is used in argumentation on things we really care about becomes readily evident in the abortion dispute, where one side chooses the term 'pro-life' to define its position while the other side chooses the term 'pro-choice.' How can anybody be against choice? How can anybody be against life? These are fundamental values, especially in a setting of democratic deliberations.

The pro-life side defines 'abortion' as the deliberate killing of a human being, equivalent to the crime of murder. For example, according to a quotation from Pope John Paul II's encyclical letter on the value and inviolability of human life (Mazilu 2011: 1212), the Second Vatican Council defines abortion, together with infanticide, as an "unspeakable crime": "[P]rocured abortion is the deliberate and direct killing, by whatever means it is carried out, of a human being in the initial phase of his or her existence, extending from conception to birth." By classifying the action of an abortion under this category, this definition of abortion has attached to it a conclusion drawn by inference that abortion is wrong.

In contrast, the pro-choice definition of an abortion describes the embryo, a newly fertilized ovum, or fetus that is removed as a clump of tissues that is a product of conception and definitely not a baby, that is, a human being. To support this definition, a distinction is drawn between a potential human being and a real human being, where the embryo, newly fertilized ovum, or fetus (however you describe it) is classified as only a potential human being (Mazilu 2011: 1216). The opposition between this pro-choice definition and the pro-life one can be specified clearly. On this definition, we can no longer classify what is removed during the procedure of an abortion as a human being, since it is only a clump of cells that may have the potential to be a human being but is not a *real* human being. By classifying the action of an abortion under this different category, the pro-choice definition of abortion cancels the conclusion drawn by inference that abortion is wrong.

The abortion dispute has become so polarized and stylized as a public debate in recent years that those of us who are not so strongly committed to one side or the other in a dogmatic way can easily recognize that some funny business is going on when these key terms are being defined in a one-sided way to support the claims of opposing advocacy groups. But the same phenomenon is more widely present in everyday conversational arguments where many of us are more likely to be deceived by it. Indeed, for practitioners of advocating a cause, this method of strategic maneuvering using emotive language and persuasive definitions is an important rhetorical skill (Zarefsky 2006). For example, conservatives like to exploit popular prejudice by using the loaded term 'bureaucracy' when they argue for reducing spending on government agencies. Once the audience accepts the equation of government and bureaucracy, the case for reducing bureaucracy by cutting taxes becomes more acceptable. This rhetorical tactic is described in Debatepedia:[1]

Who could complain if Republicans want to reduce these "armies of bureaucrats"? Everyone knows that we would all be better off with less bureaucracy and fewer bureaucrats in our lives. So when conservatives want to make shrinking government sound attractive, they say they are cutting 'bureaucracy' – not 'programs'. Most people value government programs – especially in the areas of education, health and the environment – and do not want to see them reduced; but everyone hates

---

[1] http://debatepedia.idebate.org/en/index.php/Debate:_Big_government (accessed on 11 October 2011).

bureaucracy. Using the term 'bureaucracy' in this way is a rhetorical sleight-of-hand that obscures the real costs of cutting back on government programs.

Politicians, and indeed anyone engaged in advocacy argumentation in the marketplace, learn to be nimble in the use of emotive language in order to gain advantages over their opponents, while realizing that these opponents will use the very same tactics to try to get the best of them. Both sides become skilled in building their arguments on premises containing emotive language that has a positive spin accepted by the majority of the stakeholders that need to be convinced to move action forward.

In this book we show how such a use of emotive language and persuasive definitions is an argumentation tactic of strategic maneuvering in virtually every argument that takes place in conversational argumentation on matters we routinely discuss and argue about in politics, law, and other matters of national and international importance. We provide many examples of such arguments that reveal the scope and special characteristics of the tactic as a form of argumentation. Based on our analyses of these examples we build a theory that can be applied to these and many other common examples of verbal argumentation. We provide a theoretical understanding of how these linguistic mechanisms work to be used to deal with and counteract these clever tactics of the artfull employment of emotive language.

1

When Words Are Emotive

Some words are powerful. 'War,' 'peace,' 'death,' 'terrorist,' and 'security' are but a few of the innumerable terms that we read or hear every day, and these words clearly lead us to draw a judgment, or feel uncomfortable with, or be attracted by a certain situation. When we encounter words of this kind, we do not simply interpret the message. We do not simply acquire new information. We do not simply modify our systems of belief. We feel an emotion toward what the word is depicting. We fear a war. We are afraid of terrorists. We desire peace. We love children. These words are emotive because they trigger our emotions. They influence the way we regard the reality they represent. They affect our decisions concerning their referents. The emotive power of these words can make them extremely effective instruments to direct and encourage certain attitudes and choices. But at the same time, the very emotions that they evoke make them subtle tools to manipulate the other's decisions and feelings. Names can be used to conceal reality instead of representing it, to distort the facts instead of describing them, and to omit qualities and particulars instead of depicting them. Names have meanings that can be changed and modified, so that they can be used to classify what they otherwise could not mean. Their definitions can be altered and the emotions they carry directed toward new objects. For these reasons, ever since the ancient studies on rhetoric, emotive words have been regarded as crucial instruments for persuasion and manipulation. The first step to understand what lies beneath them is to analyze how they are used and the effects they can cause.

1. Triggering Emotions by Defining Reality

In the ancient tradition, rhetoricians, dialecticians, and philosophers noticed how the use of emotive words was an extremely effective rhetorical strategy. They investigated the different possible uses and effects according to the contexts of use and classified them as fallacies or rhetorical tactics. This ancient concern with the uses and abuses of emotive language is even more important to the study of public discourse than it was then. Orwell (1949), in his book *1984*, pointed out how words can hide and change reality, and bring people to accept and even support an otherwise unacceptable situation. The Ministry for Internal Security, in charge of social control and repression, was called the Ministry of Love; in the political campaigns war was called peace, freedom slavery, and ignorance strength (Orwell 1949: 10). The uses of loaded language have been investigated in modern studies of emotive language, as we will see in this chapter, showing how they can be strategic or deceitful and highlighting their relationship with meaning and reference.

1.1. *The Aristotelian Tradition*

The power of emotive words can be shown in several discourse contexts. However, it is in legal discussions that its effects can be clearly ascertained, and its abusive uses detected by referring to precise rules and procedures. It is from legal argumentation that it is possible to draw one of the first detailed analyses of emotive words. In his *Rhetoric*, when describing the apparent enthymemes, or fallacious techniques, Aristotle treats a rhetorical strategy called *amplificatio* (see Calboli Montefusco 2004), or "indignant language" (*Rhetoric*, 1401b, 3–7):

> We do this when we paint a highly-coloured picture of the situation without having proved the facts of it: if the defendant does so, he produces an impression of his innocence; and if the prosecutor does, he produces an impression of the defendant's guilt.

This technique is also used nowadays in courts, especially in criminal cases, where the emotions of the jury can be appealed to elicit a specific judgment. A famous case is the following (*Ivey v. State*, 113 Ga. 1062, 1901; emphasis added):

> CASE 1
>
> [...] solicitor-general, in his address to the the jury, used the following language: "Gentlemen of the jury, I want you to stand by me and help me break up this **vile den;**" and "Gentlemen of the jury, if you could go over this town and see the good mothers whose **pillows have been wet with tears over their boys who have been intoxicated by the acts of this woman.**"

This speech clearly arouses the jury's emotions. Words such as 'vile den' are used to denigrate the defendant and his witnesses; a tragic picture is drawn using terms depicting suffering ('tears,' 'pillows') and outrageous actions committed against the innocent ('boys,' 'intoxicated'). The prosecutor focused his closing statement on the effects of the defendant's actions, and the character and poor reliability of the opposing party. He amplifies the effects of the accused's crime, but the very responsibility of the crime was the actual point at stake in the trial; he attacks the witnesses' and defendant's characters without previously proving their unreliability. The prosecutor uses indignant language to "substantially prejudice the defendant or serve no purpose other than to inflame the jury" (*People v. Terry*, 460 N.E.2d 746, 1984).

As Grimaldi (1988) and Calboli Montefusco (2004) put it, amplification needs to be considered as an argument, that is, a conclusion backed by a set of implicit premises. The use of emotive language in the aforementioned case is aimed at eliciting a value judgment – that the defendant's crime was horrible and that he and his witnesses are unreliable. However, this value judgment hides a set of implicit assumptions. A crime is horrible if it is particularly violent, or unmotivated, or cruel, and so on. But first, a defendant's crime can be outrageous only if he committed it, and a witness's testimony can be unreliable only if there is a reason to believe it. Both assumptions are not stated; they are taken for granted even though they are not shared by the interlocutor. In this fashion, the emotions aroused are not based on facts (the defendant's responsibility for the crime, the false declarations of the witnesses) that have been previously accepted, shared, or at least proven. On the contrary, they are triggered by events that the speaker sets up. Emotions can therefore conceal facts not accepted or not acceptable by the interlocutor.

Aristotle noticed that the use of words has a twofold dimension. On the one hand, the use of a word needs to be grounded on facts, or rather a shared representation of the state of affairs that needs to be classified in a certain fashion. For instance, if a person is called a 'criminal,' he must have committed a crime. On the other hand, words have a shared meaning, and such a meaning is the ground for our classification of reality. For instance, we can classify a person as a 'murderer' because we proceed from the fact he willingly killed a man, and from the definition of murder as the "willful killing of a human being." In Aristotle's view, naming is a process of reasoning, as he explains in the chapter of the *Rhetoric* dedicated to the *topoi*, used to draw reasonable conclusion. The speakers, by "making definitions and grasping the essence of a thing, draw syllogistic conclusions about the subject they are discussing" (*Rhetoric*, 1398a 25–26). Aristotle gives the following example (*Rhetoric*, 1398a 23–24):

CASE 2

And [another is] the reason Socrates gave for refusing to visit Archelaus: for he said *hybris* was just as much an inability on the part of those benefited to return a favor as [it was the retaliation by] those harmed.

In this case, the problem is to classify Socrates' action as 'insolent' (or rather "aimed at shaming the victim"). Aristotle shows that Socrates' reasoning proceeds from the meaning of *hybris*, from the fundamental characteristic of "failing to requite benefits or injuries." Since Socrates suffered an injury, he did not want to be considered as insolent, and therefore requited the

insult received. In this case, the use of the emotive word (in Greek society, an extremely serious offense against honor; see Fisher, 1992) is based
on a commonly shared definition and a premise left implicit (Socrates was
offended by Archelaus).

Aristotle clarified the fundamental relationships between the definition
of a word and its use, and between the use of an emotive word and its dialogical effect. He highlighted the reasoning dimension of classifying reality,
pointing out how it can be made explicit to strengthen the classification, or
be distorted to inappropriately name a state of affairs. In discussing apparent
enthymemes, Aristotle showed how the inappropriate use of a word was also
the result of faulty reasoning. For instance, he provided the example of Paris,
who was called 'high-minded' because (*Rhetoric*, 1401b 20–22):

CASE 3

[…] in the *Alexander* [the claim] that [Paris] was "high-minded"; for looking down
on the society of the multitude he passed his time by himself on Mount Ida. [The
argument is] that because the high-minded have this quality, he, too, should be
thought high-minded.

In this case, instead of proceeding from the meaning, and therefore the
definition, of "to be high minded" the speaker uses characteristics that are
usually associated with high minded people. This type of reasoning is a form
of affirming the consequent: since high minded people usually despise society and live by themselves, a person behaving in this fashion is high-minded.

Aristotle therefore emphasized the reasoning dimension of emotive
words. They are described as forms of implicit arguments, because they are
grounded on a classificatory reasoning and lead to a further conclusion,
usually a value judgment. For these reasons, the use of emotive words can
be deceptive because they are grounded on premises left implicit but not
shared by the hearer. On the one hand, the speaker can take for granted
facts that have not been proven or accepted (the defendant is named a
"*horrible* criminal" without being proven to have committed the crime he is
charged with). On the other hand, he can distort the definition on which
he is grounding his classification, or advancing a weak conclusion, based on
a defective pattern of reasoning (a man is called high-minded because he
behaves as high-minded people usually do). This approach was later developed in the Latin tradition, where the two dimensions of emotive words,
the classification of reality (which can be called the predicative dimension)
and the emotive reaction they trigger, were investigated in Cornificius',
Cicero's, and Quintilian's rhetorical works.

1.2 *Emotive Words and Definitions in the Latin Tradition*
In the Latin rhetorical tradition, the investigation of the predicative
dimension of emotive words was strictly related to definition. In the

Rhetorica ad Herennium, Cornificius distinguishes between two strategies: the inappropriate use of an emotive word, hiding or altering the facts on which its predication rests, and the redefinition of a concept, which will be used later to support a classification. These two moves based on the meaning and the effects of words were treated under two separate stages of the ancient subdivision of argumentative discussions. In the Latin rhetorical tradition, the structure of legal (and ordinary) controversies was analyzed by means of a four-step process called *stasis* (Heath 1994; Braet 1987; Marsh 2005). These four levels of inquiry, corresponding to four types of issues or questions that can be raised and dealt with in a discussion, were the *conjectura* (question of fact), *finis* (question of definition), *qualitas* (question of quality or rather qualification), and *translatio* (question of jurisdiction, or procedure) (see Barwick 1965: 96, Ciceronis, *De Inventione,* 10–11). After establishing the *facts* (e.g., the defendant killed the victim using a knife), the problem is to name them, that is, to *define* reality. For instance, was the killing murder or manslaughter? Depending on the definitions of the crimes, and the concepts thereof, the classification may be different (Ranney 2005: 118). For instance, in some definitions the killing needs to be intentional; in others, it is only sufficient that the homicide caused intentional harm from which unintentional death resulted (*R. v. Buzzanga and Durocher* 49 C.C.C. (2d) 369, Ont. C.A. 1979). If manslaughter is the "unlawful killing of a human being without malice or premeditation, either express or implied," depending on how 'malice' is defined, a homicide can be immediately classified as murder, or may be subject to controversies. Is the use of a weapon a definitional characteristic of malice? Once facts have been named, they can be qualified. The seriousness of a crime can be mitigated, or aggravated, by the circumstances. Finally, the procedure is assessed. Is the jurisdiction the right one? Is the judge competent? The statuses of definition and qualification are the sources of two different strategies of uses of emotive words: redefinition and amplification, or rather, persuading by altering the meaning and altering the facts.

1.2.1. Emotive Redefinitions – Hiding the Meaning As seen previously, the classification, or naming, of a fragment of reality is grounded on a particular definition of the word used. However, in Quintilian's view, definitions are instruments that serve a particular purpose, and therefore should be chosen according to one's communicative goal (*Institutio Oratoria,* VII, 3, 20, 21):

> On the other hand, we shall ensure the right definition, if we first make up our minds what it is precisely that we desire to effect: for, this done, we shall be able to suit our words to serve our purpose.

A definition, from this perspective, is an extremely effective instrument for a speaker to achieve his goal in a discussion or to prevent the other party from achieving his own. A definition can be broadened or narrowed, so that the name can be applied to certain facts (Tellegen-Couperus 2003: 175). For instance, consider the following case (*Institutio Oratoria*, VII, 3, 21–22):

DEFINITION OF 'SACRILEGE'

A man who has stolen private money from a temple is accused of sacrilege. [...] It is therefore debated whether the act constitutes sacrilege. The accuser employs this term on the ground that the money was stolen from a temple: the accused denies that the act is sacrilege, on the ground that the money stolen was private property, but admits that it is theft. The prosecutor will therefore give the following definition: "It is sacrilege to steal anything from a sacred place." The accused will reply with another definition: "It is sacrilege to steal something sacred."

In this case, the definition of 'sacrilege' was at stake. This concept was controversial at the time. The narrow, legal definition[1] (stealing something sacred from a sacred place) conflicted with a commonly accepted broader meaning (stealing from a sacred place) (see Schaff 1894: 2094). In this case, the prosecutor chose to use the commonly shared meaning in order to classify the deeds as a more contemptuous crime than simple theft.

The principle that Quintilian applied to legal discussions was previously described by Cicero as a strategy of rhetorical reasoning. Cicero underscored how, by changing the definition of a word's commonly positively or negatively understood value, it is possible to modify the value judgment of the subject matter of the predication. For instance, by redefining wisdom, it is possible to deny that great philosophers are wise (*De Inventione*, I, 90):

CASE 4

That man cannot be wise who neglects money. But Socrates neglected money; therefore he was not wise.

In this case the way the word 'wise' is used is altered, so that it can be shown not to apply to Socrates or other people who neglected money. The redefining of concepts can be used for two purposes. On the one hand, by redefining it is possible to broaden or narrow the application of an emotive word to include or exclude some states of affairs. On the other hand, a concept can be redefined with emotive words in order to support a specific value judgment. An example of the first strategy is the following (*De Inventione*, I, 91):

CASE 5

He is seditious who is a bad and useless citizen.

---

[1] Sacrilege. Enclyclopaedia Britannica. http://www.theodora.com/encyclopedia/s/sacrilege.html (retrieved on 03 June 2011).

Here, under the label of 'seditious' fall several types of citizens who do not necessarily lead toward insurrections against the established order, such as the ambitious, the calumniator, or the wicked.

The definition also can be used to radically modify the way a word is used. The speaker can advance a new definition of a commonly shared concept, so that the word, together with the conclusions that it originally supported, can be used to refer to noticeably different entities or qualities. For instance, we can consider the following redefinition of 'personal enemy' set out in Cicero's speech against Verres. In classical Latin, 'personal enemy' (*inimicus*) is opposed to 'public enemy' (*hostis*). *Hostis* is a war enemy (Sini 1991: 163), a specific type of enemy from a legal point of view. *Inimicus* is a personal enemy: "*inimicus sit qui nos odit, hostis qui oppugnat*" (*inimicus* is the one that we hate; *hostis* is the one that we fight a war against) (Forcellini 1831: 427). Cicero wants to rebut the attack made by the counsel for the defense, Hortensius, who suggested in his speech that Cicero was driven by personal inimities (*inimicitiae*) and interests. Cicero replies by redefining the concept of *inimicus* (Ciceronis, *Actionis in C. Verrem Secundae*, 1, § 38), showing that Verres needs to be considered as the common personal enemy (*inimicus*) of any citizens, as he used to be the public enemy of his own people (even though he could not use the word *hostis* because there was no war involved). In this fashion, he leads Roman citizens to condemn Verres' actions for offending and breaching their deepest religious and public values (Ciceronis, *Actionis in C. Verrem Secundae*, 3, § 6)[2]:

REDEFINITION OF 'PRIVATE ENEMY'

Do you think there is any greater enmity than that arising from the opposite opinions of men, and the contrariety of their wishes and inclinations? Can he who thinks good faith the holiest thing in life avoid being an enemy to that man who, as quaestor, dared to despoil, to desert, to betray, and to attack his consul, whose counsels he had shared, whose money he had received, with all whose business affairs he had been entrusted?

Here the concept of *inimicus* is redefined by Cicero as the enemy of any good citizen. The use of the term 'personal enemy' to denote a type of public enemy underscores the private dimension and the burden of any good citizen to condemn a man who is damaging the Roman state.

The second strategy consists in using the definition to elicit a value judgment. For instance, accidental features can be mentioned to describe the meaning of the word, so that from such characteristics a negative

---

[2] "Fidem sanctissimam in vita qui putat, religionem qui colendam esse existimat, is sine dubio **inimicus** est ei qui fana spoliavit, omnia templa violavit, delubra polluit': hic etiam iam Verris idem factum, id de quo specialiter quaeritur, ita continetur et includitur, ut simul cum approbatione et deductione definitionis in speciem clausum teneatur."

judgment can easily follow. An example can be found in Cornificius' *Rhetorica ad Herennium* (II, 41):

CASE 6

An informer, in short, is worthy of death; for he is a wicked and dangerous citizen.

The purpose of such definitions is not to clarify the meaning of a word, or to describe it; on the contrary, the meaning is altered and extended, but to highlight the negative features of the *definiendum*, the person classified as 'informer' in this case, supports the further conclusion that he needs to be put to death.

The two strategies, aimed at altering the classification and the evaluative (or legal) judgment, can be also combined. The meaning of a word carrying a specific value judgment, or no value judgment at all, can be narrowed down to include concepts commonly considered as positive or negative. For instance, consider the following case (*De Inventione*, I, 91):

CASE 7

Folly is a desire of inordinate glory.

The evaluation of the concept of 'folly' (*stultitia*) is altered by restricting its meaning to one of its types, in particular the most admirable one, the desire of inordinate glory. Folly is therefore presented as an admirable quality, or at least a not completely despicable one. The alteration of the positive or negative judgment commonly associated with a concept can be more complex, not involving the restriction or extension of the existent meaning, but a redefinition. For instance, we can consider the following example (*De Inventione*, I, 91):

CASE 8

Wisdom is a knowledge how to acquire money.

By redefining wisdom in terms of financial knowledge it is possible to praise a speculator as a 'wise' man. In this case the concept is actually redefined, presenting a skill as a form of knowledge, and explaining the result of knowledge and other qualities as it amounted to one specific ability. Here the *definiendum* alters the judgment commonly associated with the *definiens*.

1.2.2. Emotive Qualifications and Classifications The counterpart of the redefinitions of emotive words or emotive redefinitions of words is the illicit use of emotive words, or words carrying a value or legal judgment. A classification is illicit because there is a disagreement between the accepted definition, and therefore the requirements of the word used, and the commonly known state of affairs. By using a specific word the speaker can describe a state of affairs that does not, or cannot, correspond to reality. The speaker can describe a situation taking for granted certain characteristics or events that have not been previously proven, or that are known to be false. A descriptive word becomes in this fashion a manipulative instrument, as it triggers emotions or judgments that are unrelated to the actual or known state of affairs. This strategy can be used both in the stasis of definition and qualification.

The classification of an entity or an event is grounded on a process of reasoning based on the definition of the word and the facts or qualities that can be observed or are shared by the interlocutors. The strategies of redefinition allow the speaker to use a word even when the facts do not match the shared meaning of the word. However, the facts can also be altered in order to fit the requirements of the use of a term. For instance, consider the following case (*Institutio Oratoria*, VIII, 4, 1):

CASE 9

If a widow lives freely, if being by nature bold she throws restraint to the winds, makes wealth an excuse for luxury, and strong passions for playing the harlot, would this be a reason for my regarding a man who was somewhat free in his method of saluting her to be an adulterer?

Quintilian (ibid), commenting on the aforementioned passage from Cicero's *Pro Caelio*, shows how facts can be presented as granted even when they are unproven, or unknown to the hearer, or when they have not been supported by evidence. The goal of the speaker was to prove that the man did not commit adultery, even though he had been proven to have 'saluted' an immoral widow. The strategy adopted was to show that no adultery was committed, as the immodest woman was actually claimed to be acting as a prostitute and the lover was shown to be simply saluting her in a freer fashion. For this reason, the speaker used the word 'harlot' (*meretricio more*) to describe the woman's behavior. This word becomes loaded in this context, as it carries with it the classification of the woman as a prostitute instead of simply an immodest widow. By means of this word, the alleged adulterer becomes in fact a simple client, while the sexual relationship becomes a Platonic friendship, ill interpreted by whomever regards his spontaneous salutations as a sign of an affair. This tactic is grounded on an implicit alteration of the shared facts. The woman, not known or proven to be a prostitute, is unduly and implicitly classified as such. The word 'harlot,' not necessarily negative in meaning, becomes extremely powerful in this case, triggering a specific value (and legal) judgment. The relationship between classification of reality and emotions was also shown by Quintilian in his account of the strategy of amplification. He noticed how a description can be modified by taking for granted some circumstances, introducing unsupported evidence, and at the same time hiding it in the use of an unwarranted classification. By changing the classification of a fact, or using a different word, its evaluation can also be altered, such as in the following case (*Institutio Oratoria*, VIII, 4, 1):

CASE 10

For example, we may say that a man who was *beaten* was *murdered*, or that a *dishonest* fellow is a *robber*, or, on the other hand, we may say that one who *struck* another merely *touched* him, and that one who *wounded* another merely *hurt* him.

As in the previous case of the widow (case 9), this example demonstrates how false or unwarranted facts are taken for granted as true through the use of an emotive word. The rhetorical strategy of amplifying a situation can be extremely effective, since it triggers a value judgment appealing not only to a critical evaluative process, but to an emotional one. The goal is to arouse emotions, which in this fashion can hide the manipulation of the facts.

Emotive words play a crucial role in the *status quaestionis* (or issue) of qualification, in which the purpose of the parties is to cause indignation or arouse pity.[3] While the accusation depicts the alleged fact as discreditable by means of indignant language, the defense presents that same fact as not discreditable, usually by looking at the circumstances in which it occurred and to the intentions of the defendant (Ciceronis, *De Inventione*, II, 33). The most common strategies that can be used are indignant language, exaggeration of the offenses, and qualification of facts that are still matters of dispute. If the purpose is to arouse indignation, a person will not be a "simple fornicator, but a violator of all chastity," "not a mere assassin, but a most cruel executioner of our countrymen and allies" (*Institutio Oratoria*, VIII, 4, 2). The actions of the defendant are exaggerated and depicted using adjectives expressing intentionality or lack of pity. A clear example of the argumentative function of indignant language can be found in the *Rhetorica ad Herennium* (II, 49):

CASE 11

By means of the seventh commonplace we show it is a foul crime, cruel, sacrilegious, and tyrannical; such a crime as the outraging of women, or one of those crimes that incite wars and life-and-death struggles with enemies of the state.

Here indignant language is used to move the affections of the hearers and support the judgment. The same strategy of qualifying established facts can also be used to rebut an appeal *ad misericordiam*, by exaggerating the offences (*De Inventione*, II, 36):

---

[3] Compare also to Cicero's *On Invention*: "And the offence of which he is now accused must be extenuated and made to appear as trifling as possible; and it must be shown to be discreditable or at all events inexpedient, to punish such a man as he is" (Ciceronis, *De Inventione*, II, 35).

CASE 12

But the adversary will exaggerate the offences; he will say that nothing was done igno-
rantly, but that everything was the result of deliberate wickedness and cruelty. He will
show that the accused person has been pitiless, arrogant, and (if he possibly can) at all
times disaffected, and that he cannot by any possibility be rendered friendly.

These tactics do not alter the facts, only the evaluation of a classification.
A more mischievous use of emotive words consists in arousing emotions in
order to hide the problem of establishing the facts. Instead of qualifying an
action or a fact already proven by evidence and classified, the speaker can
amplify the seriousness of what has not already been established. In this
fashion, the emotions stem from a false or unacceptable description. The
emotions are used to prevent a critical evaluation of the facts. Indignant
terms can also be used to describe a situation that is still in dispute and
whose characteristics are not shared by the interlocutors. In this case,
the prerequisite for the attribution of a predicate, that is, the agreement
on the fundamental features presupposed by the predicate, fails and the
move appears as unreasonable. For instance, consider the following case
(Ciceronis, *De Inventione* I, 92):

CASE 13

That is a disputable definition, when the very thing which we are amplifying is a
matter in dispute. As if any one, while accusing Ulysses, were to dwell on this point
particularly, that it is a scandalous thing that the bravest of men, Ajax, should have
been slain by a most inactive man.

The speaker arouses emotions by showing how scandalous the killing of
the bravest of men by the most inactive one is. The emotive reaction of
indignation triggered by the description can be a powerful instrument to
prevent the hearer from assessing the unproven facts underlying it. By per-
ceiving the killing as unacceptable, the hearer is led to overlook the fact
that Ulysses was never proven to have killed Ajax.

Emotive words were described in the ancient tradition considering their
relationship with definition, meaning, and representation. The ancient
authors underscored the danger of the implicit dimension of emotive
words. Words, in this view, risk becoming instruments for hiding reality
through emotions instead of tools for representing it. The ancient accounts
are mirrored in the modern and contemporary studies on the relationship
between words and reality.

2. When Words Are Masks

The ancient studies show a close relationship between words, meanings,
and the representation of reality that triggers the emotions. In modern and

contemporary studies, emotive words have been studied as instruments to 'frame' reality (Schiappa 2003), distorting, hiding, and redefining facts and qualities. Words, in this view, become an instrument of persuasion, and definitions a matter of choice. The ancient theories are mirrored in more recent approaches to the persuasive use of language, which show how the connection between words and reality can be used to distort states of affairs to spark emotions and influence the interlocutor's decisions.

George Orwell (1946), in his article "Politics and the English Language," explains how words can be used to trigger emotional responses by altering the hearers' perception of reality. Orwell highlights some types of tactics used in political discourse, aimed at preventing the reader from understanding what they actually refer to. These strategies can be considered as instruments to use words as masks, instead of as signs. The first strategy consists in the use of *euphemisms* and *loaded words* to distort the perception of facts. Euphemisms can be used as tactics to provide a vague and generic representation of the facts, omitting all details and specific features. For instance, 'pacification' may refer to different types of processes aimed at resolving conflicts, among which are war campaigns. Loaded words introduce a picture of the facts with more or false details. A second strategy is the use of words having an unclear or vague referent, such as 'Fascist', 'Communist,' or 'der Wille des Volks' (the will of people) (see also Rigotti 2005). The first two words are commonly negatively evaluated; however, their meaning, when they are used to classify the present state of affairs or decisions, is unclear or even undetermined. The will of people, on the contrary, is usually associated with a positive state of affairs; however, what is actually the will of people in a given situation cannot be known, and it is often extremely hard to ascertain. The positive evaluation the speakers usually associate with such a concept is often directed toward an unknown referent. The third and subtlest strategy is the exploitation of *definitions* for categorizing reality. This technique is grounded on a fallacy of ambiguity: the speaker introduces an ambiguity by introducing a new, not shared definition of a concept. Such an ambiguity is then used to direct the emotions usually associated with the old definition toward the new referent of the word. For instance, dictatorships often redefine the concept of democracy to classify their regime as 'democratic.' The new definition often clashes with the commonly shared understanding of what a democracy is; but the word, carrying a positive evaluation, can be attributed to a form of government that is usually condemned.

All these techniques show how emotive language can be used to distort reality and lead the hearers or readers to evaluate a situation that they do not fully know. Lacking a clear-cut reference, the precise and contextual meanings of such names cannot be wholly understood, and therefore cannot lead the interlocutor to an evaluation of a situation that is left indeterminate (see Schiappa 1998, 2003). Zarefsky represents the structure of this persuasive technique, called argument *by* definition, as follows (Zarefsky 1998: 4; see Schiappa 2003: 131):

X is *Y*

A fact *X* is classified as *Y*, where *Y* stands for a name conveying a determinate set of values, which may be positive or negative. The predication of such names attributes the values associated with them to the state of affairs *X*, without any need of arguments. For example, the term 'quarantine' conveys positive values, because it represents a therapeutic intervention. However, in 1962, President Kennedy imposed a 'quarantine' of a kind on Cuba to prevent shipments of weapons from arriving there. This word, when used to describe the sanctions against Cuba, implicitly defended a hostile resolution, attributing this act of war with the positive values associated with the concept of "isolating a person suspected of carrying a contagious disease." This act of war is presented as if it was a necessary and peaceful intervention. This type of argument, however, includes several different strategies, grounded on omission or distortion of facts and concealment of reality or redefinitions.

2.1. *Omitting and Distorting*

Euphemisms are usually used to soften a harsh reality. They are commonly used to associate a positive evaluation with a situation by pointing out its generic positive characteristics, leaving out the less desirable details or qualifications. For instance, by referring to the concept of death as 'to pass away' omits the way that this passing happens or its consequences. Euphemisms in such cases can assume a precise conventional meaning: For instance, if a person has 'passed away,' nobody would think that he is not dead (see Groarke & Tindale 2004). This strategy is absolutely legitimate in many contexts of dialogue. Undesirable situations or not positively qualified states of affairs are described using generic words (Engel 1980: 50, 1994: 104):

CASE 14

We call third class today tourist class. A travelling salesperson is now a field representative, a janitor is a custodian, and garbage collectors have become sanitation engineers.

In this case, in order to refer to an object commonly perceived as negative, a generic new or old term is used. The use of the genus instead of the specific predicate does not prevent the audience from understanding what the word means or refers to, or from judging it. 'Sanitation engineers' can be used to classify people carrying out jobs different from collecting garbage (just as a 'field representative' need not necessarily be a salesperson). For this reason, the fragment of reality that the more generic categorization refers to is wider and points out the positive dimension of the actual facts.

The discrepancy between the name and the concept is useful to prevent one from automatically associating an evaluation to a word.

Euphemisms, however, can be used to conceal some aspects of reality, leading the interlocutor to draw a conclusion based on a partial representation of the situation. For instance, we analyze the following examples from Orwell (1946):

CASE 15

1. Defenseless villages are bombarded from the air, the inhabitants driven out into the countryside, the cattle machine-gunned, the huts set on fire with incendiary bullets: this is called pacification.
2. Millions of peasants are robbed of their farms and sent trudging along the roads with no more than they can carry: this is called transfer of population or rectification of frontiers.
3. People are imprisoned for years without trial, or shot in the back of the neck or sent to die of scurvy in Arctic lumber camps: this is called elimination of unreliable elements

Here words are used to conceal the facts instead of describing them. In the first case, 'pacification' presupposes a situation of war or insurgency, and may include different ways of bringing a conflict to an end. However, in this case, villages that were not *at* war, but *in* a war, were destroyed. They were pacified because they could not be in a situation of war anymore, as they were annihilated. In the second case, "transfer of population" can refer to a temporary relocation, or any type of moving. However, since human beings are not simply cattle, the most common inference that can be drawn from this phrase is that they have been moved to other dwellings. The generic word conceals the peculiarity of the 'moving,' consisting in expropriating and expelling people from their homes and country without guarantee of a place to live. In the third case, 'elimination' is used instead of the specific terms for killing and sending people to die. Moreover, 'unreliable elements' can refer to objects, animals, and human beings that are lacking the undefined quality of 'reliability,' which could potentially include any type of implicit or explicit expectation.

The counterpart of such a strategy is distorting reality by including false or unacceptable details in the representation of the situation. For instance, consider the following cases (Manicas & Kruger 1968: 326):

CASE 16

a) You cannot let this man go free because your sister or your wife may be his **next victim**.
b) Now, let's consider some disadvantages of the **immoral** policy of legalized gambling.

In the first sentence, the speaker assumes that the man already killed a person, while in the second sentence legalized gambling is presupposed as something against morality. Such assumptions do not need to be supported by arguments. They are presented as already granted, while they are controversial in nature. In this sense, they are actually or potentially begging the question (Bentham 1952: 139).

The aforementioned strategies of omitting and distorting can be combined in the process of framing (Schiappa 2003: 152). Framing consists of amplifying some of the details of a situation and omitting others that may elicit unwanted judgments. For instance, consider the following descriptions of the same event (Schiappa 2003: 152):

CASE 17

1. A tree is being cut down.
2. A cylindrical organic object is being rotated from a vertical to a horizontal position.
3. A tree is being murdered.
4. A mean old man is cutting down that nice shady tree.

The state of affairs is the same in every description. However, different judgments are encouraged by amplifying some details, introducing false or unwarranted properties (the human nature of a tree in 3; the negative character of the woodcutter in 4), and excluding others (the nature of the object in 2). Names therefore can be used like magnifying glasses, which broaden some particulars and lead us to evaluate a whole picture on the grounds of some of its details.

2.2. *Hiding Reality*

The argument by definition can also be used to conceal the facts or to prevent the interlocutor from understanding the state of affairs that is referred to. Words are used to elicit emotions without representing a specific situation. For instance, Orwell provided the following example (Orwell 1946):

CASE 18

The word *Fascism* has now no meaning except in so far as it signifies "something not desirable."

According to Orwell, this word does not describe, or refer to, a fragment of reality; on the contrary, its meaning is so vague and indeterminate that the only possible communicative effect is to trigger a negative value judgment, bound not to a specific concept but instead to a vague negative idea of past tragedies.

The speaker can use familiar words in a metaphorical way, or technical terms or abbreviations, incomprehensible to a layperson, to describe a certain situation or entity. The purpose is to prevent the hearer from understanding what the word is actually referring to, and at the same time achieving the argumentative goal of triggering positive or non-negative emotions. For instance, the use of a metaphor can easily hide a threatening state of affairs under a desirable image, while an acronym or a specialized word can convey the argument that the subject matter is inaccessible to non-experts. In both cases the speaker mystifies, makes concepts incomprehensible, because the metaphors are impossible to explain and the technical terms undecipherable (Schiappa 2003: 134).

For instance, the term 'quarantine' was used by President Kennedy instead of 'blockade' to describe the American measures taken against Cuba. The aggressive nature of the decision was hidden in a medical and "therapeutic" word (Zarefsky 1998: 4). Similarly, nuclear bombs were called 'nukes' (Schiappa 1989), and intercontinental ballistic missiles, designed to annihilate the Soviet Union, were named 'Peacekeepers' (Zarefsky 2004: 617):

CASE 19

Though he tried, President Carter was unable to enlist the imagery of war on behalf of his energy program, just as President Reagan was unable to change public understanding of the MX missile by his choice to refer to it as the "Peacekeeper".

The dreadful concept, reduced to a familiar notion, is usually positively or neutrally evaluated (for a discussion on the names of weapons, see Kauffman 1989; Taylor 1998).

The use of technical terms, or bureaucratization, is based on a different strategy of concealment. Policies or events are made inaccessible to the public through the use of acronyms or scientific jargon. For instance, naming a neutron bomb a 'radiation enhancement weapon' prevents most people from understanding the concept to which such a name refers. If the interlocutors cannot understand the concept, they cannot evaluate it, and therefore they cannot make any decisions about it.

3. Modifying Meaning and Emotions: Persuasive Definitions

As shown in the previous section, words can be used to hide, omit, and distort reality. Zarefsky (2006: 404) pointed out how these persuasive and manipulative strategies can be represented by the argument *by* definition. This argument can be used in two fashions. On the one hand, the meaning and the definition can be shared but the reality referred to by the word is not. In this case, words can depict a state of affairs different from the real or shared one. On the other hand, a state of affairs can be shared or partially known by the interlocutor. In this case, the speaker can modify or choose to use an unshared definition of the word. The argument is based on an unconventional definition, allowing an otherwise unaccepted use of a term. This view can be thought of as a modern interpretation of the ancient intuition that pointed to the crucial importance of definitions and how choosing or changing a definition amounts to an act of persuasion. The ancient rhetorical theories taught us the lesson that the classification of reality depends on the meanings we give to names. This ancient idea can be expressed by the modern description given by Schiappa (1998: 3): "All definitions are political."

In ancient rhetoric, changing the meaning of a word was regarded as pleading a cause. In modern theories, the choice of a definition is considered an act of persuasion. Instead of using a word with its shared meaning to hide or alter facts, the very meaning of words can be modified so that they refer to something that otherwise could not be classified as such. The clearest and saddest example of this strategy is the classification of Sudan as a "presidential representative democratic consociationalist republic." Sudan has actually been governed by "President" Omar al-Bashir since 1989, who held and exercised absolute control over the country and the army ("Prosecutor's Application under Article 58," ICC-02/05–151-US-Exp) and indirectly perpetrated the genocide in Darfur (*Prosecutor v. Al Bashir*, Case No. ICC-02/05–01/09–3). A man who has been ranked number one in the list of the worst dictators in the world[4] has been referred to as the *president* of a *democratic* country. What does 'democratic' mean in this case? What does 'republic' refer to? Many countries are democratic republics, even though people can vote only for one party, or candidates running for elections are arrested and imprisoned. What is a 'president'? These words are vague, and at the same time positively evaluated. In the case of Sudan, they are improperly used to avoid referring to a dreadful political and social situation with its true name, dictatorship. They are not generic or metaphorical words; they are simply words used inappropriately.

This strategy was described by Orwell (1946):

CASE 20

The words *democracy, socialism, freedom, patriotic, realistic, justice* have each of them several different meanings which cannot be reconciled with one another. In the case of a word like *democracy*, not only is there no agreed definition, but the attempt to make one is resisted from all sides. It is almost universally felt that when we call a country democratic we are praising it: consequently the defenders of every kind of regime claim that it is a democracy, and fear that they might have to stop using that word if it were tied down to any one meaning. Words of this kind are often used in a consciously dishonest way. That is, the person who uses them has his own private definition, but allows his hearer to think he means something quite different. Statements like *Marshal Petain was a true patriot, The Soviet press is the freest in the world, The Catholic Church is opposed to persecution*, are almost always made with intent to deceive. Other words used in variable meanings, in most cases more or less dishonestly, are: *class, totalitarian, science, progressive, reactionary, bourgeois, equality.*

---

[4] http://www.parade.com/articles/editions/2006/edition_01–22–2006/Dictators#. TflK0FuwRI4 (Accessed on October 11th, 2011).

The speaker can use a word whose shared meaning is different from the attributed one. He redefines it to use it or its new definition as a premise for the wanted conclusion. This particular use of definitions has been analyzed by Stevenson (1938a), who labeled it as a "persuasive definition" (PD). In Stevenson's view, a persuasive definition is a definition of an ethical word, a word carrying a value judgment. From this perspective, meaning is conceived as a particular dispositional property (Stevenson 1944: 54), consisting in the relation between a stimulus (a sign) and a psychological reaction brought about in the addressee. Words can cause a cognitive and an emotive reaction. Such reactions correspond to two different dimensions of meaning: the cognitive (or descriptive) and the emotive. Cognitive meaning is the tendency of words to record and communicate beliefs (Stevenson 1937: 23), that is, to alter the interlocutor's knowledge (the indicative function of a word, in Robinson's view; see Robinson 1950: 57). Emotive meaning is the disposition to produce affective responses in people (Stevenson 1937: 23), and therefore it does not affect the interlocutor's beliefs, nor does it provide information, but rather it influences the hearer's interests and decisions (Stevenson 1937: 18). For instance, a man can refer to a fifty-nine-year-old unmarried woman using the term 'old maid.' The woman can be offended, as the use of the emotive word 'old maid' does not simply describe her as the phrase 'elderly spinster' would, but encourages the hearer to have contempt for her. The purpose of the utterance cannot be simply descriptive. 'Old maid' has a strong disposition to influence the interlocutor's emotions, to change his affective response, and for this reason it manifests an intention to alter the other's intentions, instead of altering his beliefs. Depending on whether the emotive meaning is strong or weak, the words will be used to alter interests or belief, to describe, or to influence.

Persuasive definitions are redefinitions of ethical words, namely, words whose descriptive meaning cannot be distinguished from the emotive one (Stevenson 1944: 206). For instance, 'culture' and 'freedom' are ethical words, because they describe a situation and at the same time direct the interlocutor's interests toward their referent. The redefinition of an ethical term results in redirecting the interlocutor's interests (Stevenson 1938a: 332):

REDEFINITION OF 'CULTURE'

Let us now suppose that one member of the community had no wholehearted regard for mere reading, or mere acquaintance with the arts, but valued them only to the extent that they served to develop imaginative sensitivity. [...] For this reason he proceeded to give "culture" a new meaning. "I know", he insisted, "that so and so is widely read, and acquainted with the arts; but what has that to do with culture? The real meaning of 'culture', the true meaning of 'culture', is *imaginative sensitivity*." [...]

It will now be obvious that this definition was no mere abbreviation, nor was it intended as an analysis of a common concept. Its purpose, rather, was to redirect people's interests. "Culture" had and would continue to have a laudatory emotive meaning. The definition urged people to stop using the laudatory term to refer to reading and the arts, and to use it, instead, to mean imaginative sensitivity. In this manner it sought to place the former qualities in a poor light, and the latter in a fine one, and thus redirect people's admiration.

The redefinition "changed interests by changing names" (Stevenson 1938a: 333) and directed the positive emotions aroused by the emotive meaning of the word toward an object that is different from the commonly accepted definition of culture as formal education and acquaintance with the arts. The redefinition is persuasive because it changes the hearer's attitude toward the referent.

Persuasive definitions are extremely useful to direct public interests and concerns, and move citizens to action. A famous case is the redefinition of the concept of security. Security has usually been regarded as protection against *external military threats*. However, this concept has been redefined in the last decades to refer to environmental concerns and to promote public and social intervention on some naturalistic, economic, and political issues crucial for international relations (*Report of the World Commission on Environment and Development: Our Common Future*, 1987, Ch. 11, 37; 44):

REDEFINITION OF 'SECURITY'

The first step in creating a more satisfactory basis for managing the interrelationships between security and sustainable development is to broaden our vision. Conflicts may arise not only because of political and military threats to national sovereignty; they may derive also from environmental degradation and the pre-emption of development options. [...]

Action to reduce environmental threats to security requires a redefinition of priorities, nationally and globally. Such a redefinition could evolve through the widespread acceptance of broader forms of security assessment and embrace military, political, environmental, and other sources of conflict.

Myers (2004: 4) noted that the modification of the global balances affected the way security was considered. The prime "components of a nation's environmental foundations" that constitute the grounds for the stability of a nation needed to be related to security: Securing such resources results in protecting social, political, and military equilibrium, while the degradation thereof causes instability and conflicts. For instance, national policies about oil consumption and nuclear power directly affect other countries' economies or military systems of defense (Brown 1977: 10). Security, therefore, needed to be redefined to include the environment: "Thus the definition reflects security in its proper broad sense: security for all, security for ever" (Myers 2004: 4). The redefinition of security was an instrument to reshape political and military problems (Broda-Bahm 1999: 165):

Recasting such threats as security concerns promotes an association of immediacy and a need for quick action that is otherwise not present in common perceptions. As Mische (1992) writes, "the word security is a power word. It is related to the primary need to survive."

The concept of security was redefined by means of several arguments supporting the relationship between the old meaning and the new needs. The old persuasive and political effects of the term were maintained and redirected toward a new object, even though reasons were advanced to support this linguistic decision.

The persuasive definitions in the previous cases are explicit and supported by arguments. However, sometimes ethical words are redefined without advancing explicit arguments. A word is simply used in a new and unconventional way to trigger the old attitudes, such as in the following redefinition of freedom (Huxley 1955: 122–123):

REDEFINITION OF 'FREEDOM'

- 'But if you w-want to be f-free, you've g-got to be a p-prisoner. It's the c-condition of freedom – t-true freedom.
- 'True freedom!' Anthony repeated in the parody of a clerical voice. 'I always love that kind of argument. The contrary of a thing isn't the contrary; oh, dear me, no! It's the thing itself, but as it truly is. Ask a diehard what conservatism is; he'll tell you it's true socialism. And the brewers' trade papers; they're full of articles about the beauty of True Temperance. Ordinary temperance is just gross refusal to drink; but true temperance, true temperance is something much more refined. True temperance is a bottle of claret with each meal and three double whiskies after dinner. Personally, I'm all for true temperance, because I hate temperance. But I like being free. So I won't have anything to do with true freedom.'
- 'Which doesn't p-prevent it from being t-true freedom,' the other obstinately insisted.
- 'What's in a name?' Anthony went on. 'The answer is, practically everything, if the name's a good one. Freedom's a marvellous name. That's why you're so anxious to make use of it. You think that, if you call imprisonment true freedom, people will be attracted to the prison. And the worst of it is you're quite right. The name counts more with most people than the thing. They'll follow the man who repeats it most often and in the loudest voice. And of course "True Freedom" is actually a better name than freedom tout court. Truth – it's one of the magical words. Combine it with the magic of "freedom" and the effect's terrific.'

Just like 'culture,' 'freedom' in this case is redefined to refer to the condition of a prisoner, leading the interlocutor to positively evaluate a condition in which there cannot be actually freedom. However, differently from the explicit persuasive definition of 'culture' as 'imaginative sensitivity,' 'freedom' is implicitly redefined. The speaker does not advance a new definition, nor does he try to persuade the interlocutor of it. He simply takes it for granted by using it. He claims that what may appear as a loss of freedom is actually true freedom, presupposing that true freedom means being deprived of the condition of being free from restraints.

The implicit redefinition of a concept can be an extremely effective and dangerous persuasive tactic. An example of this force can be the introduction and redefinition of the concept of "enemy combatant" in the case of *Padilla v. Rumsfeld* (352 F.3d 695, 2d Cir. 2003). After the terrorist attack on the Twin Towers, several alleged terrorists were imprisoned in Guantanamo Bay detention camp as "enemy combatants," that is, war enemies to be tried by the martial courts, not subject to the Geneva Conventions. The term "enemy combatant" was introduced in 2002 "when the administration imbued it with a new and particular meaning designed to circumvent the Geneva Conventions and international human rights laws" (Honigsberg 2007: 5). The term was never defined in law, and was first applied in 2002 to refer to "an individual who, under the laws and customs of war, may be detained for the duration of the armed conflict."[5] The absence of the definition and the extreme vagueness of the term allowed the president to issue an order to detain an American citizen, Padilla, as an enemy combatant. He was arrested based on his relationships with members of Al Qaeda, but he was not carrying weapons or bombs. Padilla attacked the classification as an enemy combatant on the basis that there was no definition for such a term, and his categorization was the result of a lawmaking function of the president (*Padilla v. Rumsfeld*, 352 F.3d 695, 714, 2d Cir. 2003):

Padilla contends that the June 9 Order mandating his detention as an "enemy combatant" was not the result of congressional action defining the category of "enemy combatant." He also argues that there has been no other legislative articulation of what constitutes an "enemy combatant," what circumstances trigger the designation, or when it ends.

The definition (or redefinition) in this case was not stated. The president did not set out the criteria and the reasoning underlying Padilla's categorization as an enemy combatant. He simply stipulated an implicit definition and applied it. The Supreme Court in 2004 found that the term was undefined and provided generic criteria to limit the possibility of redefining it (*Hamdi v. Rumsfeld*, 542 U.S. 516, 2004):

There is some debate as to the proper scope of this term, and the Government has never provided any court with the full criteria that it uses in classifying individuals as such. It has made clear, however, that, for purposes of this case, the "enemy combatant" that it is seeking to detain is an individual who, it alleges, was "'part of or supporting forces hostile to the United States or coalition partners'" in Afghanistan and who "'engaged in an armed conflict against the United States'" there.

---

[5] *Letter from Russell D. Feingold & Carl Levin to Attorney General and Secretary of Defense Donald Rumsfeld* (Sept. 5, 2002). Retrieved from http://levin.senate.gov/newsroom/press/release/?id=b44bb013–3bdd-40c6-a4bb-62f75d190570 (Accessed on June 9th, 2011).

By implicitly redefining a word it is possible to name reality without any need to support the classification or advance a definition that can be rejected or challenged. The force of implicit redefinitions consists in the effect of defending a claim and at the same time preventing the other party from challenging it. As Zarefsky (2004: 618) put it, "to choose a definition is, in effect, to plead a cause, as if one were advancing a claim and offering support for it. But no explicit claim is offered and no support is provided."

Implicitly or explicitly modifying the meaning of a word to slant the interlocutor's positive or negative emotions toward a state of affairs is not the only strategy for altering or manipulating his attitude and relationship with reality. The speaker can redefine the word to stress its appealing or threatening dimension, so that a neutral word can spark positive or negative reactions in the hearer. Stevenson described this technique as the mirror image of persuasive definitions and named it a "quasi-definition." In quasi-definitions what is modified is the emotive meaning, while the descriptive meaning remains untouched. The speaker does not actually redefine the word, as the definition is not altered. He provides a description of the referent, presenting such a description as capturing the essence of the thing. Stevenson gives the following example to clarify this strategy (Stevenson 1944: 280, 281, from Artsybashev 1915: 27):

QUASI-DEFINITION OF 'BLACKGUARD'

- "Blackguards are the most fascinating people."
- "You don't say so?" Exclaimed Sarudine, smiling.
- "Of course they are. There's nothing so boring in all the worlds as your so-called honest man.... With the programme of honesty and virtue everybody is long familiar; and so it contains nothing that is new. Such antiquated rubbish robs a man of all individuality, and his life is lived within the narrow, tedious limits of virtue.... Yes, blackguards are the most sincere and interesting people imaginable, for they have no conception of the bounds of human baseness".

In this example the word 'blackguard' and the phrase 'honest man' are not redefined but simply described in a way that the speaker is led to judge blackguards positively and honest men negatively. The descriptive meaning is not altered. The speaker does not challenge or modify the reference of the words, but simply what Stevenson calls the "emotive meaning."

Quasi-definitions have been analyzed as particular strategies used to create pseudo-agreements or pseudo-disagreements. In a discussion, definitions are often used to avoid situations in which the interlocutors can incur the risk of talking about the same words and not about the same things (Aristotle, *Topics*, 108a 20–22). However, sometimes apparent agreements are extremely useful in contexts of dialogue in which the purpose of the speaker is not to find the most reasonable conclusion but simply to win the discussion. Quasi-definitions can be used to specify the words used in a way that their meanings are not really clarified or made more specific but simply described in an eulogistic or dyslogistic fashion. For instance we can consider the following redefinitions of 'democracy' (Naess 1966: 92–93):

QUASI-DEFINITION OF 'DEMOCRACY'

1) Democracy is the policy of government that tries to bring morality and politics closer to one another until they coincide.
2) Democracy is the form of government which gives, or tries to give, the people the illusion of their own sovereignty.

In both cases, the meaning of 'democracy' is not defined. Instead, the speaker describes the alleged purposes of this form of government using words that everybody accepts or needs to accept as positive or negative. In the first case, the ideal of "moral politics" is or shall be pursued by everybody, and for this reason 'democracy' will be positively evaluated. In the second case, the speaker points out that the goal of democracy is only to give people an illusion eliciting a negative attitude. In both cases he uses quasi-definitions not to describe what the discussion is about but to implicitly distort the subject matter. The speaker is creating an apparent agreement on the concept of democracy. He is actually describing the 'ideal' or the 'bad' democracy, but through his pretense to express and clarify the meaning, he is presenting an idealization or degeneration as the generic concept.

Quasi-definitions can be used for extremely powerful sophisticated purposes. Both of the previous examples are clear and overt tentative distortions of viewpoints using definitions. The aforementioned definitions of 'democracy' cannot deceive anybody; at most they can be funny. The previous quasi-definition of 'blackguard' was more a provocation than a tentative manipulation or persuasion of the interlocutor. The novel from which this passage is drawn was actually intended to scandalize the Victorian tastes of the Russian society, by depicting a hero openly breaching the morality and values of the old *intellighenzia*. His description of honesty and immorality is in open contrast with the shared view, and for this reason it can be read as funny or immoral, but not as potentially deceitful or persuasive. However, quasi-definitions can be used more subtly to alter an already existing "emotive meaning" in order to achieve a different purpose. They will increase (or decrease) the negative or positive attitude a word evokes in the interlocutor; however, these emotions are not the end, but simply a means. In such cases, quasi-definitions can be effective instruments to arouse indignation and passions, and hide weak or controversial reasoning. For instance, consider the following quasi-definition of 'terrorist,' provided by the Russian Foreign Minister on September 11, 2004, in a speech concerning the fights in Chechnya and the negotiations proposed by the Chechen militia and welcomed by the international community[6]:

---

[6] *Putin rules out talks with Chechen rebel leaders*, The Guardian, 16 September 2004, http://www.guardian.co.uk/world/2004/sep/16/chechnya.russia (Accessed on June, 10th 2011).

QUASI-DEFINITION OF 'TERRORIST'

Terrorists are bandits who hide behind political, religious or nationalist slogans to try to resolve questions that have nothing to do with what they publicly state.

The quasi-definition had a twofold purpose. Putin aroused emotions against terrorists on the third anniversary of the attack against the Twin Towers. By stressing their illegal and unreasonable purposes, he wants to underscore the similar reasons behind the American war against terror and the Russian one against the Chechen militia.[7] His quasi-definition points out that the slogans behind which the "bandits" hide can be religious, political, or *nationalist.* In this fashion, he includes under the same concept Al-Qaeda, moved by religious motives, and the Chechens, driven by nationalistic ideals. He provides implicit arguments supporting the same treatment and the same classification for Al-Qaeda and the Chechens, but at the same time he already categorizes the latter as 'terrorists,' challenging the international opinion that regarded them as fighters.[8] A similar quasi-definition of terrorism was used to point out the global dimension of terrorism and present it as a global enemy against which all countries need to fight[9]:

Terrorism is the Nazism of the 21st century.

This quasi-definition is aimed at stressing the hideous nature of this phenomenon, and at the same time it is used to encourage action and social responsibility against it. Like the previous case, this description of terrorism also hides the very problem, that is, the international acceptance of naming Chechen guerrillas 'terrorists' (see also Simons 2006).

4. Conclusion

Words are instruments to refer and describe reality. However, at the same time they can be used to hide and distort reality. Since ancient times, the persuasive force of names has been analyzed in two dimensions: their function of depicting reality, and their power of arousing emotions. They refer

---

[7] See *Angry Putin rejects public Beslan inquiry,* The Guardian, 7 September 2004. http://www.guardian.co.uk/world/2004/sep/07/russia.chechnya?INTCMP=ILCNETTXT3487 (Accessed on June 10th, 2011).

[8] The Chechen war against Russia was referred to as 'guerrilla' (see *No softening as Putin plans direct rule for Chechnya,* The Guardian, 6 May 2000, http://www.guardian.co.uk/world/2000/may/06/chechnya.russia?INTCMP=ILCNETTXT3487 (Accessed on June 10th, 2011)) and the fighters as 'rebels' (see *Chechen rebels ready for talks,* The Guardian, 28 September 2004. http://www.guardian.co.uk/world/2001/sep/28/russia.chechnya?INTCMP=ILCNETTXT3487 (Accessed on June 10th, 2011)).

[9] Russian Foreign Ministry: New-generation terrorism has put itself on the world map, RIA Novosti, 11 September 2004: http://en.rian.ru/onlinenews/20040911/39768956.html (Accessed on June 10th, 2011). See also Russia Rejects "Double Standards" in Dealing With Terrorism, Interfax: www.interfax.ru, 11 September, 2004 (Accessed on June 10th, 2011).

to reality by providing a representation of it, but they can also give rise to an emotive response and influence the attitude of the hearer toward the referent. The use of a word in this sense can affect decisions and judgments. The speaker can use a name to represent facts unknown to the hearer by altering reality. He can omit, conceal, and distort events and qualities, so that the representation does not correspond to the actual state of affairs. The speaker can also change the meaning of a term in order to modify the way he classifies reality. He can choose or use a new definition of a name, so that the interpretation of its referent is altered and the interlocutor's attitude toward it is modified. Names are therefore instruments for influencing our emotions and our perception of the world. They can affect our knowledge and our decisions. But what is the relationship between emotions and representations? What is the link between decisions and knowledge or belief? What lies beneath the "emotive meaning" of words?

2

The Emotions in Our Words

Some words have a particular force. Terms such as 'war,' 'peace,' 'security,' or 'terrorism' trigger emotions. They lead us to appreciate, hate, fear, or reject a state of affairs. These terms are instruments for influencing affections and choices. In this sense, words are emotive. Stevenson (1944) pointed out how this power of words can be considered as a dimension of meaning, the disposition of a word to change a hearer's attitudes and emotional reactions instead of altering his structure of beliefs. In the first chapter we showed how emotive words can be used to hide and distort reality. However, the crucial issue to be considered in order to explain such a power of words is to understand what emotive meaning is, and how it affects our feelings, attitudes, and decisions. Where is such meaning? Why is it a characteristic of some words only? Do ethical terms trigger the same emotions in any culture, or is the emotive meaning dependent upon context and knowledge? Is emotive meaning rational?

The starting point for our investigation is a quotation from Huxley's *Brave New World*. In this fantastic and metaphorical world, children were produced in laboratories, and the notion of family disappeared. Reality had been drastically modified and the laws of nature completely subverted. In this world, however, words acquired new meanings, and in particular new *emotive meanings* (Huxley 1998: 22–23):

- "And 'parent'?" questioned the D.H.C.
- There was an uneasy silence. Several of the boys blushed. They had not yet learned to draw the significant but often very fine distinction between smut and pure science. One, at last, had the courage to raise a hand.
- "Human beings used to be … " he hesitated; the blood rushed to his cheeks. "Well, they used to be viviparous."
- "Quite right." The Director nodded approvingly.
- "And when the babies were decanted … "
- "'Born,'" came the correction.

- "Well, then they were the parents – I mean, not the babies, of course; the other ones." The poor boy was overwhelmed with confusion.
- "In brief," the Director summed up, "the parents were the father and the mother." The smut that was really science fell with a crash into the boys' eye-avoiding silence. "Mother," he repeated loudly rubbing in the science; and, leaning back in his chair, "These," he said gravely, "are unpleasant facts; I know it. But then most historical facts are unpleasant."

The words 'to be born,' 'parent, ' 'father,' and 'mother' were considered as obscenities and sparked emotions diametrically opposite to the real and ordinary ones. Instead of triggering happiness, they evoked negative feelings and caused unpleasantness, confusion, and shame. How is it possible to change the emotions that words can arouse? What is the relationship between emotive words and the way we judge the fragment of the world that they represent? In order to answer these questions it is necessary to inquire into the explanations that have been advanced in ancient and modern studies.

1. The Force of Ethical Words

Ethical, or rather emotive, words have been described by Stevenson as words that have the power of directing attitudes. The redefinition of such words amounts to an act of persuasion, aimed at redirecting interests and choices (Stevenson 1944: 210):

Ethical definitions involve a wedding of descriptive and emotive meaning, and accordingly have a frequent use in redirecting and intensifying attitudes. To choose a definition is to plead a cause, so long as the word defined is strongly emotive.

The most evident feature of Stevenson's account is the strict relationship between ethics, or rather value judgments, and emotions. On this view, ethical words affect attitudes because they are value judgments. The force of value judgments does not simply consist in arousing an emotion, but affecting the other's system of choices, the reasons underlying his or her decisions. The force of emotive words needs to be understood by inquiring into the different dimensions of the so-called "emotive meaning."

1.1. *The Dimensions of Emotive Meaning*

Stevenson analyzed emotive meaning in relation to ethics, or rather with the crucial ethical question, "What is good?" From this perspective, ethical terms involve a value judgment, a classification of reality as 'good' or 'bad.' Stevenson regarded value judgments as having a twofold dimension. They are grounded on reasons, as they can be used to change the interlocutor's interests and attitudes affecting his or her future actions. Ethical words are instruments of persuasion, not simply commands or orders. They do not only provoke a change in an action, but a modification of the interests on which all future actions of that kind are based. They are instruments of persuasion, and their force consisting in permanently influencing one's desires is to provide reasons (Stevenson 1938b: 57). Ethical judgments can be objects of disagreements and discussions. For instance, people may disagree about the fact that a form of government is good or bad and advance reasons pro and contra about such judgments. Reasons can be advanced to rebut value judgments. For instance, a criticism (negative judgment) of a decision or an action ("It was really bad to declare war") can be rebutted by putting forth a different description of the state of affairs negatively evaluated ("It was inevitable") (Stevenson 1938b: 50–51). On the other hand, the classification of something as good or bad is not a simple description of one's preferences or common interests; it amounts to a "magnetic effect" (Stevenson 1937: 16), an imperative force. Ethical terms have the tendency to influence the interlocutor's decisions (Stevenson 1937: 18–19):

Instead of merely describing people's interests, they change or intensify them. They *recommend* an interest in an object, rather than state that the interest already exists.

These words have a tendency to encourage future actions (Stevenson 1938b: 49–50), to lead the hearer toward a change by affecting his system of interests (Stevenson 1944: 210). This tendency does not correspond to the effect, but with a disposition to be used to achieve a specific effect, to move the hearer, to change his attitude toward action. They are in this sense words that are used dynamically. The relationship between emotive meaning and descriptive meaning is complex. Some words have a positive emotive meaning because their descriptive meaning refers to a state of affairs commonly evaluated as positive by the speakers. For instance, the word 'democracy' has an emotive meaning determined by the descriptive one (Stevenson 1944: 72). In other cases, the two meanings are independent from each other. For instance, Stevenson notices how the differences between 'cur' and 'dog' and 'steed' and 'horse' are only in their emotive meaning. 'Cur' designates the same entity as 'dog' does but encourages the others to have contempt for the being so named; on the contrary, 'steed' is used to refer to what is neutrally named 'horse,' but it evokes a positive attitude (Stevenson 1937: 23, 1938a: 334–335).

Stevenson showed how the force of emotive, or ethical, words lies in their two dimensions. The first one consists in the reasons used to attribute an ethical term to a fragment of reality or challenge such a predication. For instance, it is possible to use the word 'genocide' to describe a particular situation because it involves a systematic killing. The second dimension is an imperative effect, leading the interlocutor to modify his choices. For instance, the claim that "This man was responsible for a genocide" is not a simple description but an invitation to act (for instance, despising him, or condemning him if the hearer is in position

FIGURE 2.1. Toulmin's model

to do it). The two dimensions are strictly connected, as ethical words are not simply instruments for moving or arousing passions, but tools for influencing future decisions, for persuading. The relationship between reasons and the modification of a person's interests and future choices that characterizes ethical words can be understood considering the path that brings reasons to affect actions.

1.2. *The Reasons behind Value Judgments*

The first crucial step is the attribution of a value judgment. Stevenson noticed how this process is deeply grounded in reasons that account for the persuasiveness of ethical terms, and the possible discussions focused on their predications. However, Stevenson did not analyze how reasons are related to value judgments; on the contrary, he identified the grounds of ethical judgments with psychological reasons instead of logical ones (Stevenson 1944: 113). Stevenson's proposal was followed by the discussion between Toulmin and Hare on the logical dimension of ethics, which shed light on the logical reasons on which value judgments are based (Kupperman 2002).

In Toulmin's (1950: 68) view, ethical judgments consist in the attribution to a subject of a property, which might represent the opinion that the subject is desirable or praiseworthy, such as in the following sentence:

1. Jones is a good man.

In Toulmin's view, this attribution of an ethical property to a subject is always grounded on a factual reason. For instance, a reason that may be given to support the ethical judgment above might be "Jones is extremely generous." Toulmin represented a common relation between the factual reason and the conclusion as shown in Figure 2.1 (Toulmin 1958: 162).

The judgment is a claim that needs to be supported by factual elements (*D*) and an established warrant (*W*), a more generic principle commonly accepted in a community, linking facts with conclusions. However, Toulmin noticed how ethical judgments are different from other types of judgments and reasoning. Ethical judgments are grounded on descriptive premises but lead to action. They are the combination of a descriptive statement and a prescriptive one. For this reason, Toulmin did not classify ethical reasoning as strictly deductive. Instead, he characterized it as a different type of inference, coined as "evaluative inference" (Toulmin 1950: 38; for

C

FIGURE 2.2. Toulmin's model of ethical judgments

the notion of evaluative inference, see Brown 1955; Welsh 1957). The previously mentioned structure of reasoning was therefore further specified to describe the prescriptive force of ethical judgments. Toulmin distinguished the ethical conclusion (E), characterized by the element of approval or condemnation, from descriptive claims. Moreover, he introduced the notion of a reason (R), the ground for an ethical judgment that does not correspond to data as it relates to norms of conduct of a community, as a code (C). Such code does not simply establish relations between facts, but between facts and actions (Nakhnikian 1959: 78) (see Figure 2.2).

For instance, the sentence "John is a good man" is an ethical conclusion because it leads to praising John based on the norm of conduct shared by his community. In Toulmin's view, the goodness of an ethical judgment depends on the goodness of the reasons supporting it. A good reason depends on the moral code of the community and more generic principles. A good reason is an argument that shows that an action ought to be carried out (1) to comply with the moral code or (2) to avoid problems for the community (Toulmin 1950: 132; Nakhnikian 1959: 60–61; Kupperman 2002: 113). Even though an action can be positively evaluated as it abides by the moral code, it can be contemptible because it breaches a more general principle of respecting the others' lives. The strict relationship between ethical judgments and the common ground of a community is underscored by the possible contradiction of ethical judgments in the case of a man belonging to two communities, such as the Ku Klux Klan and the American society. According to one moral, racism is praiseworthy, while according to the other it is condemnable (Nakhnikian 1959: 66). Depending on the commonly shared warrant, the ethical judgment will be different. This conflict of common ground can be solved by appealing to the second ground of ethical judgments, the values shared by everybody, such as the respect of life and avoidance of sufferance.

1.3. *Reasons and Meanings*
Toulmin combined Stevenson's dimensions of meaning into a sole description of ethical inferences. Hare interpreted the relationship between reasons and ethical judgments distinguishing descriptive meaning from prescriptive. In Hare's view, the inference, "This strawberry is good; in fact, it is sweet and juicy" is grounded on a culture-dependent criterion, "A good

strawberry must be juicy" (Hare 1952: 111). Such a criterion is a rule, a set of properties that an entity or action needs to meet in order to justify the attribution of the value judgment (Hare 1963: 21):

[W]hen we make a moral judgement about something, we make it because of the possession by it of certain non-moral properties. [...] moral judgements about particular things are made for reasons; and the notion of a reason, as always, brings with it the notion of a rule which lays down that something is a reason for something else.

Hare noticed how value judgments are actually grounded on definitions, rules for the correct use of words, and factual considerations (Hare 1963: 23). This characteristic of value judgments, however, is only one of the two dimensions of their meaning. Ethical terms do not simply describe a behavior or an action. They have the force of influencing others' actions and interests. The prescriptive force is the second dimension of meaning that makes ethical judgments different from any other types of predications. In his analysis of the language of morals, Hare noticed that ethical terms, instead of simply describing reality, lead the interlocutor to action by giving reasons to do it. The descriptive meaning provides the implicit reasons (Hare 1963: 15; Olscamp 1970: 241), while the prescriptive force can be considered as a moral instruction (Hare 1963: 23) that leads the interlocutor to act based on shared rules of conduct. For instance, we can consider the following inference (see Hare 1952: 44):

You must do your homework. It is your duty.

Here the conclusion is grounded on a missing premise that can be represented as "You must do your duty," belonging to the shared values and norms of behavior. Ethical judgments, in other words, are means to lead the interlocutor to action on the basis of common knowledge. These two components of meaning can be considered as the result of two different types of reasoning, respectively grounded on factual and prescriptive reasons, which can be related to each other, such as in case of 'good' or independent. As Hare (1963: 24) put it:

Let us imagine a society which places a negative value upon industry; there seem to be such societies in the world, in which the industrious man is regarded as a mere nuisance. Such a society could never (if it spoke English) express its moral standards by using the word 'industrious', like us, for commending people, only with a totally different descriptive meaning – i.e. commending them for totally different qualities, for example that of doing as little work as possible. If they did that, we should say that they had changed the meaning of the English word 'industrious'. The descriptive meaning of 'industrious' is much too firmly attached to the word for this sort of thing to be allowed; these people would be much more likely to use the word in its normal descriptive meaning, but neutrally or pejoratively; i.e. to give it no, or an adverse, prescriptive meaning.

Hare underscores how the two types of meanings are grounded on two different types of reasonings. The descriptive meaning of a word is based on definitional criteria and the prescriptive one on moral standards or shared values. This idea is crucial for understanding the reasoning structure of ethical judgments.

2. The Structure of Emotive Words

Ethical judgments can be considered as having a twofold dimension. They are grounded on factual reasons and lead to actions. They have a descriptive meaning and at the same time a prescriptive one. Their predication is supported by their meaning and the data, but their effect is not limited to a description or the attribution of a quality to an entity. Instead, they invite the interlocutor to change his or her interests and influence his or her decisions. These two faces of ethical terms stem from two different grounds: the meaning of words, and implicit value judgments, which can be implicit in the words or shared evaluations of the referents thereof. In order to distinguish and describe these different grounds, it is necessary to highlight their complexity, starting from the theories on the most controversial ethical term, 'good.'

2.1. *The Descriptive Meaning of Ethical Terms*

Hare grounded his theory of value judgments on the distinction between the descriptive dimension of value judgments and the prescriptive one. In his view, any ethical term has a descriptive component, even if it is vague and culture dependent. For instance, he underscored how, in order to be called a 'good man,' a person has to fulfill some requirements that can change over time and depend on the culture of a society. However, at the same time, the use of the ethical word amounts to a moral instruction (Hare 1963: 23):

The rule will still say that it is proper to apply the word 'good' to a certain kind of man; but in saying this (in enunciating the rule) we shall be doing more than specifying the meaning of the word. For in saying that it is proper to call a certain kind of man good (for example a man who feeds his children, does not beat his wife, etc.) we are not just explaining the meaning of a word; it is not mere verbal instruction that we are giving, but something more: moral instruction. In learning that, of all kinds of man, this kind can be called good, our hearer will be learning something synthetic, a moral principle.

Even the more vague word, 'good,' has a descriptive component. In order to be used, some "non-moral" requirements need to be met. For instance, as Hare pointed out, a man needs to meet the "standards of human excellence" that, even if they can be explicit and fixed in a society, change.

The two dimensions of ethical judgments, namely, the inference supporting their predication and their pragmatic effect of leading to action, can be analyzed from Aristotle's *Nicomachean Ethics*. The level of justifying the predication can be examined by taking into consideration Vendler's semantic analysis of 'good' (see Vendler 1964). Vendler notices how the grounds for the predication of 'good' are different according to the different possible uses of this predicate (Vendler 1964: 461):

Going into details, we can say that a person or thing can be called good on three different grounds. First of all, for what it habitually does or can do (good$_3$). A good dancer is a person who can dance well and habitually dances well, a good king is a monarch who rules or governs his country well, and so forth. Second, something (or somebody) can be called good on the basis of what can be done with it, what it is good for (good$_4$): a good meal is good to eat and a good pen is good for writing. Third, somebody (or something) can be called good because of what he actually does, did, or will do (good$_5$): John may be good to help the poor, and it may be good of Mary to have cooked dinner. Finally, what simply happens, or is the case, may be called good (good$_7$): we often say that it is good that it is raining or that it is good that John has arrived.

Vendler pointed out the predication of 'good' is always mediated by a verb class, usually specified by a noun. For instance, while the sentence, "Venus is a good planet" is incomprehensible, "Venus is a good planet to observe" is perfectly clear. The verb acts as a specification of the activity or function with respect to which the subject is called 'good' (Vendler 1964: 462). This predicate always refers to a role or function that the subject plays or performs. For instance, a good poet is a man who fulfills certain standards for writing poetry (quality, quantity, etc.); a good father is a man who meets certain social cultural and social standards in taking care of his children (providing them with food, assistance, care, etc.). Certain nouns already indicate their prototypical function. For instance, a good dinner is a dinner that performs well the function of being eaten (it is abundant, tasty, etc.). In other cases, there are more functions that an entity can carry out. For instance, a 'good dog' is usually a dog that is good at being a friend of man, behaving faithfully and obediently, but it can also be a dog that is good at being a guardian. Other words, such as 'baboon' or 'planet,' do not refer to entities having a prototypical function, and therefore the phrases 'good baboon' and 'good planet' are unclear, as there is no function such entities can perform according to certain standards. On this perspective, ethical words can be predicated based on their semantic structure, further specified by cultural standards. The classification of a person as 'industrious,' 'honest,' or 'virtuous' is established on the basis of the definitions of such words, or rather the fundamental features of the concepts they refer to (Hare 1963: 24). Such features are vague and culture dependent, as they refer to standards that vary with society and common knowledge over time. The definitions of ethical terms can be changed in order to classify a fragment of reality that otherwise would not fall within their meaning. However, such a change may conflict with deeper definitions and standards of a community.

For instance, we can consider the redefinition of the descriptive meaning of 'natural man' in this dialogue between Sanin, the hero of a novel by Artsybashev, and his interlocutor (Artsybashev 1915: 23):

REDEFINITION OF 'NATURAL MAN'

"Now a blackguard, a real, genuine blackguard is quite another matter. To begin with he is a perfectly sincere, natural fellow."

"Natural?"

"Of course he is. He does only what a man naturally does. He sees something that does not belong to him, something that he likes – and, he takes it. He sees a pretty woman who won't give herself to him, so he manages to get her, either by force or by craft. And that is perfectly natural, the desire and the instinct for self-gratification being one of the few traits that distinguish a man from a beast. The more animal an animal is, the less it understands of enjoyment, the less able it is to procure this. It only cares to satisfy its needs. We are all agreed that man was not created in order to suffer, and that suffering is not the ideal of human endeavour."

In this example, Sanin alters the definition of the ethical term 'natural' by identifying the ordinary course of man's nature with the course of animals' nature. What is considered to be natural depends on what a culture identifies with the "nature of man." By redefining the concept, Sanin redefines what human nature is and identifies it with following basic animal instincts. Definitions and values, in this perspective, are strictly interrelated.

2.2. *Emotive Meaning: Emotions Dependent and Independent of Reality*

The second dimension of ethical word is their prescriptive effect. Stevenson uses the term "emotive meaning" to refer to two different types of emotive dispositions within words. Some words have an emotive meaning dependent on the descriptive one, while in others the two components are independent. Dependent and independent emotive meanings need to be analyzed as two different concepts, characterized by different features. In the first case, the emotive meaning is a characteristic of the word. We can describe it by defining the value judgment as "inside" the word. In the second case, the value judgment is a shared evaluation of the referent of the word. In this case, the emotive meaning is caused by the use of the word.

The notion of emotions "inside" the word is a metaphor describing in its turn two different characteristics of some words: the so-called connotation, and the implicit essential properties of predicates. Connotation is a controversial notion (Mostovaia 2009), often referred to as the "real world experience" of a word use, "encyclopedic knowledge" (Leech 1974: 15), "common associations" of a word (Mill 1869: 243–244; Robinson 1950: 109), or "shade" (Sinclair 2004). Along with these meanings, largely corresponding to Stevenson's emotive meaning, connotation also refers to the stylistic use or "tonality" of a word, also called the expressive dimension of language (Green & Kortum 2007) Frege (see the specific works on this issue by Dummett 1973: 2; Aberdein 2000) notices that some words evoke positive or negative associations For instance, couples such as 'steed' and 'horse,' 'dead' and 'deceased' refer to the same entities but evoke different associations and emotive reactions. As Frege (1897:140)put it:

> If we compare the sentences 'This dog howled the whole night' and 'This cur howled the whole night', we find that the thought [i.e., the propositional sense] is the same. The first sentence tells us neither more nor less than does the second. But while the word 'dog' is neutral as between having pleasant or unpleasant associations, the word 'cur' certainly has unpleasant rather than pleasant associations and puts us rather in mind of a dog with a somewhat unkempt appearance. Even if it is grossly unfair to the dog to think of it in this way, we cannot say that this makes the second sentence false. True, anyone who utters this sentence speaks pejoratively, but this is not part of the thought expressed.

Such evocative meaning is often exploited to persuade the interlocutor. For instance, according to the policy to be encouraged toward people without a dwelling place, they will be referred to as 'vagrants' or 'homeless.'

The evocative meaning has been described in some linguistic approaches as a specific type of content (Rigotti & Rocci 2006). For Hjelmslev (1961), connotation corresponds to a level of content associated not with the expression of the sign, such as denotation, but with the sign itself. The expression plane of a connotative language is a semiotic system, which carries content, while denotative language is a semiotic system because there is an association between an expression plane and a content plane. The contents of connotative languages are, for instance, dialects, voices, and genres. The very fact that a person uses the word 'steed' instead of 'horse' connotes literariness. Connotation, at least, has been associated by Eco (1976) with pragmatic implications drawn from a common ground. However, it is the notion of this type of implication which is particularly interesting in Eco. The implication coincides, in fact, with the knowledge of the connotative semiotic code. In other words, the knowledge upon which the inference is grounded is part of the knowledge of the connotative code. Connotation, in these terms, becomes de-codification (Rigotti & Rocci 2006: 7).

This dimension of emotive meaning, related to the linguistic code, needs to be distinguished from the value judgments implicit in the linguistic structure. From this perspective, value judgments can be conditions required by the predicate to be attributed to a certain entity. This relation between a noun or a predicate and the entity it can be attributed to can be explained in terms of presuppositions. The core of congruity theory (Rigotti 2005) is a semantic analysis grounded on the necessary conditions a predicate needs to be fulfilled in order to be correctly predicated of an entity. In this theory, a predicate presupposes a number of arguments having certain qualities. These qualities are conditions for its correct and meaningful attribution to certain entities. We can represent the abstract structure of a predicate as shown in Figure 2.3 (Rigotti 2005: 79).

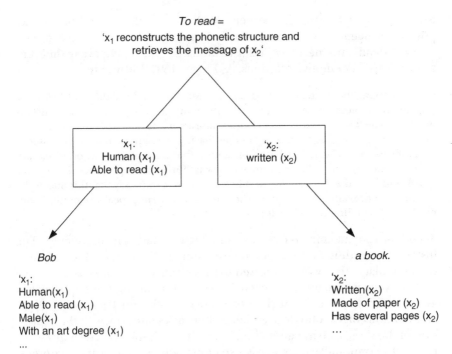

FIGURE 2.3. The abstract structure of a predicate

In this case, the verb is described according to its syntactic structure, pointing out the number of its arguments (see Partee 1992) and the conditions, or presuppositions, that impose on its arguments (Lakoff 1971: 239–240). For instance, we can consider the following analysis of the verb 'to hit' (Katz & Fodor 1963: 202):

Hits → Verb → Verb transitive → (Action) → (Instancy) → (Intensity) → [Strikes with a blow or missile] (Subject: (Human) v (Higher Animal), Object: (Physical Object), Instrumental: (Physical Object)

Katz and Fodor (1963) interpret the selectional restriction of the verb in terms of general semantic features that the arguments of this syntactic relation need to satisfy. For instance, I cannot *hit a dance*, or *the light*, nor can I read the table or the air. The conditions need to be fulfilled in order for the predicate to be reasonably attributed to the entity. Similarly, nouns, which are monadic predicates, presuppose types of predicates with which they can be associated. 'Journal' can be an argument of predicates presupposing a solid entity (for instance 'to take'), or ones requiring as an essential feature 'to be a good' (such as 'to buy'), 'to be breakable' (such as 'to tear'), or 'to be written' (such as 'to read') (for a first account of the relation between nouns [or arguments] and predicates, see Aristotle, *Topics*, 134a 20–24). Arguments, therefore, belong to more generic categories, such as 'solid entity' or 'written surface.'

In the semantic structure of predicates, values can be presupposed. For instance, the predicate 'to accuse' presupposes that the action of which the person is accused is illegal or immoral, or somehow breaches some rules. As Lakoff puts it (Lakoff 2004: 30):

The verb 'accuse' is decomposed into two statements, one declared and one presupposed. The badness (illegality or immorality) of the offense is presupposed by the accuser, who is declaring that the accused did perform the offense.

For example, in the sentence:

The Democrats accused Bush of spying on U.S. citizens.

the illegality of the action of spying is presupposed by the predicate 'to accuse' (see Lakoff 2004: 30). Value judgments, in some predicates, are part of the requirements of the predicate. An action needs to be good in order to be an argument of a predicate such as 'to congratulate,' while it needs to be negative to be the object of a verb such as 'to regret.' The object of a promise needs to be good for the promisee, whereas an agent can only *threaten* another with an action negative for the latter. Such value judgments do not depend on the evaluation of reality, but simply on the structure of the predicates. The evaluation is presupposed and does not depend on the speaker's or hearer's values. It is a choice of the speaker to 'regret' working too much, but the negative evaluation of the regretted action is a linguistic feature implicitly communicated and does not depend on values or circumstances.

2.3. *Emotions Triggered by Words: Values in the Frames*

Emotive words can also be emotive because they refer to a fragment of reality that is usually positively or negatively evaluated (Halldén 1960: 73). Words are emotive because they are related to a system of values that is commonly shared by the interlocutor and affects his evaluation and choices. The relationship between words and values is mediated by a set of common information, called common knowledge. Every word, in order to be understood and to represent a specific concept, needs to be related to, and presuppose, other knowledge. Every word implicitly takes for granted a fragment of culture, which becomes an integral part of the language itself. Fillmore (2003: 267) called a "frame" the background information every word presupposes[1] (see also Lakoff 1999):

[E]very definition consist of two parts: a frame-setting part, which characterizes the frame or conceptual background to each word sense, and a word-specific meaning. By *frame* I mean a structure of knowledge or conceptualization that underlies the meaning of a set of lexical items that in some ways appeal to that same structure.

For instance, in order to understand the concept of a *bachelor*, which can be defined as "a man who has never been married," we need some basic

---

[1] This relationship includes values and hierarchies, in addition to all kinds of factual information (see Perelman & Olbrechts-Tyteca 1969: 170).

background conceptual information, such as the notion of marriage, and some shared values, such as "a man should marry when he is *x* years old" (Fillmore 1982). No one could understand the concept of bachelor without knowing what marriage is, and by what customs and uses it is characterized in Western countries. For instance, it would be unreasonable to predicate 'bachelor' to a child or a teenager nowadays; however, in more ancient times, when the marrying age was much lower, such usage would not have been incorrect. In a comparable way, the concept of contract in law can be defined as having four elements: parties competent to contract; a consideration; a subject matter; and agreement, or meeting of the minds, by offer on the one hand and acceptance on the other (Page 1919: §49). However, this definition by essential parts can be understood only given the concepts of agreement and consideration. Moreover, it presupposes certain legal values, such as the notion of what is 'sufficient' for consideration and what can be a 'subject matter' in a contract. Such knowledge can be not only encyclopedic but also ethical. For instance, what counts as sufficient regarding consideration is determined by what is regarded as a value (see Gano & Williams 2008: 29; *Bishop on Contracts*, Second Enlarged Edition, Sec. 38, 14).

Frames are deeply rooted in the semantic structure of words, as we can see in the structure of the word 'carrion' (Fillmore 2003: 269):

The definition [rotting meat of a dead animal] does not inform me that I can't legitimately use the word carrion to refer to meat that had been left out of the refrigerator while the family was vacationing, nor can I use it to refer to dead animal parts that I accidentally stepped on while walking in the woods. Carrion is the word used for the food of scavengers, that is, animals that are opportunistic, non-hunting carnivores: their diet is evolutionarily specialized to include the meat of animals that they find dying or already dead. The word belongs to a larger conceptual framework of the ethology of this group of animals.

In the previous section we showed how the structure of predicates admits some arguments and excludes others. On the other hand, arguments can be the object of predication of certain predicates but not of others. For instance, a surface can be 'colored' but not 'heavy' (Aristotle, *Topics*, I, V). Similarly, in the previous example of Bob reading a book, the book can be an argument of some predicates but not of others. It can 'be read' or 'be interesting' but not 'be drunk' or 'be hard-working.' This principle can be applied to the semantic structure of words to understand the implicit information they trigger or presuppose. For instance, the word 'carrion' is commonly negatively evaluated. If we analyze it, we notice that it can be the argument of the predicate 'to eat,' as it falls under the category of 'food,' and in particular 'food of scavengers' (see Figure 2.4).

The semantic structure of a word often presupposes predicates and paradigms that in their turn are related to implicit information and values. For

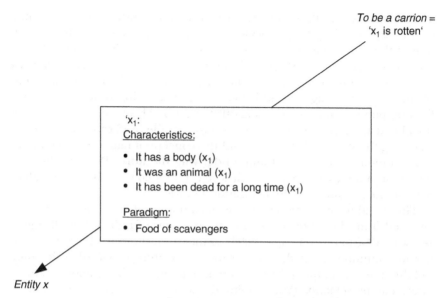

FIGURE 2.4. Arguments presupposing categories

instance, the concepts of *scavenger* and *dead body* are not positively evaluated in our society. Such concepts are part of the semantic structure of the predicate even though not necessarily part of the definition of the word itself. The frame of a word, in this perspective, is constituted of and is triggered by definitional and structural semantic features of a word, and includes fundamental features and background information needed to understand the concepts it refers to (see Fillmore 2003).

The concept of frame encompasses semantic features of words, and shared knowledge and values needed to understand the meaning of certain concepts presupposed by the *definiendum* itself. From this perspective, values, along with factual information, constitute an integral part of the semantics of a word. Words and values therefore become indissoluble, and redefinitions of ethical, or rather emotive, words can be considered renegotiations of the shared values. The debate on the definition of 'marriage' is a clear case in which the redefinition of the semantic structure (the persuasive definition) has been challenged with the redefinition of the underlying values, knowledge, and assumptions (Lakoff 2004: 47):

REDEFINITION OF 'MARRIAGE'

President Bush chose not to use the words "gay marriage" in his State of Union Address. I suspect that the omission occurred for a good reason. His position is that "marriage" is defined as between a man and a woman, and so the term "gay marriage" should be an oxymoron, as meaningless as "gay apple" or "gay telephone."

The alleged redefinition, attributed to President Bush, alters the quality of the arguments of the predicate 'to marry.' In this fashion, the attribution of the word itself to homosexual couples becomes impossible. On the other hand, instead of reshaping the argument qualities, specifying them as 'heterosexual humans,' the advocates of gay marriages reshaped the frame of the word, defining it as an ideal, as "the realization of love through a lifelong public commitment" (Lakoff 2004: 46). This latter redefinition is not aimed at altering the semantic structure of the predicate, but rather at changing the system of values behind the concept of marriage, and homosexual unions, namely, the frame underlying the word. Denying the possibility of same-sex marriages implies rejecting a commonly shared value, namely, the possibility of the realization of love.

This relationship between frame, meaning, and definition has been analyzed from the point of view of the strategies of redefinition. Burgess-Jackson (1995) and Schiappa (2004) emphasized the role of the set of values and common knowledge underlying the meaning of a word, which they call the "theory," showing the effects that redefinitions bring about on their interlocutors. Schiappa (2003) pointed out how the act of defining a word amounts to the act of imposing an interpretation of reality. Definitions, for Schiappa, have nothing to do with the essences of things, but only with perceptions of reality. Language, for Schiappa, depends on learning, that is, on the persuasive process that leads to organizing reality in a certain fashion. When a person accepts a definition, he or she also accepts the evaluation and the perspective on reality it imposes, and the course of actions and decisions it implies. For this reason, for Schiappa definitions are always political – that is, they are always aimed at attaining certain goals by means of altering or framing our valuation of reality. Defining 'rape' or 'death' does not only mean embracing a theory but imposing a whole organization of beliefs and values, such as the role of woman or of human life. Since the evaluation of a situation depends on the theory presupposed by the definition, the definer will choose the definition that better supports his goal. Explicit and implicit definitions are instruments to impose a frame and lead the interlocutor to evaluate reality in a certain fashion.

Burgess-Jackson (1995: 426–427) underscored the relationship between frame and definition by taking into consideration not the effects of redefinitions but their possibility. He noticed that the definition of the word 'rape' is grounded upon a particular theory, i.e., a specific point of view on the role of women in marriage and society. Can a sexual abuse perpetrated by a man against his spouse be considered as 'rape'? Defining 'rape' as a violent sexual act against a woman who is not the aggressor's spouse, or as the sexual abuse of a woman, means defending existing conceptions of marriage. The different definitions presuppose different theories about the nature of marriage that are already shared. Redefinition, from this perspective, amounts to the modification of the extension of the world, but its possibility is rooted in a specific theory that needs to be shared or accepted. Vague words can be redefined because the theories underlying them are somehow controversial.

The notions of connotation, predicate conditions, and frame can be explained from a cognitive and linguistic point of view, demonstrating how the emotive meanings of a word are triggered and where they are rooted. In the case of connotation and presupposition, the value judgment is part of the decoding process or in the semantic structure. The relationship between frame and emotive meaning is more complex, as it involves a cultural dimension and an evaluation mechanism that is dependent on values and common knowledge. The independent emotive meaning (or rather the dimension of emotive meaning rooted in the referent of the ethical term) involves a reasoning step grounded on what is considered to be desirable or condemnable in a specific society. How can a word trigger a process of reasoning? What does this reasoning amount to?

3. The Logical Dimension of Emotive Meaning: Reasoning from Values

How can emotive words persuade us to accept a specific conclusion? In the previous sections we showed how the frame of a word influences the evaluation of the concept itself, but how is this process possible? How can reality and values affect our decisions? A suggestion for a possible answer to these questions can be found in Anscombe and Ducrot's theory on argumentation within language (Anscombe & Ducrot 1983). In this view, the persuasive effect of words, or rather their argumentative force, is grounded in different patterns of reasoning implicit in the linguistic system. The conclusion of what a word suggests is the result of an inferential process that constitutes the very meaning of the word itself. Building on this idea, we can show from an argumentative perspective how values are related to words, and how they can support a specific conclusion.

3.1. *The Reasoning Process within Words*
Oswald Ducrot (1972a; 1972b), developing his theses on argumentative structuralism, claimed that the meaning of sentences corresponds to their argumentative effects, that is, the conclusions they lead to. Ducrot noticed how sentences can be described as having two different types of content: a stated content and a presupposed content. For instance, the sentence "I have quit smoking" states that "I no longer smoke" and presupposes that "I used to smoke." The combination of the two types of contents can explain some types of argumentative conclusions drawn from the sentences (see Ducrot 1972a). Ducrot developed this account by introducing an argumentative content in the sentence description. In order to explain his account, we can compare the two sentences "Bob and Tom are the same height" and "Bob is as tall as Tom." Even though they express the

same idea, the second sentence conveys a "rhetorical" meaning absent in the first one. Grice (1975) would have explained this difference in terms of maxims external to the linguistic structure. Ducrot instead included the principles of inference *within* the sentence meaning. In his view, the second sentence has an argumentative content that can be described as "there is a content r (in this case, Bob is tall) that the asserted content supports" (see Anscombre & Ducrot 1978: 352). This rule is a presupposition of the sentence. In this fashion, the Gricean implicature maxims, conceived as rules of discourse, become presupposed contents.

This account, however, did not explain how the implicit content r can be supported, and it did not develop the argumentativeness of words in a way much different from Stevenson's emotive meaning (Stevenson 1937). For this reason, Ducrot introduced the idea of *topos*, retrieving the ancient idea of generic and specific principles of inference and applying them to analyze why and how a word can support a specific conclusion. His intuition can be explained by means of an example (Anscombre & Ducrot 1983: 159). If we consider the sentence "The glass is full," we can notice that it has an effect on the interlocutor, an 'emotive' effect (for instance, satisfaction), that we can represent as r. This effect depends on a quality, R, which in this case is 'fullness.' The link between R and r is represented by a *topos*, a path of inference of the kind "The more a glass is full, the more the satisfaction." *Topoi*, namely, argumentative inferences from a premise (or premises) to a conclusion, are part of the meanings of words. The meanings of words correspond to the possible conclusions to which they can lead the interlocutor. Ducrot defined words as bundles of *topoi* or modifiers of *topoi*,[2] that is, words that have as their meanings a set of *topoi* and words (such as the connectives 'but' and 'and' as well as adjectives and adverbs) that select among these *topoi*, or enhance or weaken the strength of the *topos*. For instance, a word such as 'to work' is seen as a set of *topoi*, such as "The more work, the more remuneration" or "The more work, the more fatigue." If a person asserts, "Bob worked hard," the conclusion "he must be tired" is in the structure of the language, or better yet, in the meaning of 'to work.' We can illustrate the structure of Ducrot's system as shown in Figure 2.5.

The possible conclusions are bundles of *topoi* leading to further conclusions. In this fashion, the meaning of 'money' corresponds to *topoi* such as, "The more money, the more satisfaction," and so on. The emotive meaning

---

[2] A predicate, such as the verb 'to work,' is described by Ducrot as a bundle of *topoi*. Linguistic competence consists in establishing a relation between scales corresponding to areas of activities. For instance, the statement "I worked hard today" is connected to the conclusion "I am very tired." The relation between the scale 'to work' (hard, normal, a bit ...) and the scale 'to be tired' (much, not very much ...) is a *topos*: "The more work, the more tired." Every correspondence between different paradigms of activities is a *topos*. The predicate 'to work' is therefore described as the bundle of all its possible correspondences (Anscombre & Ducrot 1986: 89).

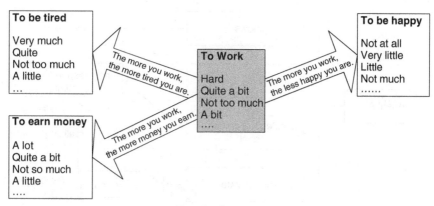

FIGURE 2.5. *Topoi* in the semantic structure

becomes a complex reasoning structure that merges reasoning processes with semantic information. This account risks making Stevenson's emotive meaning more complex and interpreting disagreements on values as semantic misunderstandings, reducing reasoning to decoding. However, it highlights a crucial dimension of emotive words: their role as premises in implicit arguments. Ducrot's account cannot explain how and why a conclusion implicit in the word meaning can affect our decisions. He developed the concept of emotive meaning but ignored the most powerful dimension of it, the alteration of interests and choices. In order to account for this pragmatic effect it is necessary to consider language as an instrument of real agents holding their own systems of beliefs and values. It is necessary to investigate the reasoning underlying our decision making and inquire into what makes a value a principle of action and decision making.

3.2. *The Prescriptive Meaning: Values as Principles of Action*
If Ducrot pointed out how emotive words are related to implicit patterns of reasoning, his theory cannot account for what Hare (1952) described as the 'prescriptive' dimension of meaning. Stevenson and Hare explained how certain words can affect our interests and move us to action, influencing our decisions. In order to explain this effect of ethical terms, we need to explain the crucial link between words and actions, or, rather, words, values, and choices.

Aristotle grounded the basic notions of his ethical and dialectical systems on the notions of good and desirable. In his view, a decision is always relative to a goal, and the goal can be what is good, or what appears to be good (*Nicomachean Ethics*, 1113a15). Such ethical principles are the basis of decision making. In the *Topics* Aristotle showed how a choice can be reduced to the classification of what is better, "for everything aims at the good (ταγαθον)" (*Topics*, 116a 18). From this perspective, the good, the

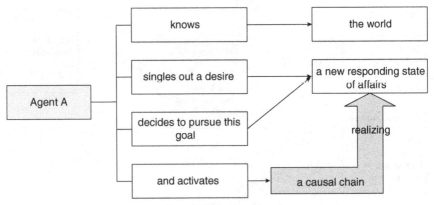

FIGURE 2.6. Values and action

pleasant, and the useful, namely, the desirable (αἱρετόν) (118b 27–30), are considered the principles of will and action: "Choice is desire pursuing what reason asserts to be good" (Burnyeat 1980: 83). The objects of choice are "the noble, the advantageous, the pleasant," while the objects of avoidance are "the base, the injurious, the painful." Pleasure, in particular, "accompanies all objects of choice; for even the noble and the advantageous appear pleasant" (*Nicomachean Ethics*, 1105a 1–2). Happiness and goodness can be identified as the ultimate goals of actions, which directly or indirectly aim at them. The teleological interpretation of action can be represented as in Figure 2.6 (Rigotti 2005: 64).

In Figure 2.6 we can notice how the final cause of action is the agent's desire, which the agent decides to realize through a causal chain. The desirable, which is what is good, is what moves an agent to action. The first crucial step is to establish what is good.

While in the *Nicomachean Ethics* Aristotle defends an absolute perspective on goodness that is related to the goal or function of life, in the *Rhetoric* and *Topics* he relates the concept of good to the reasons given to support a choice. For instance, we can consider a list of topics that are useful to classify something as good (*Rhetoric*, 1362b 2–18):

And the virtues are necessarily a good; for those having them are well-off in regard to them, and virtues are productive of good things and matters of action. Something must be said about each [virtue] separately, both what it is and what quality it has. *Pleasure*, too, is necessarily a good; for all living things by nature desire it. Thus, both pleasant things [*hēdea*] and fine things [*kala*] are necessarily goods [*agatha*]; for some are productive of pleasure; and in the case of fine things some are pleasant, others desirable in themselves. To speak of these one by one, the following are necessarily good: happiness (it is both desirable in itself and self-sufficient, and we choose other things to obtain it); justice, courage, temperance, magnanimity, magnificence, and similar dispositions (for they are virtues of the soul); and health and beauty and such things (for they are virtues of the body and productive of

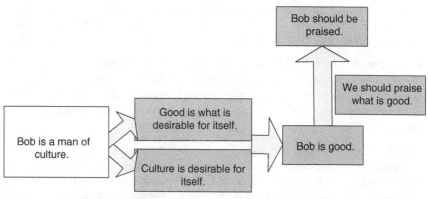

FIGURE 2.7. Values and actions – Culture

many things, for example health of pleasure and life, so health seems to be the best because it is the cause of the two things most honored by most people – pleasure and life).

In all these topics, we can notice there is a reason given to support the classification. We can apply such principles to emotive words and show how they work in their implicit reasoning structure. For instance, we can consider the redefinition of 'culture' provided by Stevenson (1938a: 332). The purpose of the speaker, in this case, was to praise a person having outstanding sensitivity and originality but little formal education. Why did the speaker choose to classify him as a man of 'culture'? The structure of the reasoning that he is triggering can be represented as shown in Figure 2.7.

In this case, the grey boxes represent the implicit premises that constitute the grounds of the attribution of the value judgment (Bob is good) and support a possible choice of action (to praise Bob).

This general structure relies on ideal values that are shared by everybody. However, this is not always the case, as men have different hierarchies of values. For some, culture is the ultimate good; for others, it is not desirable in itself, but only if it is a means to money. Therefore, the principle of action needs to be applied to men's dispositions, characters, and hierarchies of values. Aristotle recognizes that, along with an absolute and abstract concept of goodness, there is a relative one:

And most of all, each category of people [values as a good] that to which their character is disposed; for example, those fond of victory [value something] if it will be a victory, those fond of honor if it will be an honor, those fond of money if there will be money, and others similarly. Persuasive arguments [*pisteis*] on the subject of a good and the advantageous should be taken from these [elements or topics]. (*Rhetoric*, 1363b 1–5)

In the same way also it is in certain places honourable to sacrifice one's father, e.g. among the Triballi, whereas, without qualification, it is not honourable. Or possibly this may indicate a relativity not to places but to persons; for it makes no difference wherever they may be; for everywhere it will be honourable for them. Again, at certain times it is a good thing to take medicines, e.g. when one is ill, but it is not so without qualification. (*Topics*, 115b 24–27)

Culture and character, but also circumstances, influence what is good for the different speakers. From this perspective, different hierarchies of values (or rather principles of choice and possible classifications of what is to be held as 'good') are the source of conflicts of interests (*Nicomachean Ethics*, 1095a 18–27):

Verbally there is very general agreement; for both the general run of men and people of superior refinement say that it is happiness, and identify living well and doing well with being happy; but with regard to what happiness is they differ, and the many do not give the same account as the wise. For the former think it is some plain and obvious thing, like pleasure, wealth, or honour; they differ, however, from one another – and often even the same man identifies it with different things, with health when he is ill, with wealth when he is poor; but, conscious of their ignorance, they admire those who proclaim some great ideal that is above their comprehension.

When two things appear desirable in the same way to the interlocutors, it is necessary to solve a kind of conflict of values. In the *Topics* and in the *Rhetoric*, Aristotle deals with conflicting values by formulating the topic of the preferable. For instance, a topic of this kind is (*Topics*, 116a 28–34):

That which is desired for itself is more desirable than that which is desired for something else; e.g. health is more desirable than gymnastics: for the former is desired for itself, the latter for something else. Also, that which is desirable in itself is more desirable than what is desirable *per accidens*; e.g. justice in our friends than justice in our enemies: for the former is desirable in itself, the latter per accidens: for we desire that our enemies should be just *per accidens*, in order that they may do us no harm.

We should notice that there is an essential difference in arguing starting from a shared absolute notion of 'good' or 'goal of life' and conflicts involving the very concepts of happiness and goodness (see *Nicomachean Ethics*, 1095b 1-1096a 10). For some people the goal of life and happiness is pleasure; for others it is honor. There are levels of agreement and corresponding levels of conflict that can arise from values. Therefore, ethical words can have different effects depending on the interlocutors. The more shared the values are, the more effective the use of a specific emotive word will be.

4. The Logic of Values

Aristotle pointed out in his *Ethics* the connection between values and actions. In his *Rhetoric* and *Topics* we can notice how he described the reasoning mechanism underlying values and decisions. He showed how values affect the interpretation of what is good, and how different values lead to different value judgments. The existence of different human characters and contingent situations affect the hierarchies of values and the way we assess states of affairs. For this reason, the evaluation of a situation can lead to different or conflicting conclusions, to a conflict of values that can be solved by establishing what is better. In modern studies, this process of decision making has been represented as patterns of argument, called argumentation schemes (Walton, Reed & Macagno 2008). Argumentation schemes are abstract representations of the relationship between the material link (the semantic connection; see Van Dijk 1977) between the sentences constituting the premise and the conclusion, and the logical rule governing the passage from the former to the latter. Arguments can have deductive, inductive, or abductive logical forms and proceed from causal connections between things, from the meaning of terms, from the relationship between the interlocutors, or from the status of the speaker. The premises can be rules, dialogical norms, or accepted opinions (Walton & Macagno 2005a). In order to analyze the persuasive structure of emotive words, we need to consider the two types of reasoning governing their two dimensions: their 'emotive' and their 'descriptive' components.

4.1. *Argument from Values*

In the modern tradition the concept of desirable and the ethical action model are the basis of a pattern of inference called *argument from values* (Bench-Capon 2003: 429–448, 2002: 231–245). This abstract structure of reasoning is grounded on specific elements that have been described as follows (Atkinson, Bench-Capon & McBurney 2005: 1261):

SCHEME FOR VALUE-BASED PRACTICAL REASONING

In the current circumstances R
we should perform action A
to achieve New Circumstances S
which will realize some goal G
which will promote some value V

The structure of this inference has been investigated in argumentation theory in syllogistic terms as a relationship between a rule of inference, a 'factual' premise, and a conclusion (see Bench-Capon & Atkinson 2009). In this fashion, the relationship between desire and values is underscored and considered as the core of the reasoning pattern. From this perspective, 'value' is intended to mean the quality (positive or negative) that renders something desirable or valuable. It is the characteristic that makes the state of affairs the goal that leads an agent to action. The argument from values represents the process of reasoning based on two steps. The interlocutor is invited to consider a certain state of affairs as desirable, and therefore as a reason for action. Regarding a certain situation as desirable can change the interlocutor's interests and modify his commitments and decisions. For this reason, the argument from values is a kind of teleological argumentation grounded on commonly shared premises expressing what is or may be desirable and objectionable, and can be described as follows: *x* (a state of affairs) is classified as *V* (a value, which can be positive or negative on the ground of the shared knowledge, or *endoxa*[3]); value *V* (which represents the reason of the [non] desirability of *x*) implies that agent *A* should consider positively (negatively) goal *G*, which is necessary to carry out *x* (Walton, Reed & Macagno 2008: 321):

ARGUMENTATION SCHEME 1: ARGUMENT FROM POSITIVE VALUE

Premise 1	The state of affairs *x* is *positive* as judged by agent *A* according to value *V* (value judgment).
Premise 2	The fact that *x* is *positive* affects the interpretation and therefore the evaluation of goal *G* of agent *A* (if *x* is *good*, it supports commitment to goal *G*).
Conclusion	The evaluation of *x* according to value *V* is a reason for retaining commitment to goal *G*.

ARGUMENTATION SCHEME 2: ARGUMENT FROM NEGATIVE VALUE

Premise 1	The state of affairs *x* is *negative* as judged by agent *A* according to value *V* (value judgment).
Premise 2	The fact that *x* is *negative* affects the interpretation and therefore the evaluation of goal *G* of agent *A* (if *x* is *bad*, it goes against commitment to goal *G*).
Conclusion	The evaluation of *x* according to value *V* is a reason for retracting commitment to goal *G*.

This type of reasoning proceeds from a value judgment grounded on values to an action. The structure of the inference can be represented considering a clear case in which values affect decisions:

1. You should marry Sean. He is tall, bright, and incredibly rich.

This piece of advice is grounded on a value judgment: Sean is good as a husband. The whole reasoning is based on the definition of what is a 'good husband.' In this case, the speaker holds that richness is a quality of a husband

---

[3] The relation between desirability, choice, and *endoxa* can be found in Cicero's *De Inventione*. Cicero, analyzing deliberation, gives a value scale: "Rerum expetandarum tria genera sunt; par autem numerus vitandarum ex contraria parte. Nam est quidam, quod sua vi nos adlicitat ad sese, non emolumento captans aliquo, sed trahens sua dignitate, quod genus virtus, scientia, veritas. Est aliud autem non propter suam vim et naturam, sed propter fructum atque utilitatem petendum ; quod <genus> pecunia est. Est porro quiddam ex horum partibus iunctum, quod et sua vi et dignitate nos inlectos ducit et prae se quandam gerit utilitatem, quo magis expetatur, ut amicitia, bona existimatio" (Ciceronis, *De Inventione*, II, 52).

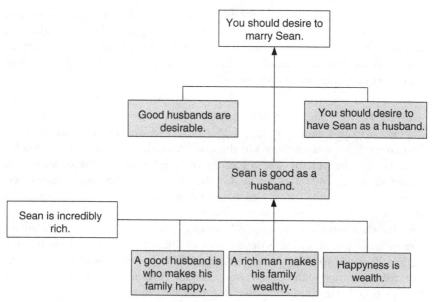

FIGURE 2.8. Argument from values

that is sought after, and therefore a reason to invite the interlocutor to desire him as a husband. We can represent the structure of the explicit and implicit reasoning as shown in Figure 2.8.

The grey boxes represent the implicit premises that support the conclusion. The value judgment is grounded on what is commonly accepted. In this case, the argument is reasonable, as wealth is commonly understood as a possible value, a possible (even though not necessarily upheld) criterion for classifying what is a good husband. Moreover, in (1) other criteria are put forward to influence the decision. Sean is described as 'tall' and 'bright,' which can lead to attribute to him him the quality of being attractive or desirable from a physical and intellectual perspective. All such qualities and values (intelligent men are desirable; good-looking men are desirable; brightness is a sign of intelligence; tallness is nice) are culture dependent. Even if the hearer does not believe that richness or physical qualities make a good husband, he knows that this can be a standard of evaluation. Even though the hearer may consider the argument as non-persuasive, he would still regard it as reasonable. The reasonableness of the arguments that the use of ethical terms implies can be understood from the following example:

2. You should marry Sean. He is fat, violent, and incredibly poor.

This argument would sound ridiculous if advanced in a Western society. It would breach the commonly shared criteria of classification, as the afore-mentioned qualities cannot count as a 'handsome man' or a 'good husband.'

However, in some cultures fat men are usually regarded as wealthy or hand-some, and violent men as passionate. *Understanding* the values, or rather the implicit criteria of classification, needs to be distinguished from *disagreeing* about values. The organization of the values in hierarchies is different from considering a value as a criterion of classification.

4.2. *The Logical Components of Prescriptive Meaning*

Argument from values is a complex pattern of reasoning. It proceeds from certain qualities to an action. On the one hand, the qualities are criteria for establishing whether the state of affairs referred to by the use of an ethical term is desirable or contemptible. On the other hand, desirability and objec-tionability are reasons to act in a certain fashion. These two components emerge clearly from the aforementioned example. Sean's richness is a crite-rion for classifying him as a good husband, based on some accepted values. Since choice pursues what is desirable, and the good is what is desirable, the agent will decide to carry out the action needed to pursue the object of desire. For instance, since Sean is good as a husband, the hearer should try to pursue the desire of having a good husband by marrying him.

The first type of reasoning can be considered as an instance of reasoning from verbal classification (Hastings 1963: 36–52). This pattern of reason-ing proceeds from certain qualities to the attribution of another property to the subject. It can be represented as follows (Walton 1996: 54, 2002: 51; Walton, Reed & Macagno 2008: 319):

ARGUMENTATION SCHEME 3: ARGUMENT FROM VERBAL
CLASSIFICATION

Premise 1	If some particular thing a can be classified as falling under verbal category C, then a has property F (in virtue of such a classification).
Premise 2	a can be classified as falling under verbal category C.
Conclusion	a has property F.

CRITICAL QUESTIONS

CQ_1	Does a definitely have F, or there is room for doubt?
CQ_2	Can the verbal classification (in the second premise) be said to hold strongly, or is it one of those weak classifications that is subject to doubt?

In case of ethical terms, the property to be attributed (F) corresponds to a value judgment, such as 'to be good' or 'to be objectionable.' The relation-ship between the quality possessed by the entity (category C) and the value judgment is supported by commonly shared criteria, a particular kind of major, or classification premises. Aristotle lists such commonly shared criteria in his *Rhetoric* as topics for the classification of an object or fact as good or desirable. Such topics can be more general or more specific. For example, in the previous section we mentioned specific topics regarding things that are good. Different people may have different values, different specific ways of classifying something as good. However, such specific topics can be traced back to some generic principles constituting the most important and essential criteria for classifying something as good (*Rhetoric*, 1362a 23–30):

Let a good [*agathon*] be [defined as] whatever is chosen for itself and that for the sake of which we choose something else and what everything having perception or intelligence aims at or what everything would [aim at] if it could acquire intelligence. Both what intelligence would give to each and what intelligence does give to each in individual cases is the good for each; and whatever by its presence causes one to be well-off and independent; and independence itself; and what is productive or preservative of such things; and what such things follow upon; and what is preventative and destructive of the opposite.

What "is to be chosen for its own sake" can be established on the basis of a person's experiences or culture. Value judgments, therefore, are forms of classification based a particular kind of 'definitional' premise, namely, values. In this view, moral judgments can be considered as the product of a classificatory reasoning process, in which the endoxical premise is drawn not from the shared knowledge of the language but from the shared values.

The second component of reasoning from values is the reasoning passage from moral judgment to action. For instance, in the case mentioned previously, Sean's richness is considered as a criterion (neither necessary nor sufficient) for classifying him as a 'good husband.' The values are premises used to establish whether a certain state of affairs (Sean as a husband) is desirable. This value judgment leads the hearer to make a decision about how to act. The relationship between judgment and action can be conceived as a pattern of reasoning connecting an action, or rather a declaration of intention (von Wright 1972: 41), or commitment, with its grounds (Anscombe 1998: 11). Such an argument is based on the Kantian principle that "Who wills the ends wills (so far as reason has decisive influence on his actions) also the means which are indispensably necessary and in his power" (von Wright 1972: 45). Along with this transmission of intentions the reasoning proceeds from the specific relationship between means and ends. This pattern, called practical reasoning, is represented by the following scheme (Walton, Reed & Macagno 2008: 323).

ARGUMENTATION SCHEME 4: PRACTICAL REASONING

Premise 1	I (an agent) have a goal G.
Premise 2	Carrying out this action A is a means to realize G.
Conclusion	Therefore, I ought to (practically speaking) carry out this action A.

For instance, if Sean is desirable as a husband, a way to pursue the desire of having a good husband is to marry Sean.

Emotive language also triggers other types of reasoning, or rather other connections between judgments and intentions. For example, we can consider negative value judgments such as "Bob is a criminal." In this case, the reasoning leading to action is not to pursue a goal, but to avoid a consequence. The reasoning is not from end to means, but from consequences. A criminal is not good, and in particular he is not good because he can be dangerous for us. In order to avoid bad consequences (the quality of "being bad for our safety") the agent will avoid the possible actions leading to such a situation, such as getting close to him. This complex scheme, called argument from consequences, presupposes a judgment and practical reasoning (Walton 1995: 155–156):

ARGUMENTATION SCHEME 5: ARGUMENT FROM POSITIVE
CONSEQUENCES

Premise 1	If *A* is brought about, then good consequences will plausibly occur.
Conclusion	Therefore *A* should be brought about.

ARGUMENTATION SCHEME 6: ARGUMENT FROM NEGATIVE
CONSEQUENCES

Premise 1	If *A* is brought about, then bad consequences will plausibly occur.
Conclusion	Therefore *A* should not be brought about.

The schemes from classification, practical reasoning, and consequences describe the deep structure of argument from values. Emotive language is, from a logical point of view, a mistake, as it leads from descriptive premises to a prescriptive conclusion. However, the passage from the evaluation of a state of affairs to the intention to act can be interpreted in terms of ground of action. Building on the ancient Aristotelian account of action, we can conceive the decision-making process as a passage from desire to the intention to pursue one's desire, which needs to be adequate to reality, considering the goal and the possible and reasonable means to achieve it (Von Wright 1972: 45). From this view, ethical terms trigger a complex process of reasoning that is ultimately based on general criteria establishing what is good. Specific values determine what is desirable in a particular case for a particular culture, society, or character. The generic and abstract scheme allows for different interpretations. However, the specific premises establishing what is good in a particular situation need to be shared in order for the reasoning to be effective.

5. Hierarchies and Conflicts of Values

Values are the most crucial and potentially controversial constituent of emotive words. They are fundamental for the prescriptive effect, for the relationship between the description of the state of affairs and the influence of the interlocutor's interests. Their controversial character can be described by considering Aristotle's account of the different types of men and the different contingent conditions that make some values more desirable than others. Perelman and Olbrechts-Tyteca distinguished the relativity of values from their sharedness. In their view, most of the differences in judging a state of affairs and support for a decision or behavior are rooted not in values but in the way they are organized in hierarchies (Perelman & Olbrechts-Tyteca 1951: 252):

> All audiences accept values as well, whether abstract values, such as justice, or concrete values, such as one's country. These values are generally accepted only by a particular audience. Some of them are considered universal values, but it could doubtless be shown that they are so regarded only on condition that their content is not specified. Besides, it is not so much the values to which they adhere as the manner in which they arrange the values in a hierarchy, which makes it possible to describe a particular audience.

The way we consider one value superior to another characterizes our interests and therefore our evaluation of the states of affairs. The conflict of values can be described by using an example examined by Bench-Capon (2002, 2003). He offered the case of Hal and Carla as an example. Diabetic Hal needs insulin to survive but cannot get any in time to save his life except by taking some from Carla's house without her permission. The argument from positive value for preserving life is pitted against the negative value of taking someone's property without his or her permission. If we consider reasoning from values only in terms of the values shared, we face a decisional deadlock. The conflict of values risks leading to the so-called Buridan's ass dilemma, where a donkey, equally hungry and thirsty, when confronted with water and a pile of hay, cannot choose and dies both of hunger and thirst. For this reason, the argument from values is grounded not only on the shared knowledge establishing what is good, but also on the *endoxa* leading to classify one value as better than another. In this case, life and honesty are the conflicting values that can be ordered in a hierarchy considering the aforementioned topics of the better (see Figure 2.9).

The argument from values, or rather the component of the argument from values proceeding from reasoning from classification, in this case is aimed at establishing what is *better*, not simply what is *good*. The topics, or rather the implicit shared premises used to classify what is to be considered as "preferable," are used to support a potentially controversial decision.

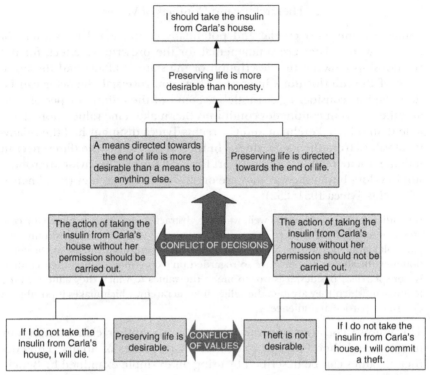

FIGURE 2.9. Conflict and hierarchies of values in Hal and Carla example

The interlocutors in a dialogue can have conflicting values. In this case, the dialogue may lead to opposed viewpoints grounded on conflicts of values. In order to find an agreement or at least try to solve the difference of opinions, the interlocutors need to find the clashing hierarchies of values, the different ways they regard what is 'more desirable.' For instance, we can examine the Douglas–Lincoln debate on the abolition of slavery in the United States (Bench-Capon and Atkinson 2009: 48). Whereas Douglas refused to accept the uniformity of the abolition in all states, defending the legislative freedom of the states, Lincoln supported that decision on the grounds of inviolable human rights. The two arguments can be represented by the following statements (Basler 1946: 436; Hammond, Hardwick & Howard 2007: 1052):

Douglas: [U]niformity in the local laws and institutions of the different States is neither possible or desirable. If uniformity had been adopted when the Government was established, it must inevitably have been the uniformity of slavery everywhere, or else the uniformity of negro citizenship and negro equality everywhere. ... I ask you, are you in favor of conferring upon the negro the rights and privileges of citizenship? ("No, no.") Do you desire to strike out of our State Constitution that clause which keeps slaves and free negroes out of the State, and allow the free negroes to flow in, ("never,") and cover your prairies with black settlements?

Lincoln: This declared indifference, but, as I must think, covert real zeal for the spread of slavery, I cannot but hate. I hate it because of the monstrous injustice of slavery itself. I hate it because it deprives our republican example of its just influence in the world – enables the enemies of free institutions, with plausibility, to taunt us as hypocrites – causes the real friends of freedom to doubt our sincerity, and especially because it forces so many really good men amongst ourselves into an open war with the very fundamental principles of civil liberty – criticizing the Declaration of Independence, and insisting that there is no right principle of action but self-interest.

In this case, both parties acknowledge the values of equality among men, civil liberty, and the interests of the white (richer) men. However, the two parties have different hierarchies. Douglas holds that the interests of the white man are better than civil liberty. On the contrary, Lincoln supports the ideal of equality, preferring it to the whites' interests. The two viewpoints are apparently not conflicting from the point of view of values. Douglas does not mention the need to defend civil liberties and Lincoln does not directly challenge the risks of extending citizenship. They simply focus their argument on the highest value. The two different hierarchies are shared among the audience they are directing their arguments to. Douglas knows that for the Southern landed gentry, granting civil rights to the high number of slaves employed in agriculture would result in an economic disaster. Lincoln is representing the interests of the Northern and more industrialized states, not economically dependent on slaves' work. For them, the hierarchy between civil values and interests was easier to establish. The argument can be represented as in Figure 2.10.

The conflict of hierarchies is much more complex than a simple conflict of values. It is not a matter of considering a different value and weighting it accordingly, but analyzing two different criteria for weighting values. For Douglas, "If the consequences be evil, that is more desirable which is followed by the less evil" (*Topics*, 117a 8–9). Since the abolition of slavery would cause great damage to the white people's interests, for the white people slavery would be a lesser evil. The contrary argument applies to northern workers and entrepreneurs for whom the commercial interests and the image of their country prevailed: "The one which is followed by the greater good is the more desirable" (*Topics*, 117a 7–8). Lincoln does not stress just this one such principle ("Slavery deprives America of its influence") but also a more generic one (slavery is said to be a 'monstrous injustice' and to be against freedom): what is good absolutely is more desirable than what is good for a particular person (*Topics*, 116b7–8). In this fashion, he stresses the particular interests of his audience and at the same time challenges the

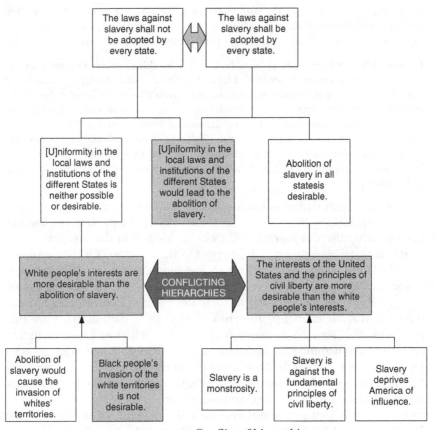

FIGURE 2.10. Conflict of hierarchies

particular interests that Douglas is defending ("There is no right principle of action but self-interest").

This complex mechanism of implicit hierarchies underlies another persuasive strategy, the quasi-definition. In quasi-definitions the definition, or rather the descriptive meaning of the term, is maintained but the system of values associated with the fragment of reality it refers to is modified. Quasi-definitions are strategies to alter the hierarchies of values that a word supports and can be more or less dependent on implicit moves. For instance, we can consider the following quasi-definition, in which Don Juan is trying to persuade his interlocutor, Sganarelle, of the negativity of marriage and fidelity (Molière 2000: 98):

QUASI-DEFINITION OF 'MARRIAGE'

Don Juan: What! Would you restrict a man to staying chained to the first woman who takes his fancy, have him give up everything for her and never look at any others again? The idea is ludicrous – making a bogus virtue out of being faithful, being trapped forever in the same relationship and as good as dead from youth onwards to the other pretty faces that might catch our eye! No no: fidelity is for imbeciles. All beautiful women are entitled to our love, and the accident of being the first on the scene shouldn't deprive the rest of the rightful claims they have on our affections.

In this example, Don Juan explicitly claims his sheer refusal of the hierarchy of virtue-pleasure. He quasi-defines 'marriage' by rejecting the superiority of the value of faithfulness over pleasure.

In modern rhetoric, the best example that can be found is perhaps Obama's Nobel Prize address. The entire speech is aimed at quasi-defining war (or rather 'just war,' one of its species). In order to justify the wars waged by the United States, Obama needed to show that wars can be positive, contradicting the common evaluation of them. For this reason, he begins his speech by describing a new (even though accepted) kind of war, just war (Barack Obama, *Nobel Peace Prize Acceptance Address*, Oslo, Norway, December 10, 2009):

The concept of a "just war" emerged, suggesting that war is justified only when it meets certain preconditions: if it is waged as a last resort or in self-defense; if the forced used is proportional, and if, whenever possible, civilians are spared from violence.

The definition of this kind of war introduces definitional elements that can lead to a positive evaluation. In this fashion, Obama manages to focus his speech on a new concept where the negative judgment is associated with a positive one, counterbalancing it. The limitation of violence mentioned in the definition of 'just war' is combined with its quasi-definition (emphasis added):

QUASI-DEFINITION OF 'WAR'

The **service and sacrifice of our men and women in uniform has promoted peace and prosperity** from Germany to Korea, and enabled democracy to take hold in places like the Balkans. We have borne this burden not because we seek to impose our will. We have done so out of enlightened self-interest – because we seek a better future for our children and grandchildren, and we believe that their lives will be better if other peoples' children and grandchildren can live in freedom and prosperity. So yes, **the instruments of war do have a role to play in preserving the peace.** And yet this truth must coexist with another – that no matter how justified, **war promises human tragedy.**

This quasi-definition of 'war' introduces a new standard of evaluation of war, presenting it as an 'instrument for preserving peace,' coexisting with the undeniable one of 'human tragedy.' With these two definitional moves, Obama restricts the concept of 'war' to a specific kind, where the 'human tragedy' is limited, which is further quasi-defined in a positive fashion, even though admitting its negative face.

Obama's quasi-definition of 'war' is explicit and is based on commonly accepted principles and hierarchies of values. Everybody accepts that peace, freedom, and prosperity are good, and that violence is bad. For this reason, Obama advances two arguments to support his viewpoint that just wars should be praised (emphasis added):

This becomes particularly important when the purpose of military action extends beyond self-defense or the defense of one nation against an aggressor. More and more, we all confront difficult questions about how to **prevent the slaughter of civilians by their own government**, or to **stop a civil war** whose **violence and suffering** can engulf an entire region.

I believe that **force can be justified on humanitarian grounds**, as it was in the Balkans, or in other places that have been scarred by war. Inaction tears at our conscience and can lead to more costly intervention later. That is why all responsible nations must embrace the role that militaries with a clear mandate can play **to keep the peace**.

The definition of 'just war' and its quasi-definition were successful in this speech because Obama set out a new specific hierarchy of values associated with the new concept of war. The deadlock between the contrasting positive and negative values is solved by showing that certain situations of (apparent) peace are violent and involve human tragedy, while war can bring true peace. In this fashion he introduces and defends the hierarchy "freedom, prosperity and peace (just war) vs. continuing human tragedy (apparent peace)." However, a potential problem can arise with these new concepts (apparent peace, unjust war), namely, their boundaries, as we will show in the following chapters.

The explicit quasi-definition is not the only strategy to challenge and alter the hierarchies of values. The speaker can also decide to undermine the hierarchy from its roots, attacking the grounds on which it is based. For instance, we can consider the quasi-definition of 'blackguard' mentioned in Chapter 1. The speaker quasi-defines the word in order to support the view that unfaithful people are to be praised, as they are 'original,' 'sincere,' and 'interesting,' as they live according to nature and without the limits of virtue and old-fashioned and boring honesty. This argument can be described as a double attack on the traditional system of values. A new hierarchy dominated by the couple boringness–originality replaces the traditional hierarchy of values organized according to the principle "that is more desirable which serves the better purpose, e.g. that which serves to promote virtue more than that which serves to promote pleasure" (*Topics*, 118b 33–34). The hierarchy in which virtue was considered better than pleasure is redefined as a new hierarchy: originality, sincerity, and individuality vs. dullness, artificiality (unnaturality), and lack of creativity. However, this new hierarchy redefines the deep concepts of vice and virtue. The original argumentation from values (virtue is more desirable than pleasure; therefore it should be pursued) is not challenged, but simply substituted with a new one (unfaithfulness is original and fun; originality and fun are more desirable than boringness, dullness, and unnaturality, and therefore unfaithfulness should be praised). However, this alteration of hierarchies of values is not made explicit, nor is it supported by arguments. The speaker simply takes the new hierarchy as granted by the whole community of speakers and tries to get his thesis accepted on these grounds.

Hierarchies of values and reasoning from what is 'better' are the two basic concepts on which the prescriptive dimension of emotive language rests. An emotive word often conceals an implicit attack on values and hierarchies, which can be solved only by reconstructing the new hierarchy that is implicitly advocated and the implicit moves that the speaker implicitly performs.

6. The Reasonableness of Emotions

In the previous sections, emotive language has been referred to as the use of ethical or emotive words. What is the relationship between ethics, or rather judgments based on values and desires, and emotions? The prescriptive effect of ethical words can be understood as a pattern of reasoning leading to an action. How can this decision-making process be somehow related to emotions? Stevenson (1944), Hare (1963), and Halldén (1960) pointed out how, to a certain extent, emotive meaning is dependent on culture and evaluation of reality. How can emotions be grounded on thought and judgment?

Contrary to common wisdom, "emotions and thought do not displace one other" (Pugmire 1998: 7). Judgments and emotions are strictly interwoven. For instance, a condition of hope is a value judgment on what is hoped for. If it is not considered as worth, it cannot be hoped (Pugmire 1998: 7). This relationship between value judgment and emotions has been stressed by several studies (Pugmire 2005: 12):

Most notably, as many philosophers and psychologists have delightedly insisted, emotions are not just feelings, when they are feelings at all. They involve thoughts, and they involve them essentially. For, as many would have it, first and foremost in an emotion one represents something to oneself in a characteristic way (I can only be disappointed at what I perceive to be the dashing of my hope). An emotion's thought-content is very often what makes sense of it and even determines its identity. Thus, a compromising situation that is my fault is shaming, whereas one that is just awkward luck is embarrassing; so that my belief about how I got into this situation decides which of these emotions my discomfiture at it amounts to.

Emotions are not simply feelings (Leighton 1984), even though feelings are rooted in reasons that can be cognitive or physical, and feelings such as like and dislike need to be grounded on reasons, which can be personal standards or cultural considerations (Manicas & Kruger 1968: 427). There is a valuation whenever an emotion arises. For this reason, emotions can be considered as reactions to appraisals, to judgments on a specific object or state of affairs (Pugmire 2005: 16). The relationship between physical reaction and evaluation can be shown in the analysis of the emotion of fear (Leighton 1988: 205):

[...] certain contextual judgments seem necessary for the plausible attribution of emotion. To describe you as afraid of a bear requires not only an object of fear, but also that you view the object as in some way dangerous. Other wise, you may have bodily upset, feelings, desires, even behavior – these, though noteworthy in themselves, do not seem sufficient to account for the matter being one of fear.

The value judgment can be conceived as the ground of emotions and their identity (Pugmire 2005: 13). On this view, to feel an emotion amounts to implicitly appraising a state of affairs (Solomon 2003: 7–8):

[...] emotions are interestingly similar to beliefs. We can now explain this similarity by claiming that emotions are judgments – normative and often moral judgments. "I am angry at John for taking ("stealing" begs the question) my car" entails that I believe that John has somehow wronged me [...]. The moral judgment entailed by anger is not a judgment about my anger [...]. My anger is that judgment. If I do not believe that I have somehow been wronged, I cannot be angry (though I might be upset, or sad). Similarly, if I cannot praise my lover, I cannot be in love (though I might want her or need her, which, traditional wisdom aside, is entirely different). If I do not find my situation awkward, I cannot be ashamed or embarrassed. If I do not judge that I have suffered a loss, I cannot be sad or jealous. [...] emotions in general do appear to require this feature: to have an emotion is to hold a normative judgment about one's situation.

The judgment (or rather the cognitive change) is the reason for a physical and psychical reaction that can drive us to action (Frijda & Mesquita 2000: 46). Emotions are motivations to action (Pugmire 2005: 78). For instance, we care about a person because we love him or her; we run away from a dangerous situation because we fear it. But emotions are also means to value reality. Emotions are grounded on implicit appraisals that we experience through a physical reaction. In this fashion, when we admire or are disgusted by someone or something we vividly experience a value judgment and at the same time we are lead to certain decisions or readiness to act in a specific fashion (Frijda & Mesquita 2000: 64), such as praise whom we admire or attack or avoid what we despise (Pugmire 2005: 78). However, how are emotions related to actions? A possible answer lies in the system of values.

The system of desires, or rather values, assumes a crucial importance in the mechanism of emotions. Values are both the grounds of appraisal and judgment, and the reasons for action. The relationship between emotions and values can be explained starting from the ontology of emotions that can be found in Aristotle's *Rhetoric*. In *Rhetoric* II, Aristotle analyzes emotions in terms of representations, or, using the modern cognitive studies terminology, sceneries (Solomon 2003; Pugmire 2005: 13). For instance, the feeling of anger can be examined as presupposing the perception of an offense together with the desire of action (Solomon 2003: 92). Other emotions, such as fear, presuppose that the feared situation is not desirable, together with the desire of avoiding it (Solomon 2003: 107). Desire, we can notice in these examples, is the key notion for understanding the link between subjectivity and perception, and it is the essential component of every emotion.[4] Without a system of values, that is, a system of reasons to act (or objects of desire), a situation or state of affairs cannot be assessed as 'good' or 'bad' for the agent. Without assessment, the agent cannot relate himself to the situation. Consequently, he cannot be interested in it, and thereby cannot experience an emotion (see, e.g., Damasio 1994: 191 for the notion of emotions as voluntary evaluative processes). Emotions are in fact assessments that are perceived as particularly important for the agent (Solomon 2003: 104). For this reason, emotions play a crucial role in the process of decision making. Damasio (2000: 302, 1994: 269–272) showed how people incapable of experiencing emotions because of brain injuries were incapable of making decisions. Emotions, in fact, derive from the positive or negative experiences (which might be individual or common) associated with a certain situation through learning. Plantin notices how a described event could arouse emotions because it represents a possible source of happiness or pain (Plantin 2004: 272); on this view, a description can direct the interlocutor's choices in relation to what he considers desirable or objectionable, namely in relation to his values. The perception of an event as pleasant or painful can be subjective (such as the pleasure of the smell of the flowers) or social, stemming from the values shared in a community. For instance, money might be a socially accepted value, and therefore it generates an emotion of pleasure and in this fashion influences the interlocutor's choices.

The last fundamental dimension of emotions is their cultural dimension. Emotions are based on a system of values, which can derive from an agent's past experiences or culture. The past experiences of the positive or negative consequences brought about by a determinate state of affairs determine the criteria for judging similar situations in relation to their possible future outcomes. For example, the negative experience of a bee sting constitutes a criterion for forecasting certain possible outcomes of a situation, such as, for instance, the sight of a bee (Damasio 1994: 246). The experiences of past emotions are therefore cognitive instruments, through which an individual interprets a situation and emotively reacts to it. People appraise a state of affairs or entities on the basis of their personal past experiences of what can cause positive or negative consequences. However, the knowledge of positive or negative outcomes

---

[4] "[...] emotions essentially involve desires, expectations, purposes, and attitude. Emotions are motivated by desires, sometimes distinguished by desires, and in virtually every case some desire is essential to an emotion" (Solomon 2003: 20).

is the result of the process of learning (see Frijda & Masquita 1998); in other words, values are in part culture dependent (Solomon 2003: 87):

An emotion is a system of concepts, beliefs, attitudes, and desires, virtually all of which are context-bound, historically developed, and culture-specific.

Depending on the culture, value judgments may vary and so can emotions. The same action can be considered as offensive in a culture and arouse rage or indignation, while in another social context it can be assessed as normal. For instance, jealousy is strictly related to monogamy. In a polygamic culture a person can evaluate his or her spouse's extramarital affairs as not offensive. Such a situation would not lead the agent to the conclusion that he or she has been "robbed by another of vital physical attention" (De Sousa 1987: 255) and, therefore, the emotion of jealousy would not be aroused (De Sousa 1987: 185).

The relationship between emotions, value judgments, and decisions is the ground for the strategies of emotive language. In ancient rhetoric, the analysis of passions was pivotal for their arousal. The rhetorician needed to know how to amplify or distort judgment in order to generate the wanted emotion in the audience so that "The judge, when overcome by his emotions, abandons all attempt to enquire into the truth of the arguments, is swept along by the tide of passion, and yields himself unquestioning to the torrent" (*Institutio Oratoria*, VI, 2, 6). This mechanism of genesis of emotions is rooted in the distortion of the value judgment on the state of affairs (Leigh 2004: 128):

The Stoic account of the passions represents them either as feelings attendant on a judgment or as inseparable from the judgment itself. The former position is associated with Zeno and the first Stoics, the latter with Chrysippus. In the first case, the judgment is that x is good or bad and the passion the feeling generated by that judgment. In the latter, the judgment is that x is good or bad and that it is right to react passionately to it. In both cases the crucial factor is that the judgments involved are false.

The relationship between value judgment and emotions is grounded on the concept of vivid representation mentioned by Quintilian (*Institutio Oratoria*, VI, 2, 34; see also the notion of "vividness effect" described by Frijda 1998: 276). In his view, the purpose of the lawyer was to use words to depict a situation in which the essential components of emotions emerge. The speaker needs to feel the emotions and act as if he were the victim or the disgraced party. In this fashion, the audience can be emotionally involved and can emotionally identify themselves with the feelings of the allegedly wronged person (Quintiliani, *Institutio Oratoria*, VI, 2, 34). For this reason, the speaker can arouse strong passions by distorting or amplifying the facts so that the jury will reach an incorrect assessment or will be led to excessive conclusions on the wave of emotions. The instrument to pursue this goal lies in the strategies of amplification mentioned in Chapter 1.

The speaker will distort the facts or use metaphors to hide their real nature (*Institutio Oratoria*, VI, 2, 23–30):

> Meanwhile I will content myself with the observation that the aim of appeals to the emotion is not merely to shew the bitter and grievous nature of ills that actually are so, but also at once make ills which are usually regarded as tolerable seem unendurable, as for instance when we represent insulting words as inflicting more grievous injury than an actual blow or represent disgrace as being worse than death. For the force of eloquence is such that it not merely compels the judge to the conclusion toward which the nature of the facts leads him, but awakens emotions which either do not naturally arise from the case or are stronger than the case would suggest. This is known as deinosis, that is to say, language giving additional force to things unjust, cruel or hateful, an accomplishment in which Demosthenes created immense and special effect.

Metaphors and amplifications are one of the possible instruments of emotions. However, Quintilian also acknowledges another type of power of words, the power of depicting the scene (see Cigada 2006: 113) and highlighting the judgments that trigger the emotions (*Institutio Oratoria*, VI, 2, 29–31):

> But how are we to generate these emotions in ourselves, since emotion is not in our own power? I will try to explain as best I may. There are certain experiences which the Greeks call φαντασίαι, and the Romans *visions*, whereby things absent are presented to our imagination with such extreme vividness that they seem actually to be before our very eyes. It is the man who is really sensitive to such impressions who will have the greatest power over the emotions. Some writers describe the possessor of this power of vivid imagination, whereby things, words and actions are presented in the most realistic manner, by the Greek word ευφαντασίωτος; and it is a power which all may readily acquire if they will. [...] I am complaining that a man has been murdered. Shall I not bring before my eyes all the circumstances which it is reasonable to imagine must have occurred in such a connexion? Shall I not see the assassin burst suddenly from his hiding-place, the victim tremble, cry for help, beg for mercy, or turn to run? Shall I not see the fatal blow delivered and the stricken body fall? Will not the blood, the deathly pallor, the groan of agony, the death-rattle, be indelibly impressed upon my mind?

Words can depict a past or possible situation connected to the interlocutor's experiences, which can evoke emotions previously experienced. While mentioning abstract concepts such as pain, sorrow, injustice, and violence cannot awake the interlocutor's emotions, the use of words to depict painful, cruel, or unjust scenarios can actually evoke in the hearer anger, compassion, or contempt. The hearer experiences a representation that can be related to his memories, and live the depicted state of affairs by feeling the emotions.

7. Conclusion

Emotive meaning can be conceived as an instrument for leading the interlocutor to act. If we consider values in relation to choice, namely, what makes an action worthy, it is clear how decision making and arguing from values are consequences of emotions generated by the representation of a state of affairs. Emotions are both the result of past choices and past experiences, and evaluations of present and future states of affairs. The notion of representing a situation, which corresponds to generating emotions in connection with the interlocutor's system of desires (his interests), is the pivotal link between words and actions. This account can explain the relation between emotive and descriptive meaning on the basis of an ontological structure of values grounded on the notions of desire, emotion, and judgment. This account of emotive meaning leads us to consider the other dimension of ethical words, descriptive meaning. As seen in the first chapter, the emotive 'meaning' of words can be directed toward objects that normally would not be classified as such. This strategy cannot be simply considered as a misuse of a word, but a form of alteration of its meaning, an implicit redefinition. For this reason, in order to investigate the possibility and the effects of modifying the meaning of an emotive term, we need to inquire into the nature of the principle of classification, definition.

3

When Words Are Reasoning

Definitions as Strategies of Classification

Words are instruments for modifying our beliefs and affect our decisions. Stevenson (1944) underscored that words have a tendency to alter our knowledge, which he named "descriptive meaning." Words describe, and at the same time hide, reality (Schiappa 2003). They frame a certain state of affairs by pointing out specific features and leaving out others. This two-fold dimension of names, their nature as instruments for providing and excluding information, is crucial for understanding the strategies of meaning listed in the first chapter. Selecting information always results in hiding some characteristics of a situation. Amplifying, or rather emphasizing some features of a complex state of affairs inevitably results in leaving out other characteristics. According to the selection of features, certain emotions can be triggered and others prevented. The strategies of selection are grounded on the power of words to represent, describe, and refer to reality. Sometimes words are not simply used to select what is important for the conversation, but to distort reality. Dictatorships are called 'democracies' while the word 'pacification' conceals massacres and human tragedies. However, sometimes the boundary between selecting the relevant aspects of reality and lying becomes, or is made to become, blurred. The meanings of words are altered, and also what they represent. The meanings of some words are altered, and a powerful ambiguity is introduced. Sometimes the effect is funny or ridiculous, but sometimes it is extremely effective. We can open the newspaper and notice how difficult it is to judge the boundaries of the words, between 'true freedom' and 'slavery,' 'treason,' and 'true patriotism,' 'war-making' and 'peace enforcement' (Doyle & Sambanis 2006: 1).

The problem of modifying the meaning of a word leads us to the crucial problem of definition. Since Aristotle, definition has been regarded as the instrument for classifying reality. It is the essential premise that supports the attribution of a property to an entity having specific qualities (Walton 1996: 54). It represents the relationship of identity between a predicate (the *definiendum*) and other predicates (the *definiens*). Such a relationship was for a long time regarded as the expression of the immutable essence of the thing. This view led to a deadlock: How can this essence be known? How can the mutable and often unshared meanings of words be related to a fixed and unchangeable essence (Sager 2000: 217; Walton 2005a: 169–173)? The distinction between essential and unessential characteristics became more and more controversial (Sager 2000: 216–217) and led to relativistic approaches to definition (Schiappa 2003). From this perspective, if essence cannot be known or does not exist, any definition advanced can be good, as it cannot be verified or falsified. Is definition only a matter of choice? Do the meanings of words only depend on our purpose?

If we want to analyze how definitions are used to name reality and when they can become strategies of manipulation, we need to go back to their function. Our crucial claim is that we need to first understand what the purpose of a definition is in order to analyze its possible structures and its possible force. From this perspective, the questions concerning why, how, and when it is possible to alter the meaning of a word can be tackled by shifting the problem of definition from metaphysics to the realm of reasoning and argumentation. We maintain that definitions need to be considered as premises in the complex reasoning that we trigger when we want to classify reality. Definitions will be inquired into as instruments of classification, as premises having different possible structures and different possible purposes and conditions. In this view, the question of what a definition is turns into the problem of determining the possible strategies in the reasoning used to classify reality.

1. Why Definitions Cannot Be Persuasive

Stevenson claimed that some definitions are persuasive. They can be used to modify our attitude toward reality and affect our choices. However, the two concepts of definition and persuasion seem to be somehow conflicting. A definition, using the ancient Aristotelian account, is supposed to represent the shared meaning of a word, the elements commonly considered to be accepted by everybody (*Topics*, 101b 38-102a 8):

A 'definition' is a phrase signifying a thing's essence. It is rendered in the form either of a phrase in lieu of a term, or of a phrase in lieu of another phrase; for it is sometimes possible to define the meaning of a phrase as well. People whose rendering consists of a term only, try it as they may, clearly do not render the definition of the thing in question, because a definition is always a phrase of a certain kind. One may, however, use the word 'definitory' also of such a remark as 'The "becoming" is "beautiful"', and likewise also of the question, 'Are sensation and knowledge the same or different?', for argument about definitions is mostly concerned with questions of sameness and difference.

Definitions describe what a thing is, or rather what the meaning of a word or phrase is for a specific community. For instance, the most famous definition in the ancient tradition was the definition of man as a 'mortal rational animate being.' The famous syllogism proceeded as follows (see Abaelardi, *Dialectica*, 271):

> Socrates is a man.
> A man is a mortal rational animate being.
> Therefore Socrates is a mortal rational animate being.

This piece of reasoning is perfectly sound. However, it does not add much to our knowledge. Any possible interlocutor who maintains the classic definition of man cannot dispute that Socrates is a mortal, rational being. How can something that is shared or accepted by everybody be used to modify an attitude of the interlocutor? How can definitions be persuasive? These questions can be answered starting from the concept of persuasion.

Persuasion was the ground of the ancient rhetorical and dialectical theories. Persuasion had in ancient times a meaning different from what we sometimes associate with embellishment or rhetorical features (Kelly & Bazerman 2003). The word 'persuasion' semantically stems from *pístis*, that is, the credit that a speaker obtains by means of his speech, namely, the recipient's agreement (Rigotti 1995: 11). In this ancient view, "The relation constituted by *pístis* is not only cognitive, but goes through the whole area of human relationships, both institutionalized and personal" (Rigotti 1995: 11). Persuasion is characterized by the freedom of choice, and is the result of a process of modification of one's beliefs, more specifically propositions he or she is committed to (Walton & Krabbe 1995). When our interlocutors find an argument persuasive, it is generally because they think it is reasonable and it proceeds from premises that they accept or are committed to (Walton 2007a: 86).

The effect of persuasion can be compared to a conceptual change (Baker 2003). It amounts to adapting a viewpoint to the audience's background knowledge, in order to make it more acceptable. In Baker's view, this amounts to changing the epistemic status of the solution (Baker 2003: 48). The issue presented needs to be tailored to the interlocutors' knowledge and interests, and its relevance and importance shown (Sutton 1996: 146; see also Martins et al. 2001). The act of persuasion is aimed at modifying the other's perception of reality, and therefore influencing his or her autonomous judgments and actions (Simons, Morreale & Gronbeck 2001: 7; Chi & Roscoe 2002). The process of persuasion is therefore an activity that is grounded on what the interlocutor already holds, in order to lead him to modify his view of a controversial standpoint. For instance, if I want to persuade my interlocutor that going to the swimming pool is good, I need to proceed from what *he* holds to be good for him, such as 'being fit' or 'being more attractive.' If my purpose is to show that the Greek insolvency can affect the whole European Union, I need to start from premises that are accepted by my audience, such as "When a state becomes insolvent it cannot pay its debts off." Persuasion is therefore a dialogical process that has been described in argumentation in the models of dialogue called critical discussion and persuasion dialogue. Both models outline normative procedures intended to set out the structure of persuasion.

The first model, developed by Walton (1984; Walton & Krabbe 1995), is grounded on the notion of commitment. Arguments in persuasion dialogues are conceived as patterns of reasoning that transfer the acceptability of the premises, or rather the strength of the interlocutor's commitments, to the conclusion (Walton 2007a: 87; see also Hahn & Oaksford 2006). This model of dialogue is based on two parties, called the proponent (or speaker) and the opponent (or hearer), and each tries to persuade the other to accept a claim by using arguments. Persuasion dialogues stem from a conflict of opinion, consisting in the respondent's denial or questioning of the proponent's position, and presuppose that each party has the capacity and freedom for defending its point of view (see Vanderveken 2001). The dialogue is aimed at altering a dialogical situation in which the interlocutors are committed to incompatible positions (A: Bob stole the milk; B: Bob did not steal the milk), or where the hearer refuses to accept the speaker's viewpoint (A: Bob stole the milk; B: Why do you say that?). The interlocutors intend to change the other party's commitments, which can be the description of a state of affairs (Bob stole the milk) or a judgment (Bob is a thief). The instrument to lead the interlocutors to change their position is a chain of arguments following from premises belonging to the knowledge shared by the latter.

The theoretical model of critical discussion has been developed by the Pragma-Dialectical school. In van Eemeren and Grootendorst's view (see van Eemeren & Grootendorst 1984, 1992, 2004), a dialogue aimed at resolving a difference of opinion, called a critical discussion, is characterized by four stages: the confrontation stage, the opening stage, the argumentation stage, and the concluding stage. The confrontation stage represents the starting point of the dialogue, namely, the point in which a point of view is expressed by one party and is not accepted by the other party, who challenges it or cast doubts on it. The second stage is a level in which the parties "try to find out how much relevant common ground they share" (van Eemeren & Grootendorst 2004: 60). At this level the format of the dialogue, background knowledge, the values, and the roles are compared and discussed. At the argumentation stage the participants advance their arguments to support their viewpoint, whereas at the concluding stage the parties establish "what the result is of an attempt to resolve a difference of opinion" (van Eemeren & Grootendorst 2004: 60).

Both models are grounded on a similar notion of persuasion as a change of attitude stemming from a shared or common ground. The interlocutors can persuade each other because they proceed from a set of shared propositions. At the same time, however, the conclusion needs to be debatable, or at least less acceptable than the premises. In order for a conceptual change to happen, there must be room for a change of a kind. If we maintain that definitions represent a form of truth, or a meaning that everybody agrees upon, how can they be used to persuade the other party? On the other hand, if definitions are only a matter of choice, how can they add any force to the conclusion? If I choose to define a man as 'a luminous being,' how can I persuade my interlocutor that he is luminous, if he does not agree with my premise? What is the argumentative foundation of reasoning from definition? What is the structure of classification and how can it be persuasive?

2. Definitions as Premises: Reasoning for Classifying

Reasoning by definition has often been regarded as an indefeasible type of reasoning. Mill (1869: 539) describes it in the following fashion:

Some particular properties of a thing are selected, more or less arbitrarily, to be termed its nature or essence; and when this has been done, these properties are supposed to be invested with a kind of indefeasibleness, to have become paramount to all the other properties of the thing, and incapable of being prevailed over or counteracted by them.

Mill regarded the appeal to the definition as an irrefutable argument. The classification could not be attacked, as it was based on essential features of the thing defined. For instance, in order to prove the absence of a void, the following reasoning was put forward. First, a body was defined as "what can move up and down." Then, it was applied to a specific case: In the void a body cannot move up and down. From such a premise, by definition, in the void a body is not a body anymore (Mill 1869: 539). This argument was used to disprove the existence of a void, and was wholly grounded on the 'nature' of the bodies. However, what is commonly considered as an immutable truth is often a rhetorical strategy to refer to a shared and accepted view, which can be hardly rejected, or rather whose rejection would hardly be considered. The appeal to the definition or the essence becomes a rhetorical strategy of prevention by blocking any possible attack.

From a reasoning perspective, the appeal to the fixed essence of things hides the dialogical and logical roles of definition. Both in the essentialistic and relativistic perspectives, definitions are used to support a conclusion, which can be an absolute truth or a plausible viewpoint. In both cases, definitions are used or chosen to classify reality and are principles that can be shared, or controversial, from which a conclusion follows. However, just as the essence cannot be known, the choice of a definition cannot be arbitrary, at least from a purely strategic point of view. Just as with all the possible premises on which we ground our reasoning, the force or acceptability of a definition affects the force or acceptability of the conclusion. In the first chapter we noticed how the term 'enemy combatant' was implicitly redefined to classify potential terrorists. However, even though the defining authority was the president himself, the redefinition was unsuccessful, as it was promptly rejected.

Within both the essentialist and relativistic approaches, however, only one argumentative dimension is pointed out. Definitions are regarded as the premises supporting a conclusion, but the force of such premises and the effect of such a force are not analyzed. Perelman and Olbrechts-Tyteca, in their *The New Rhetoric* (1969), advance a view of definitions both as standpoints that need to be supported by arguments (such as etymology or consequences) and as arguments grounding a thesis. Definitions, for this reason, are analyzed as the result of an argument and as the premises for an ulterior argumentative move. The correspondence of identity between the *definiens* and the *definiendum* is regarded as a quasi-logical relation, argumentatively warranted (Perelman & Olbrechts-Tyteca 1969: 213).

Definitions, from this perspective, are argumentative instruments for classifying reality. They are argumentative for two reasons: They are premises of an argument and they are sustained by arguments. In order to understand the nature of the force of definition, and how and why some definitions can be better than others, it is necessary to first analyze the structure of the reasoning based on them.

2.1. *The Logical Structure of Classification*

The concept of reasoning from classification can be approached starting from modern accounts. The first to introduce the idea of an argument from classification, or rather a pattern of reasoning aimed at classifying states of affairs, was Hastings. In his Ph.D. thesis (1963), he identified two schemes that can be treated under the label of argument from classification. The first scheme leads from a set of characteristics to the attribution of a predicate to a subject. For instance, we can consider the following argument (from Windes & Hastings 1965: 160):

CLASSIFICATION OF 'MONOPOLY'

Bounce – O Company controls the manufacture of all Ping-Pong balls in the U.S. Therefore Bounce – O Company is a Ping-Pong ball monopoly.

The logical link between the classificatory conclusion and the premise can be reconstructed as a premise stating that, "Monopoly is control of the market." Such a premise is a principle of classification, a possible definition of 'monopoly.'

In the second scheme, a subject, classified as *X*, is predicated on the definition of *X*. In other words, first a predicate is attributed to a subject (the subject is classified); then, by virtue of the definition of the predicate, some fundamental characteristics are attributed to the subject. For instance, from the classification of Bounce – O Company as a monopoly the conclusion that Bounce – O Company has no rivals in the market can be drawn. We can notice that the second scheme is the mirror image of the first. The definition used to classify a subject in the latter scheme is applied to the classified subject. We can represent the two argument schemes as follows (see Hastings 1963: 36–52):

ARGUMENT FROM CRITERIA TO VERBAL CLASSIFICATION

Event or object X has characteristics A, B, C...
If x has characteristics A, B, C..., then x is Q
Therefore, event or object X is Q.

Hastings gives the following example, which can be represented in Figure 3.1 (1963: 36):

In voluntary health insurance you generally get a poor return for your money because overhead and profits of the insurance company eat up huge chunks of the premiums you pay. On individual policies these companies spend for overhead and profits an average of about 60% of what you pay them and only about 40 cents of your premium dollar goes for benefits to policyholders. Obviously such insurance is a mighty poor buy.

Hastings pointed out that the principle of classification needs to be shared by the audience in order for the argument to be acceptable. In order to assess the strength and acceptability of the classification, he listed seven

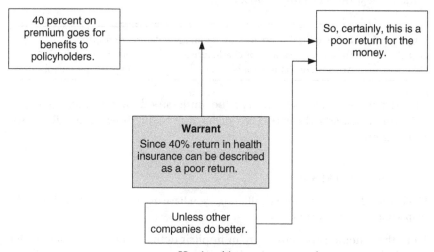

FIGURE 3.1. Hastings' insurance example

critical questions that can be asked to test the premises and the relationship between premises and conclusion (Hastings 1963: 42–45):

CQ₁	What is the implicit definition being used?
CQ₂	Is the definition acceptable? Are the criteria acceptable as a definition of the classification, label, adjectival category, etc.?
CQ₃	Are there exceptions or qualifications to the definition and criteria?
CQ₄	Are other criteria necessary for an adequate definition?
CQ₅	Do the characteristics described meet the criteria?
CQ₆	Are enough characteristics described to justify inclusion in this category?
CQ₇	Could the event fit better into another category, or be classified differently on the basis of its characteristics?

In Hastings' argument from criteria to verbal classification we notice that the critical questions play a fundamental role. In the structure of the inference nothing is said about the nature of the conditional proposition, whereas the critical questions specify that the strength of the inference depends on the acceptability of the definition.

If the argument from criteria to verbal classification represents the conditions of the predication of a name, an argument from definition to characteristics highlights the structure of the inferences that can be drawn from the predication itself. In his account of argument from definition to characteristics, Hastings (1963: 46–54) underscored that the characteristics predicated in the conclusion may be semantic characteristics stated in the definition, or implications drawn from the definition. As in the case of an argument from classification, the classificatory premise, i.e. the definition, must be acceptable and accepted by the interlocutors, as specified in the critical questions (Hastings 1963: 53):

C.Q. 1	Is the definition an accurate or an agreed upon definition?
C.Q. 2	Do the implications or characteristics follow from the premises?
C.Q. 3	Are any conflicting, inconsistent, or superseding principles involved?

The structure of the scheme can be understood by considering Figure 3.2, which displays the structure of an argument drawn from Robinson (1947: 200).

CASE 1: TOLERANCE

Since you believe in tolerance in all things, you have no right to be so critical of this man's ungentlemanly conduct.

Here the scheme proceeds from an implicit definition of 'tolerance' (tolerance is the acceptance of any kind of behavior or position) that the audience or the interlocutor may agree upon. Such a definition does not correspond

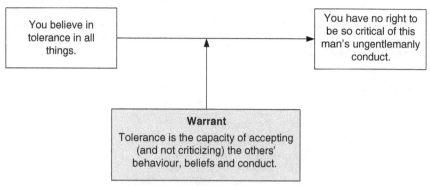

FIGURE 3.2. Inferences from tolerance

to the dictionary, which supposedly reports the common and shared meaning of words. However, the vagueness of the concept of 'respecting other's opinions,' which constitutes the meaning of the word, makes the definition taken for granted somehow acceptable. From a predicate of the definition the conclusion is drawn. Since 'accepting any kinds of behavior' is contrary to criticizing them, the interlocutor is not tolerant in criticizing a man's conduct.

The argument from definition to characteristics can be considered as a form of circular reasoning. Since the definition is taken to be accepted, the conclusion simply states a property of a premise. An argument of the kind, "Bob is a man; therefore he is an animate being" can be formally valid reasoning but an ineffective or at least useless argument. This type of argument becomes dialogically effective when the purpose of the conclusion is not to provide information or support for a potentially debatable viewpoint (which would not be the case, as the definition is already shared) but to perform another type of act, such as condemning, reminding, and so on, as shown in case 1 earlier. The speaker intended to point out an inconsistency rather than persuade the interlocutor. The speaker can also support a controversial conclusion using an apparently accepted or acceptable definition. For instance, we can consider the following case, diagrammed in Figure 3.3 (Hastings 1963: 48):

CASE 2: RESCISSION OF A CONTRACT

If the United States be not a government proper, but an association of States in the nature of contract merely, can it, as a contract be peaceably unmade, by less than all the parties who made it? One party to a contract may violate it – break it, so to speak, but does it not require all to lawfully rescind it?

In this example, the speaker does not use the definition of 'rescission,' but the description of a more specific concept, 'rescission by agreement.' While a contract can be rescinded for different reasons, a contract can be rescinded by agreement only if the parties thereto actually agree on it. The tautology is only apparent, as the definition only *seems* to be shared.

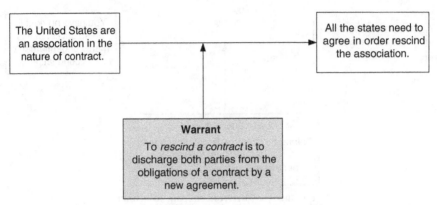

FIGURE 3.3. Structure of contract example

Hastings' description of reasoning from classification points out the crucial importance of the acceptability of the definition, or rather the principle of classification. But he does not inquire into what a definition is, and why a definition can support a conclusion.

2.2. *Reasoning from What Is Acceptable*

Why can a definition support a conclusion? As seen previously, definitions are not absolute truths. They do not hold valid for everything. The structure of logical inferences proceeds from quantifiers, in particular from the relationship between the universal quantification and the specific instance. For instance, the inference,

SYLLOGISM 1

Socrates is a man.
Every man is a mortal rational animate being.
Therefore, Socrates is a mortal rational animate being.

This syllogism is based on the relationship between 'every man' and 'a man,' in this case Socrates. However, reasoning from classification is much more complex than a relation between quantifiers. If we depart from the realm of logic and analyze what is persuasive, we need to acknowledge that while the aforementioned argument can be reasonable, even though it is not persuasive, the following ones cannot be persuasive because they are completely unreasonable (see Van Dijk 1977: 47):

SYLLOGISM 2

Socrates is a man.
Every man is a green without.
Therefore Socrates is a green without.

SYLLOGISM 3

Socrates is a man.
Every man is an inexistent stone without a surface.
Therefore Socrates is an inexistent stone without a surface.

Even though these definitions are universally quantified, they can hardly be reasonable. They cannot be accepted as descriptions of man, or as descriptions of an entity at all from a grammatical or categorical point of view. Reasoning from classification cannot be simply based on the logical principles of quantification. Moreover, from a purely epistemic point of view, our limited knowledge cannot support a universal statement about the entities. What is the foundation of reasoning from classification?

In the ancient dialectical studies, the relationship between premises and conclusions was supported by a material link, a semantic or causal relationship between the terms. In the Middle Ages, dialectical inferences were analyzed by combining a rule of reasoning, such as the deductive *modus ponens* (if *p* then *q*, *p*; therefore *q*) with a specific relation between the terms (Stump 1989: 6; Abaelardi, *Dialectica*, 264). The terms need to be connected by a reasonable and acceptable relationship. For instance, we can consider the following consequences:

He is a man; therefore he is a rational animate being.
*He is a man; therefore it is sunny today.

The first consequence is valid only because it is known that a "rational animate being" *can* be the definition of 'man,' and there is a generally accepted rule of inference, or *maxima propositio* (Boethii, *De Topicis Differentiis*, 1176d), that links the *definiendum* with the definition. On the contrary, no relationship between the terms can be found in the second reasoning. The acceptability and reasonableness of the inference depends on the local semantic connection between the terms (genus–species; cause–effect ...), which was called *habitudo*.[1] Such a *habitudo* needs to be reasonable and acceptable. For instance, in syllogisms 2 and 3 the relationship between the terms is unreasonable and unacceptable, and therefore the conclusion cannot follow.

The logical structure of reasoning from classification was developed by Kienpointner (1992). In *Alltagslogik* he analyzed the principles supporting

---

[1] "Unde sit locus, requiritur, a specie respondemus scientes 'hominem' ad 'animal' secundum hoc quod species eius est antecedere; cuius quidem interrogationis sententiam diligenter inquiramus" (Abaelardi, *Dialectica*, 264)."Itaque tam ex loca differentia quam ex maxima propositione firmitas inferentiae custoditur, alio tamen et alio modo; ex differentia quidem hoc modo quod ipsa in antecedenti posita uim inferentiae tenet secundum habitudinem ex qua consequenti comparatur. Oportet enim in ipso antecedenti semper de loco differentia agi [qui] secundum habitudinem ex qua ad illatum terminum inferendum adducitur." (Abaelardi, *Dialectica*, 263–264).

a classification, some of the *maximae propositiones* that allow a categorization of a state of affairs to follow from a definition. Two schemes from definition were identified and can be represented as follows (Kienpointner 1992: 250–252):

Schemes – Argument from definition

What is predicated of the definition is also predicated of the *definiendum*, and vice versa.
X is predicated of the definition.
Therefore *X* is predicated of the *definiendum*.

What the *definiendum* is predicated of, also the definition is predicated of.
The *definiendum* is predicated of *X*.
Therefore the definition is predicated of *X*.

These schemes are descriptive, as they support a description of reality instead of an action or a decision. In these schemes, the definition can be substituted by the interpretation of the name (Kienpointner 1992: 259). According to this perspective, definition is necessary to the process of classification. Without a unique definition of a term, the same reality can be contradictorily classified. For instance, the word 'full employment' can be defined as 'a situation in which only 5.5% of the population of a country is unemployed.' If this definition is considered, a country like the United States can be classified as and characterized by 'full employment.' On the other hand, the same term can be defined as 'a country in which all the employable adult people have a full-time activity.' In this case, the same country would not be classified or characterized as 'full employment.'

Kienpointner's account, we can notice, revives the ancient tradition on topics. The major premise of the schemes, such as "What is predicated of the definition is also predicated of the *definiendum*, and vice versa" represents the ancient maxim of the *locus* from definition (see, e.g., Boethii, *In Ciceronis Topica*, 1059c). However, in its scheme it is not clear how the general principle (the maxim) is related to the premise that needs to be accepted or acceptable, namely, the definition.

Classification can be conceived as a type of reasoning grounded on plausible, or defeasible premises, and a semantic principle connecting them. How can the logical structure be related to the semantic link? How are the two dimensions of classification connected?

2.3. *The Structure of Reasoning from Classification*
As noticed previously, the relationship between premises and conclusion in a classification needs to be grounded on a principle that is shared or acceptable by the interlocutor. It would be unreasonable to claim, "This is a table, as it moves fast and is really funny." The existence of several

ways of classifying the same state of affairs does not result in the fact that any method of classification is good, or that they are all equally acceptable or effective. Interpreting the ancient concept of definition developed in Aristotle's *Topics* (Giuliani 1972: 130), definitions can be conceived as *endoxa*, or commonly accepted opinions. From this view, definitions are a matter of commitment, that is, they depend on what is shared or can be shared between the interlocutors. How can the acceptability of a premise be included in the reasoning structure of an inference? How can the semantic relation be considered in a quasi-logical inferential structure?

As seen in the previous chapter, in Walton (1996: 54) Hastings' argument from criteria to verbal classification was developed specifying the nature of the consequence. Instead of expressing the relationship between characteristics and classification as a generic consequence (if p, then q), Walton specified the nature of the link as classificatory and expressed it as follows: "If some particular thing a can be classified as falling under verbal category C, then a has property F in virtue of such a classification." This type of reasoning proceeds from a universal generalization that cannot describe ordinary reasoning, subject to default and based on incomplete knowledge. Reasoning from classification needs to be described as a type of inference grounded on an acceptable and plausible premise. From a logical point of view, such a major premise, or warrant, to use Toulmin's term,[2] is a qualified generalization. This generalization is subject to exceptions, and hence the argument based on it is *defeasible*. This means that the argument can default if it is found that the case in point constitutes an exception to the rule. Such reasoning typically takes a form of argument studied in Walton (2004, chapter 4) and can be applied to the aforementioned scheme as follows (Walton 2005b: 107):

DEFEASIBLE *MODUS PONENS* FROM CLASSIFICATION

Premise 1	Generally, but subject to exceptions, if something has property C, you can also expect it to have property F.
Premise 2	Object a has property C.
Conclusion	Object a has property F.

This form of argument is called "defeasible *modus ponens*" (DMP), as opposed to the deductively valid form of *modus ponens* that is so familiar in deductive logic: If A then B; A; therefore B. A DMP is a special subtype

---

[2] Toulmin (1958: 103–107). Toulmin clearly saw inference warrants as defeasible in his model of argument. He expressed the conclusion using the wording "so, presumably," basing it on an inference containing an "unless" qualifier. If the qualifier is supported by evidence of an exception, the warrant is subject to default and the conclusion may not follow from the premises (1958: 105).

of *modus ponens* argument that applies to defeasible arguments.[3] DMP is a common form of reasoning in argumentation, especially in arguments from and concluding to a classification.

The etymology of the term 'defeasible' comes from medieval English contract law, referring to a contract that has a clause in it that could defeat the contract in a case where special circumstances fit the clause. However, the origin of the term in modern philosophy is from a paper entitled "The Ascription of Responsibility and Rights" by Hart (1949; 1951). According to Hart, defeasible claims can be challenged either by a denial of the facts upon which they are based, or by a plea that circumstances are present that bring the case under some recognized head of exception (1951: 147–148). Hart (1961) also showed that defeasible reasoning arises from the use of defeasible concepts, using his famous example of the rule that no vehicles are allowed in the park. This rule could be defeated by issues of classification. For example, a car is classified as a vehicle, but what about a bicycle? Is it a vehicle? Both sides could be argued, in the absence of a law making a specific ruling. The best way of dealing with such disputes, we will contend, is to view arguments based on classification as defeasible.

The notion of *defeasible modus ponens*, however, seems to beg the question. The inference proceeds from a premise that cannot be universal, but only valid for most of the times. If the major premise is not universal, how can the inference be valid? A possible answer can be found in the ancient dialectical tradition that Kienpointner (1992) revived in his schemes. Kienpointner showed that the inference was based on the specific semantic principle connecting the definition to the thing defined. The link between premise and conclusion, or rather properties and classification, is not conceived as a relationship of quantification, but a semantic link based on the meaning of 'definition' (see the scheme from definition in Walton, Reed & Macagno 2008: 319). For instance, we can apply Kienpointner's scheme as follows:

The *definiendum* is predicated of *X*.	Bob is a man.
What the *definiendum* is predicated of, also the definition is predicated of.	If Bob is a man, then Bob is a rational animal.
Therefore the definition is predicated of *X*.	Therefore Bob is a rational animal.

We can notice that if the semantic link is clear, the logical one is missing. The relationship between the semantic principle and the logical one is not stated: The endoxical (or commonly accepted) premise that a "rational

---

[3] Verheij (2003) has recognized DMP as a form of argument widely used in legal argumentation.

animal is the definition of man" is lacking here. The only possible inference that can be drawn from the premises is the following:

The *definiendum* is predicated of *X*.	Bob is a man.
What the *definiendum* is predicated of, also the definition is predicated of.	If Bob is a man, then the definition of man is predicated of Bob.
Therefore the definition is predicated of *X*.	Therefore the definition of man is predicated of Bob.

In order to account for the relationship between semantics and logic, we can represent the structure of the inference as follows (see Rigotti & Greco 2006):

Maxim	Endoxon
What the *definiendum* is predicated of, also the definition is predicated of.	
	Rational animal is the definition of man

Preliminary conclusion:
What man is predicated of, also rational animal is predicated of.

The *definiendum* is predicated of *X*.	Bob is a man.
Therefore the definition is predicated of *X*.	Bob is a rational animal.

This structure of inference accounts for the double reasoning passage, in which the semantic principle logically applies to the premises. This complex pattern can be summarized in an argumentation scheme in which the defeasibility of the scheme is bound to the semantic relation. We can represent such as scheme by developing the scheme presented in Walton, Reed and Macagno (2008: 319; see Macagno & Walton 2009a: 96):

ARGUMENTATION SCHEME 7: REASONING FROM DEFEASIBLE CLASSIFICATION

Definition Premise	*a* fits definition *D*.
Classification Premise	For all *x*, if *x* fits definition *D*, and *D* is the definition of *G*, then *x* can be classified as *F*.
Conclusion	*a* has property *F*.

In this scheme, we can notice that the reasonableness of the inference is guaranteed by the relation between the definition and its *definiendum*, whereas the relation between the endoxical premise and the relation between *definiens* and *definiendum* is represented by the additional premise "*D* is the definition of *G*." The classification premise could also be represented as, "What the *definiendum* is predicated of, also the definition is predicated of, and *D* is the definition of *G*." The universal quantification of the semantic relation is defaultive, in the sense that it is valid only if the condition "*D* is the definition of *G*" applies. *D* needs to be accepted by the interlocutor as the definition of *G* for the inference to be acceptable. The critical questions appropriate for this version of the argument from verbal classification are the following (from Walton, Reed & Macagno 2008: 319):

CQ$_1$	What evidence is there that D is an adequate definition of G, in light of other possible alternative definitions that might exclude a's having G?
CQ$_2$	Is the verbal classification in the classification premise based merely on a stipulative or biased definition that is subject to doubt?
CQ$_3$	Does *a* actually fit definition *D*?

The first two critical questions represent the possible reasons for not accepting that *D* is *the* definition of *G*, while the last one is aimed at undermining the factual premise (*a* is *D*). A definition can be attacked based on a comparison with alternative accounts (CQ$_1$) or reasons internal to the definition itself (CQ$_2$). For instance, the definition may not be convertible with the *definiendum*, or it may describe a different concept.

3. Definitions and Definitional Structure

The analysis of the argument schemes from verbal classification shows how the link between the premises and conclusion is grounded on a semantic link, called *maxim* in the ancient dialectical tradition, and an endoxical, or commonly shared premise (the definition). In the previous section, we took into account the structure of the inference, showing how the conclusion depends on two conditions:

1. The object *x* must fit the definition *D*.
2. *D* must be accepted as the definition of *G*.

How can the concept of definition be related to a principle of inference? How is the maxim connected with a semantic principle (*to be the definition of*)? What is a definition?

If we analyze the way we classify reality or argue from definitions, we can notice that there are several definitions for the same concept (see Gallie 1956). We often argue because we do not have the same understanding of a concept, because our definition does not correspond to our interlocutor's. What is democracy? What is peace? The problem, however, is not simply limited to the existence of different definitions intended as definitional discourses. The fact is that there are also different definitions in the sense of definitional methods. Victorinus, in his *Liber de Definitionibus,*[4] lists fifteen different types of definitions. For instance, a concept such as 'man' can be defined as 'the rational animal,' 'the animal that can pity the Gods,' 'the featherless biped,' 'the being composed of two legs, a head, two arms...,' 'the being to which *Homo sapiens sapiens* and *Homo sapiens idaltu* belong,' and so on. Definitions can be different for their semantic content ('Man is the rational animal' and 'Man is the laughing animal') but also for their structure ('Man is the rational animal' and 'Man is the being composed of two legs, a head, two arms, etc').

The acceptability of a definitional discourse needs to be distinguished from the strength of a definitional structure. For instance, we can consider the following arguments grounded on two different definitions of 'monopoly':

Pop Cola is *controlling the soft drinks market.* Therefore it is a monopoly.	A monopoly is a company that exclusively controls the market.
Pop Cola is a *big soft drinks company.* Therefore it is a monopoly.	A monopoly is a big industry in a field of activity.

The second argument is based on a definition that cannot be accepted. 'Big industry in a field of activity' might describe what a corporation or specialized firm is, but it cannot define 'monopoly.' The acceptability of the definitional discourse is different from the acceptability and strength of the structure of a definition. For instance, if we analyze the following argument, we can notice that it is clearly unreasonable:

3. This object is white. Therefore it is a bag

'To be white' cannot be considered as a definition of 'bag.' It does not tell what a bag can be, nor does it describe its possible properties. The relationship between the premise and conclusion cannot even be retrieved, as it cannot even be identified with a possible definition. The alleged definitional link is not simply unacceptable, but unreasonable. On the contrary, the following cases would be commonly accepted as reasonable arguments.

4. This object is a container of flexible material that is used for carrying or storing items. Therefore it is a bag.
5. This object is something which you can carry by hand and you can put stuff into. Therefore it is a bag.
6. This object is used for baggage (*bagage*). Therefore it is a bag.
7. This object has two handles and a sack. Therefore it is a bag.

Such arguments are grounded on a specific and clear definitional relation between the qualities mentioned in the premise and the property

[4] See also Boethii *Liber de Diffinitione.*

When Words Are Reasoning

Genus-species definition		Definition by parts	
This object is a container of flexible material that is used for carrying or storing items.	A	This object has two handles and a sack.	B
(A bag is a container of flexible material that is used for carrying or storing items.)	A ↔ B	(A bag is characterized by two handles and a sack.)	A → B
Therefore it is a bag.	B	Therefore it is a bag.	A

FIGURE 3.4. Logical properties of definitions

attributed to the object in the conclusion. The features that the object is claimed to possess are forms of definition of the property attributed to the object in the conclusion. However, these arguments differ because of the nature or structure of the definition they are based on. Definition (4) is commonly considered to be the genus-difference definition of 'bag,' that is, a definition showing the most generic semantic features, and the characteristics distinguishing the *definiendum* from other concepts of a language. Definition (5) is a definite description, that is, a definition in which only the attributes proper to the *definiendum* are pointed out, or some of its characteristic accidents. Definition (6) is a definition by etymology, in which the *definitum* is described by showing its relationship with the words from which it historically stemmed. Definition (7) is a definition by parts, highlighting the material or quantitative parts of the object that the *definiendum* refers to is made of.

These definitions are different from a logical, semantic, and pragmatic perspective. Definitions (4), (5), and (6) are commonly considered as convertible with the *definiendum*, as they represent respectively its fundamental semantic features, the attributes or the combination of attributes that can refer only to it, and its etymology. In contrast, the definition by parts is not convertible; even if a bag always has two handles and a sack, two handles and a sack can be something entirely different from a bag if the way they are combined is not specified. The parts in themselves (and not their specific connection, which would constitute a genus) can be conceived only as signs or presumptions that the object is a bag, just like the fact that a being has two feet and no feathers is a possible sign that it can be a man. From a logical perspective, it is apparent from the previous examples how different definitions have different logical properties. An argument from genus-difference definition (4) is much stronger from a logical point of view than an argument from mereological definition (7). The former is convertible with the *definiendum* and represents the semantic features that the interlocutors are supposed to share in order to understand each other. On the contrary, a simple list of the quantitative parts an object is made of cannot be convertible. We can represent the different logical structures of the two definitions (indicated in the column on the right of each definition) in Figure 3.4.

While in the first case the definition allows a type of deductive reasoning, in the second case a different form of reasoning is triggered that proceeds from a necessary condition, but not a sufficient one.

The logical structure of the definition can also be affected by the specific semantic relation between the *definiendum* and the predicates in the definition. For instance, the definition of a bag as 'a container' has logical properties different from its description as a 'white thing with the logo of a shop on it.' In the first case we are pointing out a necessary condition of being a bag, while in the second we are listing some characteristics that can be said of many different entities. Depending on the semantic relationship, the logical properties may vary. For instance, arguments based on definite descriptions (such as Definition 5) can be convertible or not, depending on whether they describe the concept using a property that can be attributed only to it or a generic and common characteristic. For instance, if we claim that this being is a horse because it whinnies, we are proceeding from a property that only horses have. On the contrary, if we support such a conclusion maintaining that it is a proud or noble animal, we are defining 'horse' using prototypical or stereotypical attributes that can be predicated of many other animals or beings. Independently from the acceptability of the shared knowledge expressed by the definition, the propositional structure of the definition itself can determine the logical properties of the arguments proceeding from it.

From a pragmatic perspective, the argumentative effectiveness of a definition depends on the context of its use and the knowledge it presupposes. An argument based on an essential definition can be used only when the essential features of the object are already known by the hearer. The interlocutor needs to share the taxonomy, or rather the structure of the semantic system. For instance, in (4) the hearer needs to know that the entity is used for carrying items in order to classify it as a bag. In contrast, an argument based on a definition by parts can be used when only physical evidence is given. For instance, even in cases in which the purpose of the object is unknown, it is possible to cite its physical characteristics. A definition from etymology leads to arguments from classification especially aimed at generating the possible implications of the already classified object (you are a counselor; therefore you should advise, not advocate). Definitions by descriptions are the most argumentatively and rhetorically powerful, as from the choice of the properties a value judgment can be suggested. For instance, we can consider the following definitions of 'embezzlement':

8. Embezzlement is theft of assets (usually money) entrusted to your care.
9. Embezzlement is the siphoning of another's money.
10. Embezzlement is a fraud committed by many employees.

Definition (8) is a definition by genus and species in which the most important semantic features of the *definiendum* are pointed out. The *definiendum* is explained by connecting it to the more generic and shared concept of 'theft,' and differentiating the thing defined by the other types of theft using the difference 'of assets entrusted of your care.' On the contrary, (9) and (10) are not aimed at describing a concept, but rather at hiding it behind a metaphor (in Definition 9) or eliciting a value judgment in Definition 10, where it corresponds to a justification based on an appeal to popular practice. In (10), in particular, the *definiendum* is described by means of one of the possible properties that can be attributed to it, but in this fashion its meaning is only vaguely explained. As noticed in the previous chapter, knowing what a concept is, and situating it within one's own system of desires, is essential for judging the thing defined. Whereas in (8) the concept of 'embezzlement' is clearly connected with notions the interlocutor is acquainted with (theft, company money), in (9) and (10) a clear value judgment is harder to be elicited. Where the notion of 'theft' is shared and commonly judged as negative, 'siphoning' or 'fraud' are vague and less known, and the popularity of a crime can make it more acceptable or at least less contemptible (see Blakey 1982 for the use of euphemisms in law).

Definition refers to different types of phrases, using an Aristotelian term (*Topics*, 101b 39). Aristotle refers to all phrases that may be advanced to establish the identity between two concepts as *definitory* (102a 6). All such definitions have different purposes and different logical properties. Who advances a definition claims that an identity exists between the *definiendum* and the definition. Such an identity can be based on semantic features or physical properties. However, some definitions can structurally establish an identity, while others cannot. What makes a definition a good one? What are the characteristics of a definition? How is it possible to assess a definition? In order to answer these questions it is necessary to introduce the Aristotelian semantic system and his theory of logical properties of semantic relations.

4. The Nature of Definition: The Tradition and the Theory of Predicables

In the ancient rhetorical tradition the types of definitions were described according to their argumentative and strategic force. However, the strongest definition was considered the genus-difference definition, also called "essential," which was identified as the only proper one.[5] Together with the definition by parts and etymology, the essential definition was considered

---

[5] "Quaerit homo quid sit: huic ùtique genus est animal. Cum igitur in definitione qua explicabo quid sit homo 'animal' dixero ac deinde reliqua conectam, erit substantialis definitio; substantiam enim hominis declaravi, cum dixi 'animal'. [...] Haec substantialis esse dicetur et haec propria, haec integra, haec a philosophis probata, ita ut alio modo facta definitio numquam esse dicatur." (Victorini, *Liber de Definitionibus*, 7, 23–8, 4). "Ergo praeceptis et dialecticorum et philosophorum illud tenere debemus: non esse definitionem nisi solam quae in ea re quam definitam volumus, primum quam eius rei 'esse' intelligimus, declaret atque ostendat substantiam. Hoc ut apertus fiat, hic docebimus nullam esse definitionem certam integram approabandam nisi eam quam dicunt philosophi substantialem." (*Liber de Definitionibus*, 7, 10–16).

as "substantial," as it made clear what the defined concept was. The force of such a definition depended on the inferences that its structure allowed.

Aristotle, in his *Topics*, laid the fundamentals of his dialectical studies of classification. In this work, Aristotle distinguished between the four predicables, which are four classes of semantic-logical relations of predication. These relations are formulated in the form of intrinsic topics, namely, instruments of discovery and inference warrants, which are directly connected to the subject of discussion. Aristotle distinguished four predicables: **genus** (e.g., 'A house is a building'), **definition** (e.g., 'A house is a building that serves as living quarters for one or a few families'), **property** (e.g., 'Do up a house,' which is said of 'house' only), and **accident** (e.g., 'red' or 'nice' said of 'house'). All the predicables can be predicated of the species, which in these examples is 'house.' The species, conceived by Aristotle as a thing, can be interpreted as a categorization of a fragment of reality that we can describe as the meaning of a word.[6] The species (or concept) is that which can be predicated of more individuals different in number (e.g., 'house' can be predicated of my house, or my neighbor's house….), and falls outside the domain of dialectic. Dialectic is concerned with relations between concepts, not about reasoning relative to the particular objects (Crowley & Hawhee 1999: 54; Green-Pedersen 1984: 119)[7].

The predicables are divided into two groups according to their semantic properties. The first class incorporates the predicables that can reveal the essence of the thing, that is (see Rigotti & Greco 2006) what the concept is or, rather, its fundamental characteristics (Stebbing 1933: 429). Genus and definition fall into this group. The second class is characterized by not expressing the essence of the thing, and incorporates property and accident. On the other hand, a second division of the predicables is advanced in *Topics* and is relative to the logical properties. While definition and property are convertible with the species they are predicated of, genus and accident are not. We can represent such a classification as shown in Figure 3.5.

From this broad division it is possible to understand the definition of the predicables. The **genus** answers the question *"What is it?"* and reveals the essence of the thing, without being convertible with the species it is

---

[6] This interpretation is coherent with Aristotle's perspective of dialectic. Dialectic does not deal with objects and individuals (what we can call 'things'), but with species, namely, linguistic organizations of reality. He is not interested in the matter, but in the form, that is in the relevant semantic properties of the concepts.

[7] Aristotle (*Topics*, 104a 7–13) considers a dialectical proposition to be a proposition held by everybody, or the majority, or the wise. Dialectics (*Topics*, 105b 30–33) is about philosophy, and philosophy is not concerned with particulars. In the Middle Age, the account of the predicables is different. Medieval tradition stems, in fact, from Porphyry's *Isagoges*, in which the species is considered to be a predicable, along with property, difference, genus, and accident. This distinction is extremely helpful in the process of *stasis*.

SEMANTIC DIMENSION / Logical dimension	SHOWING THE ESSENCE		NOT SHOWING THE ESSENCE	
	Definition	**Genus**	**Property**	**Accident**
Convertible with the thing.	Ex: Man is a **reasonable animal**.		Ex: **to laugh** (man).	
Not convertible with the thing.		Ex: Man is an **animal**.		Ex: This man is **strong**.

FIGURE 3.5. The predicables

predicated of. It is predicated of several species. For instance, the genus (or rather the proximate genus) of man is an 'animate being': in fact, it would be meaningless to say "*This is a man, but he is not an animate being.*" The **definition** is that which is convertible with the species it is predicated of and reveals the essence of it. It is constituted by the proximate genus and the specific difference.[8] For instance, the definition of man that was agreed upon in the Middle Ages was "animal, mortal, rational," as "being animate" distinguished man from plants, "being rational" from the beasts, and "being mortal" from the other rational being, God. The difference divides the generic feature in its species, which in their turn are inferior genera to be divided by a further difference. Obviously, the same genus can be divided differently. The structure of division can be represented as in Figure 3.6 (Boethii, *Porphyrii Isagoge, Translatio Boethii*, II; Damasceni, *Dialectica*, 30, 7–24).

The **property** is what is convertible with the subject it is predicated of, without expressing the essence of the thing. In other words, the property is absolutely or relatively predicable of only one thing. In order to explain this concept, it is useful to use some examples. The adjectives indicating colors, such as 'yellow,' 'blue,' and so on, can be attributed only to what can be a 'surface' (or a metaphor for an entity having a surface). The famous example of 'green ideas' clearly shows how the breach of the property results in ungrammaticality. Similarly, only animate bodies can 'sleep.' The adverb 'pitch' can only be predicated of the term 'black,' just like the phrase 'as a bull' of the adjective 'strong.' '*Grammaticus*', in the Aristotelian and medieval tradition, was considered the property of man, since it cannot be predicated of any other being. This property differentiates the concept from everything else.

---

[8] A good example of this procedure is found in Cicero's *Topics* (Ciceronis, *Topica*, XXVIII): "Hereditas est pecunia. Commune adhuc; multa enim genera pecuniae. Adde quod sequitur: quae morte alicuius ad quempiam pervenit. Nondum est definitio; multis enim modis sine hereditate teneri pecuniae mortuorum possunt. Unum adde verbum: iure; iam a communitate res diiuncta videbitur, ut sit explicata definitio sic: Hereditas est pecunia quae morte alicuius ad quempiam pervenit iure. Nondum est satis; adde: nec ea aut legata testamento aut possessione retenta; confectum est."

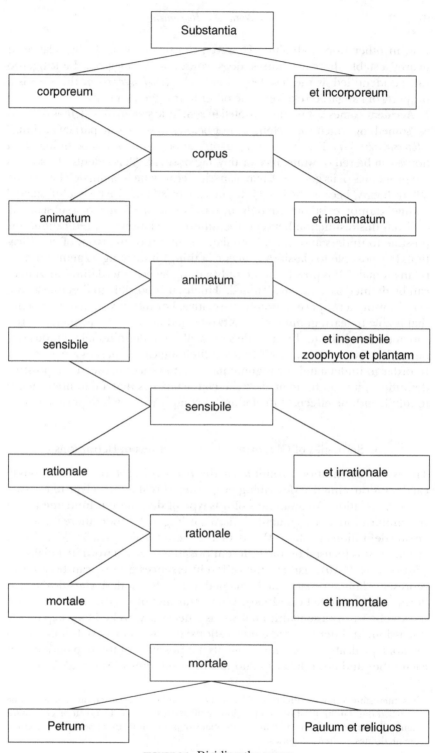

FIGURE 3.6. Dividing the genus

It is, in other words, absolute. However, the property might be relative. If nearby a stable there are horses, dogs, cows, and a kangaroo, the kangaroo can be identified as the 'two-legged animal.' *Two-leggedness* in this case is a property of kangaroo relative to the other four-legged animals.

Accident comes last in the Aristotelian semantic system. Accident is defined as "something which can belong or not belong to some one particular thing" (*Topics*, 102b 6–7). For instance, a person can be sitting or not be sitting,[9] or a house can be red or white, nice or tiny, big or small. All accidents of a species are properties of its genera: A man can 'sit' because he is 'animate'; he can 'be tall' or 'heavy' because he is a 'body'; he can 'exist' because he is a 'substance' ('white' cannot 'exist' but can only 'be dark' or be predicated of a substance).

From this distinction between the different relations of predication, it is possible to understand the Aristotelian treatment of the types of classification. It is possible to classify a concept (a thing) indicating its genus: A man is 'an animal.'" It is possible to identify a thing by using its definition: A man can be defined as 'a rational animal.' Finally, it is possible to describe a concept by using a property, absolute or relative. For instance, a man is 'a being that is able to learn grammar,' or 'a two-legged being,' or 'the animal at the top of the food chain.' In Aristotle's view, all these definitional methods can be used to clarify the concept. However, their logical properties are different. In order to understand the argumentative differences between the possible definitions, it is useful to analyze the characteristics that a definition needs to fulfill, and the effects of the failure to comply with such requirements.

5. Strategies of Obscurity: The Correctness of Definitions

The essential definition, as outlined in the *Topics*, is therefore not a metaphysical definition, aimed at describing properties of reality, but a type of logical–semantic relation. An awareness of this type of definition is fundamental to communication and argumentation. According to Aristotle, there must only be one definition of a thing, that is, of a concept (*Topics*, 141a 32–34; 143a 1). His interest is focused on the different possible uses of a word in a dialogue (*Topics*, 106a 9–10), namely, the different essences a word can be used to represent. This approach can be named, using the modern classification, as 'terminological' (De Bessé 1990). Making distinctions between the different senses of a word (a semantic analysis) is a necessary preliminary step to any discussion, in order to avoid equivocations. In other words, only if the interlocutors speak about the same concepts it is possible for them to understand each other and avoid fallacies and misunderstandings (Naess 2005 (1953):

---

[9] It is interesting to notice (Rigotti 1997) that a man can be sitting or standing, or he can be stretched out, but he must be in a position. Similarly, a stone can be green or grey, but it cannot jump. Accident is related to the possibility of predication, to the semantic genera of the predicates, the ten categories.

151). The method to achieve this result is to share the same definitions of the concepts. The methodology of definition given in the *Topics* is based on two crucial characteristics: the correctness of the definition, and the ability of the definition to express the essence of the thing. For a definition to be **correct**, two requisites must be respected (*Topics*, IV, 3):

a) Avoid obscurity and unclear expressions.
b) Avoid unnecessarily long descriptions.

Aristotle lists a series of topics that can be understood as rules for the assessment of a definition. For instance, we can analyze the following topics:

Obscurity	
1. The definition contains equivocal words.	a. A house is a *place* where a family lives (it can be any place).
2. The definition does not distinguish between the different meanings of the *definiendum*.	b. A house is *a building with a roof* (Dwelling? Shelter?).
3. The definition contains words used in a metaphorical sense.	c. A house is the *heart* of a family.
4. The definition contains words whose use is unusual (not very well established and known).	d. A house is a *gaff* where people live.
5. The definition contains terms whose proper meanings do not describe the things and that are not metaphors. The senses of these words cannot be recovered.	e. A house is a building that can have an *e-space*.

Length	
1. The definition contains attributes universally applicable (attributes that are not the proximate genus or that apply to all the things under the same genus).	a. A house is a building that *has a foundation*.
2. The definition contains an attribute that is useless, that is not necessary to distinguish the thing from all the other concepts.	b. A house is a dwelling, *sometimes very nice*, which serves as living quarters for *big or small* families.
3. The definition is not peculiar of the species defined, since it does not belong to all the individuals falling under the same species.	c. A house is a *big* dwelling that serves as living quarters for families.
4. In the definition the same attributes are predicated more than once of the same thing.	d. A house is a dwelling *built by humans* that serves as living quarters for families.

The topics of obscurity and length distinguish the essential definition from the definitions built to direct the interlocutor's value judgments. For instance, metaphors are used to establish an analogy between the *definiendum* and other entities or qualities that do not describe it. For example, the definition of house as the 'heart of a family' or of man as 'the microcosm' (Victorini, *Liber de Definitionibus*, 28, 6–7) allows the speaker to draw inferences based on analogy. Since the house is the heart of a family, it cannot be changed, as it is impossible or cruel to change the heart. If man is referred to as the 'microcosm,' it can be claimed that man reflects the natural order of things, and so on. Metaphorical definitions trigger arguments from analogy, whose structure can be represented as follows (Walton 1995: 135–136; Macagno & Walton 2009b):

ARGUMENTATION SCHEME 8: REASONING FROM METAPHORICAL
DEFINITIONS

Premise 1	Generally, case C_1 is similar to case C_2.
Premise 2	Proposition A is true (false) in case C_1 / property G is attributed to C_1.
Conclusion	Proposition A is true (false) in case C_2 / property G is attributed to C_2.

Metaphorical definitions are not used for the dialogical purpose of clarifying a concept and avoiding misunderstanding. They are rhetorical instruments to trigger specific inferences, supporting classifications that could not be grounded on the simple essential definition. Metaphors can also be used to trigger value judgments. For instance, the definition of youth as the 'flower of life' supports a positive judgment grounded on the positive evaluation of flowers and transferred to 'youth' by means of an analogical reasoning (Victorini, *Liber de Definitionibus*, 22, 8–9; Ciceronis, *Topica*, VII, 32, 2–5). The other obscure definitions can serve for various argumentative purposes. The vagueness of a concept can be used to hide reality and elicit a value judgment not connected with the reality referred to, or simply pursue specific rhetorical or strategic goals. For instance, we can consider the following definition of 'peace' (Barack Obama, *Nobel Peace Prize Acceptance Address*, Oslo, Norway, December 10, 2009):

DEFINITION OF 'PEACE'

A just peace includes not only civil and political rights – it must encompass economic security and opportunity. For true peace is not just freedom from fear, but freedom from want.

What is 'security'? What is 'freedom'? What is 'want'? Such terms are vague, or have been redefined to include several concepts. However, they are all considered as positive and supported by everybody.

Definitions may include technical terms, unclear to the interlocutor (what Schiappa called "bureaucratization") in order to hide the concept and at the same time exclude the audience from the community able to judge and understand it. Sometimes technical terms are used only to prevent the audience from making an independent judgment. For example, in medical litigations, technical expert testimony sometimes has the effect of impressing and at the same time confounding the jury (Mahadevan & Garmel 2005: 665). The purpose of such definitions is to misuse authority: Since it is impossible for me to even understand the issue, I have to follow what the expert says. This type of argument is not simply an argument from authority, which is subject to assessment (Walton 2002: 49–50):

ARGUMENTATION SCHEME 9: REASONING FROM AUTHORITY

Premise 1	Source E is an expert in subject domain S containing proposition A.
Premise 2	E asserts that proposition A is true (false).
Conclusion	A is true (false).

This argument needs to be evaluated by considering six critical questions. In particular, the *Backup Evidence Question* is extremely relevant for the case. Such a question, which can be expressed as "Is E's assertion based on evidence?" presupposes an understanding of the issue by the interlocutor (see the role of authority in doctor–patient interactions in Buchanan et al. 1998). He or she can accept the argument only if it sounds reasonable. The role of 'bureaucratic' definitions is to exclude understanding, and therefore assessment.

Definitions can be excessively long because the purpose of the speaker is to describe a specific instance of the *definiendum*, not the generic concept. For instance, in Chapter 1 we mentioned the definition of 'wisdom' as 'knowledge of how to acquire money' and of 'folly' as 'desire of inordinate glory.' In both cases the definition, in addition to being too specific, provides a description that is useless to outline 'wisdom' or 'folly.' On the contrary, they can only be attributed to specific kinds of wisdom or folly. However, the properties attributed have the purpose to elicit reasoning from values. Similarly, in the ancient definition of 'informer' as 'a wicked and dangerous citizen,' the properties can be attributed to several kinds of criminals or citizens breaching the law. Such attributes, again, simply point out such qualities to lead the interlocutor to negatively evaluate the informers. Victorinus called such definitions "definitions *per laudem* e *per vituperationem*" (Victorini, *Liber de Definitionibus*, 26, 16–27, 1; 27, 13–14) and provided the following example (Isidori Hispaniensis, *Etymologiarum sive Originum Libri XX*, II, 29.13):

DEFINITION OF 'SLAVERY'

Slavery is the last of all evils, and should be repelled not only by war, but also by death.

The exaggeration of the negativity of the concept is increased by emphasizing its evil character, comparing it to war and death. The purpose of this definition cannot be the clarification of the concept, but rather the simple devaluation or amplification of 'slavery.'[10]

6. Strategies of Circularity: The Logic of Prior Terms

In Aristotle's view, the definition must express the essential property of a thing, in other words, its fundamental semantic features. The notion of an essential property, or a "semantically fundamental characteristic," depends upon the concepts of intelligibility and differentiation (*Topics*, VI, 4). The definition must make known the meaning of the concept, by describing it using the prior and more intelligible concepts,[11] that is, the genus and the *differentia*. The genus is more intelligible than the species, since the species is more complex, being constituted by the genus and the difference. The same applies to the difference. The basic principle is what can be taken for granted. In genus-difference definitions, the genus is presupposed to be known by the interlocutor, and therefore it is taken to be already part of his commitments (Tarello 1980: 195).

The first basic requirement for advancing a definition is the logical and epistemological priority of its terms. Aristotle sets out the following rules:

Topic of Prior Terms	
1. An opposite cannot be defined by means of its opposite (when it is possible to avoid this circular definition).	Good is what is not bad.
2. A thing cannot be defined by its opposite belonging to the same division.	A man is a being that is not a beast.
3. A definition cannot contain the term defined.	A house is a building that is a house for a family.
4. A thing cannot be defined by using its species.	A boat is a vehicle a ferry belongs to.

Aristotle provides such rules to distinguish the essential definition from three other types of definitions with different logical properties. A definition should

---

[10] "Non enim aut consequens eius est aut aliquid horum quae ενvoημaτικη definitioni dedimus, sed sola vituperatio est, quae servitutem malorum omnium dicit esse postremum; nec accipitur rursus malum quasi genus esse ad servitutem – nam malum qualitas est, servitus ad aliquid –_ unde, cum diversae sint res, malum genus esse non potest ad servitutem; iure igitur per vituperationem facta dicitur servitutis supra posita definitio?" (Victorini, *Liber de Definitionibus*, 27, 21–28)

[11] For the notion of basic elements of meaning see Mel'cuk's Meaning-Text theory (Mel'cuk 1997).

not be circular (either by including the very *definiendum* in the definition or by denying its contrary) and inductive (mentioning some or all the specific concepts falling under the *definiendum*).

Victorinus analyzes the definition by negation of the contrary (*per privantiam contrarii*) and the definition by species as two definitional strategies. The definition by species was classified as "essential" and "not essential" according to its structure. It is possible to define by species either by listing all the possible more specific concepts that can fall within the generic *definiendum*, or by providing only one or more examples as illustration (ὡς τύπος). For instance, we can consider the following definitions by essential parts (Ciceronis, *Topica*, 10, 6–8):

DEFINITION OF 'TO FREE'

If someone has not been freed by either having his name entered in the census-roll or by being touched with the rod or by a provision in a will, then he is not free. None of these apply to the individual in question. Therefore he is not free.

The definition of 'to free a man' is provided by listing all the possible ways a slave can be freed. If all such possibilities are denied, the generic concept is denied. This pattern of reasoning is grounded on a logical principle and a semantic one. The logical principle is the combination of the *modus tollens* and the rules of the inclusive disjunction. The *definiendum* is posited as equal to the disjunction of its species. The only way of denying the disjunction is to deny that an entity can fall within any of the species. By denying all the species it is possible to deny the generic concept, the *definiendum*.

Modus Tollens	Inclusive Disjunction
If x is A, then x is B. x is not B. Therefore, x is not A.	$\neg(A \vee B) \equiv (\neg A \wedge \neg B)$

Denying the species
If x is A, then x is A_1, or A_2, or A_3, etc. x is not A_1, and x is not A_2, and x is not A_3, etc. Therefore, x is not A.

As can be seen here, since the reasoning is only plausible and is not subject to quantification, the link between the antecedent and the consequent needs to be supported by a rule of inference, which can be expressed as follows: "It is impossible for something to be predicated of the genus if it is not predicated of one of its species" (*Topics*, 121a 28–29). These axioms and the rule of inference can be applied to reasoning from classification and result in the following scheme:

ARGUMENTATION SCHEME 10: REASONING FROM SPECIES

Classification Premise	For all x, if x fits A, and A_1, A_2 and A_3 are the only species of A (only A_1, A_2 and A_3 can be classified as A, x fits A_1, or A_2, or A_3).
Negation Premise	x does not fit A_1, and x does not fit A_2, and x does not fit A_3.
Conclusion	x does not fit A.

The list of the species needs to be exhaustive in order for the reasoning to follow. In law, these types of definitions are extremely dangerous, as they need to include all the possible entities that the predicate may refer to (Tiersma 1999: 119). For instance, consider the following definition of 'securities' (18 USC Section 2311):

DEFINITION OF 'SECURITIES'

'Securities' includes any note, stock certificate, bond, debenture, check, draft, warrant, traveler's check, letter of credit, warehouse receipt, negotiable bill of lading, evidence of indebtedness, certificate of interest or participation in any profit-sharing agreement, collateral-trust certificate, preorganization certificate or subscription, transferable share, investment contract, voting-trust certificate; valid or blank motor vehicle title; certificate of interest in property, tangible or intangible; instrument or document or writing evidencing ownership of goods, wares, and merchandise, or transferring or assigning any right, title, or interest in or to goods, wares, and merchandise; or, in general, any instrument commonly known as a "security", or any certificate of interest or participation in, temporary or interim certificate for, receipt for, warrant, or right to subscribe to or purchase any of the foregoing, or any forged, counterfeited, or spurious representation of any of the foregoing.

The risk is that a new type of security is introduced. In this case, the interlocutor can show that it is not a security from a legal point of view, and therefore that it is not subject to the law on securities. The defeasibility of such a definition rests on the completeness of the enumeration. The species need to be completely exhaustive.

From a dialectical perspective, definitions by enumeration are useful for shifting the burden of providing all the possible evidence concerning a concept. For instance, we can consider the following definition of 'no consent' in the Canadian Criminal Code (section 244(3), see Temkin 2002: 117):

DEFINITION OF 'NO CONSENT'

For the purpose of this section, no consent is obtained where the complainant submits or does not resist by reason of:

(a) the application of force to the complainant or to a person other than the complainant
(b) threats or fear of the application of force to the complainant or to a person other than the complainant
(c) fraud
(d) the exercise of authority.

The concept is defined by providing the genus (failure to resist) and a list of circumstances in which there is no consent. Such an enumeration is aimed at shifting the evidential burden onto the defendant (Tadros 2006). If the prosecution proves that one of such circumstances apply, "the accused will have to introduce evidence if he wishes the issue to reach the jury" (*R. v. Robertson*, 1 S.C.R. 918, 1987). For instance, if the victim has been shown to have consented out of fear, a presumption is raised that there was no consent, and the accused needs to introduce evidence supporting the absence of *mens rea*.

Another dialectical property is the rule of negation. In order to deny a classification, the speaker does not have to simply deny the attribution of a property, but rather provide evidence that all the specific instances are not the case. For this reason, the definition by enumeration has a counterpart in the definition by exclusion, or defining a concept by denying all the contrary instances. For instance, 'non-strategic nuclear weapons' were defined as "all weapons not covered by strategic arms control treaties as nonstrategic nuclear weapons" (Woolf 2004: 6). In such a case, the speaker presupposes both the knowledge of the genus (weapon) and the excluded species (weapons covered by arm control treaties) (Tarello 1980: 206).

Definitions by illustration are grounded on a type of reasoning from example. Such definitions do not include all possible instances of predication of the *definiendum*, but only the most prototypical ones (Victorini, *Liber de Definitionibus*, 26, 8). For instance, in the following case, instead of explaining the meaning of 'artificial means,' the drafter simply listed the most common types of operations classified as such (Bayles 1991: 262):

DEFINITION OF 'ARTIFICIAL MEANS'

My living will states that if I would not recover from a disability I "not be kept alive by artificial means or 'heroic measures', including, but not limited to, any resuscitation efforts, the transplant of any vital organ, or the use of a respirator."

This type of definition is useful for a rhetorical and explanatory purpose. For instance, Victorinus provides the following definition by illustration (Victorini, *Liber de Definitionibus*, 26, 8):

DEFINITION OF 'ARTIFICIAL MEANS'

Animate being, such as man.

This case provides the interlocutor with a clear instance of a particular type of animate being. From such an example, he can abstract the trait of rationality as fundamental, and therefore could have concluded that dogs or cats are not animals. The rhetorical power of such a definition lies in the characteristics of the examples chosen. If we define 'peacekeeping missions' as 'missions such as Operation Restoring Hope in Somalia,' we allow the interlocutor to draw the conclusion that peacekeeping missions are actually operations of war (Mayall 1996: 110; Blokker 2000: 557). The nature of this type of inference can be understood by analyzing the structure of argument from example (from Macagno & Walton 2009b: 173):

ARGUMENTATION SCHEME 11: REASONING FROM EXAMPLE

1. Example Premise	If x is like y, then x is A.
2. Factual Premise 1	y also has property G.
3. Abstraction of the Property	What is A is also G.
4. Factual Premise 2	x is G.
Conclusion	x is A.

In this case, the hearer is led to abstract the property of 'being a war operation' from the comparison between the two examples. Since the operation in Sudan is known to have become an operation of war, peacekeeping missions can be concluded to be war operations (step 3 of the scheme) and further instances can be classified as such (step 4 and conclusion).

Aristotle points out that a concept shall not be defined by negation of the contrary of the *definiendum*. An example of a definition "*per privantiam contrarii*" is the definition of 'good' as "what is not evil" (Victorini, *Liber de Definitionibus*, 23, 9–11). Such definitions presuppose the knowledge of the contrary, and do not describe what a thing is, but what it is not. The problem with this type of definition is the nature of the paradigm to which the two predicates (the contraries) belong. The paradigm can be constituted of only two elements, such as in the case of dead–alive (either a man is dead or he is alive). Otherwise, the paradigm can include more elements. For instance, the paradigm of 'moral qualities' can be characterized by the contraries good–bad, but in between there are several other types of intermediate predicates. Moreover, definitions by contrary do not specify the meaning of the concept, and therefore do not specify the meaning of a word in case of polysemy. For instance, if we define 'dead' as 'not alive,' we do not specify the generic property the two species fall within. Are they instances of 'vital condition'? Or are they rather included in the generic quality of 'responsiveness' or 'level of productivity'? From a dialectical perspective, definitions by negation of the contrary trigger only one type of reasoning, whose correctness depends on the type of paradigm of the predicates. The classification is grounded on the exclusion of the alternative, and proceeds from the following logical rule:

Disjunctive Syllogism
Either A or B.
Not B.
Therefore A.

While binary paradigms allow for this type of reasoning, paradigms with more than two elements do not. The only conclusion that can be drawn is that the contrary predicate or the other possibilities are the case. When the contrary predicates belong to a non-binary paradigm, the conclusion that *A* is the case from the negation of *B* is a logical fallacy (see Engel 1994: 140–142). This reasoning is useful when the speaker wants to suggest that an intermediate predicate, which cannot be precisely identified, applies. Definition by negation is extremely useful to shift the burden of proof. To illustrate, we can consider the case *Adams et al. v. United States*, in which the defendant (the Health and Human Services Division, hereinafter HHS) wanted to prove that the plaintiffs (working as investigators) were not entitled to overtime pay as their duties were administrative, and administrative works are not entitled to overtime pay. In order to show that the job was to be classified as administrative, they advanced the following reasoning (*Adams et al. v. United States* No. 90–162C and Consolidated Cases [doc. 661, 2007: 9–10]):

DEFINITION OF 'ADMINISTRATIVE WORK'

Defendant sees the production work of HHS as the sponsoring of federally-funded health care and benefit programs, not the investigation of abuses in the delivery of those programs. [...] Defendant argues that performing criminal investigations cannot be part of the production work of HHS. [...] Defendant concludes that plaintiffs were exempt administrative employees of HHS during the relevant time period.

The defendant's argument was grounded on a definition by negation of the contrary, and, in particular, the negative definition of 'administration work' as 'work that is not productive.' Since the defendant's work did not consist in sponsoring health care and benefit programs, it was shown to be administrative. The defendant in this case could not proceed from the definition of 'administration work,' as the work was not characterized by managerial tasks. But the negative definition allowed him to shift the burden of proof onto the other party.

The rhetorical force of definitions by negation of the contrary consists in the attribution of contrary qualities to contrary predicates. Such a line of argument was described by Aristotle as follows (Aristotle, *Rhetoric*, 1397a 7–10):

One *topos* of demonstrative [enthymemes] is that from opposites [*ek tōn enantiōn*]; for one should look to see if the opposite [predicate] is true of the opposite [subject], [thus] refuting the argument if it is not, confirming it if it is: for example, that to be temperate is a good thing; for to lack self control is harmful.

This argument is based on two interrelated paradigms. 'Temperance' is presented as contrary to 'lack of self-control' and 'to be a good thing' as contrary to 'to be harmful.' The two paradigms are connected by a relationship of "quality of the consequences." When the two paradigms are binary, such an argument can be extremely effective, as the negative definition can be used simply to point out the difference between the two concepts and deny the predication of a quality. For instance, we can consider the following example (Ciceronis, *Topica*, III, 17, 10–18):

DEFINITION OF 'CONSUMPTION'

The woman to whom the man bequeathed the usufruct of 'all his goods' should not believe that, if the oil and the wine cellars were left filled, their content belonged to her. For it is use (*usus*) not its consumption (*abusus*) which was granted (the two are opposite to one other).

In this case, 'consumption' is defined as the opposite of 'use.' Since from a legal point of view either a good is expressly bequeathed or it is not bequeathed at all, the fact that the consumption is not the use supports the conclusion that the use has not been mentioned. For this reason, it cannot have been bequeathed.

Definitions by negation can be powerful tools that can be used to redefine a concept and elicit value judgments based on the topic from contrary qualities. If we define 'wisdom' as 'what is not ignorance' or 'what is not erudition,' we redefine the *definiendum* by selecting only one of its possible characteristics or causes ('The ability to discern or judge what is true, right, or lasting'). We place the concept under the genus of 'educative condition' or 'learning,' altering its genus (ability). At the same time, we trigger specific conclusions based on the positive value we associate with wisdom. For instance, we can argue that "wisdom is good" or "useful" and conclude that erudition is bad or useless, or we can maintain that "wisdom is honorable" and show that ignorance is shameful.

7. The Logical Force of Definition by Genus and Difference

For a definition to express an essence, it must be constituted by its genus and difference. Aristotle provided a set of rules to attribute the genus and the difference correctly, which at the same time constitute the logical proprieties of the components of the essential definition.

7.1. *The Logic of the Genus*

The concept of genus can be clarified by the most important topics by which it is characterized (Aristotle, *Topics*, 120b 12–123a 27):

Topics	Examples
1. The genus must include all the members of the species it is predicated of.	1. Theft is a crime. Therefore embezzlement is a crime.
2. The genus is predicated in the category of essence. Genus and species must fall in the same category.	2. Theft is an action. Therefore embezzlement is an action, not an omission.
3. The species can be predicated of the definition of the genus, not vice versa.	3. Embezzlement is theft. Therefore embezzlement is an act of stealing.

4. The genus is predicated of what the species is predicated of.	4. This manager embezzled the company's money. Therefore he stole the company's money.
5. It is impossible for something to be predicated of the genus if it is not predicated of one of its species.	5. Bob never embezzled, robbed, skimmed, and rustled. Therefore you cannot call him a thief. If you are a white collar worker, it does not mean that you cannot be a thief. White collar workers often commit embezzlement.
6. What is placed in the genus cannot be predicated of the definition of anything contrary to the genus.	6. Embezzlement is a crime. Therefore it cannot be honest.

The topics of the genus allow the inferences proceeding from the more generic concept to the more specific ones and from the more specific to the more generic. These topics play a crucial role in the inferences triggered by persuasive definitions. For instance, we can consider the previous redefinition of 'peace' as "not just freedom from fear, but freedom from want." According to such a definition, the war in Afghanistan was made for peace, as it was waged to free the Afghans (from their political slavery). Moreover, it is possible to claim that Greece cannot be at peace now, as peace is the absence of necessity or constraints and Greeks are subject to the rules of International Monetary Fund and now have many necessities. It is also possible to claim that the population in Greece needs peace, and therefore has the need to be freed from their necessities. Since the process of freeing the Afghans from their political oppression was violent, peace can also be claimed to be violent. Finally, the war against the Taliban cannot be said to be a form of oppression, as it was a mission of peace.

7.2. *Specifying the Genus*
The second characteristic of the genus is that it needs to be the most proximate to the species and needs to be specified by means of the difference. Aristotle in book VI of his *Topics* provides some rules to correctly specify the genus, which can be summarized as follows:

Topics of the Difference	
The definition must divide the species by means of the difference from something else. There must be an opposite of the species in the division.	Embezzlement is a fraud committed by employees (are there frauds that cannot be committed by employees?).
The difference must be a difference of the genus considered.	Embezzlement is the appropriation of assets (it is the dishonest appropriation).

The genus cannot be divided by negation.	Fraud is what is not honest. Peace is what is not war.
The difference must not be a species of the genus or the genus of the one stated.	A fraud is a crime like embezzlement.
The difference must signify an essential (not accidental) quality of the subject. It cannot signify affections, special or temporal indications.	Embezzlement is a larceny committed by white collar workers.
The genus is predicated of the species; the difference is predicated of the species. The genus cannot be predicated of the difference, or vice versa. The species cannot be predicated of the difference.	Embezzlement can be committed only by people to whom assets are entrusted, as it is the misappropriation of assets entrusted to one's care.
The difference of relatives must be relative and relative to the primary relation of the term. In case of an artifact, the difference must be relative to its natural purpose.	Money is a medium for the happiness of the people (not the natural purpose).
The difference must not be an affection of the genus.	Embezzlement is a contemptible crime (if no one holds it in contempt, it would be still embezzlement).

The concept of difference is fundamental for understanding the difference between the semantic analysis and the definition by parts. The difference divides a generic concept in its more specific ones. It is based on the formal properties of a concept. Such parts are not physical, but merely categorical. On the contrary, it is possible to define a concept by showing its physical components. The definition by integral parts has two main schemes:

Definitions		Inferences
X is A and B.	A house is walls, the foundation, a roof, etc.	There are walls, the foundation, a roof, etc. Therefore there is a house (there might not be).
X is made of A and B.	A house is made of walls, the foundation, a roof, etc.	A house is destroyed. Therefore walls, the foundation, a roof are destroyed (they might be not destroyed).

In all these schemes, we should notice that the subject cannot be identical with the single part. In the first scheme, the whole is not identical to the compound of the parts. In other words, the subject is not convertible with the *definiens*. In the second scheme, the subject and the *definiens* are not convertible since they cannot be subject to the same predications. For instance, if a house is destroyed, the parts it was made of can still be intact. The definition must indicate the specific composition of the parts, in order to indicate the essence of the compound. Definitions by material parts are useful only for destructive purposes (Ciceronis, *Topica*, 9): If there are no walls, there cannot be a house. However, such definitions are the ground of fallacious arguments by composition and division. A soccer team can be defined as having eleven football players; however, if the team is strong, it does not follow that one single player is strong.

The definition, in addition to being convertible with the subject,[12] must therefore express its fundamental characteristics. In other words, the definition must not be merely wider or narrower than the *definiendum*, but also must comply with semantic and logical conditions. The argumentative power of an essential definition is based on its being hardly questionable. Semantics can be conceived as the deepest level of *endoxa* (or shared commitments): To refuse to accept the most basic semantic characteristics may result in refusing to accept a fragment of the shared semantic system. For instance, if we refuse to claim that a man is an animate being, we deny the possibility of attributing him predicates such as 'to walk' or 'to breathe.' For most of the concept the semantic analysis can be highly controversial, as there is not one agreed upon meaning. Moreover, the essential definition is always convertible with the *definiendum*, and it can be used to develop inferences based on the genus. For instance, if we consider the definition of 'free speech' as 'the human right regarding the freedom of expression,' by showing that 'free speech' has been forbidden, we can support the conclusion that a human right has been violated (what is said of the species is said of the genus as well). These observations can be useful to understand the difference between an essential definition and the other kinds of definitions.

7.3. *The Logical Force of the Genus-Difference Definition*
In definitions by genus and difference, the definition is convertible with the *definiendum*. Such a property is the foundation of different inferential patterns that underlie different uses of the argument from classification and constitute different schemes (Petri Hispani, *Summulae Logicales*, 1990: 52–54):

---

[12] For the use of the Aristotelian topical relations in rhetorical speech, see Weaver (1953). Analyzing the definition of 'human referred to the black slaves,' for instance, he notices that the category of 'not human' applies only in certain circumstances to the slaves and not to all the black people.

1a. Thing defined/definition as subject of predication (Positive)	1b. Thing defined/definition as subject of predication (Negative)
Maxima: Whatever is predicated of the thing defined is predicated of the definition as well, and vice versa.	Maxima: Whatever is removed from the thing defined is removed from the definition as well, and vice versa.
Example. A person stealing the assets entrusted to his care betrays the trust. Therefore, who embezzles money betrays someone's trust.	*Example.* A person stealing the assets entrusted to his care cannot be trusted. Therefore, who embezzles money cannot be trusted.
2a. Definition as predicate (Positive)	2b. Definition as predicate (Negative)
Maxima: Whatever the thing defined is predicated of, the definition is predicated of as well, and vice versa. *Example.* Bob embezzled his company's funds. Therefore, Bob stole the funds entrusted to his own care.	Maxima: From whatever the thing defined is removed, the definition is removed as well, and vice versa. *Example.* Bob did not embezzle his company's funds. Therefore, Bob did not steal the funds entrusted to his own care.

Such topics make the argument from classification much more complex. They represent the two directions of the argument from classification and the two axioms from which it proceeds. In the argument from classification, only the positive and negative topics concerning the attribution of a definition to a subject are represented. We can represent all the topics of the definition as a predicate as follows:

ARGUMENTATION SCHEME 12: REASONING FROM CLASSIFICATION OF AN ENTITY

Definition Premise	a is classified as G. / a is classified as D.
Classification Premise	For all x, if x is classified G, and D is the definition of G, then x can be classified as D.
Conclusion	a is classified as D. / a is classified as G.

The other schemes, based on the attribution of a property to the defined thing, can be represented with the following argument scheme:

ARGUMENTATION SCHEME 13: REASONING FROM/TO CLASSIFICATION OF A DEFINITION

Definition Premise	$G(a)$ is classified as F. / $D(a)$ is classified as F.
Classification Premise	For all x, if x is G, and D is the definition of G, then x is D.
Conclusion	$D(a)$ is classified as F. / $G(a)$ is classified as F.

In addition to being convertible, the essential definition is constituted by the genus and therefore it is characterized by the aforementioned logical properties of the genus (Petri Hispani, *Summulae Logicales*, 56; Aristotle, *Topics*, 120b 12-123a 27). For this reason, the critical questions mentioned in Section 1.3 need to be developed further to include the properties and purposes of definition as follows:

CQ$_1$: *Purpose.*	What is the purpose of definition *D*? Is it aimed at describing the meaning of *D*, or rather qualifying it or providing criteria for heuristically classifying a state of affairs as *D*?
CQ$_2$: *Fundamental characteristics.*	Does the definition express what the *definiendum* is? Or does it not answer such a question, or beg it?
CQ$_3$: *Convertibility in predication.*	Can all entities or states of affairs classified as *G* be also classified as *D*? Are there any entities or states of affairs that are *G* but cannot or are not *D*?
CQ$_4$: *Convertibility in qualities.*	Can all entities or states of affairs referred to as *G* be classified in the same fashion as entities or states of affairs referred to as *D*?
CQ$_5$: *Clarity.*	Does the definition explain the meaning of the *definiendum* using more generic and simpler concepts? Or does it use metaphors or vague terms? Does the definition include terms less understandable than the *definiendum*?
CQ$_6$: *Non-circularity.*	Is the *definiendum* described using more specific concepts, or denying its contrary?

An essential definition, as shown in the previous subsections, is characterized by semantic and logical properties that allow one to situate the concept defined within a conceptual system. This system, being grounded on necessary semantic features, can be common to different types of ontological classifications. In such a fashion, in a clarification dialogue, an essential definition can play a fundamental role by constituting the more basic classification system common to different types of conceptual representations. Moreover, topics from genus and definition characterize essential definitions by means of necessary rules of inference.

8. Conclusion

Words can direct and trigger emotions, suggest, influence, or alter our evaluation of reality. The emotive force of words lies in the value judgment that stems from their use and is ultimately grounded on the state of affairs that they are used to represent. Stevenson pointed out how words have a descriptive and an emotive dimension, which are often related to each other by an identifiable pattern of reasoning. If the value judgment cannot be severed from what the judgment is about, it is however possible to modify the descriptive meaning of a word in an explicit or implicit fashion. The quasi-logical instrument to analyze how the (cognitive or descriptive) meaning of a word can be changed is the definition. The definition is the logical-semantic link between what a word means and the different types of reasoning aimed at using such a word to classify reality, or classifying the reference of such a word. On this argumentative perspective, a definition is the premise of reasoning from classification, and like all other arguments, it needs to be accepted to support a conclusion. This characteristic of reasoning from classification reflects the structure of our knowledge. Definitions need not be true or false, but simply acceptable or accepted.

The apparent relativism of this account of definition is actually grounded on strong logical criteria that distinguish what can be an acceptable definition from what cannot. Definitions cannot be all the same, but they need to be assessed through logical tests and counterarguments. A strong and acceptable definition is a definition that can resist all possible objections, which have been broadly summarized in the critical questions mentioned in Section 6.3. Such questions represent the generic criteria to establish whether the interlocutor can accept a definition based on his classification of reality and his use of language, which are his more basic commitments.

The manipulative use of persuasive definitions and emotive words is ultimately based on either an alteration of the properties of a state of affairs, omitting some qualities or details or falsely presupposing the existence of others, or the use of a definition that the interlocutor would not accept. In both cases, the target is the two basic premises of the argument from classification. The speaker can either alter the factual premise or the definition. However, only in conditions of the interlocutor's total lack of knowledge about facts or language would such an argument be a strong one. In normal conditions, the hearer can simply assess the premises and reject the conclusion or consider it as extremely weak. Why, then, is the use of emotive language so effective? Why are persuasive definitions powerful and sometimes dangerous instruments? The answers cannot be found in argumentation schemes, in which premises and conclusions are represented simply as propositions that can be evaluated and objected. A different approach is needed, which investigates the strategies used to hide reality and prevent the interlocutor from detecting and objecting to redefinitions and omissions or misrepresentations of states of affairs. We need to enter the domain of pragmatics and see how these schemes and these patterns of reasoning are actually used to act. We need to analyze the acts of language in order to understand how their inner logic actually works.

4

The Acts of Defining

The act of naming is based on a factual premise and a definition, or classificatory principle. Like all conclusions in arguments, the classification depends on the strength of the acceptability of the premises supporting it. The interlocutor can rationally explain that he cannot accept the conclusion because he does not agree with one of the premises supporting it. Emotive words can be used as dialectical instruments of manipulation. They can hide reality or conceal the controversial nature of a definition. In both cases, the interlocutor is prevented from judging a classification and challenging it. Dialectical strategies of hiding facts or meaning can explain the force and the danger of arguments from classification, and help in analyzing the pragmatic dimension of definitions.

The meaning of words can be controversial, vague, or unshared. In these cases, the definition cannot be considered as acceptable by the interlocutor, and becomes the standpoint of a discussion. In the previous chapter we showed how a definition can be evaluated and rejected by showing that it does not fulfill semantic and logical conditions. If 'true peace' is defined as 'waging war against nations breaching civil rights,' it is possible to attack the definition and show that war cannot in any case be considered as peaceful. There is nothing inherently wrong in redefining a concept, as long as the freedom of altering, choosing, or précising the meaning does not limit the other party's freedom to accept or challenge it. The thin line between negotiating, discussing, proposing a definition, and imposing it lies in the pragmatic nature of the conversational framework.

If we analyze the deceptive uses of language, we notice that something is always missing. Some redefinitions can be controversial, or at worst ridiculous, such as Stevenson's redefinition of 'culture' or Huxley's sarcastic description of the meaning of 'true freedom.' In such cases, the interlocutor can evaluate the definitional discourse and choose whether to accept it or challenge it by means of criticisms or counterarguments. Other redefinitions are subtler. They are often unnoticed and therefore unchallenged.

They are presupposed, taken for granted, and therefore not subject to criticism. They are hidden in a classification of reality, as they are simply used to name a state of affairs in a specific fashion, to lead the interlocutor to the wanted conclusion or judgment. This strategy, called argument by definition, is a dialectical technique to position into place a meaning that the interlocutor does not or cannot share. From a dialectical point of view, the speaker rules out the interlocutor's possibility of challenging a premise. From a pragmatic perspective, his assertion is based on conditions that are known to be not shared, and it is intended to be infelicitous. Finally, the move rhetorically increases the burden of challenging and rejecting the unacceptable argument.

In this chapter we will analyze the dialectical effects of defining, starting from the distinctions between the different acts of defining. Building on Viskil's (1994) idea of classifying definitions under different types of speech acts, we will apply the tools of the pragmatic approaches to describe the requirements and the effects of every kind of act of defining. In this fashion, we will show the differences between the preconditions, for example, of the act of reminding of and the act of imposing a definition. The pragmatic profile will provide a set of pragmatic changes that can be developed in a dialectical perspective. Defining can be analyzed as an act that modifies the possible moves of the interlocutor and alters his set of commitments. The acts of defining will be classified according to two distinctions: positive–negative (or rather non-negative) and explicit–implicit. The first distinction points out the two different possible modalities to act with respect to a definition. The speaker can provide a definition in order to avoid vagueness or ambiguity, or omit a definition when it is necessary, in order to achieve a specific dialectical effect. The second distinction captures the two modalities the speaker can choose for providing or putting into place a definition. He can make it explicit, or simply take a definition for granted. All these types of actions presuppose different conditions and result in various dialectical effects and strategies, ranging from opening possible attacks and criticisms to imposing commitments and impeding rejections.

This theoretical framework will be applied to and tested against some political discourses, in which the different acts of defining play a crucial role in building not only a shared meaning but also the ground for his further dialectical moves. In particular, the effects of the explicit and implicit moves in Obama's speeches will be examined, and the role and strategic force of implicit definitions will be compared with the teachings of the ancient rhetoricians.

1. How Definitions Can Change Reality

In Chapter 3 we introduced different types of definitional structures, or discourses. Definitions may proceed by genus and difference, enumeration of the parts, or description. Each definitional structure has specific logical properties and can be used to achieve different specific argumentative goals. The propositional structure needs to be distinguished from its use, or rather from its role as a discourse move (Gobber 2007: 461; Rigotti 1993; Stati 1990).

As shown in the last chapter, definitions are instruments to name reality. They are often implicit and are left unstated as hidden premises of our reasoning from classification. We never realize how important and crucial definitions are until something goes wrong, until our interlocutor or ourselves need to state, change, or reject them, or simply until we understand that the definitions we take for granted do not correspond to the definition that our interlocutor is using or maintaining. In such cases, they cease to be implicit components of our reasoning and become the propositional content of real discourse moves, having as a common purpose the alteration of the interlocutor's classificatory grounds. However, the way such a modification is brought about can vary. In order to understand the different strategies of introducing a new definition, we can analyze some uses in political discourse, beginning from one of the most famous contemporary speeches, Obama's Nobel Peace Prize speech.

In this address, Obama needs to reconcile two "irreconcilable truths": Wars can be used to preserve the peace, but they promise human tragedy. The most powerful instruments he uses are the definition and redefinition of crucial concepts. One of the first moves he makes is to support the claim that the wars waged by the United States are or can be justified. To do so, he reminds his audience of the concept and meaning of 'just war' (Barack Obama, *Nobel Peace Prize Acceptance Address*, Oslo, Norway, December 10, 2009):

DEFINITION AS A PIECE OF INFORMATION OR A REMINDER: 'PEACE'

The concept of a "just war" emerged, suggesting that war is justified only when it meets certain preconditions: if it is waged as a last resort or in self-defense; if the force used is proportional, and if, whenever possible, civilians are spared from violence. [...]What I do know is that meeting these challenges will require the same vision, hard work, and persistence of those men and women who acted so boldly decades ago. And it will require us to think in new ways about the notions of just war and the imperatives of a just peace.

Obama relies on one of the essential communicative characteristics of definitions, i.e. the fact that they are presumed to be shared by the interlocutors. Definitions are the basic grounds of understanding, and therefore they are taken to be known by the audience. However, sometimes the speaker needs to inform the audience of the meaning of an uncommon or possibly unshared term, or simply remind them of such a meaning, in order to make sure that the definition is part of the interlocutors' common ground. Obama needed to inform and remind the audience that wars can be justified, in order to show that U.S. wars were waged for just reasons and support the new concept that he needs to introduce, 'just peace.'

Therefore, in this passage he states the definition, or rather the sufficient and necessary conditions of the concept, introducing as a commitment a meaning that the hearers might not share. He points out that it was a concept introduced in the past, to reinforce the hearers' commitment to such a proposition.

Further on in the text, Obama uses the word 'peace' in an unconventional fashion, without having first advanced any new definition for it. He claims that soldiers should not be honored as "makers of war" but rather "wagers of peace":

IMPLICIT REDEFINITION: 'PEACE'

Peace requires responsibility. Peace entails sacrifice. That is why NATO continues to be indispensable. That is why we must strengthen UN and regional peacekeeping, and not leave the task to a few countries. That is why we honor those who return home from peacekeeping and training abroad to Oslo and Rome; to Ottawa and Sydney; to Dhaka and Kigali – we honor them not as makers of war, but as wagers of peace.

The verb 'to wage' presupposes an activity to be carried on, an action (usually a campaign or a war). By using 'peace' as an argument of such a predicate, he bends its meaning, which can no longer be considered as a condition or state of affairs, as an "absence of conflict." He implicitly redefines this concept. He uses it with a definition that his audience cannot share, as it clearly departs from the ordinary and accepted use of the term. Through this move he introduces as a metaphorical and paradoxical expression a redefinition that he later makes explicit.

The pivotal strategic move in this speech is to alter the audience's commitments to the meaning of peace. The first definition he introduced, the description of 'just war,' split the notion of war into two species: just and unjust war. However, if there is a just war, there also must be a just peace, "for of necessity the contrary species must be in the contrary genus, if there be any contrary to the genus" (Aristotle, *Topics*, 123b 7–9). This implicit step of reasoning leads him to advance a new definition:

DEFINITION AS A STANDPOINT: 'PEACE'

For peace is not merely the absence of visible conflict. Only a just peace based upon the inherent rights and dignity of every individual can truly be lasting. [...]

For true peace is not just freedom from fear, but freedom from want.

Here we notice that the move consists of two steps. First, Obama defines the new species of 'peace,' 'just peace.' He counters the commonly accepted definition as too vague and proposes to introduce a species, "just peace," which is claimed to correspond to the new 'true' meaning of peace, "freedom from want." Obama provides an apparently sound argument to support such a claim, maintaining that the only way of having a lasting peace is to avoid the causes of possible instabilities. He advances such a definition as a proposal that needs to be borne out, even though the very structure of the discourse he was giving could not allow possible counterarguments.

The structure of this speech can be analyzed in terms of commitments. Obama wishes to support a specific viewpoint, and in order to do so, he builds up a new definition proceeding from what the people have already accepted, or from what they should accept. The only definitional move that forced this dynamic is the implicit redefinition, which Obama made explicit later on, without relying on it. From a dialectical perspective, we can say that Obama supports new definitional claims using past commitments. His purpose is to bind himself and the audience to the new redefinition of peace and lead his listeners to accept it.

In his Inaugural Address (*In a Dark Valley: Barack Obama's Inaugural Address*) Obama uses a strategy of redefinition completely different from the ones just mentioned. The definitions of 'just war' and 'peace' are aimed at modifying the interlocutors' understanding of the concept of war and peace. For this reason, they are open to criticism, as they can be compared with the shared meaning. In contrast, the following move is not intended to alter the commitments of the listeners, but only Obama's:

DEFINITION AS A COMMITMENT: 'WE-NESS'

We – and in this presidency, when I use that word, I will mean you and me, not the royal "we" to which American presidents have become far too attached – we can, I think, hope to accomplish much, but only if we're honest with ourselves.

Obama commits himself to a specific meaning of 'we.' He is not simply specifying its reference, but distinguishing the meaning of the pronoun as a *pluralis maiestatis* from the ordinary meaning. By refusing the royal definition, he commits himself to a meaning that includes the speaker as one of a number (the audience) performing an action. Obama not only clarifies the meaning of his words, he commits himself to a definition that wants to mirror his political attitude, consisting in making the people part of the decisions that need to be made.

These uses of definition that we just analyzed are purely persuasive. They are meant to lead the audience to a specific viewpoint, which can be the definition itself, or what the definition implies. The force of definitions can go far beyond the power of persuasion. Crucial concepts can be politically defined and redefined, in order to apply a specific law or politics to a state of affairs. When the speaker is the lawmaker, he has also the authority of deciding what the words in the laws mean. In this case, he is not simply using or proposing a definition, but actually imposing it. He stipulates a new meaning for a word in order to establish new behavior. Schiappa showed the mechanism of this strategy by analyzing the redefinition of 'wetland' (Schiappa 1996; 1998), which since its coming into broad use in the 1960s and 1970s was vague. The coexistence of several definitions allowed President Bush to redefine it, restricting its meaning in order to meet the promises made to the environmentalists, who were seeking the protection of the areas labeled as wetland, and at the same time allowing for the development of such lands (Schiappa 1998: 31). Similarly, the concept of "homeland security," first introduced and defined in 2002 primarily as powers to prevent terrorist attacks, was redefined in later 2007 and 2010 to include other types of threats to the national security. In 2002 'homeland security' was defined as follows (Office of Homeland Security, *National Strategy for Homeland Security* (Washington, DC: Office of Homeland Security, 2002: 2; see also *Homeland Security Art. I sec. 101*):

IMPOSING A DEFINITION: 'HOMELAND SECURITY'

Homeland security is a concerted national effort to prevent terrorist attacks within the United States, reduce America's vulnerability to terrorism, and minimize the damage and recover from attacks that do occur.

However, since 2007, the types of threats to security multiplied. In order to deal with the emergencies of Hurricane Katrina, proposals for a definitional change were advanced to include "*man-made and natural hazards*" (see Bellavita 2008), until 2011, when a new definition was advanced (Quadrennial Homeland Security Review Report Page, 11 February 2010: 13):

IMPOSING A REDEFINITION: 'HOMELAND SECURITY'

Homeland security is meant to connote a concerted, shared effort to ensure a homeland that is safe, secure, and resilient against terrorism and other hazards where American interests, aspirations, and way of life can thrive.

In this case, not only is the war on terror and environmental security included, but all other types of hazards, including cyber-terrorism. The new definition was meant to face a growing number of dangers and guarantee prompt responses to emergency situations.

The choice and imposition of a definition can set or change categories and rules. However, sometimes the new definitions conflict with commonly shared concepts, creating dangerous ambiguities. Such definitions do not only set a rule, but also have a persuasive or potentially manipulative function, exploiting the different meanings of the redefined word (see Zarefsky 2004). For instance, we can consider the following proposed amendment to the National Defense Authorization Act (Section 1034 of H.R. 1540, 2 and 3), in which 'armed conflict' is contextually redefined with respect to the meaning established in the 1949 Geneva Conventions. It is aimed at including not only the actual non-international conflict in Afghanistan but also all forms of terrorism or suspected support of terrorism:

IMPOSING DEFINITIONS: 'ARMED CONFLICT'

[...] (2) the President has the authority to use all necessary and appropriate force during the current armed conflict with al-Qaeda, the Taliban, and

associated forces pursuant to the Authorization for Use of Military Force
(Public Law 107–40; 50 U.S.C. 1541 note);

(3) the **current armed conflict** includes nations, organization, and persons
who –

(A) are part of, or are substantially supporting, al-Qaeda, the Taliban, or
associated forces that are engaged in hostilities against the United
States or its coalition partners; or

(B) have engaged in hostilities or have directly supported hostilities in aid
of a nation, organization, or person described in subparagraph (A).

Here an ambiguity is created with an acknowledged meaning of (non-internationalized) 'armed conflict.' Under the laws of war, it refers to armed
conflicts "which take place in the territory of a High Contracting Party
between its armed forces and dissident armed forces or other organized
armed groups which, under responsible command, exercise such control
over a part of its territory as to enable them to carry out sustained and
concerted military operations and to implement this Protocol" (Article 1
of Additional Protocol II – Geneva Convention 1949). This definition is
much narrower than the one advanced in Section 1034 and would exclude
terrorist attacks (that do not exercise control over a part of U.S. territory),
let alone supporters of such organizations, from the concept of armed
conflict. According to the Geneva definition, the United States is at war in
Afghanistan, while the operations against terrorists could not be classified
as armed conflicts. To the contrary, in order to allow the application of the
National Defense Authorization Act, the president redefined the crucial
concept and broadened it to include any possible member or supporter
of terrorist groups. The Act, introduced to take prompt measures in war-
time, also applies to a situation that cannot be commonly considered as
an 'armed conflict' under the laws of war. This new definition, however,
implicitly redefines other concepts that depend on it, or rather leaves such
terms without a definition. For instance, in the aforementioned amendment 1034, two concepts are mentioned, whose meanings cannot correspond to the ordinary one:

OMITTING DEFINITIONS: 'BELLIGERENT' AND 'HOSTILITIES'

(4) the President's authority pursuant to the Authorization for Use of Military
Force (Public Law 107–40; 50 U.S.C. 1541 note) includes the authority to
detain **belligerents**, including persons described in paragraph (3), until the
termination of **hostilities**.

What does 'belligerent' mean, if the very concept of armed conflict does not
correspond to the ordinarily accepted one? What does 'hostilities' mean?
Only in 2009 was this term first defined as "any conflict subject to the laws
of war" (10 U.S.C. § 948a 9); however, the broad concept of 'armed conflict'
exceeded the categories of the laws of war. The imposition of a definition sets
a rule, which can be attacked, discussed, or amended. It imposes a criterion

of classification that constitutes a position, a commitment of the speaker. The most powerful and dangerous definitional move is exactly the contrary of imposing a definition, namely, failing to do so. The speaker introduces a term, a key concept upon which the application of the rule depends, but he does not define it, leaving it open to a wide range of interpretations. This strategic move was used by Reagan to avoid any commitment to the (indiscriminate) cuts he wanted to make to the welfare system (Weiler 1992: 243). He introduced a new concept of 'needy,' the *truly needy*, which was not defined (Zarefsky, Miller-Tutzauer & Tutzauer 1984). Its contrary, the "apparently" needy, or rather the people who illegitimately benefited from the welfare system, were condemned as a fraud to the United States and the poor, but the two categories were never described in a fashion to clearly establish classificatory boundaries. Reagan could reduce the welfare budget heavily hitting the poor, as 'truly needy' potentially meant any poor and none.

The absence of a definition, or its vagueness, opens up a dialogical move, the possibility of defining or redefining a concept. Such a move is extremely powerful when implicit. The possibility of leaving it unexpressed comes directly from the absence of a conflicting shared definition. One of the most famous contemporary cases is the implicit redefinition of 'hostilities' used by Obama to classify the American intervention in Libya. Under the War Powers Resolution (US Code 1541), the president needs to obtain the authorization of the Congress to continue the hostilities within sixty days after the beginning thereof (War Powers Resolution, sec 5b, Public Law 93–148). However, the concept of 'hostilities' was not provided in such an act, and the aforementioned definition is extremely vague, not giving any criterion to classify the American involvement in a conflict. This vagueness allowed Obama to redefine 'hostilities' to exclude the American strikes in Libya. He implicitly redefined such a concept in a narrower way, including only ground troop intervention, sustained fighting, and exchanges of fire. From this definition airstrikes are excluded, especially if missiles are fired and bombs are dropped by unmanned aircraft (Obama Administration letter to Congress justifying Libya engagement, June 15th, 2011, p. 25):

IMPLICIT REDEFINITION: 'HOSTILITIES'

The President is of the view that the current U.S. military operations in Libya are consistent with the War Powers Resolution and do not under that law require further congressional authorization, because U.S. military operations are distinct from the kind of "hostilities" contemplated by the Resolution's 60 day termination provision. [...] U.S. operations do not involve sustained fighting or active exchanges of fire with hostile forces, nor do they involve the presence of U.S. ground troops, U.S. casualties or a serious threat thereof, or any significant chance of escalation into a conflict characterized by those factors.

Instead of explicitly arguing for a new definition, or rather a specification, of the concept, Obama takes it for granted. He does not reject the shared one, nor does he attack it based on its vagueness. He does not even suggest that it should be better clarified. Instead, he supports the claim that the United States is not engaged in any hostilities in Libya (and therefore he does not need the Congress' authorization) based on the fact that ground troops have not been deployed and ground battles have not been fought. He presupposes that 'hostilities' means only active fighting by ground troops, which does not correspond to any accepted definition of the term under the U.S. laws or military dictionaries.

These examples from political discourse show how definitions can be used in a dialogue. They can be proposed or imposed; they can remind the interlocutor of a commitment or inform him of a shared one. However, they can also be omitted or simply hidden. In political discourse, such uses appear as strategies that can be used for persuasive reasons. However, these strategies represent dialectical moves that have specific preconditions and effects. They are acts that occur in a dialogue, and at the same time are affected by the dialogical context and the previous dialogical moves (Kramer 2003). In order to analyze such conditions and consequences, we will analyze the use of definitions in law, where specific and explicit rules set out the limits and the effects of the different types of definitions, or rather acts of defining. By analyzing the rules of the acts of definition in law it is possible to understand their potential effects and conditions in ordinary language, governed by social and moral constraints.

2. The Acts of Defining

Definitions can be used for different purposes and have different dialectical effects, or rather effects on the dialogical situation. They are the propositional content of acts of language. Definitions can be used to impose a meaning, or advance a proposal of clarification or disambiguation, or inform the interlocutor. However, we usually imagine acts as positive actions. We often forget that we can voluntarily bring about a state of affairs by refraining from performing a specific action. The omission of expected behavior or words is an instrument to perform a specific action, not committing the speaker (or rather the non-speaker) to a specific decision or proposition (see Tannen 1985: 97). Silence can be regarded as a speech act of a kind (Ephratt 2008: 1921). Within the category of non-positive acts it is possible to classify (unduly) an actual non-act, consisting in taking for granted a proposition. Like omitting and silence, taking for granted cannot be considered a form of intentional conveyance of a communicative intention or the performance of a dialogical effect unless it breaches a dialogical expectation, agreeing upon what is not shared.

These distinctions can be useful to analyze how the use of a definition can affect the structure of dialogical commitments. In order to show the structure of such different types of acts, they will be analyzed within a specific context, that of legal dialogue and in particular legal discussions, including civil and criminal cases. The rules of the legal context highlight crucial dialogical features of the different acts, showing their conditions and requirements.

2.1. *Positive Acts of Defining*

Definitions can be used to create a new classification. This use has been referred to in the tradition as the stipulative (Robinson 1950: 59) or hortatory (Leonard 1967: 286) definition. The act of imposing a definition corresponds to a norm recommendation, where a rule is given to the interpreter. As Aarnio (1987: 57) puts it:

A stipulative definition can never be true or false: It is to add to, simplify or clarify the "agreed-upon" use of language. In this view a stipulative definition corresponds to a norm recommendation. To be more exact, it is a question of defining stipulatively a term in a law text so that a norm recommendation with a corresponding content can be given. Thus, if "surviving spouse" is defined as being similar to the term "widower", we can arrive at norm recommendation where all legal instructions pertaining to surviving spouses express norms that deal with widowers.

Such definitions are common in legal discourse. For instance, statutes provide statutory definitions of key concepts, such as the following (Iowa Code § 4.1[39]; 554D103):

DEFINITION OF 'WRITTEN'

Written – in writing – signature. The words "written" and "in writing" may include any mode of representing words or letters in general use, and include an electronic record as defined in section 554D.103.

"Electronic signature" means an electronic sound, symbol, or process attached to or logically associated with a record and executed or adopted by a person with the intent to sign the record.

Such definitions may conflict with the ordinary or shared meaning of the word, and in this sense the legislature may act as its own lexicographer, binding the interpreter to a specific intended meaning (Tiersma 1999: 117):

For example, burglary includes an "entry," but the image summoned by ordinary speech – a man inside a house – is not the legal meaning of 'entry.' Part of a hand inside a window, engaged in raising it, a bullet shot into a room, and even a hole bored in the floor of a granary, through which the grain drops into sacks held below the floor, are entries in the legal sense. The common-law definition of murder is killing a human being with "malice aforethought"; but "malice" does not mean malice, and "aforethought" is not premeditation in the dictionary sense.

For instance, in *State v. Fisher* (785 N.W.2d 697, 2010) the aforementioned definition of 'written' conflicted with the ordinary one. An officer used a computer screen to make a 'written request' to withdraw a bodily substance for testing from a driver suspected of operating while intoxicated.

Should checking a box on an electronic document count as 'writing'? In this case, as the statutory definition imposes a rule on the interpreter, the court found that it was to be considered as such.

The act of imposing a definition is, however, a complex concept. In statutes the nature of the act is clear, as it is provided by law.[1] In other contexts, however, ambiguities may arise. For instance, if we consider the legal domain, in which definitions and their communicative effects are clearly governed by rules, we notice that in contracts the interpretation of the acts of defining is less clear. In contracts, definitions are used to impose a criterion of interpretation. However, contracts are legally enforceable agreements between two or more parties, not enactments. The drafter needs to take into consideration that he cannot impose a new meaning unless the other party agrees. For this reason, the act of imposing a definition can be troublesome.

On the one hand, the drafter can exploit the ambiguity between the existing and shared definitions of a term and its new contractual definition. On the other hand, the imposition of a new meaning to an already existing *definiendum* is not completely free, but needs to be acknowledged and accepted; otherwise the shared meaning prevails in case of disagreement. For instance, in *Cmi Corp. v. Gurries* (674 F.2d 821 [10th Cir. 1982]) CMI agreed to pay Gurries' stockholders supplemental payments on the net sales prices of 'motor graders.' The disagreement was as to what machines were to be considered as 'motor graders.' The contract provided the following definition (emphasis added):

DEFINITION OF 'MOTOR GRADER'

"(c) 'Motor grader', as used herein, shall mean a grader having **control systems** incorporated therein or thereon for automatically controlling grade and/or slope, or constructed to receive a system for automatically controlling the elevation or angle of the main frame."

This definition conflicted with the ordinary one, which instead included all types of machines, with or without control systems, constructed for the purpose of controlling grade. The ambiguity between the imposed and not accepted definition and the shared one was resolved by considering the act of imposing a definition (*Cmi Corp. v. Gurries*, at 824):

Technical words are to be interpreted as usually understood by persons in the profession or business to which they relate, unless clearly used in a different sense. [...] a party to a contract cannot fail to disclose a meaning he attaches to a term which

---

[1] For instance, in the aforementioned case the rule was provided by previous decisions, setting out the nature of the statutory definitions and their effects (*Henrich v. Lorenz*, 448 N.W.2d 327, 332 [Iowa 1989]; Inter-State Nurseries, *Inc. v. Iowa Dep't of Revenue*, 164 N.W.2d 858, 861 [Iowa 1969]).

is not in accordance with the accepted meaning in the industry when he is aware or should be aware that the other party is using the term in its accepted sense.

Even though definitions in contracts impose rules of interpretation for the text they belong to, they cannot avoid considering the common ground. While statutory definitions resemble the act of imposing a name to an unshared or new concept, contractual definitions either are used to clarify an ambiguous concept or a meaning that needs to be acknowledged. The act of imposing a clarification needs to be distinguished from the act of imposing a new meaning in order to avoid ambiguities.

Imposing a definition presupposes that the interlocutor does not share or may not have previously shared such a meaning and results in his knowledge of the definitional discourse. When the legislator introduces a new definition, the *definiendum* is presupposed to be different from the accepted meaning. When a word is defined in contracts, it is presupposed that either it describes a new meaning, not existing or not conflicting with the accepted ones, or clarifies it by choosing between its possible meanings. The act of declaring a definition has radically different conditions. The speaker presupposes that the definition is shared and accepted, based on a previous agreement. For instance, we can consider the following use of definition taken from the famous mock trial *Regina v Ojibway* (8 Crim.L.Q. 137, 1965):

DEFINITION OF 'BIRD'

Fred Ojibway, an Indian, was riding his pony through Queen's Park on January 2, 1965. Being impoverished, and having been forced to pledge his saddle, he substituted a downy pillow in lieu of the said saddle. On this particular day the accused's misfortune was further heightened by the circumstance of his pony breaking its foreleg. In accord with Indian custom, the accused then shot the pony to relieve it of its awkwardness. The accused was then charged with having breached the Small Birds Act, s. 2 of which states: "2. Anyone maiming, injuring or killing small birds is guilty of an offence and subject to a fine not in excess of two hundred dollars." The learned magistrate acquitted the accused holding, in fact, that he had killed his horse and not a small bird. With respect, I cannot agree.

In light of the definition section my course is quite clear. Section 1 defines "bird" as "a two legged animal covered with feathers." There can be no doubt that this case is covered by this section.

In this case, the definition is simply stated to the jury or the judge, in order to persuade them of the desired classification. This definition is mentioned to point out that a proposition, the description of what 'bird' means for the law, had to be part of the audience's commitments.[2] Instead of imposing a

---

[2] "He submitted that the evidence of the expert clearly concluded that the animal in question was a pony and not a bird, but that is not the issue. We are not interested in whether the animal in question is a bird or not in fact, but whether it is one in law. Statutory interpretation has forced many a horse to eat birdseed for the rest of its life" (*Regina v. Ojibway* "Criminal Law Quaterly" 8, 1965, p. 137).

new commitment, the declarative definition simply brought a (forgotten or ignored) commitment to light.

Finally, a definition can be advanced as a standpoint, when the meaning of a word is not agreed on, and such meaning is actually or potentially controversial. The definition is the object of a proposal, which needs to be supported by reasons and accepted by the other party. It is not simply stated as part of the common ground; it is put forward as a proposition that can be rejected as not shared or acceptable. Also in this case, it is necessary to distinguish between the purpose of the definition, whether to propose a new definition or choose between possible existing meanings (interpretations). In the first case, the definition is presupposed to be different from the existing ones, and is aimed at covering a conceptual area not governed by any meaning descriptions. In science the most famous case is the discussion on the redefinition of 'planet' (Soter 2007), in which a new definition of planet was discussed by the International Astronomical Union in 2006. In law, the discussion about new definitions or redefinitions is usually recorded as *travaux préparatoires*. In the legislative discussions definitions are proposed and supported by arguments, rejecting previous proposals and advancing amendments. For instance, we can consider the following discussion of the General Assembly of the United Nations on the definition of an 'organized criminal group'[3]:

DEFINITION OF 'ORGANIZED CRIMINAL GROUP'

The term "organized criminal group" is defined in article 2 *bis* of the Convention as a structured group of three or more persons existing for a period of time and having the aim of committing a serious crime in order to obtain, directly or indirectly, a financial or other material benefit. In the same article, the definition of "serious crime" is given as conduct constituting a criminal offence punishable by a maximum deprivation of liberty of at least [...] years or a more serious penalty.

Even Greenpeace, with its spectacular campaigns, and manufacturers of home-distilled fruit vodka might also be counted as transnational organized criminal groups under the criminal legislation in force in some States.

Ajerbaijan would propose the following definition of an organized criminal group: "'Organized criminal group' means a structured group of two or more persons operating for a period of time and having the aim of obtaining a material or other benefit of any form through the commission of serious crime covered by this Convention, or existing for a period of time on account of such benefit."

In this case, the speaker rejects a definition by pointing out an unacceptable consequence of such an account and makes a new proposal, and then bears it out showing the possible positive consequences of his account. For instance, he claims that extending the notion of 'benefit' would avoid

[3] United Nations, Ad Hoc Committee on the Elaboration of a Convention against Transnational Organized Crime Seventh session Vienna, 17–28 January 2000 A/AC.254/5/Add.17, pp. 2–3.

the exclusion of crimes such as the murder of officers or judges which are aimed at no financial or material goals.

A definition can be advanced as a standpoint aimed at clarifying or disambiguating a polysemic concept. The speaker presupposes the existence of two or more possible definitions of the concept, incompatible for the purpose of the discussion. He takes for granted that they are or can be controversial. While in the case of definitional standpoints the speaker advances a new possible object of commitment ("Shall we define *x* as *yz*?"), clarificatory standpoints presuppose an alternative definition that is or can be agreed upon by the audience or the interlocutor. The speaker needs to counter the alternative viewpoint and show the superiority of his claim. A clear case can be found in the legal discussions on statutory interpretation. In *Muscarello v. United States* (524 U.S. 125, 1998), for instance, the dispute regarded the meaning of the verb 'to carry,' in order to establish whether the defendant, who transported a handgun in his truck used to transport marijuana for sale, fell within the law providing for a five-term prison sentence for anyone who "uses or carries a firearm" "during and in relation to" a "drug trafficking crime." The defendant claimed that "to carry a firearm," as used in the statute, meant uniquely to bear them, excluding the aggravating circumstance to apply to the case, quoting the authorities of dictionaries and appealing to the principle of lenity (*Muscarello v. United States* 96–1054, dissenting opinion). The court replied by supporting the definition of such term including "carting about in a vehicle," quoting dictionaries and literature and newspapers excerpts:

The New York Times, for example, writes about "an ex-con" who "arrives home driving a stolen car and carrying a load of handguns," Mar. 21, 1992, section 1, p. 18, col. 1, and an "official peace officer who carries a shotgun in his boat," June 19, 1988, section 12WC, p. 2, col. 1; cf. *The New York Times Manual of Style and Usage, a Desk Book of Guidelines for Writers and Editors*, forword (L. Jordan rev. ed. 1976) (restricting Times journalists and editors to the use of proper English). *The Boston Globe* refers to the arrest of a professional baseball player "for carrying a semiloaded automatic weapon in his car." Dec. 10, 1994, p. 75, col. 5. *The Colorado Springs Gazette Telegraph* speaks of one "Russell" who "carries a gun hidden in his car." May 2, 1993, p. B1, col. 2. *The Arkansas Gazette* refers to a "house" that was "searched" in an effort to find "items that could be carried in a car, such as ... guns." Mar. 10, 1991, p. A1, col. 2. *The San Diego Union-Tribune* asks, "What, do they carry guns aboard these boats now?" Feb. 18, 1992, p. D2, col. 5. [...] We recognize, as the dissent emphasizes, that the word "carry" has other meanings as well. But those other meanings, (e.g., "carry all he knew," "carries no colours"), see post, at 6, are not relevant here. And the fact that speakers often do not add to the phrase "carry a gun" the words "in a car" is of no greater relevance here than the fact that millions of Americans did not see Muscarello carry a gun in his car. The relevant linguistic facts are that the word "carry" in its ordinary sense includes carrying in a car and that the word, used in its ordinary sense, keeps the same meaning whether one carries a gun, a suitcase, or a banana (*Muscarello v. United States*, 524 U.S. 125, 1998).

Here the speaker presents arguments based on the authority of newspapers that are supposed to report the ordinary use. Since several words have no statutory definitions, as "legal language is itself ordinary language" (Aarnio 1977: 101), words not defined by statute "should be given ordinary or common meaning" (*Perrin v. United States*, 444 U.S. 37, 42, 1979). The arguments in such a case are aimed at bringing evidence of the most common usage.

2.2. Non-Negative Definitions

The uses of definition mentioned previously are forms of positive actions. The speaker performs a speech act (imposing/recommending, proposing or stating a definition) in order to achieve a specific effect (commit himself and the others; commit the interlocutor to accept or rebut the proposal; bring an implicit commitment to light). However, effects also can be brought about intentionally by failing to act. For instance, deciding not to report a crime results in the possibility that the authorities may not be informed of it. Failure to take care of a child may result in the possibility of the death of child. In law, omissions are defined in terms of the duties to act (Williams 1983: 148–149; Fusco 2008: 86). An omission can be generally considered as a breach of an affirmative duty to perform the omitted action. In cases of written instruments, such as contracts, it requires knowledge of the items (*Inter-Ocean Casualty Co. v. Banks*, 32 Ala. App. 225, 227, 1945) or words left out (Page 1919: sec. 1243). However, if we depart from the legal domain, we can notice how the concept of omission is complex. Walton (1980) analyzed omission as an act of a kind where the agent decides not to perform an action that was sufficient for the occurrence of a specific consequence at a later time (Aqvist 1974; Chisholm 1976; Walton 1980: 317). In this sense, an omission can be seen as the deliberate decision to leave open the possibilities of the occurrence of a state of affairs. By omitting to report a crime an agent leaves open the possibility that the authorities are not informed of it, even though he is not preventing them from knowing it. In this sense, omission can be considered as a form of action (Walton 1980: 318):

[...] we can see and understand a notion that at first seems highly paradoxical, namely that of an omission (a negative action) bringing about (positively) some outcome. It almost seems like an omission, so described, is a non-negative action, and in a way it is. Accordingly, we might say that someone's failure to treat a patient brought about the death of that patient.

The last type of use of definition can be called the omission of a definition. A speaker can deliberately avoid defining a word in order to bring about interpretative ambiguity. In the case of the contractual definition mentioned previously (definition of motor grader) the drafter deliberately failed to inform the hearer of a redefinition that caused a contractual ambiguity. When this non-negative action is performed at the level of law-making, the effects can be extremely dangerous.

In order to clarify how the non-performance of a definitional act can affect decision making, we can analyze the non-definition of torture in the criminal codes of some countries such as Russia and Armenia. Before 2003, Russian criminal law contained no definition as such of the concept of 'torture' (CAT/C/34/Add.15, 15 October 2001, art. 1 [4], p. 3). As pointed out in the CAT, 28th session, 13 May 2002,[4] even though the Russian laws prescribe legal liability in the event of an official's or domestic use of torture, the absence of the definition of such a concept allowed the lawful detaining of suspects for up to thirty days, even without sufficient reasons, while tens of thousands of complaints against the actions of the internal affairs agencies' security units were filed, of which only a small percentage resulted in disciplinary actions (demotion and dismissal). Similarly, Armenia has disregarded the UN recommendations (CAT/C/SR.246, 1996; EUR 54/02/00, April 2000, par. 2),[5] leading to attacks moved by the United Nations and Amnesty International. In particular, the allegation of the international reports pointed out that Armenia deliberately considered it "not appropriate" to introduce a definition of such a term. The United Nations clearly stated the effects of such an omission (AI Index: EUR 54/02/00, April 2000, par. 2):

OMISSION OF THE DEFINITION OF 'TORTURE'

Although torture is prohibited under the Armenian Constitution, a major obstacle in bringing alleged perpetrators to justice is the lack of a specific offence of torture, as defined under Article 1 of the Convention against Torture, in the Criminal Code of Armenia. (*Armenia – Torture and ill-treatment: Comments on the Second Periodic Report to the United Nations Committee against Torture*)

In both the cases of Russia and Armenia, the act of omitting a definition was a specific classificatory decision.[6] This was extremely clear in Russia, where the absence of a definition allowed the officials, the police, and the military in general to avoid serious criminal sentencing and only incur minor

---

[4] *Committee against Torture Takes up Report of the Russian Federation,* CAT 28th session, 13 May 2002:   http://www.reliefweb.int/rw/rwb.nsf/db900SID/ACOS-64CSAN?OpenDocument (accessed on 5th September 2011).

[5] http://www.ishr.ch/archive-upr/766-armenia-reviewed-by-the-upr-expected-political-tensions-barely-disrupt-review.

[6] This is clear in Russia, where the purpose of non-persecuting the crimes committed by officers and the military was also achieved by providing a definition of 'torture' that was clearly different from the one put forward by the Convention. According to the international reports, the definition "applies only to acts committed by private individuals," therefore excluding that officers can commit torture (*Russian NGO Shadow Report on the Observance of the Convention against Torture and Other Cruel, Inhuman or Degrading Treatment or Punishment by the Russian Federation for the period from 2001 to 2005*).

punishments for charges of "exceeding of power." The following example clearly shows the classificatory effects of the omission of a definition[7]:

OMITTING DEFINITIONS AND RECLASSIFYING CRIMES: 'TORTURE'

Oleg Fedorov had been detained by two high-ranking, drunk ROVD officials on the street in Arkhangelsk. He had been interrogated by the two officials for two hours and during questioning had allegedly been severely beaten by them. Oleg Fedorov, reportedly, asked to go to the toilet and threw himself out through the window. After the incident a criminal investigation was opened against the two law enforcement officials and they were charged under Article 171(2) of the Criminal Code for "exceeding of power." In March 1996 the Department of Internal Affairs (UVD) reportedly announced publicly the dismissal of the two officers for "serious violations of the professional discipline."

The omission of a definition was a strategy aimed at avoiding any government's commitment to curb or forbid the crimes committed by police and soldiers. This move allowed the government to implicitly authorize the use of torture for interrogations, ill-treatment in prisons, and a wide range of violations of humanitarian rights in Chechnya.[8]

The act of omitting a definition can be considered as the act of allowing possible alternative classifications that a definition would forbid. In this sense, it is the choice of allowing the non-classification of a state of affairs.

2.3. *Implicit Definitions*

The omission of a definition can be considered as an act of non-defining, where silence carries a dialectical effect, opening the paradigm of interpretations and not setting the boundaries of a concept in order to allow ambiguity. The last type of use of definition is not an act in the proper sense of the word, but the omission of the manifestation of an act. In this case, the definition is not omitted, but simply used and taken for granted. Just as in cases of omissions, such non-actions become non-negative actions when they become failures to perform an action. Definitions in law can be left unexpressed because they are already shared. However, sometimes the speaker does not simply fail to remind the interlocutor of a commitment, but actually defines or redefines a word and sets new commitments, without making such a move explicit. He simply uses a new definition, which can be reconstructed through the context (in this sense, the implicit definition corresponds to the scientific axiomatic definition, namely, a definition of a concept through the axioms in which it is

---

[7] *Torture in Russia: "This man-made hell."* AI Index: EUR 46/04/97. Amnesty International April 1997 (pp. 28–29). (retrieved from http://www.amnesty.org/en/library/info/EUR46/004/1997/en on September 21st, 2011).

[8] *Russian Federation: Denial of justice.* AI Index: EUR 46/027/2002. Amnesty International October 2002 (chap. 3). (retrieved from http://www.amnesty.org/en/library/info/EUR46/027/2002/en on September 21st, 2011).

contained; see Gorsky 1981: 38). The speaker is not refraining from defining, but is implicitly using a definition that has never been stated. In this fashion, the responsibility of defining or redefining is not taken on by the speaker, who can avoid supporting the definition, as it is not set forth as a standpoint, or assuming the responsibility of imposing it, as it is not the content of a stipulation. Let's consider two different cases: the implicit act of imposing a redefinition (or a definition), and the implicit act of advancing a redefinition (clarification).

The imposition of a definition is possible only when the speaker (or rather non-speaker) is in a position to do so. States can redefine the terms in the laws. The omission of an *imposition of a redefinition* prevents the speaker from explicitly exercising a right but risks creating dangerous pragmatic ambiguities. A clear case is the redefinition of *mens rea* in the case *Montana v. Egelhoff* (518 U.S. 37, 1996), where the defendant was convicted of deliberate homicide on the count of having killed his friends while voluntarily intoxicated. In order to establish such a charge, the state had the burden of proving all the elements of the crime, which is defined as "purposely or knowingly causing the death of another person." However, the court instructed the jury not to consider his voluntary intoxication in determining the existence of the requisite mental state, based on a rule (Mont. Code Ann. § 45–2–03) providing that "an intoxicated condition is not a defense to any offense." The crucial point was that the jury instruction prevented the defendant from negating the *mens rea* element of the crime (Sweitzer 1997: 274). The Supreme Court interpreted the State of Montana's introduction of a new rule as an act of implicit redefinition (Sweitzer 1997: 284–285):

Justice Ginsburg, [...] concluded that Montana's exclusionary statute in fact implicitly redefined the mens rea element of deliberate homicide, changing it from "purposely or knowingly" to "under circumstances that would otherwise establish knowledge or purpose 'but for' [the defendant's] voluntary intoxication."

On this view, the Supreme Court took into consideration the argument from classification used by the Montana First Instance Court and the new rule. The context of the statute implied a redefinition of the term, as it limited the mental element of the offence.

The implicit act of *advancing a redefinition* can be extremely powerful, as it allows the speaker to avoid grounding his decision. The case of *Sahi v. Gonzales* hinged on the implicit redefinition of 'persecution.' Before leaving his country, Sahi, an alien member of the Ahmadi religious sect discriminated against by Muslims in Pakistan, had been beaten by orthodox Muslims and his property destroyed. The Board of Immigration Appeals denied his application for asylum, because he could not be considered as a victim of 'persecution.' The argument advanced by the judge was the following (*Sahi v. Gonzales*, 416 F.3d 587, 589, 7th Cir. 2005):

IMPLICIT REDEFINITION OF 'PERSECUTION'

While this Court [i.e., the immigration judge] fully recognizes that Ahmadis are discriminated against and face harassment in Pakistan because of their religious beliefs, I do not find that this fact, coupled with the general risk of random violence singles the respondent out or establishes a pattern and practice of persecution of all Ahmadis.

The Board never defined such a concept, and the judge had no power to impose a new definition. Instead of using the shared definition, or advancing a new one and supporting it, he simply took for granted the meaning of 'persecution' as "systematic violence directed against a group," which was not accepted or acceptable. By means of the implicit redefinition, the judge evaded the burden of providing reasons for adopting a new interpretation of the concept. The Court of Appeals reversed his judgment on this basis, requesting the Board to provide an explicit definition.

The two acts of omitting and implicitly defining can be closely related to each other. The omission of a definition opens up the possibility of implicitly interpreting the concept, namely, implicitly defining or redefining the term. One of the most famous cases in which the effects of the (voluntary or involuntary) omission of a definition emerge is the non-definition of 'enemy combatant' mentioned in Chapter 1. This designation was used by the Bush administration to denote a specific class of combatants, falling outside the boundaries of the Geneva Convention. However, no definition was provided. Subsequent to the attacks on September 11, the government arrested and detained some American citizens with the charge of being an 'enemy combatant.' The government never defined or redefined such a term (*Hamdi v. Rumsfeld*, 542 U.S. 516, 2004), which was simply used until two American citizens, Hamdi and Padilla, were arrested and designated as enemy combatants. Before such cases, the administration simply used the term, charging the defendant of a crime that would not allow him to have any rights of protection. In other words, the other party could not have the possibility of rebutting the classification. Since Hamdi and Padilla were American citizens, they brought the case to court, and the problem of the implicit definition of the term came to light. Padilla was detained as an enemy combatant based on an order of President Bush (see President Bush order [June 9, 2002] to hold Padilla as an enemy combatant[9]), where the reasons provided were that he was "closely associated with al-Qaeda" and engaged in "hostile and war-like acts" including "preparation for acts of international terrorism" directed at this country (June 9 Order, pp. 2–5; *Padilla*, 233 F. Supp. 2d 568). Hamdi was considered an enemy combatant on the grounds of a declaration of the Special Advisor to the Under Secretary of Defense for Policy (the Mobbs declaration). The reasons

---

[9] Retrived from http://cjc.delaware.gov/terrorism/padilla.shtml (accessed on 9 September 2011).

provided for his designation were "[b]ased upon his interviews and in light of his association with the Taliban," a series of tests that determined that Hamdi met "the criteria for enemy combatants," and "a subsequent interview of Hamdi" (*Hamdi v. Rumsfeld* 542 US 507, 513, 2004).

The implicit definition did not provide any criteria for the classification, and the Court had to reconstruct a possible meaning relying on the definition accepted in law, which amounted to the previous cases. The court interpreted the term as equivalent to 'unlawful combatant,' based on the Quirin case (*Padilla v. Bush*, 233 F. Supp. 2d 564, 2002), to refer to foreign spies and saboteurs (Ex parte Quirin, 317 U.S. 1, 37–38, 1942):

Citizens who associate themselves with the military arm of the enemy government, and with its aid, guidance and direction enter this country bent on hostile acts are enemy belligerents within the meaning of the Hague Convention and the law of war.

However, Hamdi did not "enter the country" (he was captured in a field of battle thousands of miles from America), nor was he proved to have known of or participated in any plots against Americans. Moreover, neither Padilla nor Hamdi were members of an enemy state, but were American citizens. The implicit definition led to controversies that were solved only in 2004, when it was made explicit by the Supreme Court (*Hamdi v. Rumsfeld*, 542 U.S. 516, 2004). The power of implicit redefinition is clear from this case. The government introduced a term without explicitly redefining it. Its meaning had to be found in previous cases and reconstructed from the definition of 'unlawful combatant,' which was further interpreted to also include any person who is "part of or supporting forces hostile to the United States or coalition partners."

The acts of defining can be divided into the broad categories of acts and omissions, and explicit and implicit acts. Whereas explicit acts or omissions set or deny actual commitments, implicit acts can be more dangerous. The definitions or the redefinitions can be simply taken for granted, and the speaker can introduce an otherwise unaccepted or potentially controversial meaning without supporting it. The hearer needs to reconstruct the unacceptable proposition and reject it by providing a reason of a kind.

3. Describing Speech Acts

As mentioned previously, in order to understand the dialogical constraints of the different acts of defining we need to look at contexts that crystallize their effects and conditions. The legal institutional context clearly shows the relation between the possibility of redefining and common knowledge (see Clark 1992: 72–73), and between the nature of the act of defining and the authority of the speaker. In the first section the different types of uses of definitions were presented, and in the second one such uses were described as acts of a kind, having specific conditions. The acts of defining can be described from a dialectical perspective by analyzing their structure as moves in a dialogue, combining the generic theoretical background on speech acts with the specific constraints that the different definitions have and impose in a dialogue.

As noticed previously, definitions are used for different types of purposes and can be considered as the propositional content of different types of speech acts. Searle (1969: 31) and Searle and Vanderveken (2005: 122–130) described the minimal units of human communication, the speech acts, as a combination of an illocutionary force, referred to as F, and a propositional content, p. The same propositional content, for instance, "You will leave the room," can be used in different utterances, such as "Leave the room!", or "You will leave the room," or "Will you leave the room?", having different illocutionary forces. Illocutionary force is an essential component of meaning, as any proposition uttered in a context constitutes the attempted performance of an act. Such forces can be analyzed in their different components. The most relevant ones for our analysis are the following:

1. *Illocutionary points* represent the purpose of an act. For instance, the point of statements is to tell people how things are; the point of orders is to get people to perform an action.
2. *Propositional content conditions* represent the requirements of the illocutionary force on the propositional content. For instance, orders presuppose an action to be performed (I cannot order you to be tall); promises presuppose a future action (I cannot promise you that I went to London).
3. *Preparatory conditions* represent the pragmatic presuppositions of a speech act, the relationship between the dialogue move and the common ground. For instance, if I utter the statement "Bob has been at home the whole day," I presuppose that my interlocutor knows who Bob is, and that he is interested in him. If I promise my friends to steal all their money, my promise would sound paradoxical, as a promise presupposes that the promised action is in the hearers' interest.
4. *Sincerity conditions* are any speech act that expresses a psychological state. For instance, a statement expresses the speaker's belief in what he says, even though the speaker himself can be insincere.

Such components represent the conditions that need to be fulfilled for a speech act to be successful and non-defective (Searle & Vanderveken 2005: 128). Searle and Vanderveken identified five fundamental types of speech acts according to their purpose (Searle & Vanderveken 1985: 52):

One can say how things are (assertives), one can try to get other people to do things (directives), one can commit oneself to doing things (commissives), one can bring about changes in the world through one's utterances (declarations), and one can express one's feelings and attitudes (expressives). Often one can do more than one of these things in the same utterance.

Speech acts have four different directions of fit (Searle & Vanderveken 1985: 53), which can be thought of as the relationship between their purpose (the intentional alteration of a state of affairs), their propositional content, and reality. They represent, from a logical perspective (Vanderveken 1990: 105), how the speech act affects the relations between propositional content and a state of affairs.

1. *The word-to-world direction of fit.* The propositional content of the move fits an independently existing state of affairs. For instance, an assertion ("You are tall") is aimed at representing a state of affairs, and it achieves success of fit if it is true.

2. *The world-to-word direction of fit.* The purpose of the move is to achieve an alteration in the world (action), so that the world is made to correspond to the propositional content of the move. For instance, orders are aimed at getting the world to match what is ordered. An order, for instance, "Open the door," achieves success of fit if the door is opened.

3. *The double direction of fit.* The move is aimed at altering the world to fit the propositional content by representing the world as being so altered. For instance, in a declaration such as "You are fired!," the propositional content represents a state of affairs already altered, and such a declaration makes the world fit to the content. In this case, it achieves success of fit if the interlocutor actually loses the job.

4. *The null or empty direction of fit.* The purpose of the move is neither to represent the world nor to get the world altered to correspond to the words. For instance, an expression of enthusiasm simply represents the speaker's attitude towards a specific situation.

This structure represents only one dimension of a speech act: the conditions for a communicative move to be understood. However, assertions, orders, requests, and many other speech acts are performed with an interactional purpose. The speaker asserts a specific proposition because he intends to impress, persuade, or shock the interlocutor. In other words, he does not merely want his speech act to be understood, he wants it to be accepted (van Eemeren & Grootendorst 1984: 24–25). Even though the interlocutor is not impressed, shocked, or moved by the assertion, the move is still an assertion in the communicative situation, as long as the listener understood it. The illocutionary dimension is in this fashion distinguished from the perlocutionary (or interactional) one. In order to clarify better this concept, it is useful to provide some examples (van Eemeren & Grootendorst 1984: 25) (see Table 4.1).

The link between understanding and acceptance can be found in Austin's notion of invitation to respond (Austin 1962: 116), which he considered as part of the understanding of the illocutionary act. A question can be answered in several ways, or even not answered at all. A request can be accepted or not. An argument can result in a counterargument or an acceptance of the viewpoint. However, a question (Where is London?) can

Table 4.1. Communicative and Interactional Aspects

Communicative Aspects		Interactional Aspects		
Illocution	**Illocutionary Effect**	**Perlocution**	**Inherent Perlocutionary Effect**	**Consequent Perlocutionary Consequence**
Advising	Understanding the advice.	Cheering up	Accepting the advice.	Enrolling for a new course.
Arguing	Understanding the argumentation.	Convincing	Accepting the argumentation.	Desisting from opposition to a point of view.
Requesting	Understanding the request.	Persuading	Accepting the request.	Abandoning the intention to leave.
Informing	Understanding the information.	Instructing	Accepting the information.	Henceforth using contraceptives.
Warning	Understanding the warning.	Alarming	Accepting the warning.	Keeping mouth shout.

be considered as understood, or felicitous, if the hearer is committed to a specific type of answer on a specific topic (It is in ... .). He can reject the commitment (I have no time now) or provide a non-informative answer (It is in a place unknown to me). However, independently from his reply, his communicative situation has been changed in a conventional fashion. The speech act introduced a choice that he did not have before. On this perspective, the analysis of the previous commitments of the interlocutors become extremely important for the analysis of the dialectical characteristics of the acts of defining (see Connor-Linton 1991: 98–99).

This methodology of analysis can be applied to the different uses of definition shown in the previous sections. However, as noticed previously, the most crucial differences lie in the preparatory conditions, or rather the structures of commitments and presuppositions of the interlocutors. Depending on the different roles and common ground, the definitional move can have different purposes and effects.

4. Speech Acts of Defining

In Viskil (1994) four types of definitions are distinguished: stipulative, lexical, stipulative-lexical, and factual definition. This classification, however, merges the purpose of a speech act with its content and does not account for other purposes that definition may have. The definitional acts will be described in the following subsections according to the type of speech act that they represent, and will be classified according to their dialectical purpose.

4.1. *Defining for Informing*

In the first section, the first definition analyzed was the description of 'just war' provided by Obama. The purpose of such a move was to provide the audience with information about the meaning of a concept. According to the classification of speech acts, this use of definition would fall within the class of assertion, whose conditions are represented in Table 4.2 (Searle 1979: 12; Searle & Vanderveken 1985: 54–55; Vanderveken 1990: 105).

From a dialectical point of view, however, we can notice that the act of informing requires a further specification of the preparatory conditions. In order to be informative, a speech act needs to provide information that is not known or presumed to be already shared by the interlocutors. Obama could not *inform* the audience of his speech that the Nobel Prize is an international award. Moreover, the dialectical analysis of the move also needs to consider its sequel effects, or rather the dialectical possibilities that it allows (Searle & Vanderveken 2005: 118), and the reasons supporting the claim that the speaker is supposed to have. From a dialectical perspective, this preparatory condition can be analyzed as a possible move that the speech act allows, the request for further grounds. Finally, providing a piece of information is different from proposing a course of action or expressing a viewpoint. The propositional content needs to express a description of a state of affairs, and not a prescription or a judgment. We can represent the dialectical profile of the act of informing as shown in Table 4.3.

The effect of the definition, in this case, is to add a proposition to the speaker's commitments, and the purpose is to have this proposition inserted in the audience's common ground. In the case of the Nobel Prize address, the audience could not reply or reject the definition, and accepted it (even tentatively or for the sake of the discourse). Then, it became part of the shared knowledge (the concept was introduced in the interlocutor's knowledge) and it could be used for the further reasoning step.

In ordinary conversation we often use a specific type of act of informing of a definition, the so-called specification or usage clarification. For instance, we can state that "with x I mean y" in order to inform our interlocutor not of the shared meaning of a word, but of our contextual understanding of it. This act of informing the hearer of a contextual redefinition is used to avoid misunderstandings and clarify the purpose of a move.

4.2. *Defining for Reminding*

In the aforementioned speech, Obama addresses a wide public, largely unknown. The only prediction he could make about their background knowledge was that while some of them could know the meaning of 'just war,' others probably did not. He addressed the move to both types of audiences, presupposing different conditions and therefore expecting different effects. He informed a part of the audience, while he reminded the other part of such a notion. Similarly, in *Regina v Ojibway*, the judge

Table 4.2. Structure of the Speech Act of Defining for Informing

Illocutionary point	To represent as actual a state of affairs. To commit the speaker to something's being the case.	*[Just war:] War is justified only when it meets certain preconditions.*
Propositional content	None	
Preparatory conditions	The speaker has reasons (or grounds or evidence) that count in favor of or support the truth of the propositional content.	*Over time, as codes of law sought to control violence within groups, so did philosophers, clerics, and statesmen seek to regulate the destructive power of war.* *The concept of a just war emerged (the speaker is taking the definition from ancient sources).*
Sincerity conditions	A speaker who succeeds in performing an assertive illocutionary act of the form F(P) is sincere only if he believes the proposition he expresses.	*[…] we have a moral and strategic interest in binding ourselves to certain rules of conduct.*

used the definition of 'bird' in the Small Bird Act not to inform the interlocutors of a new meaning (they all knew the act, as it was the matter at issue), but to remind them of their commitment to such a meaning. The two cases are obviously different. In law, a legal definition is binding and can be thought of as a commitment that cannot be rejected. The judge restated the definition in order to underscore that such a definition needed to be applied and could not be disregarded. In Obama's speech, the definition of 'just war' had the effect of reminding the audience of a commitment, whose force needed to be reinforced by stating its sources. The force of such a commitment is increased by showing that it is a concept acknowledged by ancient lawmakers, politicians, and philosophers. In this fashion, Obama enhances the acceptability of his further claims based on such an ancient and acknowledged definition. These two different contexts show two different applications of the same possible effect of the act of reminding. Just like the act of informing, the act of reminding presupposes some reasons, which in this case are presumptions. The judges are presumed to know legal definitions, and that a definition in a law is a *legal definition*. The educated audience is presumed to know the history, and therefore that the notion of a 'just war' is a fundamental historical concept. The two speakers make explicit their grounds and in this fashion

Table 4.3. Defining for Informing – Dialectical Profile

Move	Content Conditions	Speaker's Commitments	Hearer's Commitments	Effects on the Speaker	Effects on the Hearer
Informing (*Hearer, p*).	*p* represents a state of affairs/ judgment / decision.	*S* has grounds supporting *p*.		*S* is committed to *H's Comm.* to *p*.	• Acknowledge (*Comm. to p*). • Reject (*Comm. to p*) based on reasons.
Just war is a war that is justified when some preconditions are met.	Meaning of 'just war.'	• Authorities in the past defined 'just war.' • People are presumed to accept the opinion of authorities.		Obama is bound to the meaning of 'just war' he gave.	The interlocutors cannot ignore the definition. The interlocutors need to accept it or show that it is not shared.

increase the binding effect of the move. We can represent the structure of the move as shown in Table 4.4 (Searle & Vanderveken 2005: 129).

Reminding a definition is therefore a more subtle act compared to the simple act of informing, as the speaker can exploit the powerful mechanism of presumptions. The judge mentioned the legal status of the definition, and Obama mentioned the ancient sources in order to suggest the presumptions on which the act of reminding was based.

4.3. *Definitions as Standpoints*

In his speech, Obama advanced a redefinition of 'peace' by supporting it with arguments based on the need to keep its effects lasting. He is not merely informing the audience of a meaning that is already shared. Instead, he is taking for granted that the meaning is not shared and needs to be supported by reasons, in this case based on reasoning from cause to effect (only freedom from want can result in lasting peace) and values (a stable peace is better than an unstable one). This type of move can be described as a speech act of advancing a standpoint, an assertion of a kind, having the following essential condition (Houtlosser 2001: 32): "Advancing a standpoint counts as taking responsibility for a positive position in respect to an opinion O, i.e., as assuming an obligation to defend a positive position in respect to O, if requested to do so." This condition can be specified in the dialectical profile of the move analyzing its different components (see Table 4.5).

Obama put forward a standpoint whose purpose was to describe the meaning of a word having a specific referent. In other words, he is correlating

Table 4.4. Defining for Reminding – Dialectical Profile

Move	Content Conditions	Speaker's Commitments	Hearer's Commitments	Effects on the Speaker	Effects on the Hearer
Reminding (*Hearer: p*).	*p* represents a state of affairs / judgment/ decision.	*S* has grounds supporting that *H* is/should be committed to / knows *p*.	• *H is / should be committed to p*.	*S* is committed to *H's Comm. to p*.	• Acknowledge *Comm. to p*). • Reject *(Comm. to p)* based on reasons.
Bird [is] a two legged animal covered with feathers.	Meaning of 'bird.'	• People are presumed to remember what mentioned before in the discussion. • Judges are presumed to know the law.	People are / should be committed to the meaning of 'bird.'		• The interlocutors cannot ignore the definition.

words (the definition) to a thing (peaceful state of affairs) that the interlocutors already share (Robinson 1950: 17). He takes for granted that his audience knows what 'peace' is and proposes a new way of describing such a concept, grasping what makes peace "truly" itself. This standpoint can be judged as correct or incorrect, considering what is the common understanding of the described concept. The legal definition of 'to carry' mentioned previously shows how the strength of a definition is assessed by considering how it reports the common understanding of the concept.

However, sometimes definitions are not matters of judgment (this definition better describes what a thing is) but of decisions. The standpoint is a proposal on a course of action, on the imposition of a definition. For instance, in the discussion on the legal definition of 'organized criminal group,' the representatives of Azerbaijan countered a proposal of a possible course of action (impose a specific definition) on the basis of its possible negative consequences. On this perspective, this type of definitional act amounts to the act of making a proposal (Kauffeld 1998: 248; 1995a: 79; Aakhus 2005: 7; Walton 2006). The difference between these two kinds of standpoints is mirrored in the types of arguments used to support them. The argument from consequences can support a decision, but not a judgment. It provides grounds to a course of action, but not to the relationship between reality (or rather common ground) and its possible descriptions or judgments.

4.4. *Declaring a Definition*

In the previous analysis of political definitions we pointed out the peculiar status of Obama's redefinitions of 'homeland security' and 'armed

Table 4.5. Defining for Advancing a Standpoint – Dialectical Profile

Move	Content Conditions	Speaker's Commitments	Hearer's Commitments	Effects on the Speaker	Effects on the Hearer
Advancing as a standpoint (p).	p represents a judgment/proposal.	• S believes that H does not (already, at face value, completely) accept p. • S believes that he can justify p for H with the help of arguments.	H is not committed to p (already, at face value, completely).	• S is committed to p. • S is committed to defend p. • S is committed to the fact p may be not accepted.	• Accept (p). • Question (p). • Reject (p). • Advance (*non-p*).
peace is not merely the absence of visible conflict. [...] true peace is based upon the inherent rights and dignity. [...] For true peace is not just freedom from fear, but freedom from want.	Definition of 'peace'.	(Obama takes for granted that the shared definition of peace is "absence of visible conflict").	(H is committed to the definition of peace as "absence of visible conflict").	Obama supports the definition with an argument (*it is the only peace that is truly lasting*).	

conflict.' In both cases the definition is not supported by arguments, nor does the speaker mention or rebut a previous and shared one. Obama simply stipulates a new meaning for the term, which is meant to constitute a criterion for the interpretation and application of the National Defence Authorization Act or granting the Defense Department the task of dealing with specific dangers. These definitions do not report a shared meaning or previous usage, or at least this is not their purpose. They establish a correspondence, valid within the text, between the *definiendum* and the definition, regardless of whether such a meaning is or can be accepted. In particular, in law we can notice that statutory, or stipulative, definitions often depart from the ordinary understanding of the word. The legal cases show specific characteristics of the act of imposing a definition. First, the speaker needs to have the authority to do so, which in law derives from the institutional setting. For instance, the lawmaker can impose a definition, or the authority invested of such powers, but a judge can only interpret it. A scientist who discovers a new entity or state of affairs can impose it on a name and a definition, but he can only argue in support of modifying a definition of a concept. Second, once the definition has been stipulated, it becomes a rule and cannot be challenged, but only substituted by another stipulative definition. Third, the definition should not introduce ambiguity. For instance, in the case of contracts, the act of stipulating a definition needs to be made clear to the other party in order to avoid misunderstandings. We can represent the speech act of imposing (or stipulating) a definition as a declarative act, altering both the speaker's and the hearer's commitments. The structure of this act is shown in Table 4.6.

The act of imposing a definition can have two different goals, depending on the epistemic nature of the definition. In the first case, this move introduces a meaning not existing before in order to establish a new rule. In the second case, the speaker chooses one of the shared meanings of a word in order to avoid potential ambiguity. In both cases a new state of affairs is imposed: A word has a new definition, or has only one meaning.

4.5. *Defining for Committing*

The aforementioned cases need to be distinguished from a particular type of act that is frequent in ordinary conversations, the use of a definition for clarifying how the speaker is using the words. A typical use of this definition is the formula "with *x*, I will henceforth mean *y*." The speaker can introduce a new definition or simply specify one of the possible meanings. However, he does not have the authority to impose such a meaning to the interlocutor. The speaker simply commits himself to use the word in the discourse or text with the stated meaning. The act of committing to a definition can be represented as shown in Table 4.7.

Through this definition, Obama implies that he is not like the other presidents, and that his program and decisions mirror what people think.

Table 4.6. Declaring Definitions – Dialectical Profile

Move	Content Conditions	Speaker's Commitments	Hearer's Commitments	Effects on the Speaker	Effects on the Hearer
Imposing (declaring) (p).	• p represents a state of affairs (*SoA*). • The *SoA* represented by p is not an actual or past one. • The *SoA* can be the case.	• S knows that H is not committed to p. • S holds the authority to impose a new state of affairs.	*H is not* committed to p.	• S is committed to p.	• H is committed to p.
Homeland security is a concerted national effort to prevent terrorist attacks within the United States, reduce America's vulnerability to terrorism, and minimize the damage and recover from attacks that do occur.	Definition of 'homeland security'.	• The Office of Homeland Security and the President have the authority to define. • The definition of 'homeland security' is new.	(*H is committed to a previous definition of 'homeland security'*).	The Office of Homeland Security shall deal with environmental problems.	The offices in charge of the environmental disasters shall refer to the Office of Homeland Security.

Table 4.7. Defining for Committing – Dialectical Profile

Move	Content Conditions	Speaker's Commitments	Hearer's Commitments	Effects on the Speaker	Effects on the Hearer
Committing to (*p*).	*p* represents a future course of action (*A*).	• *S* is not committed to *p*. • *S* normally should not be committed to *p*.	*H* knows that S is not committed to *p*.	• *S* is committed to *p*.	• *H* knows that *S* is committed to *p*.
[...] when I use that word ['we'], I will mean you and me, not the royal 'we.'	Future use of the pronoun 'we.'	Usually presidents use the pronoun 'we' as *a pluralis maiestatis*.	The audience expects the pronoun to be used as a *pluralis maiestatis*.	Obama shall use the pronoun meaning 'you and me.'	The audience will interpret the pronoun as meaning 'you and me.'

At the same time, he shows how his politics needs to be supported by everyone, as it is a commitment of all Americans.

As mentioned previously, the speaker's commitment can be a dialogical move to avoid misunderstanding or a strategy to support a thesis. The 'commissive definition' cannot be rejected, as it is a commitment taken on by the speaker that is not intended to affect the interlocutors. However, such a definition sets a condition necessary for supporting a viewpoint. It provides an artificial (conditional) ground for bearing out a conclusion: Granted that *S* with *x* means *y*, proposition *q* follows. For instance, if I define 'life' as "an object with a definite boundary, continually exchanging some of its materials with its surroundings," I can claim that life exists on many planets. The risk is to create semantic and pragmatic ambiguity by introducing a new meaning similar to the ordinary one (as in this case) or by confounding a commitment of the speaker with a commitment of both the interlocutors.

5. Acts of Non-Commitment

All the aforementioned acts are aimed at binding the speaker or the hearer to a specific definition or course of action. The acts of reminding, introducing, advancing, proposing, or imposing new commitments can be rejected by the hearer, or questioned, or at least judged as reasonable, or just, or unacceptable, or unfair. Whether the act of defining was reasonable, new commitments were created. The hearer (or the public) can always confront the speaker with his past commitments, or in law with the definitions that have become normative criteria of classification. The most powerful and dangerous definitional strategies do not consist in advancing new definitions as such, but in introducing them without taking on a specific commitment, or deliberately allowing for the possibility of freely redefining a word. These two strategies, non-commitment to a redefinition and refusal to commit to a definition, are strictly related to each other.

5.1. *Omitting Definitions*

The omission of a definition can be considered as a speech act in the sense that it is an act performed through silence (absence of a speech act). It is the use of silence to bring about a specific definitional effect. As mentioned previously, omissions are not simply non-actions, but deliberate 'non-negative' actions, consisting in refusing to perform a requested action in order to achieve a specific effect. In the case of definitions, the omission of a definition does not correspond to taking a concept for granted or forgetting to provide a definition. The omitted definition is known not to be shared, and the effects of such an omission are known by the non-speaker. The non-speaker deliberately decides not to provide a definition knowing that a specific effect will result from such a decision.

The clearest case is the omission of the definition of 'torture,' where the Russian and Armenian governments were requested to define such a crucial term in order to curb the violence denounced by Amnesty International and other international authorities. Such governments knew exactly the effects of the absence of a definition, and had the power to comply with the request of the United Nations and avoid heavy criticisms. However, they decided not to do it, without advancing any explanation or excuse. Similarly, in the United States, a few years after crucial legal cases stemming from the ambiguities regarding the concepts of *enemy*, *combatants*, and *hostilities*, a proposal of an amendment was proposed in which the definitions of these strategic notions were not provided, and the criteria for applying such categories were known not to hold in the case of war on terror. From a rhetorical point of view, Reagan chose not to define 'truly needy' when he intended to cut the welfare system. He knew perfectly well that such a concept was not shared at all, and the necessary criteria for establishing its boundaries (a decision needed to be implemented) did not exist. All such choices resulted in the same effect, known by the person that was requested or supposed to define.

We can represent the omission of a definition as shown in Table 4.8.

The omission of the definition of 'torture' clearly differs from the non-definition of 'hostilities' and 'belligerent.' In the first case the speaker's commitment to the speech act of defining (or refusing to do it) results from an explicit act (request). In the latter case, as in Reagan's discourse, the commitment derived respectively from an institutional (legal) and a communicative rule, "avoid ambiguity." In both cases the speaker is aware of the requirement (or expectation) and deliberately refuses to comply with it,

Table 4.8. Omitting Definitions – Dialectical Profile

Move	Content Conditions	Speaker's Commitments	Hearer's Commitments	Effects on the Speaker	Effects on the Hearer
Omitting (a speech act - Fp).	• Fp represents a dialogical move. • Fp can be performed by S.	• S has the commitment to perform Fp (CFp). • CFp results from an institutional or social obligation. • S knows that non-Fp causes effect E. • S knows that Fp is necessary to avoid E.		• S is not committed to Fp. • S is not committed to $refuse(Fp)$. • S is not committed to E.	• H's dialogical situation has been altered (E).
Omission of the definition of 'torture.'	Russian (Armenian) governments had the power to define 'torture.'	Russia and Armenia were requested to define 'torture' and blamed for not doing it.		Russia (Armenia) are not committed to a specific meaning of 'torture.'	The category of 'torture' can be applied arbitrarily.

knowing its effects. The omission of a definition is a discourse move because a specific effect is expected to result from it, the possibility of implicitly redefining, or rather giving the word new unshared definitions. This latter move can be considered as an act of a kind, even though it is not explicit.

5.2. *Taking Redefinitions for Granted*

In order to avoid requesting the authorization of Congress, Obama performed a move that allowed him to achieve his communicative and legal purposes without committing himself to a modification of the Constitution. He had to request the authorization of Congress in order to continue the bombings in Libya, as the War Powers Resolution provided that the president "needs to obtain the Congress Authorization to continue the hostilities." At the same time he did not want to submit such a request, but the only way to do it was to refuse to comply with the law, or change it. He opted for a third way: He chose to change the law, but avoided being committed to such an act. He defined the concept of *hostilities* without supporting this position with arguments and without committing to a proposal of a constitutional amendment to be submitted for approval. He simply used the word with a new meaning, exploiting the absence of a statutory definition of it.

He implicitly imposed a new meaning on the word, which was different from any previous use and common understanding. This move can be labeled "implicit redefinition," and can be analyzed as an implicit illocution, studied by Searle and Vanderveken (2005: 129). They noticed how

[...] sometimes by performing one illocutionary act a speaker can be committed to another illocution. This occurs both in cases where the performance of one act by a speaker is *eo ipso* a performance of the other and in cases where the performance of the one is not a performance of the other and does not involve the speaker in a commitment to its explicit performance. [...] But there are also cases, which we will call *weak* illocutionary commitments, where the speaker is committed to an illocutionary act $F(P)$ by way of performing certain illocutionary acts $F_1(P_1), \ldots, F_n(P_n)$ although he does not perform $F(P)$ and is not committed to its performance.

By excluding operations that "do not involve sustained fighting or active exchanges of fire with hostile forces" from the definition of 'hostilities,' Obama bound himself and the hearers to a specific commitment, that 'hostilities' meant *only* "active fighting by ground troops." Searle and Vanderveken (2005: 130) provided a generic rule that can be used to describe this kind of implicit speech act, the act of "taking for granted" (Hopper 1981a, 1981b):

As a general definition we can say that an illocutionary act of the form $F_1(P_1)$ commits the speaker to an illocutionary act $F_2(P_2)$ iff in the successful performance of $F_1(P_1)$:

1) The speaker achieves (strong) or is committed (weak) to the illocutionary point of F_2 on P_2 with the required mode of achievement and degree of strength of F_2.

Table 4.9. Implicit Definitions – Dialectical Profile

Move	Content Conditions	Speaker's Commitments	Hearer's Commitments	Effects on the Speaker	Effects on the Hearer
Performing (Fp) implicitly by performing F_1p_1	• Fp represents a dialogical move. • Fp can be performed by S. • The performance of Fp is a condition of the performance of F_1p_1.	(Depends on the nature of F_1p_1).	(Depends on the nature of F_1p_1).	• S is committed to F_1p_1. • S is not committed to the performance of Fp. • S is committed to p.	• Commitments resulting from F_1p_1. • Commitments resulting from Fp.
The war in Libya is not hostilities (F_1p_1), as it does not involve sustained fighting by ground forces (F_2p_2).	Obama is committed to the sincerity conditions and illocutionary point of "Hostilities" means active fighting by ground forces" (p).	• S believes that H does not (already, at face value, completely) accept p_1. • S believes that he can justify p_1 for H with the help of p_2 and p. • S believes that H accepts (knows) p and p_2	• H is not committed to p_1 (already, at face value, completely). • H is committed to p_2 and p.	Obama needs to support p_1 if requested.	H needs to attack/challenge/question p_1 or accept it.

2) He is committed to all of the preparatory conditions of $F_2(P_2)$ and to the propositional presuppositions.

3) He commits himself to having the psychological state specified by the sincerity conditions of $F_2(P_2)$ with the required degree of strength.

4) P_2 satisfies the propositional content of F_2 with respect to the context of utterance.

We can use this type of methodology to analyze the implicit redefinition. The act of classifying an entity commits the speaker to the sincerity condition that he believes the 'hostilities' has the proposed meaning, and the assertion of the classification commits the speaker to the illocutionary point that "'hostilities' only means 'active fighting by ground troops.'" We can represent the commitment structure of this implicit act as shown in Table 4.9.

In this analysis we present Obama's move as an implicit act of reminding the audience of a commitment, and he commits himself and the interlocutors to the redefinition of 'hostilities.' The nature of the implicit act, however, can be reconstructed only from the conditions and the nature of the explicit one. In this case, Obama could not have imposed such a definition, as he did not have the authority to do so, nor could he have advanced it, as the nature of his act of defending a standpoint required the previous acceptance of the definition. This move was immediately recognized and denounced as manipulative, as the implicit commitment to which it bound the hearers clashed with the shared definition of 'hostilities.' This case can explain one of the most interesting uses of implicit redefinitions. The implicit nature of the act and the process of reconstruction it presupposes allow the speaker to perform such a move to accomplish different types of implicit acts and achieve different dialogical purposes.

In the implicit redefinition of 'deliberate homicide,' the judge performed the action of informing the jury that intoxication was not a defense. However, this statement committed him to another statement, namely, that "homicide means causing the death of another person under circumstances that would otherwise establish knowledge or purpose, excluding voluntary intoxication." He had the power to provide an interpretation and therefore a redefinition, but he did not commit himself to the act of imposing a definition. The outcome was that the implicit redefinition set new commitments.

A different case is the redefinition of 'persecution.' The Board of Immigration Appeals excluded an alien member of a sect discriminated by Pakistani Muslims, a victim of violence in his country, from the category of 'persecuted individuals' based on an implicit redefinition of 'persecution.' The Board never defined such a concept, but the implicit redefinition, set as an essential requirement the use of "systematic violence," did not correspond to the common understanding of the term. In this case, the speaker did not have the authority to apply a definition that had not been previously made public. By means of the redefinition he avoided commitment to the explicit act of setting a new definition (which would not have been possible in such a situation), but at the same time he achieved the same effect.

The last case is the redefinition of 'enemy combatant.' As mentioned previously, Bush supported the classification of Hamdi as an enemy combatant as he was allegedly "closely associated with al Qaeda" and engaged in "hostile and war-like acts" including "preparation for acts of international terrorism." This statement requires, or rather hides, another act, the reminding of a definition on which the classification is based. The problem with this redefinition is that it was advanced as a reason to support a classification, and therefore it was supposed to be shared (Bush could not impose a definition and at the same time use it). However, not only was the term not legally defined, but the implicit definition did not reflect any common or shared use, let alone any previous legal use of it. The definition did not conflict with any previous definition, like Obama's redefinition of 'hostilities,' and therefore could not be condemned as mischievous or deceptive. The omission of the definition in the laws enacted to govern this category of actual or potential belligerents allowed the president to take for granted any of its possible meanings, presenting it as a legal precedent or a shared meaning. The omission of a definition allowed Bush to use any of the possible meanings of 'enemy combatant' without explicitly committing to any of them. This double act, omitting the definition of a word and implicitly redefining it, put before the court an interpretative riddle, where they had to reconstruct a missing meaning that the very legislator treated as shared.

6. Strategies of Ambiguity

The implicit act of redefining can hide a complex strategy that can be explained by inquiring further into the notion of pragmatic ambiguity. The aforementioned positive acts of defining all have a clear structure consisting in a representation of the preliminary conditions and the effects on the interlocutors' commitments. From the intended effects and the preconditions it is possible to analyze the possible moves that are allowed by the definitional move. If a definition is advanced as a standpoint, it is aimed at altering the listener's commitments and presupposes that he may be committed to a different meaning. For this reason, the speaker needs to support it by arguments and be ready to face criticisms. However, if a definition is simply stated to remind the audience of a meaning, it does not need to be borne out by reasons, while the hearer is presumed to be committed to it. Why, then, can definitions be so dangerous? A possible answer lies in the ambiguity of the definitional move. We will show how ambiguity is used and introduced, analyzing excerpts from the previously quoted speeches.

In order to explain the structure of the complex mechanism of implicit redefinitions, which will be applied to our contemporary cases, we will go back to the ancient tradition and rhetorical theories, where such a move was described and analyzed in detail.

The aforementioned moves are reconstructions of the conditions and effects of making a move. Very seldom does the speaker claim that he is redefining a word, or that the description that he is advancing is intended to state what the *definiendum* actually means. On the contrary, he often chooses to leave it up to the hearer to interpret his act. While he is presumed to know what he intends to do with his communicative move, the hearer can only reconstruct his intention, taking into consideration his own commitments and the structure of the move. The speaker can decide to create a pragmatic ambiguity that prevents the hearer from understanding the real nature of the definition he is advancing, and therefore advancing objections. The strategies to achieve this result are based on the introduction of a semantic ambiguity, consisting in disguising the new definition as if it were a commonly accepted one.

The most common rhetorical strategy of definitional ambiguity is grounded on the pragmatic confusion between an act of reminding (or informing) and an act of advancing a standpoint. The difference between these acts is in the dialogical nature of the propositional content. If the proposition is shared by the hearer or is commonly known (and perhaps unshared by the hearer), the speaker is performing an act of reminding (or informing). On the contrary, if the proposition is not shared and not known, the hearer is commonly presumed to bear the burden of proving the claim that he is advancing. This distinction is often taken for granted when the speaker advances arguments to support the acceptability of his claim (as in Obama's definition of 'peace' as "not merely the absence of visible conflict"), or when he quotes or refers to sources (as Obama does in his definition of 'just war'). However, sometimes the definition he advances is dialectically ambiguous; it can lead to pragmatic misunderstandings (as we have seen).

An example that can be used to clarify the concept of pragmatic and dialectical ambiguity is Obama's previously mentioned redefinition of 'peace.' If we examine each rhetorical step in detail, we can notice that his last act of advancing a new definition is based on a definition that was not agreed upon (emphasis added):

For peace is not **merely** the absence of visible conflict. Only a just peace based upon the inherent rights and dignity of every individual can truly be lasting.

[…] a just peace includes not only civil and political rights – it must encompass economic security and opportunity. For true peace is not just **freedom from fear**, but freedom from want.

Obama's first move consists in attacking the shared meaning of 'peace,' echoing Martin Luther King. To do so, he qualifies the shared definition

"absence of visible conflict" as a genus to be further specified by the difference "based on inherent rights and dignity of every individual." Further
in his speech he reminds the audience of the definition that they have
accepted, "freedom from fear," and from there he advances a new definition, "freedom from want," supporting it with reasons. By reminding the
hearers of the now accepted meaning, he can slightly modify it. However,
he is not simply making a commitment explicit. He is actually redefining
the term, changing the accepted meaning from "absence of visible conflict based on civil and personal rights" (paraphrasing his words) to "freedom from fear (or from the violations of such rights)." What appears to be
missing is the genus. 'Peace' is not defined as the negation of its contrary,
conflict, but the privation of fear, which is the effect of a real or possible
danger (e.g., resulting from the violation of human rights). Obama presents a redefinition as a reminder. In this fashion he avoids the burden of
supporting it.

This redefinition is at the same time hardly acceptable and crucial for
the whole speech, not so much for the explicit content as for the genus that
he takes for granted. Obama uses the predicate 'freedom' as the generic
category to which "true peace" belongs. However, 'freedom,' as used here,
can also bear the meaning of "to be released from something onerous,"
corresponding to the nominalization of the passive form of 'to free,' which
requires three arguments: an agent, a living entity to be freed, and something onerous or displeasing. Therefore, it presupposes an agent, a libera-
tor, and places the *definiendum* in the genus of actions (which can be wars)
aimed at taking the burden away. Such an implicit meaning could not have
been made explicit, as the whole argument would have sounded noticeably
different. It would have been a poor argument to claim that the only way of
preventing a possible future war is to fight one right away.

Another powerful strategy of dialectical ambiguity is the implicit redefinition (see the general structure of this strategy represented in Table 4.10).
In order to explain its characteristics, it is useful to go back to the ancient
textbooks on strategic discourse and apply the theoretical insights to our
contemporary cases. Implicit redefinitions are implicit moves hinging on
the alteration of an allegedly shared concept. For this reason, it is necessary
to know the historical and social background in order to reconstruct the
move and show its strategic use. In Chapter 1 we mentioned the redefinition of 'seditious' described in the rhetorical work *De Inventione* by Cicero:

(Case 5) He is seditious who is a bad and useless citizen.

This redefinition was analyzed by Cicero because it was actually the pivotal
move of a legal case. In order to describe it, we need to distinguish the dialectical effects of the propositional content from the dialectical effects of
the act of redefining. Considering only the propositional content, Cicero
quotes this paraphrase as a clear example of a bad definition, even though
it was actually an effective one. In Cicero's times, as now, a seditious citizen

Table 4.10. Strategies of Implicit Redefinition – Dialectical Profile

Move	Content Conditions	Speaker's Commitments	Hearer's Commitments	Effects on the Speaker	Effects on the Hearer
Performing (*Fp*) implicitly.	• *Fp* represents a dialogical move. • *Fp* can be performed by S; → • *p* is shared by H.	• (*p*) • (H knows *p*)	• (S can perform *Fp*);→ • (*Fp* is a reminder);→ • (*p* is shared).	• S is committed to *F*[*p*[*t*.→ • S is not committed to the performance of *Fp*. • S is committed to *p*.	• Commitments resulting from *Fp*.→ • H needs to reject *Fp* in order to challenge *p*.→ • H needs to provide reasons for *non-Fp*. → • H needs to provide reasons for (non-shared *p*)-
The war in Libya is not hostilities (*Fl*,*Pl*) (hostilities means sustained fighting by ground forces) (*Fp*).	• Everyone knows that *hostilities means sustained fighting by ground forces*. • Common knowledge: (hostilities is an act of warfare) (*non-p*).	• Obama is committed to "*hostilities means sustained fighting by ground forces*" • Obama is committed to the fact that his audience accepts this definition.	• The audience reconstructs the move as a reminder.	Obama does not need to advance reasons in support of his definition.	• Prove that the definition of hostilities is not shared → • Challenge the act of redefinition→ ○ Obama needs to defend the act (*p* is shared) or ○ Obama needs to defend the redefinition (provide arguments).

could be commonly considered as falling within the category of bad and useless citizens. However, this proposition was presented as a definition, confounding the genus with the species (or an accidental property with an essential or fundamental one). This similarity between the definition and propositions commonly accepted generates a first dialectical ambiguity, which was used in the implicit act of redefining and therefore combined with a second dialectical ambiguity, generated by the pragmatic confusion stemming from the speaker's act of reminding a definition that could be advanced only as a standpoint.

This definition was used in 100 BC by the *quaestor* Quintus Caepio to label the tribune of the people Lucius Saturninus as seditious, because he brought a new grain law before the people despite the veto of some senators. This decision was an action outside the bonds of the *res publica* (Gildenhard 2011: 145) but amounted only to a hostile attitude toward the senate, without involving any insurrection or attacks to the established order. The redefinition was used implicitly in a classificatory argument. Saturninus was labelled as 'seditious' based on his decision to act against the senate. The implicit aspect of the redefinition increased its strategic force. The speaker took it for granted, as if it were a shared concept, leaving to the hearer the pragmatic burden of reconstructing the implicit move and the definitional proposition, and the dialectical one of providing arguments against its acceptability and rejecting the move as an implicit reminder.

The act of implicitly redefining a concept can be considered an act of introducing ambiguity. Instead of clarifying a vague or ambiguous meaning, the speaker uses a definition that is unshared. Moreover, the implicit redefinition carries a powerful dialectical effect, as we have noted, the absence of commitments. The speaker introduces a new definition that conflicts with the accepted meaning or does not correspond to it. However, his move is implicit. He commits himself and the audience to a definition without taking on any commitment for the act of introducing it. For this reason, his new definition can be attacked only by performing a meta-dialogical move. The hearer needs to reconstruct the speaker's definitional act and reject it, denying the possibility of performing it. The hearer needs to solve first a pragmatic ambiguity: Is the speaker trying to impose the redefinition (he is in the position of power), advance it, or inform the hearer of a meaning that should be shared? Then he has to show why the move could not be performed, reconstructing the implicit definition and analyzing the conditions of the act. What is relevant is that this implicit move shifts the burden of proof onto the hearer. He is not simply bound to question the definition, accept it, or advance a contrary position. His "right to challenge" is not granted, and he needs to advance a reason for rejecting the move in order not to be committed to the implicit redefinition.

The strategic effect of the act of implicitly redefining can be represented by specifying further the commitment structure mentioned in the previous section, making explicit the consequences of the conditions of the implicit act. In Table 4.10 we show the dialectical structure of the implicit redefinition as a reminder, applying the aforementioned account to the example of the redefinition of 'hostilities.'

Implicit redefinitions are therefore strategies grounded on a dialectical ambiguity, resulting in a shifting of a burden of proof. Their force can be increased by taking for granted a redefinition that is similar to the shared one. Obama was harshly criticized for his redefinition, which openly conflicted with the military definition and the commonly shared one.

If we consider the ancient counterpart of Obama's move, we notice that Caepio's redefinition mentioned above was much more complex. Refusing to comply with the law and attacking the senate amounted to being a 'bad citizen,' as Cicero claims, of a specific kind. Far from being seditious, Caepio refused to comply with the laws and subverted them. In a metaphorical sense, he declared war on the senate. This definitional ambiguity makes the move extremely effective, as the citizens (and the court) actually had to face a subtle distortion, an extreme reinterpretation of the *definiendum.* Thus this ancient 'textbook' case can reveal crucial elements of a strategic move that is currently used in politics.

The force of the implicit redefinition lies in the dialectical ambiguity of the propositional content, that is, the definition. The speaker needs to hide his move and lead the interlocutor to take the new definition as an accepted or acceptable one. For this reason, the undefined or vague concepts are the ones that better suit the purpose of this kind of move. The omission of a definition or the introduction of different definitions artificially creates a definitional gap or conceptual vagueness and allows the speaker to be free to redefine the concept, within the limits provided by the boundaries of the alternative concepts. The vagueness of a concept increases the interlocutor's burden of proof, as he cannot rely on a specific and alternative definition to oppose it. The use of conceptual vagueness can be analyzed starting from an ancient strategic move, whose effects were analyzed in the Roman dialectical theories. Let's go back to the comparable example in the ancient rhetoric, which is very revealing, and continue the story on the grain tax.

After Saturninus had brought the bill to the popular vote, Caepio impeded and broke up the voting on it. Caepio "destroys the bridges, throws down the ballot boxes, and blocks further action on the motion" *(Ad Herennium,* I, 21). For this reason, he was accused by Saturninus of treason, or rather *maiestas minuta* (Gildenhard 2011:145). Saturninus (and the court) charged Caepio of a crime that was extremely vague, which was until that time applied to the conduct of the provincial governor (Mousourakis 2003: 227; Seager 2001: 144). He implicitly redefined a vague concept (Seager 2001: 147):

ANCIENT REDEFINITIONS OF 'TREASON'

The prosecution, he says, would claim that *maiestas* was diminished by the spurning of those elements which constituted the *amplituda* of the State. As paramount among these it would then select (from an obviously wide range of possibilities) the suffrage of the people and the powers of its magistrates. Cacpio's action in interfering with the poll deprived the people of its right to vote, Sarurninus of his right to initiate legislation. The defence, however, has a counter-definition: that man is guilty of *maiestas* who damages the amplitude of the State *(qui amplitudinem civitatis detrimenta adficit)*. With pleasing synecdoche Caepio claims that he protected the *amplituda* of the State from damage by saving the treasury from the unjustified expense which Saturninus's corn distributions would have entailed. Thus he preserved *maiestas* from utter extinction.

Both parties argued for a classification grounding it on implicit redefinitions of *maiestas*. The prosecution shifted the burden of disproving the redefinition onto the defense, who in its turn implicitly redefined what 'amplitude' was. This legal case shows how vagueness can be used as the ground for a strategic move. Vagueness can also be introduced for the purpose of allowing the speaker to redefine the concept he wishes to use.

Comparison with these ancient examples is extremely relevant in the current political and legal rhetoric. The previously presented cases of implicit redefinition clearly show the deliberate use of vagueness. The implicit redefinition of 'enemy combatant' was allowed by the deliberate omission of its definition. A term that can be used to avoid the application of the Geneva Convention was left undefined, without referring to any precedent case containing such a word. Bush used it to classify foreign alleged terrorists or combatants as well as two American citizens caught in two clearly different situations. The court had to reconstruct a possible meaning, tracing it back to the only possible similar concept, applied to foreign saboteurs during the Second World War.

Reagan supported his cuts to the American welfare system by leaving the category of the 'truly needy' (to be left unaffected by the reduction of the welfare program) undefined and therefore extremely vague. In his speech on May 1, 1971, Reagan used this concept to support his proposal of increasing spending for this category of people and improving education (Kiewe & Houck 1991: 79):

These are the truly needy ... the blind, the elderly, the disabled and those children from families with little or no outside income and no employed breadwinner.

Age and physical impairment were the two criteria used for classifying the truly needy. However, when later as a president he decided to reduce the welfare program, he could not provide such a narrow definition. In his State of the Union Addresses in 1982 and 1983 he simply identified this category as including the opposite of the 'greedy,' or rather the cheaters (Ronald Reagan, State of the Union Address, January 26, 1982):

Not only the taxpayers are defrauded; the people with real dependency on these programs are deprived of what they need, because available resources are going not to the needy, but to the greedy.

However, the cuts affected not only the cheaters, but all the needy. Reagan used in his speeches other redefinitions of 'truly needy,' narrowing down the concept to exclude people who could work but are unemployed or poorly paid (Weiler & Pearce 1992: 243). The vagueness of this concept allowed him to use it as an instrument of persuasion and at the same time as a strict criterion for excluding the needy from the welfare programs.

7. Conclusion

Definitions are crucial for setting the dialectical grounds of a dialogue or a discourse. Definitions can inform the interlocutor of a commitment or remind him of it. They can advance a description of a meaning or simply impose it, by stipulating a unique or new definition. Finally, they can commit the speaker to a specific language use and the interlocutor to a specific interpretation. However, these acts are only the explicit ones. Some actions can be performed by non-acting when it is necessary to do so, or by performing a more complex action, presupposing a non-explicit one. To describe the first case, we introduced the act of omitting a definition, while to refer to the second one we used the concept of implicit definitions. In order to analyze the structure of these acts we examined their use in a context of dialogue in which the conditions and the effects of a dialogical move are governed by specific rules and judged by a competent authority in a coherent fashion. The legal framework provided a set of requirements for the use of each act of defining and descriptions of their consequences. However, in legal discourse the admissibility of a move is (almost) always dependent on an external judgment or rule. In other contexts of dialogue, a move cannot be simply assessed as right or wrong. In politics, like in ordinary conversation, we evaluate a dialogue move as effective, felicitous, acceptable, mischievous, infelicitous, or unacceptable. In order to provide some criteria for evaluating the moves of defining, we abstracted their dialectical characteristics and pragmatic conditions and applied them to some of the most known and effective contemporary speeches.

From the definitions we analyzed in political speeches, we noticed that the most effective and strategic definitional moves are based on ambiguity. The first kind of ambiguity is *pragmatic*. Very seldom does the speaker announce his redefinition of a crucial term. Instead, he can achieve a more powerful effect by leaving it up to the hearer to reconstruct his communicative intention. Is the speaker introducing a new definition that needs to be supported by arguments and open to criticism, or simply stating a commonly accepted one? This pragmatic ambiguity rests on two crucial factors: the speaker's decision not to underscore the questionable nature of his description, and the *dialectical* ambiguity of the definition itself. In particular, the speaker treats a new definition as if it were a commonly accepted one, manipulating the interlocutors' commitments. This dialectical ambiguity is often grounded on a *semantic* one, as the redefined concept somehow resembles the one that is commonly shared.

As we noted about the political definitions, the most effective act of defining is the implicit definition. The speaker simply takes for granted a new definition of a word, using the *definiendum* with a new meaning. He leads the audience to take the new definition as an accepted or acceptable one. Vague words such as 'peace,' 'hostilities,' and 'needy' can be implicitly redefined because their boundaries are not shared, and the speaker can implicitly impose new ones without conflicting with the interlocutors' commitments. Similarly, definitional gaps created by the omission of definitions leave the speaker free to implicitly redefine the non-defined concept.

Implicit redefinitions traditionally were analyzed as extremely powerful dialectical strategies. They shift the burden of proof on the interlocutor, who needs to reject a commitment that he never took on. Vague concepts increase such a burden, as the interlocutor cannot refuse the implicit definition by opposing a commonly accepted one. Implicit moves are therefore crucial strategic moves, as they can be used to manipulate commitments, impose on the hearer a commitment that he never took on, and alter the dialectical roles between the proponent of a viewpoint and the opponent. These moves are extremely complex if we analyze them as kinds of speech acts. From a pragmatic point of view, the speaker is taking for granted a proposition. The crucial question is how this move is possible. How can the speaker "take for granted"? This problem brings us back to a fundamental and controversial issue, pragmatic presupposition. The inquiry into this topic will bring us to a deeper level of analysis, where semantics and dialectics meet epistemology.

5

What Our Words Hide

Presupposition and Dark-Side Commitments

In the previous chapter we showed the different types of acts of defining. The most dialectically powerful is the implicit definition. The speaker, instead of stating or advancing a definition, simply takes it for granted, considering it as part of the interlocutors' common ground. Zarefsky (1998) and Schiappa (2003: 111-112; 130) pointed out the implicit dimension of this act of naming reality, which they call "argument by definition." Instead of putting forward a classification and supporting it by a definitional reason, the speaker simply names reality, leaving the definition unexpressed. As seen in Chapter 4, the hearer is left with the burden of reconstructing the move, assessing the definition, and rebutting it if it does not correspond to the shared meaning. This complex mechanism, one that can be exploited for rhetorical and dialectical purposes, has been classified previously as an 'improper' act of defining, and it may even be seen as a non-act of defining. It is a definitional act, as it alters the dialectical situation restricting the interlocutor's possibilities of making further moves. It is a stipulation of a kind, as the speaker commits the hearer to a proposition, but he does not take on any responsibility for it. However, at the same it is a non-action, as it is a speech act required by the act of naming actually performed by the speaker. For this reason, pragmatic and semantic ambiguity plays a crucial strategic role in this kind of dialectical tactic. The hearer needs to retrieve the implicit move from a semantic and pragmatic perspective. At the same time, he needs to reconstruct the definition, and the type of speech act the speaker did not perform, in order to ascertain whether to continue the dialogue or attack the possibility of the implicit act.

The act of taking a definition for granted leads us to a wider and more controversial issue, presupposition. Implicit definitions can be analyzed as utilizing a pragmatic presupposition (Stalnaker 1970, 1998), where the speaker can choose whether to deploy a possible world (Stalnaker 1970: 280), or rather a set of conditions (in case of implicit definitions, the meaning of the 'key' word). He can use a shared world, or a commonly known meaning, or set a new one as if it were part of the common ground. In the latter case he is not only using a word but imposing some conditions. He is performing a specific non-act, the act of presupposing. In order to inquire into the pragmatic dimension of implicit definitions, we need to broaden our field of inquiry and consider what we hide in words.

In our words we can hide powerful acts in different fashions. We presuppose by using certain predicates, by uttering some sentences, or by performing a dialogue move. At all these levels, presuppositions can be used to alter the dialogical situation and modify the interlocutor's possible moves. We will show the different dimensions of presuppositions, explaining how they work in some rhetorical moves. From this step we will move on to analyze how they can be used strategically. For this purpose, we will take into consideration the legal context, which is the only context where the effects of such moves have been clearly described from a dialectical perspective, and where the moves are actually assessed and judged as admissible or not. This dialectical analysis of the strategies-based presupposition reveals their origin and the reasons behind them.

The problem of the implicit grounds of dialogue is twofold: It is a linguistic matter, as presuppositions are the conditions of meaning, but it is also an epistemic one, because we take the presupposed information for granted, as already shared by the hearer. We do not state such information because we believe that he can know it, or he can retrieve or reconstruct it. However, how can we know that a proposition is already known, or that it can be reconstructed? Why should we believe that our interlocutor may know or accommodate a presupposition? To answer these questions, we will analyze the linguistic and epistemic dimensions of presupposition from an argumentation theory perspective, showing the nature and effects of the reasoning underlying the possibility of presupposing. For this purpose, presupposition will be investigated as an implicit act aimed at setting forth the conditions of the continuation of a dialogue. Such an act is in its turn subject to some constraints, rooted in the epistemic problem of knowing the other's mind. This argumentation approach will provide an explanation of presenting presupposition as the result of a presumptive reasoning advanced by the speaker. From this perspective, the dialectical effect of an implicit definition can be explained as an undue act of presumption, one that shifts a burden of proof (and a risk of criticism) onto the interlocutor.

1. Presuppositions

The notion of presupposition[1] can be traced back to the discussion in logic on the problem of definite descriptions (see Frege 1897; Russell 1905; Whitehead & Russell 1927), and to the famous sentence:

1. The present king of France is bald.

---

[1] Several linguistic and pragmatic phenomena fall under the label of presupposition (Chomsky 1972: 112; Green 1996: 72). The very term 'presupposition' is ambiguous, as it may refer to

According to Frege, such a sentence cannot be proven to be true or false if there is not a king of France. The existence of the king of France is a requirement for the verifiability of the sentence: if there is not a king of France, no reference can be given, and therefore the sentence lacks a truth value (see Wilson 1975: 43–44).The sentence is said to presuppose that there is a king of France, a presupposition that in this instance fails.

However, reference can be determined only in context. Therefore, presupposition cannot be regarded as a property of sentences, but rather of the *use* of sentences, or statements (Strawson 1950, 1952; Karttunen 1973; Kempson 1975; Wilson 1975; Keenan 1971). For this reason, Strawson (1950: 325) distinguished sentences with respect to their use and utterance. From a logical perspective, presuppositions are considered as properties of the use of sentences. However, the logical criterion of truth (implying a God's eye-view) needs to be relativized in order to describe a phenomenon concerning the actual use of natural language. The famous statement (1) can be true (and therefore its assertion perfectly felicitous) among people who are used to referring to the French Prime Minister Sarkozy as "the king of France." The same statement would be controversial and less likely to be felicitous in a context in which the interlocutors cannot identify any king of France. Depending on the background knowledge, the king can exist or not, or rather be identified or not. From this view, depending on its belonging to the Pragmatic Universe of Discourse, or shared knowledge, a proposition can be *known* to be true or false (Kempson 1975: 168–170). This pragmatic concept of truth allows one to understand the relationship between the logical and the pragmatic perspectives on the use of language.

As Hamblin (1970: 240) pointed out, talking about what is true for a language user amounts to what *he knows* to be true. However, since we do not proceed from what is absolutely known to be true but from what we *believe*, or rather accept as being true, the concept of verification needs to be replaced with the weaker criterion of acceptability (Hamblin 1970: 242–243; Walton & Macagno 2005a, 2005b). Acceptability is an assessment (and therefore a decision) of the agent, and not a judgment external to him or her. This pragmatic view of verification leads to analyzing meaning in terms of effects on the audience instead of truth (Grice 1975, 1989: 220; Levinson 1983: 97; Austin 1962: 50–51). From this perspective, the nature of presupposition also needs to be enlarged to account for a failure not consisting in

the semantic conditions for the verification of a sentence (a logical relationship between two statements; see Kempson 1975: 50–51), to the background assumptions underlying discourse (intended as a chain of sentences) cohesion (Sandulescu 1975), or to a much broader pragmatic concept to denote the propositions that are taken for granted in the utterance of a linguistic expression and on whose truth, or better acceptance and knowledge by the hearer, the felicity of the statement depends (Wilson 1975: 26; Green 1996: 72). Another definition, operational, was provided by Keenan (1971: 45), who identified presupposition by means of the test of negation. In this view, the presupposition of a sentence is entailed by both the sentence and its negation (for the weakness of this definition, see Katz 1973).

non-verifiability, but rather in lack of effect (and, in the case of assertions, resulting in the impossibility of judging a statement as acceptable or not).

Conceiving presuppositions as a property of utterances, and not of sentences, affects the very definition of this concept. The presupposition becomes what the speaker assumes to be true, or rather, what is accepted by the interlocutor (Kempson 1975: 54). From this pragmatic perspective, presuppositions need to be defined as felicity conditions of speech acts. Presuppositional failure can result in the failure of a speech act to carry out its intended effect on the audience. This social dimension of felicity and presupposition was emphasized by Austin, who pointed out how the falsity of presuppositions causes the infelicity of a speech act (Austin 1962: 50–51):

Next let us consider presupposition: what is to be said of the statement that 'John's children are all bald' if made when John has no children? It is usual now to say that it is not false because it is devoid of reference; reference is necessary for either truth or falsehood. (Is it then meaningless? It is not so in every sense: it is not, like a 'meaningless sentence', ungrammatical, incomplete, mumbo-jumbo, &c.). People say 'the question does not arise'. Here I shall say 'the utterance is void'.

In Austin's example, the speaker is presupposing that there is a person called John, and that he has children. We should notice that the speaker is not presupposing the *existence* of such entities, but simply their existence in the *listener's domain of knowledge*. This pragmatic view extends the notion of presupposition to several phenomena of meaningfulness constraints (Austin 1962: 34; 51), such as selection restrictions, coherence relations, and felicity conditions. Such linguistic phenomena are conditions that need to be complied with for the interlocutor to understand the move; these linguistic presuppositions are therefore included within the pragmatic conditions for speech act felicity.

The basic distinction between logical and pragmatic presuppositions lies in how language and discourse are assessed: From a logical perspective, the basic concern is the verifiability of statements (sentences that can be true or false in some context of utterance, or possible world; see Kempson 1975: 51); from a pragmatic position, the focus is on the felicity of a discourse move, or the possible effect of a speech act on the interlocutor (for the notion of presupposition as felicity conditions, see Stalnaker 1970; Kempson 1975). The problem of the definition of presupposition hides and is grounded on the problem of the types of presuppositions, or rather, the linguistic and pragmatic phenomena that trigger presuppositions.

2. Presupposition Triggers

The problem of the definition of a presupposition is strictly related to the origin and type of presupposition. Considering the broadest notion of pragmatic presupposition from another perspective, the different kinds of presuppositional phenomena are triggered by semantic, syntactic, and pragmatic entities (or rather predicates). Therefore, they can be divided into three broad categories (Sandulescu 1975; see also Green 1996: 72–77): sentence, inter-sentence and discourse presuppositions, including in the latter category both pragmatic phenomena such as speech act presuppositions and cohesion relations between discourse moves.

2.1. *Sentence Presuppositions: Semantic Presuppositions*

The first level of presuppositions is triggered by predicates *within* a sentence, and is related to the well-formedness and what in logic is usually referred to as the verifiability of a sentence. Why can some linguistic units combine while other combinations are usually considered unsound, if not ungrammatical? Why is it possible to say, "The king of France is bald" but not "Australia is bald"? (Seuren 2000: 279). Why is the first sentence meaningful and verifiable if uttered in the seventeenth century, while unsound and not verifiable these days? (Atlas 2004).

The problem of grammaticality was deeply analyzed by Chomsky (1971) and Katz and Fodor (1963). From such approaches and subsequent studies a crucial relationship emerges between the conditions required by semantic predicates (or selectional restrictions) and the fundamental semantic features of their arguments. Selectional restrictions can be described as the conditions (or preconditions; Seuren 2000: 277) that a predicate imposes on the elements acting as its arguments (Hobbs 1979: 70; Grimes 1975: 162). Such conditions represent the categorical presuppositions of the predicate (McCawley 1971: 290; Antley 1974; Chomsky 1971: 205), i.e., the categorical conditions imposed on the denotation of a semantic structure. For instance, the predicate 'to kill' requires an animate being as a second argument, and therefore its second argument needs to have as a semantic property "to be an animate being." Similarly, the use of the predicate 'bald' carries the following preconditions (Seuren 2000: 278):

BALD:	Unary adjectival predicate.	
	Preconditions:	The term referent (a) exists, (b) belongs to a category whose members are normally covered with hair, pile or tread (for tyres) in prototypical places.
	Update conditions:	The coverage which is normally there is largely absent.

In this view, the semantic structure of predicates provides for categorical conditions (or argument types, see Pustejovsky 1991: 422, Pustejovsky 1998) and existential requirements. For instance, the predicate 'to contribute to,' in the sense of "help bring about a result," presupposes that *an agent* (a living or humanized being or collective entity) contributes to an *object* (an existing or future activity, or purpose) with an action.

There are several types of semantic presuppositions corresponding to the different types of predicates, conceiving the latter term as a logical functor that attributes a quality or binds into a relation one or more arguments (Seuren 2010: 328–331). Quantifiers and determiners impose specific conditions on nouns (it would be ungrammatical to say "*I ate *a* rice"), adjectives on nouns (I cannot say "*The apple is *happy* today"), and adverbs on verbs (it would be meaningless to say "*I slept really *fast*"). In particular, the use of the definite article carries the presupposition that the following noun phrase is in the interlocutor's domain of knowledge (Kamp & Reyle 1993: 164, 253; Zeevat 1992). The semantic characteristic distinguishing the definite from the indefinite article is the interlocutor's possibility of individuating the referent in the context or in his previous knowledge.

2.2. *Sentence Presuppositions: Syntactic Presuppositions*

At the level of the sentence, presuppositions can be also triggered by syntactic elements such as conjunctions or prepositions, or particular syntactic constructions, such as cleft sentences. In Frege's view, presupposition is not limited to existential presupposition triggered by the determinative article, but also includes facts that are presupposed by the use of certain adverbs or prepositions. For instance, consider the following cases (Frege 1948: 224, 222):

2. After Schleswig-Holstein was separated from Denmark, Prussia and Austria quarrelled.
3. He who discovered the elliptic form of the planetary orbits died in misery.

In (2), the use of the conjunction 'after' imposes a precondition on the sentence, namely that Schleswig-Holstein was separated from Denmark. Should that condition fail, as Frege pointed out, it is impossible to place the event of the quarrel between Prussia and Austria in a temporal context, and therefore verify it. Similarly, the verifiability of (3) depends on the truth of the presupposition that "someone has discovered the elliptic form of the planetary orbits." In this case it is the restrictive use of the relative clause that imposes a factual precondition. Also prepositions (when used not as syntactic markers of an argument, but with a proper meaning; see Rigotti & Cigada 2004) can be described as predicates imposing specific conditions on their arguments. For instance, we can consider the following sentences:

4. I am walking in the park with John.
5. *I am walking in the park with Australia.

In this case, the preposition 'with' is a predicate that may have the meaning of 'accompanying,' 'having,' 'being characterized by,' 'owing to,' 'availing himself of,' and so on, and connects two arguments: an action, a condition, or a state of affairs and an entity.

Another crucial dimension of sentence presuppositions is the semantic–syntactic distinction between topic and focus. In his analysis of existential presuppositions, Strawson noticed that reference failures caused truth-value gaps when they were about the sentence topic (Strawson 1971: 71). He noticed a fundamental difference between (1) and the following sentence (Strawson 1971: 67):

1. The king of France is bald.
6. The exhibition was visited yesterday by the King of France.

While (1) cannot be true or false if the king of France does not exist, in such a circumstance (6) will be simply untrue. The difference lies in the role of the definite description. In (6) it is part of the focus, in (1) it constitutes the topic: what the sentence is about. According to the old dichotomy drawn by Jackendoff (1972), sentences are functionally organized in a topic and a functional predicate, the rheme, indicating what the speaker expresses about the topic. The topic, or theme, is presupposed, or taken for granted by the speaker, while the rheme is stated (Karimi 2003: 170; Gundel & Fretheim 2004; Rebuschi & Tuller 1999). The presuppositional analysis of the distinction between topic and focus (Gundel & Fretheim 2004) was applied to more complex syntactic cases, in which the topic is manifested syntactically through cleft sentences or morphophonemically through contrastive stress (Hockett 1950). For instance, we consider the following example (Green 1996: 74):

7. It was in Los Angeles that the Sixters beat the Lakers.

This sentence, which also can be expressed through contrastive stress ("The Sixters beat the Lakers IN LOS ANGELES"; see Chomsky 1971: 205; Kempson 1975: 192), thematically presupposes that "the Sixters beat the Lakers" (Szwedek 1980: 96; Kempson 1975: 50). From this perspective, the sentence topic can be considered to be the trigger of presuppositions, as it indicates the prerequisites of the sentence (see Wilson 1975: 39, 53; Keenan 1971: 43; Hamblin 1970: 275).

2.3. *Inter-Sentence Presuppositions*
Presuppositions can be triggered by predicates of a higher level, the connectives (Karttunen 1973: 176). In this case, the arguments are both discourse sequences, and they presuppose specific relations between them. For instance, we can consider the following famous case (R. Lakoff 1971: 133):

8. John is tall, but he is no good at basketball.

Lakoff notices that (8) is composed of an assertion (John is tall, and he is no good at basketball) and a presupposition (If someone is tall, then one would expect him to be good at basketball). The effect is a denial of expectation, which was described by Ducrot as the contradiction by the second conjunct of a presupposed conclusion (in this case, "John is good at basketball") (Ducrot 1978).

Other types of connectives, such as 'therefore,' specify more precisely the type of relationship between the sequences. For instance, the predicate 'therefore' presupposes that the first sequence is a reason supporting the second one (see also Grice 1975: 44). Let's consider the following case:

9. (A) Bob murdered his friend. (B) Therefore he is a criminal.

The predicate 'therefore' expresses a relation of motivation (see Rigotti & Rocci 2006), but it needs to be specified further. The relation of motivation needs to support the attribution of a quality (to be a criminal) to the same subject of the previous sentence (A). The predication of a quality on the basis of actions or qualities attributed to the same subject usually can be presumed to be a classification. Obviously, the specification of the relation depends on several factors, such as the type of property attributed (the structure of the predicate 'to be a $P(x)$' in (B) indicates more clearly a relation of classification). This relation requires that the quality or event expressed in the first sentence represents a classificatory, or definitional, principle for the attribution of the quality in the second sentence (Bierwisch 1969; Kempson 1975: 109–110). In this specific case, the fact, event, or quality needs to instantiate a definition, or definitional principle, of 'to be a criminal.' We represent the structure of the presuppositions as shown in Figure 5.1.

The abstract relation of coherence (Hobbs 1979; Asher & Lascarides 2003: chapter 7), in this case motivation, is further specified according to the levels of analysis of the sentences. Obviously, this definitional principle is grounded on more shared definitions, of the kind "A criminal is someone who breaks the law," and classifications ("Murder is illegal"). The last step is the specification of the presupposition that in this case corresponds to a definitional principle of murder.

In both coordination and subordination text sequences are connected in a similar fashion. In subordination the predicate is explicit and imposes a set of specific coherence conditions, or presuppositions (classified as pragmatic presuppositions, see Vanderveken 2002: 47; Bach 2003: 163), on its arguments (Grimes 1975: 162). In coordination, an explicit or implicit predicate hides a deeper relationship (Ballard, Conrad & Longacre 1971), or rather a "high level notion" (Polanyi 1985: 4; Hobbs 1985) that needs to be reconstructed in order to understand the role and the conditions of the discourse segments or sequences. For instance, the connective 'and'

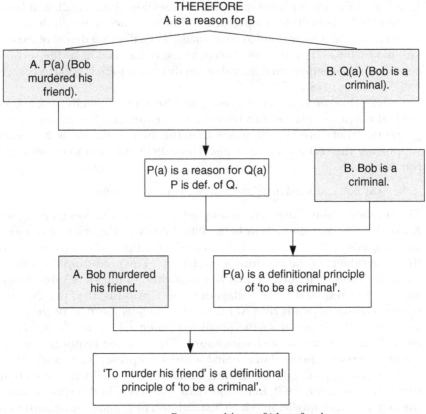

FIGURE 5.1. Presuppositions of 'therefore'

presupposes a common relevance or topic (R. Lakoff 1971: 128; Kempson 1975: 58). Let's consider the following cases (Kempson 1975: 56, 61):

10. The Lone Ranger rode off into the sunset and mounted his horse.
11. Pope John is dying and the cat is in the bath.

Both sentences are unsound and somehow nonsensical because a relationship between the two conjuncts seems to be missing, or rather is unavailable to the interlocutors in normal conditions. In (10) the conjunction presupposes a temporal sequence that is impossible, while in (11) the (causal) relationship cannot even be retrieved. These cases show how coordination can express temporal, causal, explanation relations (see Hobbs 1985; Lascarides & Asher 1993), imposing specific requirements on their sequences, such as a causal or temporal order of the sequences.

2.4. *Dialogical Presuppositions*
The last type of presupposition is relative to the use of a sentence in a dialogue to perform a specific act. At this pragmatic level, sentence and inter-sentence

presuppositions become necessary conditions for the felicity of the move. In addition to these semantic and syntactic requirements, other prerequisites are imposed by abstract predicates representing the interlocutors' communicative intentions and also involving specific background knowledge concerning the agents' roles, interests, and expectations.

This view was introduced by Austin, who maintained that the falsity of presuppositions represents the failure of some conditions of speech act, on which a particular type of meaningfulness depends (Austin 1962: 50–51):

Next let us consider presupposition: what is to be said of the statement that 'John's children are all bald' if made when John has no children? It is usual now to say that it is not false because it is devoid of reference; reference is necessary for either truth or falsehood. (Is it then meaningless? It is not so in every sense: it is not, like a 'meaningless sentence', ungrammatical, incomplete, mumbo-jumbo, &c.) People say 'the question does not arise'. Here I shall say 'the utterance is void'.

Considering presuppositions as a condition of a speech act, Austin noted how they not only stem from the use of determinative articles, adverbs, or prepositions but can be extended to a wide set of conditions that make a communicative move 'meaningful.' For instance, just as it is possible 'to inform' my interlocutor of a fact only if he can understand it by placing it in a certain place and at a certain time, the speech act of 'appointing' someone is not possible if the speaker is not entitled to do so, or if the appointee has already been appointed, or is not a person (Austin 1962: 34, 51). Just as it is meaningless to 'appoint' a horse, the appointment of a person as CEO of a company would be infelicitous (and void) if performed by a regular employee. Speech acts on this perspective have several types of presuppositions, including procedures (Austin 1962: 30), roles, and institutions in addition to factual, categorical, and existential requirements. Following Austin, if we broaden the picture of presupposition, we can notice that sentences are always in a conversational context, which not only includes the interlocutors and their roles but also their communicative intention, the dialogical rules (or procedures, interpreting Austin's concept), their values and preferences (it would be in most contexts infelicitous to say, "*Cheer up, I will fire you tomorrow!", unless the speaker is presumed to be inclined toward sadism) and the previous moves performed in the dialogue uttered (see Searle & Vanderveken 1985: 66–67).

At the pragmatic level, the interlocutor as a person becomes an element in the structure of the act. His desires and interest need to be considered as presuppositions of the act. For instance, we can consider the following example by Ducrot (1966: 46):

If, during a conversation, I abruptly say, "I have met Pierre this morning," my sentence is linguistically absurd if my interlocutor is not interested in Pierre.

As Ducrot puts it, such an assertion presupposes the interlocutor's interest (and therefore the interlocutors' acquaintance) just like the sentence

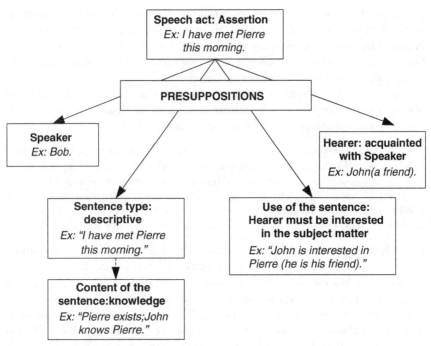

FIGURE 5.2. Structure of speech act presuppositions

"The king of France is bald" presupposes the existence of the king of France (see Ducrot 1966: 46). If we consider speech acts, the structure of the presupposition becomes wider, to include the participants in the dialogue. We can represent such a structure as shown in Figure 5.2.

We can represent presuppositions on two levels: the presuppositions triggered by the speech act of *using* the sentence as an assertion, and the presuppositions triggered by the *sentence*.

Considering speech acts as the interlocutors' communicative intentions in a dialogue leads to another consequence in the analysis of presupposition. The assertion "I have met Pierre this morning" cannot be understood in this perspective as a disconnected remark; on the contrary, it opens up certain possibilities of reply (such as "Ah, really?" or "What did he say?") and excludes others (it would be hardly meaningful, or rather felicitous, to reply "I have eaten an apple" unless I want to implicitly point out the lack of relevance of my interlocutor's act). Grice noticed that every speech act is a cooperative effort to comply with the requirements needed to reach a common dialogical purpose (Grice 1975: 45):

Our talk exchanges do not normally consist of a succession of disconnected remarks, and would not be rational if they did. They are characteristically, to some degree at least, cooperative efforts; and each participant recognizes in them, to some extent, a common purpose or set of purposes, or at least a mutually accepted direction. This

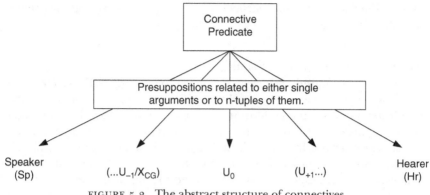

FIGURE 5.3. The abstract structure of connectives

purpose or direction may be fixed from the start (e.g., by an initial proposal of a question for discussion), or it may evolve during the exchange; it may be fairly definite, or it may be so indefinite as to leave very considerable latitude to the participants (as in a casual conversation). But at each stage, SOME possible conversational moves would be excluded as conversationally unsuitable.

From this view, every speech act needs to be interpreted within a dialogical setting, in which the interlocutors contribute to a common goal. It would be "unsuitable" to answer a question regarding the location of a specific monument with a remark on the weather or with a question on the economic situation. This common purpose can be interpreted as a higher level predicate connecting the discourse moves, which Grimes referred to as a rhetorical predicate (Grimes 1975: 209ff), later named a logical-semantic connective (Crothers 1979; Rigotti 2005) or a coherence relation (Hobbs 1979: 68, 1985), representing dialogical purposes such as explanation, alternative, support, and so on. From a pragmatic perspective, these relations can be considered as high-level speech acts (Grice 1989: 362; Carston 2002: 107–108), imposing a set of presuppositions, or felicity conditions, on the first-level speech acts (Vanderveken 2002: 28; Wüest 2001). These predicates can be either expressed or implicit, and like normal predicates they are characterized by some conditions that have to be fulfilled. If we conceive the relation between sentences as a relation between predicates and arguments, we could represent the abstract structure of connectives as shown in Figure 5.3 (Rigotti 2005: 83).

Consider, for instance, the following move:

12. Bob is a thief. He stole a wallet.

Here the speaker advances the second sequence in order to support the acceptability of the first one, which in its turn is aimed at eliciting a value judgment on Bob. The hearer needs to understand the intention of the speaker in order to understand the link between the moves. He needs to consider the common ground associated with the concept of stealing and being a thief, and then reconstruct the missing premise linking the premise with the conclusion.

2.5. *Summary: Levels of Presupposition*

Pragmatic presuppositions have been shown to be triggered at different levels of discourse. They can be conditions of the use of semantic or syntactic predicates, on which the well-formedness of sentences depends. They can be requirements imposed by connectors on the sentences they link. Or they can be dialogical preconditions, set by an abstract discourse relation on the dialogical moves, the participants, the context, and the possible future moves. The scope of presupposition is different according to the level of its triggers. Predicates can only impose categorical or existential presuppositions on their logical and semantic arguments. For instance, by using a predicate such as 'acknowledge' I can take for granted that the state of affairs acknowledged is true. At a higher level of sentence organization, I can distinguish between the roles of topic and focus. Intonation here works as a predicate of a kind, separating the functional subject, taken for granted, from the functional predicate. At a higher level of discourse organization I can also presuppose that a whole sequence has a specific purpose. For instance, by using the predicate 'therefore' I can take for granted that the antecedent is a reason supporting the consequent. Finally, discourse relations impose conditions on dialogical moves, the interlocutors, their background knowledge, and their future moves. All these presuppositions can be used from a dialectical and strategic perspective.

3. How to Presuppose

Presuppositions are the foundation of discourse. When we talk, discuss, or try to persuade our interlocutor, we leave most of the information needed to communicate implicit: We simply pragmatically presuppose it. We never remind our interlocutor of the definitions of the words that we use; we never describe people, things, or places that our interlocutor may know, or we think he may know. We draw conclusions from conditional premises that we very rarely express; we take turns speaking and prove a point without telling why we act in such a fashion, without stating the rules governing our discussion. However, presuppositions also can be used strategically. Their strategic effect derives from the fact that they can present a state of affairs or some qualities as granted, as accepted by the interlocutor. For this reason, the speaker can use them to provide some specific information without taking on the responsibility for it and present a standpoint as an accepted premise by avoiding the burden of proving it, or committing the hearer to a controversial or unacceptable proposition. These strategies are commonly used in political or ordinary discourse, but the absence of clear rules of dialogue in such contexts make it difficult to analyze the effects and the conditions of such moves. On the contrary, legal discourse provides a clear description of the dialectical consequences and requirements of the different presuppositional tactics. Analyzing strategic presuppositional moves in law can provide a detailed framework of their possible uses.

3.1. *Sentence Presuppositions*

As noticed previously, presuppositions can be triggered at a sentence, inter-sentence, or dialogue level. The type of presupposed information varies according to the nature of the triggering predicate.

The first level consists in the use of a predicate that requires specific conditions to be fulfilled. For instance, consider the following case (*State v. Childs*, 422 P.2d 898, 1967):

CASE 1. SENTENCE PRESUPPOSITIONS – PREDICATES (VERBS AND NOUNS)

Patton was then asked if he had ever had occasion to show pictures of the defendant to anyone, and he replied, "I did. I secured mug shots – " Defense counsel objected to the term "mug shots" as going to the "character" of the defendant.

This answer was given in cross-examination, where character evidence is excluded. The examined person could not introduce elements providing information about the previous criminal activity of the defendant. In this case, Mr. Patton did not *state* anything that could affect the defendant's credibility and character. He simply used the expression "to secure mug shots." He presupposed that the defendant had been portrayed in mug shots, which in their turn presuppose that the person portrayed in the picture had been arrested. The presupposition required by the complex predicate 'to take mug shots of' is in fact that the object is an arrested person.

A similar case can be found in the following excerpt from a cross-examination (*United States v. Stockdale*, 13 C.M.R. 546, 1953):

CASE 2. SENTENCE PRESUPPOSITIONS – PREDICATES

The first question of Trial Counsel on cross-examination of the accused was as follows: (R. 67.):

"Q. Stockdale, when did you first think up this story about this man handing you this package?"

Here the examiner uses a combination of two presuppositional triggers. He uses the predicate 'to think up,' presupposing that the object is not true, or not existent. In this fashion, he takes for granted that the fact at stake did not correspond to reality, which was the point to be proved. However, the examiner did not limit to advance a claim. He took the object of the whole accusation as a shared fact. He achieved this goal by using another type of sentence presupposition, grounded on the distinction between theme and rheme, or topic and focus. For instance, in the sentence "The defendant thought up the story **yesterday**," the presupposed information is that "the defendant thought up the story" while the rheme is that "the invention of the story happened yesterday." Questions on this view are instruments for obtaining the completion of the rheme. For instance, in the aforementioned question, the presupposed information is that the interlocutor actually thought up the whole story.

These types of questions are sometimes abusively used in cross-examinations or police investigations to elicit unwanted or false testimonies that can be used against the witness or to support a specific conclusion. For instance, the following question, asked by an officer of the defendant after a road accident (*State v. Frank*, 82AP-501, 1983):

CASE 3. SENTENCE PRESUPPOSITIONS – THEME

Why are you high?

This question requires an explanation of a fact presupposed to be true (defendant is high) but not proved or previously admitted. For this reason, when they are detected they are usually forbidden, or can lead to mistrial.

The distinction between theme and rheme is one of the most used and powerful instruments in law for taking states of affairs or events for granted. In this fashion, as seen previously, unsupported or inadmissible evidence can be presented as a fact that is known by everybody. Moreover, possible inferences or unsupported explanations can be taken as known information, and therefore can be treated as facts. For instance, in the following case a speculation is presupposed and presented to the jury as an established fact (*Commonwealth v. Rodriguez*, 437 Mass. 554, 565, 2002) (emphasis added):

CASE 4. SENTENCE PRESUPPOSITION – INFRA-SENTENCE SYNTACTIC PREDICATES

In his closing argument the prosecutor argued: "[The defendant] entered the store with a knife and **a bag**, and a hat **for a disguise**. ... He took **the baseball hat**. He took the bag, the tools of the trade of a robbery, and he headed out the door. ... I ask you, Ladies and Gentlemen, when an individual walks into a store armed with a knife and **a bag** of sufficient room to carry money, and a hat **to cover a distinctive scar over his eye**, is that consistent with somebody who doesn't know what he is doing ...?"

The prosecutor here is simply drawing inferences from pieces of evidence. He treats his speculation (the defendant wore a hat because he needed to cover a distinctive scar) as a fact. The defendant's very intention to rob the bank (and therefore act in disguise) was disputed throughout the trial, and was not proven or admitted.

3.2. *Intra-Sentence Presuppositions*

The two aforementioned strategies of presupposition are based on the sentence structure and are extremely evident. Loaded words can be easily detected, and the theme of questions and statements is expressed, even though it is introduced as part of common knowledge. In some cases the presupposed proposition needs to be hidden more deeply to conceal the speaker's intention. These subtler strategies can be grounded on inter-sequence presuppositions, which are more difficult to detect and leave the speaker more room for a possible defense or for denying his communicative intention. For instance, consider the following move *People v. Aguirre*, 684 N.E.2d 1375, 1376, 1997):

CASE 5. INTER-SEQUENCES PRESUPPOSITIONS – CONNECTORS

BY MS. MOE [Assistant State's Attorney]:

Question. But you told the police, you yourself said to the police, 'It's my gun,' is that correct?
Answer. Yes.

Question. And you are willing to suffer any consequences for that statement, is that correct?
Answer. Yes.

Question. Now, you are very good friends with Frankie, the defendant at the table?
Answer. No. I hardly know him.

Question. You hardly know him. But you are willing to take the fall for this, is that right?

In this case, the use of the conjunction 'but' presupposes that the second sentence, stating the witness's intention to get imprisoned for his confession made to help the defendant, is contradictory with the extraneousness between the two individuals (the defendant and the witness). The propositions that the use of 'but' presupposes are "You therefore are not willing to help him" and "Your confession is contradictory with your testimony." These presuppositions place on the examined person a burden of disproving an accusation that could not be otherwise expressed in cross-examination.

Connectors can be used in interrogative sentences to generate more complex presuppositions. One of the most known cases is the so-called disjunctive questions, where the connector 'or' forces the hearer to an obliged choice between two possibilities, presupposing that the paradigm of the possible answers corresponds to the advanced options. This presupposition can also combine with a topical presupposition, as in the following case (*People v. Aguirre*, 684 N.E.2d 1375, 1376, 1997):

CASE 6: INTER-SEQUENCE PRESUPPOSITION – DISJUNCTIVE
QUESTIONS

The prosecutor began her cross-examination with the following question: "Did you
come up with the story that we heard today or did Mr. Potkonjak [defense counsel]
come up with the story that we heard today?"

In this case the presupposition "the story was invented" is strengthened by
the disjunctive question excluding the possibility of a negative answer by
the witness.

3.3. *Dialogical Presuppositions*

The last type of predicate is dialogical in nature. They connect discourse
moves and can be explicit or implicit. In the first case, they presuppose
a set of previous moves and background knowledge that can be found
considering not simply the meaning and the role of the previous sentence but also prior or subsequent dialogue exchanges. For instance,
consider the following case (*United States v. Dixon*, 38 Fed. Appx. 549,
2002):

CASE 7: DIALOGICAL PRESUPPOSITIONS – EXPLICIT
CONNECTORS

So, if during deliberations, the jury were to look at that [bank security video tape]
and see you reaching over and taking the money like that, you're telling us that
would be the wrong conclusion, correct?

The force of this question does not only lie in the presupposed information that the defendant actually committed the crime (such a proposition
was supported by sufficient evidence and therefore did not amount to the
questioner's misconduct). The crucial problem lies in the relationship
between the question and the (unstated) previous testimony. By using the
connector 'so' the speaker presupposes that the question is a conclusion
drawn from previous evidence (see also Max 2008). The speaker presupposes that in previous instances the defendant also denied the truth of
clearly true facts.

The last type of presupposition trigger considered is the implicit connector. While explicit connectors are predicates of a kind, whose presuppositions are part of their meaning, implicit connectors need to be
reconstructed starting from the intended purpose of the dialogue move.
For this reason, they are at a dialogical level, which includes the speaker's
intentions. The relationship between the propositions is left to the reconstruction of the interlocutor. For instance, connectors indicating consequence or explanation are often left unexpressed and the meaning of the
statement is retrieved by reconstructing the implicit connector. Consider
the following case (*West v. Seabold*, 73 F.3d 81, 1996 at 86):

CASE 8: INTER-SENTENCE PRESUPPOSITIONS – IMPLICIT CONNECTORS

(Trans. at 1081, J.A. at 391) The prosecutor also implied that the victim's mother had something to hide because she called her lawyer right after the shooting:

> Why did she need a lawyer? Innocent people don't need lawyers. Justice will prevail.

Here the relationship between the moves can be understood only as a conjunction of premises leading to an implicit conclusion. A connector that can be represented as 'therefore' is left unexpressed in order to hide the needed conclusion, retrieved by innuendo. The prosecutor presupposes that the lady's need of a lawyer conflicted with the fact that innocent people do not need a lawyer, presupposing the existence of a conclusion that can be drawn from the negation of the expressed general principle of innocence. In this case, the relationships between the discourse moves are governed by abstract predicates, which can be retrieved by reconstructing the speaker's intention, articulated in different acts. The implicit connectors do not specify a further move but presuppose its existence as a conclusion from the previous premises.

4. The Dialectical and Rhetorical Force of Presupposition: The Act of Presupposing

Presuppositions represent the conditions that need to be fulfilled to construct a text that is semantically and pragmatically cohesive. This description is a purely structural perspective, as it indicates the structure of the predicate–argument relation. However, we need to enlarge the picture in order to explain the mechanism of presupposing redefinitions, making a sentence a fragment of dialogue in which the speaker and the hearer interact and take turns. We therefore need to analyze the act of presupposing from a pragmatic perspective, assess it from an epistemic point of view, and evaluate its dialectical effects.

4.1. *The Act of Presupposing*

As seen previously, the common characteristic of all the presuppositional phenomena is that a proposition p is presupposed when it is taken for granted in performing a speech act, whose felicity depends on the interlocutor's acceptance of p. To presuppose a proposition is "to take its truth for granted, and to assume that others involved in the context do the same" (Stalnaker 1970: 279). This "taking a proposition for granted" has been analyzed by Stalnaker as a propositional attitude, which can be interpreted as an action of a kind (Stalnaker 2002: 701):

Speaker presupposition is a propositional attitude of the speaker, but I and others who have emphasized the role of speaker presupposition in the explanation of

linguistic phenomena have been vague and equivocal about exactly what propositional attitude it is. To presuppose something is to take it for granted, or at least
to act as if one takes it for granted, as background information – as *common ground*
among the participants in the conversation.

Therefore, presuppositions are *made* by the speakers (Stalnaker 1970: 279), in
the sense that presupposing a proposition amounts to a form of decision made
by the speaker to treat some information as already known by the interlocutor.
This idea of analyzing presuppositions in terms of their effects, and relating
them to the speaker's intentions, is also developed by Kempson (1975). She
maintains that presupposing a proposition amounts to treating it as belonging
to the common knowledge, or the Universe of Discourse. For instance, the
utterance of a sentence containing a definite noun-phrase (used as a topic)
implies "(a) that the speaker believes that there is an object to which the noun
phrase refers, (b) that the speaker believes that the hearer believes that there
is an object to which the noun phrase refers, and (c) the speaker believes that
the hearer knows which object is referred to" (Kempson 1975: 17; see also
the weaker definition set forth in Stalnaker 1974: 200, in which the hearer is
simply assumed or believed to believe p and to recognize that the speaker is
making this assumption). However, this implication is "deliberately invoked"
by the speaker, who "wishes to convey that the hearer knows what object he is
intending to refer to" (Kempson 1975: 180). From these accounts two crucial
elements emerge: (1) A presupposition can be considered as a form of *decision*
to treat a proposition as shared, and (2) presuppositions are crucially related
to the speaker and hearer's beliefs and knowledge (Schwarz 1977: 248).
However, the definition of a linguistic phenomenon in terms of beliefs or
assumptions risks confounding the phenomenon with its accidental effects or
possible explanations. How can a speaker believe or assume that a proposition
is shared by the hearer? How would it be possible to presuppose propositions
that are *known not to be shared*, without the sentence being meaningless?
    A possible explanation of presupposition in non-epistemic terms can
be proposed by developing the first characteristic that the previously mentioned accounts seem to suggest: the nature of a presupposition as a kind
of act. Presupposing a proposition can be described as the performance
of an implicit speech act, in which the speaker subordinates the felicity
of his move to the listener's acceptance of some conditions. This idea was
put forward by Ducrot, who described presupposition as the set of conditions that need to be fulfilled in order to satisfy the pretension of carrying
out an effect on the listener (see Ducrot 1966). On this view, their failure, determined by the interlocutor's rejection, causes the infelicity of a
communicative move (or speech act). In such an event a move becomes
simply void, that is, it cannot be considered as a move anymore. Such conditions limit the field of possible moves of the interlocutor. For instance,
if he accepts the assertion that "I have met Pierre this morning," he also
implicitly agrees to a conversational situation in which the topic is *Pierre*.

On the contrary, if the hearer refuses the presupposition, he terminates the dialogue game. Ducrot accounted for this pragmatic effect of presupposition by defining it as an implicit speech act (Ducrot 1968: 87)[2]:

> Comme le joueur d'échecs doit accepter le champ de possibilités que crée pour lui la manœuvre de son adversaire, le participant d'un dialogue doit reprendre à son compte certains au moins des présupposés introduits par les phrases auxquelles il répond.

Ducrot claimed that speech acts need to be divided into an explicit act of stating (the *posé*) and an implicit act of presupposing (the *présupposé*). This latter act is aimed at setting the possible moves that can be performed by the interlocutor, that is, the possible dialogical world (Stalnaker 1970: 280) that determines the boundaries of the linguistic moves (Ducrot 1972b).[3] From this view, the act of presupposing sets the conditions of a dialogue game (Ducrot 1972a: 91):

> Présupposer un certain contenu, c'est placer l'acceptation de ce contenu comme la condition du dialogue ultérieur. On voit alors pourquoi le choix des présupposés nous apparaît comme un acte de parole particulier (que nous appelons acte de présupposer), acte à valeur juridique et donc illocutoire [...] : en accomplissant, on transforme du même coup les possibilités de parole de l'interlocuteur. [...] Lorsqu'on introduit des présupposés dans un énoncé, on fixe, pour ainsi dire, le prix à payer pour que la conversation puisse continuer[4].

By analyzing presuppositions as acts, it is possible to explain how and why the speaker can treat a proposition as part of the common ground even if it is not. While assertion can be counted as a proposal to add a proposition p to the shared propositions (see Von Fintel 2008: 139), a presupposition

---

[2] "Just as a chess player needs to accept the field of possibilities that the move of his opponent opens up, the participant to a dialogue needs to accept at least some of the presuppositions introduced by the sentences to which he replies (translation by the author).

[3] In Ducrot's view, the communicative game resembles a chess game, in which the possibilities are set by means of presuppositions: "dans ce combat simulé –qui substitue aux possibilités réelles, dues à la force, les possibilités morales dues aux conventions- les règles permettent aux joueurs de se contraindre mutuellement à certaines actions, et de s'en interdire certaines autres." (Ducrot 1968: 83); "pour trouver une description sémantique satisfaisante d'un phénomène comme la présupposition, phénomène qui est repérable selon des critères syntaxiques précis, il nous a été nécessaire de la relier aux règles qui définissent conventionnellement le jeu du langage, et de décrire la présupposition par rapport aux manœuvres dont elle fournit le thème : sa réalité, comme celle d'une règle des échecs, consiste seulement à rendre possible un jeu. " (Ducrot 1972: 27).

[4] To presuppose a certain content amounts to treating the acceptance of such a content as the condition of the continuation of the dialogue. It is clear then why we regard the choice of the presuppositions as a specific speech act (that we call act of presupposing), an act that carries a legal value, and thereby illocutionary [...]: by performing it, the dialogical possibilities of the interlocutor are immediately modified. [...] When the speaker introduces some presuppositions in a sentence, he fixes the price for the continuation of the dialogue. (Translation of the author)

can be considered as the act of treating p as already shared (see Horn & Ward 2004: xii; Atlas 2004; Lewis 1979: 339). Such an act does not depend on what the interlocutors actually share or on what the speaker believes (Burton-Roberts 1989: 26). A proposition that has been assumed as not shared can be presupposed in the sense that it has been advanced as a condition or ground of the dialogue.

4.2. *The Worlds Presupposed*

The analysis of presupposition as an act separates the linguistic phenomena eliciting it from its dialogical effects, and its effects from its epistemic conditions. These dimensions appear when we analyze the different types of 'worlds' of discourse that can be presupposed. For instance, consider the following case (Barack Obama, Nobel Peace Prize Acceptance Address, Oslo, Norway December 10, 2009):

PRESUPPOSITION 1: CHOOSING A FRAGMENT OF A KNOWN WORLD

And yet I would be remiss if I did not acknowledge the considerable controversy that your generous decision has generated.

Here Obama uses the predicate 'to acknowledge' to presuppose the truth of the argument, "the considerable controversy." He presupposes a fact that everybody in his audience knows or should know, as his nomination raised quite a few debates and discussions. With his move he indicates and chooses the world of discourse in which he is putting forward his speech, and therefore justifies his further moves aimed at explaining the peaceful role played by a war-monger nation.

Presuppositions can also impose a new world of discourse, and not simply select a fragment of a shared one. For instance, further on in his discourse Obama advanced the following claim:

PRESUPPOSITION 2: DISPLAYING A POTENTIALLY UNKNOWN WORLD

I believe that the United States of America must remain a standard bearer in the conduct of war. That is why I prohibited torture. That is why I ordered the prison at Guantanamo Bay closed. And that is why I have reaffirmed America's commitment to abide by the Geneva Conventions.

Obama addressed an international audience (the whole world interested in the Nobel Prize in fact), among which many might not know Obama's previous resolutions on torture, Guantanamo Bay (which is in its turn presupposed to be against the conduct of war), and the Geneva Conventions. By framing the topic, or theme, of his assertions, he takes for granted all his decisions and the fact that the situation they eventually changed was against the rules of war (see Hamblin 1970: 275). He does more than simply select a shared world; he displays a potentially unknown one. He implicitly informs a potentially unaware audience of all his decisions taken to comply with an ideal of war fought pursuant to certain rules, and of his modification of previous incompliant conditions.

Presuppositions can also impose a potentially controversial and unaccepted world. For instance, in the same speech Obama knew of the many controversies regarding the American intervention in Afghanistan, especially the ones regarding the invasion of a state not directly responsible for an aggression (O'Connell 2002). However, he advanced the following claim:

PRESUPPOSITION 3: DISPLAYING A POTENTIALLY
UNACCEPTABLE WORLD

The world rallied around America after the 9/11 attacks, and continues to support our efforts in Afghanistan, because of the horror of those senseless attacks and the recognized principle of self-defense.

Here Obama presupposes that the war in Afghanistan was fought for self-defence, and that this was the reason that led other nations to support the American intervention. Instead of tackling the controversial issue, Obama simply sets it as a condition shared and accepted. This use of presupposition amounts to imposing a world of discourse that the interlocutor is presumed to consider as not acceptable.

In Ducrot's view, by presupposing the speaker modifies the dialogical situation and sets the boundaries of the interlocutor's future actions (Ducrot 1972b). Presupposing therefore can be conceived as setting the conditions for the continuation of the future dialogue game (Ducrot 1972a: 91). Not accepting a presupposition amounts to ending the dialogue, something like knocking over the chessboard. However, this perspective is purely from the point of view of the structure of the dialogue move, and not from its possibility. A speech act of the kind "My brother is feeling bad today" would not make sense if the interlocutor knows that I am an only child. The speech act would simply fail to accomplish its dialogical purpose, that is, to inform the interlocutor. In order to account for the effect of a move, and therefore its possibility conditions and fallacious uses, it is necessary to take into consideration the relationship between the speaker and the hearer's knowledge.

5. The Limits of Presuppositions

The cases in the previous section show how we cannot think of presupposition in terms of what is known, or what is believed to be known. It is possible to presuppose a proposition that is known to be potentially unshared, or potentially unacceptable, or, as Ducrot pointed out, false, without incurring a communicative failure or infelicity. Ducrot (1966: 42) noticed how it is possible to imagine the enemies of Caesar or Napoleon during the Roman consulate or the French Republic talking about the magnificence, or the richness, or the wisdom of the king. In this case the speaker was presupposing false or unshared propositions ("Caesar or Napoleon are kings"). However, their assertions, far from being void, might have caused them serious troubles for their meaning. This case illustrates a crucial problem concerning presuppositions, the possibility of treating as shared a proposition that is actually not granted or that does not belong to the hearer's common knowledge, called *accommodation* (see Lewis 1979; Von Fintel 2008). By analyzing the limits of such a process of reconstruction it is possible to understand the conditions characterizing the speech act of presupposition.

5.1. *Accommodation*

Accommodation was described by Lewis as a process of adjustment of the common ground, in which the presupposed proposition comes into existence when not previously known (Lewis 1979: 340):

> If at time *t* something is said that requires presupposition *P* to be acceptable and if *P* is not presupposed just before *t*, then – *ceteris paribus* and within certain limits – presupposition *P* comes into existence at *t*.

In this definition some boundaries of accommodation are mentioned without being specified. Lewis noticed that the process of reconstruction, or rather the process of bringing into existence presupposed propositions, is not totally free. For instance, in the previous cases the hearers of Caesar or Napoleon could retrieve the presupposed information. However, in that specific historical time the same people could not state that "The King of Myanmar is bald" without being infelicitous. The limits of accommodation have been investigated by Soames, who noticed that the presupposed propositions can be reconstructed only when they have already been accepted by the interlocutor, or they do not conflict with the interlocutor's common ground (Soames 1982: 486):

> Utterance Presupposition. An utterance *U* presupposes *P* (at *t*) iff one can reasonably infer from *U* that the speaker *S* accepts *P* and regards it as uncontroversial, either because
>
> a. *S* thinks that it is already part of the conversational context at *t*, or because
> b. *S* thinks that the audience is prepared to add it, without objection, to the context against which *U* is evaluated.

These conditions, however, are based on the speaker's beliefs about the interlocutor's common knowledge. In the previously mentioned Caesar and Napoleon cases, the speaker actually *knows* that the presupposition that "Caesar is a king" is not in the conversational context, and actually conflicts with the interlocutors' common knowledge.

5.2. *The Conditions of Accommodation*

In order to analyze the conditions of presupposition, it is useful to examine when a proposition can be presupposed, distinguishing between two different dimensions of accommodation, retrieval and acceptance, or rather possibility and reasonableness. Stalnaker (1998: 8) explains the first characteristic by claiming that the speaker can only *presume* that the presupposed information is *available* to his or her audience. In his view, the speaker can presuppose a proposition only because he or she can conclude that the interlocutor can retrieve such information. For instance, consider the following cases:

13. Bob was at the party too (no parties were mentioned before and the listener does not know who Bob is).

Let's consider such a sentence used in the aforementioned context. The presuppositions that "Hearer knows which party I am talking about" (triggered by 'the'), "Hearer knows who Bob is," and "Other people were at the party" (triggered by 'too') cannot be reconstructed without a specific dialogical context. Unless the party and Bob can be identified through the context, the presuppositions cannot be reconstructed and even the meaning cannot be retrieved. The hearer can obtain the information that there was a party and that there were other people at the party as they are "implicit contents" of the sentence (Bach 1999). However, if he does not know that there was a party, he cannot reconstruct the information "the aforementioned party" triggered by the determinative article. In (13) the speaker therefore presupposes two propositions that the hearer cannot accommodate because he cannot retrieve them. The possibility of reconstructing a presupposition was underscored by Asher and Lascarides, who claimed that the mere concept of adding a proposition to a context cannot explain why and how some presuppositions can be accommodated, and why others cannot. As they put it (Asher & Lascarides 1998: 255), "presuppositions must always be rhetorically bound to the context, rather than added." Presuppositions need to be related to the propositions already known, from which they may be derived through defeasible reasoning (Hobbs 1979; Asher & Lascarides 1998: 277). Building on this view, the *possibility* of reconstructing the presuppositions depends on the possibility of drawing them from the linguistic and pragmatic data provided by means of a pattern of reasoning. From this perspective, the reconstruction of a presupposition is essentially related with the plausible reasoning underlying its retrieval.

The second characteristic of accommodation is acceptability, which can be referred to as the major premise of the reasoning or its conclusion. The possibility of reconstructing a presupposed proposition depends on the possibility of abducing it by means of defeasible reasoning, and therefore on the existence of the premises supporting the conclusion. Sometimes the reasoning is possible because the premise allowing the hearer to reconstruct the proposition is provided, but the reasoning itself or the conclusion cannot be accepted by the interlocutor. For instance, consider the following cases (see Stalnaker 1998: 9):

14. I can't come to the meeting – I have to pick up my cat at the veterinarian.
15. My dog got an A in Math.

16. I have to pick up my Martian friend at the Voodoo club.
17. Bob is tall. Therefore he is really rich.

In (14) the hearer can reconstruct the fact that the speaker owns a cat and can accept both the reasoning (if someone has to pick up his cat, he owns a cat) and the conclusion (he can accept that usually people have pets). On the contrary, the presuppositions of (15), (16), and (17) are unacceptable (in an ordinary context) for different reasons. In (15) the accommodation reasoning is based on a conditional that cannot be accepted: "If x studies, then x can be a dog." This premise conflicts with semantic rules and therefore is simply known to be false. In (16) the reasoning can be acceptable, but the conclusion ("The speaker has a Martian friend") is hardly acceptable, as usually people maintain that Martians do not exist. Similarly, in (17) the conditional can be reconstructed, but normally height is not considered as leading to richness and therefore it cannot be accepted.

The *possibility* of presupposing needs therefore to be distinguished from the *acceptability* of a proposition taken for granted. Not only does the hearer need to be able to derive the missing information from the semantic, syntactic, pragmatic, and discursive conditions that the predicates impose on their arguments, but the presuppositions also should not conflict with what is commonly known and accepted, or with the propositions that the hearer knows to be true or acceptable. Both the reasoning and the conclusion of the reasoning need to be acceptable. As seen previously, the process of reconstructing a presupposition consists of a chain of reasoning from the sentence structure; such reasoning may be grounded on three different types of principles of inference: (1) undefeasible rules of reasoning (If x is an object, x has a surface; if x studies, then x is a human being); (2) defeasible but commonly accepted propositions (If there is a party, then there are guests; if x is an adult, then x may have a car); and (3) conditionals known to be false (If x studies, then x can be a dog). The same applies to the conclusions: Some propositions are definitional elements, and therefore true; others are simply accepted while others are usually considered as unacceptable.

5.3. *The Conditions of Presupposing*
By distinguishing the two dimensions of accommodation, the possibility and the acceptability, it is possible to distinguish between four different cases:

1. The presupposition can be reconstructed and accepted as a background assumption.
2. The presupposition cannot be reconstructed.
3. The presupposition can be reconstructed but the accommodation reasoning cannot be accepted.
4. The presupposition can be reconstructed but it cannot be accepted.

These possibilities allow us to outline the possible felicity conditions of the "speech act" of presupposing, building on Austin's and Searle and Vanderveken's accounts of speech act conditions (Austin 1962: 14–15; Searle & Vanderveken 1985: 13–19; Holtgraves 2008: 13). We refer to presupposition as a speech act in a metaphorical sense. It is not performed through speech, but rather *in* speech. It is a secondary kind of 'action' that can be indirectly, even though willingly, carried out through another direct speech act.

Essential Condition:	Speaker (*S*) sets the presupposed proposition (*pp*) as a condition of the felicity of his speech act (*SA*); if hearer (*H*) does not accept *pp*, *SA* will be void.
Propositional Condition:	*pp* is a proposition / fact / value / role that can be reconstructed by *H*.
Preparatory Condition:	*S* can presume that *H* can reconstruct and accept *pp*.
Sincerity Condition:	*S* believes that *pp*; *S* believes that *H* can reconstruct and know or accept *pp*.

This "speech act," having a direction of fit from the World (of the hearer) to the Words (of the speaker), is aimed at setting what the hearer needs to accept for the dialogue to continue. The possibility of reconstructing the presupposition is set as a propositional condition: *H* needs to be able to draw *pp* from the linguistic and pragmatic elements provided. The acceptability of the presupposition is expressed by both the preparatory and the sincerity conditions. The sincerity condition expresses the conditions set out in the tradition on pragmatic presupposition as essential, while the preparatory condition, expressed in terms of a presumption, is aimed at bridging the gap between the speaker's and hearer's minds from an epistemic and argumentative perspective, without resorting to the psychological notion of belief.

This treatment of presupposition as a kind of speech act can also explain the particular types of presuppositions, such as the previously mentioned Napoleon and Caesar cases. In these cases, the speaker can presume (and believe) that the hearer can reconstruct the presuppositions, but at the same time he presumes (and believes) that he cannot accept them. Ducrot described this phenomenon as a form of connotation, in which the utterance becomes a sign aimed at communicating the conditions of its use (see Ducrot 1968: 44). Interpreting this concept of connotation within the theory of speech acts, it is possible to analyze this particular use of presupposition as an indirect speech act, where the act setting out the conditions of a move needs to be interpreted as a type of assertive (Hickey 1993: 107).

The foundations and the dimensions of the speech act of presupposition arise from another important problem, the *reasonableness* of a speaker's presupposition. In our epistemological analysis we have only considered a sentence as a fact, and not as an act. If we analyze presuppositions as acts performed by a speaker, we need to find an answer to the crucial question, why and how can a speaker presuppose a proposition? Stalnaker (1974: 200), in his first definition mentioned previously, explained the speaker's presuppositions in terms of belief of knowledge. However, such an approach cannot explain why in some cases presupposing is reasonable while in others it is absurd, manipulative, or ridiculous. A possible alternative can be developed from the analysis of presuppositions from an argumentation perspective. Instead of considering the concept of belief of the other party's knowledge as the foundation of the speaker's presuppositions, we can conceive them as the outcome of a process of reasoning. From this perspective, the speaker can presuppose what it is reasonable to be considered as known: The reasonableness of presupposing depends on the reason supporting the fact that a premise *can* be shared.

6. Presuming Knowledge: Presupposition as Presumptive Reasoning

The conditions of the speech act of presupposition include two essential elements: the possibility of presupposing, which is grounded on the linguistic information provided and the hearer's background knowledge, and the acceptability of the accommodation reasoning and the presupposed proposition. These conditions present accommodation as a reasoning process that needs to be evaluated according to the hearer's knowledge. However, this account seems to fail to explain the crucial gap between the hearer's and the speaker's knowledge. How can the speaker predict that the hearer can reconstruct and accept a proposition? A possible answer lies in the preparatory condition, setting out that the speaker can *presume* that *H* can reconstruct and accept *pp*. This concept, partially hinted at by Strawson's presumption of knowledge (Strawson 1971: 58–59; Kempson 1975: 166–167), shifts the traditional psychological explanation onto an epistemic level. The speaker's *beliefs* of the hearer's acceptance or knowledge are replaced by a process of reasoning grounded on plausible premises, presumptive reasoning. From this perspective, the hearer's possibility and acceptability of reconstructing a presupposition correspond to the speaker's possibility and reasonableness of presupposing. From the speaker's perspective, the fulfillment of the conditions of the speech act of presupposing depends on presumptive reasoning. In order to presuppose a proposition *pp*, the speaker presumes that the hearer knows or accepts *pp*. The epistemic presumption of knowledge or acceptance becomes the requirement for the linguistic act of setting the conditions of a move. In order to explain this reasoning process, it is necessary to introduce presumptive reasoning and the speech act of presumption.

6.1. *Presumptive Reasoning*
Presupposition essentially involves a gap of knowledge, as the speaker cannot know the hearer's beliefs or values, or what he holds to be true. He can

only conclude that he holds such knowledge, beliefs, and values based on a form of guess, a pattern of reasoning in conditions of lack of knowledge that is called presumptive reasoning. Presumption can be considered as an inference with three components (Ullman-Margalit 1983: 147): (1) the presumption-raising fact in a particular case at issue; (2) the presumption formula, a defeasible rule that sanctions the passage from the presumed fact to the conclusion; and (3) the conclusion is a proposition that is presumed to be true on the basis of (1) and (2). Rescher outlined the structure of this type of inference as follows (Rescher 2006: 33):

Premise 1:	P (the proposition representing the presumption) obtains whenever the condition C obtains unless and until the standard default proviso D (to the effect that countervailing evidence is at hand) obtains (Rule).
Premise 2:	Condition C obtains (Fact).
Premise 3:	Proviso D does not obtain (Exception).
Conclusion:	P obtains.

The first essential element is the principle of inference, a rational principle supporting the conclusion (Ullman-Margalit 1983: 147), which "may be grounded on general experience or probability of any kind; or merely on policy and convenience" (Thayer 1898: 314). These principles describe what generally happens, what the speaker knows or perceives as governing usual correlations between facts or events. These presumption rules may be epistemic, pragmatic, or factual. The most common presumption rules are the factual ones, correlating facts or events not connected by a causal principle, but only by a usual co-occurrence. For instance, we go to the supermarket because we presume that it has not been destroyed, as things that are in a certain condition usually remain in such a condition (during a reasonable time). Pragmatic presumptions govern linguistic behavior and social actions. For instance, a word is presumed to be used with its conventional meaning, just as an insult is usually used to offend people. Finally, epistemic presumption rules predict what a person may know, including factual and pragmatic presumptions: For instance, usually people know who the president of the United States is, just as they know the rules governing the language and the usual connections between things and events.

The second element of presumptive reasoning is the lack of evidence. Presumptions are forms of reasoning that operate when proof is not available (Louisell 1977: 290), and for this reason their conclusion is only provisional (Rescher 1977: 1):

To presume in the presently relevant sense of the term is to accept something in the absence of the further relevant information that would ordinarily be deemed necessary to establish it. The term derives from the Latin *praesumere*: to take before or to take for granted.

As Rescher (1977: 2–3) put it, presumption is reasoning *in ignorance*, which can support the best possible solution when a conclusion needs to be reached in a circumstance in which it is not possible to reach a proof (cf. Dascal 2001; Blackstone 1769: 371). For instance, if a man has not been heard from for seven years, he is presumed to be dead. The reasoning is triggered in conditions of lack of evidence: The man is not *known* to be dead or alive; the only available information is the lack of any information on him.

The last element is strictly related to the condition of reasoning in ignorance. Presumptions are rebuttable in nature and provide only a provisional conclusion that needs to be relied upon until the contrary is proved (Blackstone 1769: 371), in the sense that the interlocutor needs to accept the conclusion unless he can provide evidence to the contrary or support to some extent the contrary conclusion. This characteristic of presumption was clearly described by Wigmore (1940: sec. 2491):

A presumption, as already noticed, is in its characteristic feature a rule of law laid down by the judge, and attaching to one evidentiary fact certain procedural consequences as to the duty of production of other evidence by the opponent. It is based, in policy, upon the probative strength, as a matter of reasoning and inference, of the evidentiary fact; but the presumption is not the fact itself, nor the inference itself, but the legal consequence attached to it. But, the legal consequence being removed, the inference, as a matter of reasoning, may still remain; and a 'presumption of fact', in the loose sense, is merely an improper term for the rational potency, or probative value, of the evidentiary fact, regarded as not having this necessary legal consequence. 'They are, in truth, but mere arguments,' and 'depend upon their own natural force and efficacy in generating belief or conviction in the mind.'

The interlocutor, in short, needs to provide contrary evidence or a contrary argument to reject the presumption; otherwise, he needs to accept commitment to the presumed proposition (Walton 1993: 139). Presumptions, therefore, have a fundamental effect on the dialogical setting: They shift the burden of producing evidence, or proving a proposition, onto the other party. For instance, in law a person missing for seven years is presumed to be dead. This does not mean that the person has been proved to be dead, but simply that the other party needs to provide contrary evidence in order to reject this fallible conclusion. The legal framework provides a general idea of the structure of this reasoning in everyday argumentation. Presumptions work to move the dialogue further when knowledge is lacking. Their role is simply to shift the burden of proof onto the other party, who can reject the proposition only by providing contrary arguments or positive facts leading to a contrary conclusion. If not rebutted, the speaker can consider it as tentatively proved, and move the dialogue further.

6.2. *Presumptions as Epistemic Bridges*

Presumptive reasoning can be considered as the argumentative bridge between the speaker's beliefs about the hearer's mind, and the actual knowledge, beliefs, and values of the speaker. Presupposition has been analyzed in terms of belief, or common or shared knowledge (see Kempson 1975: 166–169); however, how can the speaker know or believe that a piece of knowledge is common to, or *shared by the hearer*? The concepts of belief or common knowledge represent respectively the outcome and one of the possible grounds of the reasoning process that underlies presupposition (see Freeman 2005: 43). It is possible to believe that the other party may know a proposition on the basis of his previous declarations (testimony), or dialogues with other people, or because such a proposition is part of the so-called common knowledge. As Freeman put it (Freeman 2005: 346):

[...] the mark of common knowledge is that everyone, or virtually everyone, in an historical or cultural situation believes that statement. As we argued [...], common knowledge is presumptively reliable.

The speaker cannot know that a proposition is common *to* the hearer; he can only *presume* it based on the epistemic rules of presumption that he knows (Kauffeld 1995b: 509). For instance, he can presume that there is a king of France because he holds two basic premises: "People usually know basic information about an important country" and "The existence of a king of France is basic information about an important country." Similarly, a speaker can tell a friend that,

18. I met Bob yesterday

because he is presuming that the hearer knows Bob and he is interested in him; such presumptions proceed from the premises that "Common friends are usually known," "Information relative to a friend is interesting," and "Bob is a common friend" (Kauffeld 2003: 140; cf. Kauffeld 1995b: 510). We can represent the presumptive structure of presupposition as shown in Figure 5.4.

Explaining the act of presupposing as grounded on presumptive reasoning allows one to evaluate a presupposition. Presupposing can be reasonable or unreasonable, depending on the conclusion and the premises of the reasoning underlying it. For instance, the assertion above would be infelicitous if the reasonings supporting its presuppositions were different. For instance, if the speaker held that "Bob is not a common friend," his act of presupposing would be unreasonable, as the underlying reasoning would be invalid or unacceptable.

There are different levels of unreasonableness, corresponding to the different ways a presupposition can fail. For instance, we can analyze from this perspective some of the cases mentioned in the previous section:

13. Bob was at the party too.
15. My dog got an A in Math.
16. I have to pick up my Martian friend at the Voodoo club.
17. Bob is tall. Therefore he is really rich.

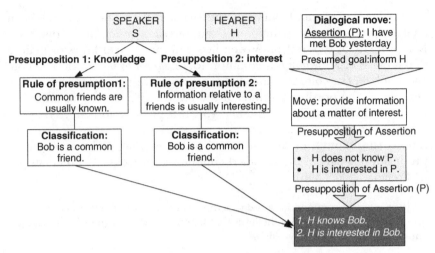

FIGURE 5.4. Presumptive structure of speaker's presuppositions

In a context in which no party was known, the speaker would ground his speech act on a presupposition resting on the premises "People usually know what has been referred to previously (or what they experienced before)" and "The party was mentioned before (or, the hearer was at the party)." The last premise is contingently false and therefore the speaker is unreasonable because he is distorting the facts. The act of presupposing in (15) is based on a different type of unreasonableness, not contingent on the fact but relative to the rules governing language. The speaker reasons on the basis of the presumptive rule that "People know the usual meaning of the words" and the premise that "If a dog can study, a dog is a human being"; this latter premise is in conflict with the commonly accepted meaning of 'dog.' Here the unreasonableness is deeper, as conflicting with a proposition rooted in language itself. Sentences (16) and (17) are grounded on instances of reasoning that is unreasonable because it is contrary to what is commonly accepted. The presuppositions that "Martians exist" and that "Tallness leads to richness" are unacceptable to different extents. The speaker proceeds from the rules that "People usually know important encyclopedic information" and "People usually know relationships between facts or states of affairs," which cannot apply to the aforementioned propositions. In (16) the speaker presupposes based on "The existence of Martians is a piece of encyclopedic information," which is simply unacceptable, while in (17) the relationship between height and economic success is posited as a common experienced relationship, contrary to what it usually maintained.

Depending on the type of violation, whether contingent or absolute falsity, or the unacceptability of encyclopedic information or relations and co-occurrences, the type of unreasonableness varies, resulting in impossible or unacceptable (to different extents) presuppositions. Evaluating the speaker's reasoning allows one to understand the grounds of his unreasonableness, and correct or challenge his act of presupposing by pointing out the premises that cannot be accepted.

6.3. *Assessing Presuppositions*

The analysis of a speaker's presuppositions as presumptions opens the possibility of explaining their force and assessing their reasonableness. A false or unacceptable presupposition is dialogically a false or unacceptable presumption. The listener, in order not to be committed to the presupposed proposition (Walton 1999: 380; Corblin 2003), needs to rebut the speaker's move, by attacking either the principle of presumption or the reasoning underlying the passage from the presumption to the proposition. For instance, considering Figure 5.4, the speaker can reject the presumption that information relative to a friend is interesting, or the fact that Bob is a common friend. Assessing the presumptive reasoning underlying the presupposition and showing its dialogical effect is necessary in order to understand when and why presuppositions are used to deceive and alter the perspective or reality.

We can show the process of assessment by taking into consideration one of the most effective and deceitful kinds of presuppositions, implicit redefinitions. Presupposed redefinitions can be instruments for hiding reality, and for this reason they need to introduce ambiguity. For this reason, their force lies in the vagueness of the concept, or in the poor knowledge of its boundaries. We will consider two extremely clear cases, where the presupposed meaning was clearly false (they have been judged as such by scholars), unshared, and for these reasons was used to hide reality.

The first strategy relies on the ambiguity of a word, used to presuppose a proposition without being committed to it or letting the interlocutor know. The speaker can use a word having a specific presumptive meaning presupposing an unshared new meaning, such as in the following case (Lifton 1986: 51):

MANIPULATION CASE 1: INTRODUCING AMBIGUITY

Physicians can carry out euthanasia (to indicate direct medical killing of "lives unworthy of life").

Euthanasia here refers to the killing of Jewish children; even though the idea of killing mental patients was considered as euthanasia, the word was presumed to refer to the killing of a man to relieve him from horrible suffering (Lifton 1986: 49). The word was used with a new presumptive meaning, while the listener constructed it based on his presumption. We can represent this fallacious presumptive move as follows:

Premise 1:	*The interlocutor should know (be committed to) the meaning of "euthanasia"* (P) *whenever such a word* is used with its commonly accepted meaning (C) (unless *the interlocutor does not master the language, belongs to a different culture or community, etc.*) (D) (Rule).
Premise 2:	The commonly accepted definition of "euthanasia" is "**killing of a man's to relieve him from horrible suffering**" (C) (Fact).
Premise 3:	It is not the case that the audience does not know the language or belongs to a different community of speaker (or culture) (*non-D*) (Exception).
(?) Conclusion:	*The audience should know that "euthanasia" means medical killing of lives unworthy of life* (P).

The Nazis presupposed not simply a potentially unshared proposition, but rather a proposition that they knew that their audience could not know. They made up a new meaning for a word advertized by their propaganda as a means to reduce suffering. However, when they gave public physicians permission to carry out euthanasia, the word was used with a different meaning. In this case, the presumptive reasoning is not simply weak or controversial. It is clearly fallacious, as the conclusion cannot follow from the premises.

The presumptive reasoning can also fail when the meaning of a new concept is presumed as shared. The speaker in this case presupposes what he clearly knows cannot be known by the interlocutor, as he is introducing a concept without having defined it. For instance, consider the following sadly famous use of a word with an unshared meaning (Lifton 1986: 42):

MANIPULATION CASE 2: PRESUPPOSING NEW DEFINITIONS

We (the Nazis) have programs of positive and negative Eugenics.

The meaning of "positive and negative eugenics" was not known at the time, but its definition was simply presupposed in Nazis propaganda. Such information could be retrieved by the known meaning of 'eugenics' ("strengthening a biological group on the basis of ostensible hereditary worth" – Lifton 1986: 24), but could not be traced back to the real definition of "sterilization of unhealthy individuals or racially inferior people and sometimes euthanasia" as the actual 'medical' description recited. In this case, it is the relationship between the second premise (the fact) and the presumption rule that fails:

Premise 1:	*The interlocutor should know (be committed to) the meaning of "euthanasia"* (P) *whenever such a word* is *used with its commonly accepted meaning* (C) (unless *the interlocutor does not master the language, belongs to a different culture or community, etc.*) (D) (Rule).

Premise 2:	**There is not a commonly accepted definition** of "positive and negative eugenics," but only of "eugenics," which means "strengthening a biological group" (*C*) (Fact).
Premise 3:	It is not the case that the audience does not know the language or belongs to a different community of speakers (or culture) (*non-D*) (Exception).
(?) Conclusion:	*The audience should know that **"positive and negative eugenics" means "sterilization of unhealthy individuals or racially inferior people and sometimes euthanasia"** (P).*

In this case, not only is the conclusion different from the facts, but the relationship between the fact and the rule fails. The audience cannot be presumed to know a concept created by the speaker without informing the public. The clear unreasonableness is disguised by the possibility of the interlocutors to guess, or accommodate the meaning based on a shared concept of eugenics, which is clearly different from the one presupposed.

6.4. *Presuppositions as Presumptions*

Presuppositions can be analyzed as the conclusion of a presumptive reasoning, where the rule of presumption applies to a fact, consisting in a proposition in the speaker's knowledge of what is or can be commonly known and accepted. The felicity of a presupposition therefore depends on the reasonableness and correctness of the presumptive reasoning underlying it. In particular, as seen in the analysis of the cases in which redefinitions were presupposed, the speaker can ground his move on a fallacious (incorrect) step of reasoning, or on an unreasonable one. In the first case, the speaker draws a conclusion different from the factual premise. In the second case, he proceeds from a factual proposition that he knows does not fit the requirements of the rule. The unreasonableness and fallaciousness of the presumptive reasoning is hidden by the vagueness of the concept and people's ignorance of the facts. However, these cases are clear because it is possible to reconstruct through historical works the meaning and the intentions. In real life it is not possible to know what the speaker really knows, unless he is introducing apparently false presuppositions. Most of the time presuppositions are not used to hide reality, but to achieve dialectical or rhetorical goals.

7. The Dialectics of Presupposition

Presuppositions are the conclusions of presumptive reasoning. Therefore, their most immediate effect is the alteration of the interlocutor's commitment store. Following Walton and Krabbe's (1995) dialectical models, we can represent a verbal exchange as an alteration of the agent's commitment store, which contains all the statements that the participant has conceded or accepted during the course of the dialogue. In a dialogue not all the commitments are explicit. The interlocutors can interact because they share the

definitions of the words used, the rules of the dialogue, procedures, and encyclopedic knowledge regarding the place where they are. Some of these *dark-
side* commitments (Walton & Krabbe 1995: 11) are the outcome of previous
dialogues; for instance, if I utter that "Bob's decision caused great trouble to
all of us," I implicitly commit myself and the hearer to the fact that Bob made
a decision. In a dialogue, presuppositions are implicit activations of dark-side
commitments (see Corblin 2003). They refer to propositions already accepted
by the parties to move the commitments further. This alteration of the dark-
side commitments carries crucial dialectical consequences, affecting the interlocutor's burden of proof.

7.1. *The Burdens of Presupposition*

Analyzing the speaker's presuppositions as the outcome of his presumptive
reasoning can help in understanding the effects of presuppositions. From a
dialectical point of view, a presupposition carries the effects of a presumption: The hearer becomes committed to it, unless he challenges and rejects it
(Walton 1999: 380; Hickey 1993: 108). Some presumptions are easier to reject
than others. For instance, if the speaker presupposes a false fact that can be
easily determined, the burden of rebutting his presumption can be easily met
by the hearer by providing evidence. However, if the same fact is not known
or little information about it is available, rejecting the presupposition can
become complex. A presumption of meaning needs to be refuted by providing a shared definition. However, when the concept is ambiguous, rejection
becomes extremely hard. Finally, the presumption of knowledge can be easily
rejected by the hearer by providing information about his own knowledge.
Such positive evidence is often much stronger than the defaultive presumptive reasoning.

However, the force of this presupposition lies in a different effect of this
act. As Kauffeld noticed, ordinary presumptions place on the interlocutor
a specific burden, the "risk of resentment, criticism, reprobation, loss of
esteem" in the event he or she does not accept a presumptive conclusion
(Kauffeld 1998: 264). The effect of potential resentment can be understood
from the following example. In this excerpt from Manzoni's *I promessi sposi*,
Father Cristoforo, once a gentlemen who became a friar after killing a man
in self-defense, is invited by a powerful lord, Don Rodrigo, to judge a controversy between two guests on violence against messengers[5]:

'With your leave, gentlemen,' interrupted Don Rodrigo, who was afraid of the question being carried too far, 'we will refer it to Father Cristoforo, and abide by his
sentence.' [...]

'But, from what I have heard,' said the Father, 'these are matters I know
nothing of.'

---

[5] http://manzoni.classicauthors.net/IPromessiSposiOrTheBetrothed/
IPromessiSposiOrTheBetrothed6.html.

'As usual, the modest excuses of the Fathers,' said Don Rodrigo; 'but you shall not get off so easily. Come, now, **we know well enough** you did not come into the world with a cowl on your head, and **that you are no stranger to its ways**. See here; this is the question...'

Don Rodrigo presupposes the fact that Father Cristoforo knows the ways of the world pretty well and in particular the acts of violence. Such a presupposition would be hardly acceptable by Father Cristoforo. However, the burden of rejecting is increased by the fact that it is presented as shared by everybody. Often definitions and facts are presupposed even though they are not shared; however, the presumptive reasoning presents them as accepted by everybody, and the possibility of challenging them is hindered by the shame of being unaware of what everyone knows.

7.2. *Dialectical Uses of Presupposition*

Presupposing unshared propositions is a twofold dialectical strategy. On the one hand, presuppositions are commitments: Presupposing an unshared proposition means committing the hearer to a view that he or she never accepted, and that has to be denied in order to be deleted from the commitment store. On the other hand, presuppositions are the conclusions of implicit presumptive reasoning, and therefore their denial needs to be supported by an argument that rebuts the presumption.

The presumptive nature of presuppositions can explain the reasonableness and the strategic effect of the different acts of "imposing a dialectical world" presented previously. If we go back to Obama's presuppositions in his Nobel Prize address, we can notice that he relies on different presumptions in the three cases. In (presupposition 1), when he claims to "acknowledge the considerable controversy" he relies on the presumption that the "people usually know the most important information regarding the event they are attending." He takes for granted that the controversies on the decision to grant him the Nobel Prize were important and widely broadcasted pieces of information, and therefore could ground his presupposition on sound presumptive reasoning. We can represent the implicit premises underlying his presupposition as follows:

Premise 1:	*The interlocutor should know (be committed to) a piece of news (P)* whenever *such information is important, relevant, and sufficiently broadcasted (C)* (unless *the interlocutor does not watch the television, or is not interested in the topic, etc.) (D)* (Rule).
Premise 2:	The controversies have been widely broadcasted and are important for the international community(*C*)(Fact).
Premise 3:	It is not the case that the audience is not interested in information regarding the event they are attending (*non-D*) (Exception).
Conclusion:	*The audience should be aware of the controversies (P).*

The presumptive reasoning is acceptable, given the context. However, the following two cases (presuppositions 2 and 3) can be more controversial.

In (presupposition 2) Obama claims that America should be a model in the conduct of war, and that was the reason why he "prohibited torture, [...] ordered the prison at Guantanamo Bay closed, and [...] reaffirmed America's commitment to abide by the Geneva Conventions." However, in this case the international audience cannot be presumed to have been informed of Obama's decisions in matters of American political decisions (especially his reaffirmation of America's commitment to the Geneva Conventions) and some controversial issues about Bush's presidency (the fact that Guantanamo Bay violated the conduct of war). Such information can be shared by many, but it would be more debatable whether it can be presumed to be known by the whole audience. In particular, the press releases focused on Obama's stress on international diplomacy and negotiations as an alternative instrument of dispute resolution. We can represent this presumptive reasoning as follows:

Premise 1:	*The interlocutor should know (be committed to) a piece of news (P)* whenever *such information is important, relevant, and sufficiently broadcasted (C)* (unless *the interlocutor does not watch the television, or is not interested in the topic, etc.) (D)* (Rule).
Premise 2:	Obama's prohibition of torture, reaffirmation of America's commitment to the Geneva Conventions, and the shutdown of Guantanamo Bay have been widely broadcasted and are relevant for the international community (C) (Fact).
Premise 3:	The audience may be not interested in information regarding America's politics (D) (Exception).
Conclusion:	*The audience should be aware of the Obama's decisions (P).*

In this case, the presumptive reasoning is much weaker than the previous case, as the conditions may not obtain, while the default can apply to the case. In this case, Obama presents his decisions as widely known and relevant for his public. He informs the audience of his politics, and at the same time avoids advancing them as arguments for his implicit conclusion, namely, the rebuttal of the controversies regarding his candidature for the Nobel Prize. If he had provided such information explicitly, he would have also had to show its role in the discourse. The most evident function was to support the conclusion that he deserved the Prize. Obviously, such an argument could have been rejected, or appear as irrelevant or insufficient. By taking it for granted, he also conceals its role in the discourse. This presupposition also carries a rhetorical effect. Obama's decisions are presumed to be known all over the world for their importance. Through this presumption, he increases their possible impact on the interlocutors unaware of them.

The last use of presupposition consists in taking for granted a proposition that the audience may not accept. As pointed out in (presupposition 3),

Obama stated that the world continues to support American war in Afghanistan "because of the recognized principle of self-defense." However, as noticed previously, the admissibility of a large-scale invasion of a state for the purpose of preventing terroristic attacks has been widely disputed. Obama cannot presume that it is a piece of accepted information, nor that it is known or shared by his audience. We can represent his presumptive reasoning as follows:

Premise 1:	*The interlocutor should know (be committed to) a proposition (P) whenever such a proposition is commonly* accepted as true, *important, relevant, and sufficiently broadcasted (C)* (unless *the interlocutor does not watch television, or is not interested in the topic, etc.*) *(D)* (Rule).
Premise 2:	It is accepted by everybody that America invaded Afghanistan for self-defense, and such information has been widely broadcast and is relevant for the international community(*C*)(Fact).
Premise 3:	It is not the case that the audience is not interested in information regarding Obama's wars (*non-D*) (Exception).
Conclusion:	*The audience* should *know and accept that Afghanistan was invaded for self-defense (P).*

In this case, the very condition of presupposition, the audience's acceptance, is controversial. As noted in the previous section, not only does a proposition need to be known by the interlocutor, but it also needs to be accepted (if not known to be true). In this case, Obama cannot reasonably presume that his presupposed proposition is accepted by everybody, but he advances it as such. In this fashion, he achieves two results. He includes in the interlocutor's commitment stores a proposition that could have raised doubts or controversies. Not only does Obama avoid providing any support for it, but he also dodges the risk of raising a potential controversial issue. Moreover, he prevents the audience from using the (controversial) fact that he is fighting an unjustified war. The presumption places on the audience the burden of rejecting the move as a whole, and proving the contrary of the presumed proposition. Another indirect effect is to hide the purpose of this implicit argument, directed to justify the fact that America is actually attacking a foreign nation (not properly an act of peace).

By means of presupposition it is possible to alter the dialogical situation by preventing the interlocutor from performing certain moves. Presuppositions insert new commitments into the hearer's commitment stores. As noted by Ducrot (1968), this move has powerful dialectical outcomes. Like a move in a game of chess, presupposition has a twofold effect. On the one hand, it allows the speaker to perform certain moves (e.g., claiming that America fights according to the highest international conduct of war), and not to perform others (e.g., Obama did not have to defend or support that Afghanistan had been invaded for self-defense). On the other hand, presupposition affects the interlocutors' possible moves, impeding them to use the contrary or the contradictory of the presupposed proposition for supporting the opposed viewpoint, or preventing them from advancing counterarguments or rejections. The power of presupposition is even greater when what is presupposed is a redefinition.

7.3. *Presupposing Redefinitions*

In the previous chapters we introduced the notion of persuasive definition (Chapter 2) and implicit redefinition (Chapter 4). As we emphasized in the previous chapter, implicit redefinitions can introduce ambiguity strategically, while at the same time hiding such a move and shifting the burden of rebutting it. Implicit redefinitions, as observed previously, can enhance the interlocutor's burden of rejection, as the redefined terms are usually vague or ill-defined. The presumptive reasoning underlying presupposition can explain why and how this mechanism works.

A clear case of a presupposed redefinition is Obama's redefinition of 'hostilities.' In Chapter 4 we quoted a passage from his letter to Congress, in which he claimed that U.S. military operations in Libya do not fall within the category of 'hostilities' because they

[...] do not involve sustained fighting or active exchanges of fire with hostile forces, nor do they involve the presence of U.S. ground troops, U.S. casualties or a serious threat thereof, or any significant chance of escalation into a conflict characterized by those factors. (Obama Administration letter to Congress justifying Libya engagement, June 15th, 2011, p. 25)

He presupposed a definition of 'hostilities' not shared by Congress and conflicting with the military one. The structure of his presumptive reasoning is grounded on the presumption of meaning. The hearer is presumed to know the meanings of the words used, and the speaker at the same time is presumed to use the words with their ordinary meanings if he does not explicitly define them. However, in the previous case the presumption of meaning fails:

Premise 1:	*The interlocutor should know (be committed to) the meaning of 'hostilities'* (P) whenever *such a word* is used with its commonly accepted meaning (C) (unless *the interlocutor does not master the language, belongs to a different culture or community, etc.*) (D) (Rule).
Premise 2:	The commonly accepted definition of 'hostilities' (in politics, military, etc.) is "action involving ground troop intervention, sustained fighting and exchanges of fire" (C) (Fact).
Premise 3:	It is not the case that the audience does not know the language or belongs to a different community of speaker (or culture) (*non-D*) (Exception).
Conclusion:	*The audience should know that 'hostilities' includes only ground troop intervention, sustained fighting and exchanges of fire* (P).

The strength of the presumption lies in the vagueness of the concept. There are no explicit definitions thereof, but Obama's definition could not be accepted by the military and caused many controversies. At the same time, however, this definition could not be easily rejected, as no statutory definitions supported a different account of the meaning of 'hostilities.'

The effect of a presumption of meaning is much greater when a concept is "essentially contested" (Gallie 1956). For instance, concepts such as 'art,' 'freedom,' and 'peace' are vague and controversial. They can have different accepted definitions, even though all these accounts can have a shared basis, or some of them can be easily rejected. 'Peace' is a vague notion and therefore can be used effectively in implicit redefinitions. However, all definitions (etymological, by description, by qualitative parts) usually share one fundamental feature, that the most generic description is the absence of conflict. If we analyze Obama's redefinition of 'peace' in his Nobel Prize address, we can notice that he performs two moves. The first one consists in introducing a new difference in the commonly accepted genus "absence of visible conflict," namely, the quality "to be based on inherent rights and dignity [...] economic security and opportunity." Then he replaces the genus, without arguing against it, claiming that "true peace is **not just freedom from fear**, but freedom from want." He presupposes that the second sequence replaces an accepted meaning, but the very definition he corrects presupposes a new genus for peace, 'freedom,' instead of "absence of conflict."

ACCEPTED MEANING: ABSENCE OF CONFLICT

Premise 1:	*The interlocutor should know (be committed to) the meaning of "peace"* (P) whenever *such a word* is used with its commonly accepted meaning, or when the speaker redefined it supporting it by reasons (*C*) (unless *the interlocutor does not master the language, belongs to a different culture or community, etc.*) (*D*) (Rule).
Premise 2:	The commonly accepted definition of 'peace' is "absence of conflict," and the speaker redefined it as "absence of conflict based rights and opportunities (based on freedom from want)..." (*C*) (Fact).
Premise 3:	It is not the case that the audience does not know the language or belongs to a different community of speaker (or culture) (*non-D*) (Exception).
Conclusion:	*The audience should know that 'peace' means "freedom of a kind"* (P).

In this case, Obama grounds his implicit redefinition on the vagueness of 'peace' and on the similarity between the conclusion of his presumptive reasoning (peace is known to mean "freedom from want") and its premise (the speaker has redefined it as "absence of conflict based on rights and opportunities"). Ambiguity and vagueness increase the effect of this implicit move.

7.4. Redefining Values

Persuasive definitions can be analyzed as implicit redefinitions of emotive words. However, the structure of a presupposition can also explain when and how the strategy of quasi-definitions is used mischievously. As seen in Chapter 2, quasi-definition refers to an improper definition, in which words denoting concepts positively evaluated are presented as negative, or dyslogistic terms are redefined in a positive fashion. In quasi-definitions the definition of the term is maintained, but the system of values associated with the fragment of reality it refers to is modified. As noticed in Chapter 2, quasi-definitions can be explicit or implicit strategies. Obama in his Nobel Prize address relies on a hierarchy of values that is commonly accepted. Everybody agrees that violence is bad and peace is good. By redefining the concepts of war and peace as 'just war' and 'true peace,' he associates the values of peace and justice to 'just war' and violence, fear, and want to 'false (or apparent) peace.' This move allows him to modify the system of values, showing that wars can be justified and desirable, while peace (or rather the new concept he introduces for it) can be violent, unjust, and oppressing.

As noticed in Chapter 2, quasi-definitions can be implicit strategies based on hidden alterations of the hierarchy of values. Building on our account of presuppositions, we can show how this tactic is based on unacceptable presumptive reasoning. For instance, in the following excerpt from the scandalous novel *Sanine*, the protagonist subverted the system of values commonly shared in Russia at the beginning of the twentieth century and took for granted that his interlocutor, Sarudine, shared the same view (Artsybashev 1915: 22):

- "Very well, then, enjoyment is the aim of human life. Paradise is the synonym for absolute enjoyment, and we all of us, more or less, dream of an earthly paradise. This legend of paradise is by no means an absurdity, but a symbol, a dream."
- "Yes," continued Sanine, after a pause, "Nature never meant men to be abstinent, and the sincerest men are those who do not conceal their desires, that is to say, those who socially count as blackguards, fellows such as – you, for instance."

In this case, Sanine presupposes that "intemperance and adultery is natural," redefining the very concept of "nature of man." He takes for granted that the "nature of man" corresponds to the nature of animals and is guided by instincts instead of reason. This premise supports his following implicit redefinition of values, which we mentioned in Chapter 1, made explicit in Chapter 2, and report here again (Stevenson 1944: 280, 281, from Artsybashev 1915: 27):

- "Blackguards are the most fascinating people."
- "You don't say so?" Exclaimed Sarudine, smiling.

- "Of course they are. There's nothing so boring in all the world as your so-called honest man. … With the programme of honesty and virtue everybody is long familiar; and so it contains nothing that is new. Such antiquated rubbish robs a man of all individuality, and his life is lived within the narrow, tedious limits of virtue. … Yes, blackguards are the most sincere and interesting people imaginable, for they have no conception of the bounds of human baseness."

This argument does not advance or support a new hierarchy of values, substituting the commonly accepted one. On the contrary, Sanine presupposes key value judgments at the basis of his new hierarchy. For instance, he takes for granted that "honest men are boring"; "honesty and virtue are tedious, narrow, antiquated rubbish"; and "virtue is base." He presumes that his interlocutor (a respected officer) accepts that "Vice is sincerity" and that "Virtue is hypocrisy," stemming from the previous implicit move ("Those who socially count as blackguards, fellows such as – you, for instance"). We can represent the unacceptability of this presumptive reasoning by showing the conflicting hierarchies and definitions of values as in Figure 5.5.

In the figure, the dotted boxes represent the propositions that the speaker (Sanine) takes for granted and presumes to be shared by his interlocutor. In the grey boxes the values that Sarudine holds are indicated (corresponding to the shared values and definitions), or rather the values he is commonly presumed to hold, as a respectable officer. The conflict of values is shown with a double arrow. This alteration of hierarchies of values is not made explicit, nor is it supported by arguments. The speaker simply takes the new hierarchy as granted by the whole community of speakers and tries to get his thesis accepted on these grounds. In addition to the redefinition of the moral virtues, Sanine supports his new hierarchy by also redefining the vice of being unfaithful. Such an implicit strategy of redefinition of values and hierarchies can be represented as shown in Figure 5.6.

In the analysis shown in Figure 5.6, we can notice how the speaker presupposes hierarchies and definitions of key concepts such as 'faithfulness' and 'honesty' as commonly accepted. In fact, the presupposed propositions are in conflict with the accepted common knowledge. There would have been nothing wrong in quasi-defining the concepts at stake explicitly and supporting the view with arguments. However, in this case the controversial propositions are objects of acts of presupposition. The speaker improperly inserts them in the hearer's commitment store and grounds his move on a presumptive reasoning that is unacceptable. If those values had been accepted or were acceptable, the redefinition would have been a reasonable persuasive move. In this case, in the novel at least, the presupposition is a manipulative act, aimed at introducing unaccepted *endoxa* without defending them.

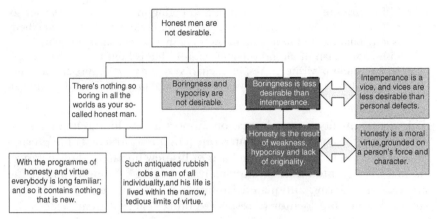

FIGURE 5.5. Conflict of hierarchies and redefinitions of values

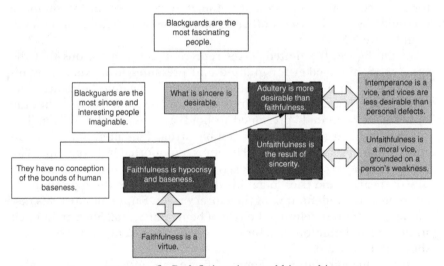

FIGURE 5.6. Redefining vices and hierarchies

8. Presuppositions as Rhetorical Strategies

As seen in the previous chapter and earlier in this chapter, the pragmatic function of presupposition is to take a proposition for granted. This pragmatic role can be translated into a dialectical approach as the function of committing both the speaker and the hearer to a proposition, shifting the burden of disproving it onto the interlocutor. This effect, described in the previous chapter, is not allowed in legal discourse. In law the act of presupposing, or rather the act of taking for granted specific information and considering it as already admitted or shared by the interlocutor, is limited by the rules of evidence. In cross-examinations, questions "may not assume facts to have been proven which have not been entered into evidence" (FRE 611; see the interpretation of the rule at *Essex v. Millikan*, 88 Ind. App. 399, 164 N.E. 284, 1928). For this reason, in law the purpose of presuppositions is not dialectical in nature, corresponding to leading the witness or the opposing party to a commitment that otherwise he or she would not have admitted. The goal is rhetorical in nature, and consists in exploiting a pragmatic and dialectical instrument to perform an indirect move. By presupposing, the speaker does not commit the hearer, but insinuates to the audience that the presupposed proposition is true, or informs the jury of the presupposed and inadmissible fact. There are several strategies of communicating inadmissible facts through presuppositions, depending on the type of legal dialogue (Hickey 1993). Their strength is noticeable, and can lead to a mistrial.

8.1. *Presuppositions as Implicit Character Attacks*

In legal witness examinations, statements on witness's character are not allowed. Presupposition in this case plays a crucial role. By asking the witness questions presupposing his bad character, the speaker can convey to the jury inadmissible information, without taking on responsibility. Moreover, when denied or objected to, such questions can also mislead the jury (*People v. Enis*, 139 Ill. 2d 267, 1990): "The danger inherent in such questioning is that the jury will ignore the denial and presume the accuracy of the impeaching insinuation contained in the question."

The first and most evident strategy of presupposition is the loaded question (Bocchino & Sonenshein 2006: 28), in which a proposition to which the interlocutor is not committed is taken for granted. Given the strict rules of evidence, the most obvious goal, namely altering the witness's commitments, is often only a possible side effect.

In fact, one of the most powerful effects of presupposing facts not in evidence is to lead the jury to distrust the witness (for the exclusion of witness's character evidence, see Phillipps 1815: 921). For instance, in case 2, the speaker asked the defendant, "When did you first think up this story about this man handing you this package?" (*United States v. Stockdale*, 13 C.M.R. 546, 1953). This question, presupposing the falsity of the witness' statement, was not asked to elicit an answer from the witness, but in fact to depict him as not reliable, without providing any evidence to support such a conclusion. This move, when not repeated further in the examination, is a potential strategy to "arouse passion and prejudice" (*United States v. Stockdale*, at 547) without incurring the risk of a mistrial.

Loaded questions also can be used to attack a defendant's credibility on cross-examination, when he is acting as a witness. Facts supported by evidence, but not admissible as evidence, can be taken for granted in order to inform the jury and undercut his credibility. For instance, a defendant's prior convictions are not relevant in a cross-examination and should not be admitted in trials, in order to prevent prejudice (FRE 609, a). A common strategy is to inquire about character issues ("Have you ever been convicted"?), but this technique is often blocked by the court without producing dangerous effects. A subtler strategy is to presuppose evidence that cannot be considered as false, even though not admissible. For instance, consider the following move (*United States v. Sanchez*, 176 F.3d 1224, 1999):

CASE 9: CROSS-EXAMINATION: PRESUPPOSING DEFENDANT CHARACTER

During cross-examination, the prosecutor asked the defendant the following question: "Can you explain to me, Mr. Sanchez, why you have a reputation [for] being one of the largest drug dealers on the reservation but you don't have more than one source of supply?"

This question presupposes a fact that could not be introduced as evidence, because it falls into the category of "evidence of prior bad acts." The effect of such a move was indicated by the court: "The question was not harmless to Sanchez's right to a fair trial because it suggested to the jury that the defendant had a reputation for being one of the largest drug dealers on the reservation" (*United States v. Sanchez*, at 1225). Attacks of this kind to the defendant's character can be highly detrimental to his credibility, and prejudice the whole process.

The hidden argumentative strategy used exploits a common relationship between moral qualities and reliability, which is the ground of the relationship between a person's testimony and the acceptability thereof. This link can be represented as follows (Walton 1995: 152; Walton, Reed & Macagno 2008: 336):

ARGUMENTATION SCHEME 14: ETHOTIC ARGUMENT

Major Premise	If x is a person of good (bad) moral character, then what x says should be accepted as more plausible (rejected as less plausible).
Minor Premise	a is a person of good (bad) moral character.
Conclusion	Therefore, what x says should be accepted as more plausible (rejected as less plausible).

Especially in the second aforementioned implicit attack, the speaker takes for granted the defendant's negative moral character and undercuts the credibility of his statements. More generally, the speaker depicts the defendant as a bad person (he has a bad reputation as a drug dealer) and exploits this stronger negative judgment to enhance the force of the conclusion. We can represent this stronger attack as follows (Walton 1998: 249; Walton, Reed & Macagno 2008: 336):

ARGUMENTATION SCHEME 15: *Ad hominem* ARGUMENT

Premise	a is a bad person.
Conclusion	Therefore, a's argument α should not be accepted.

These cases show how presuppositions can be used not as dialectical ends in themselves but as premises for a further argumentative move.

8.2. *Presuppositions as Instruments to Alter the Weight of Evidence*

Presuppositions are also used in cross-examinations to alter a jury's perception of the evidence by taking for granted unsupported information or increasing the probative weight of some proofs. When pursuing the strategy of discrediting the witness, the speaker does not need to have the presupposition accepted; he simply needs to convey the information that the proposition is obviously true. Such a proposition can undermine the credibility of the witness and arouse prejudice. The speaker can also use presuppositions to influence a jury's perception of the evidence, by presenting information as granted or altering its probative weight. In order to achieve this goal, the speaker needs to disguise the altered evidence, that is, he needs to present it as similar to the presumed, admitted, or proved propositions. For instance, consider the following case (*School City of Gary v. Claudio*, Ind.App., 413 N.E.2d 628, 1980):

CASE 10: CROSS-EXAMINATION: PRESUPPOSING FACTS NOT IN EVIDENCE

Was Joey breaking the instructions he had been given out there that day?

This question was asked during a cross-examination in a claim for damages brought by a student who was run over by a bus. However, from the evidence provided it appeared that such instructions were not provided; by asking this question, the attorney wanted to exploit the presumption that "usually schools give instructions" to take for granted new evidence that could be useful for the theory.

The speaker can also take for granted that some propositions have been already proved, while they are still controversial. For instance, in the following dialogue the attorney presupposes that the hair found on a piece of tape was the defendant's (Giangrande); however, the hair evidence was only a possibility envisaged by a forensic scientist, and not a fact (*People v. Giangrande*, 428 N.E.2d 518, 1981):

CASE 11: CROSS-EXAMINATION: ENHANCING EVIDENTIAL WEIGHT

[Ms. Propes]: Don't you find it a little suspicious that Michael Giangrande's head and arm hair would have ended up on the underside of the tape?
Mr. Bradley: Objection, that's not the evidence.
The Court: I think you could be a little more accurate on that, Ms. Propes.
Ms. Propes: Don't you find it suspicious that limb hair of Michael Giangrande would be on the tape?

Mr. Bradley: Objection, that's not the evidence.
The Court: That's not the evidence.
Ms. Propes: Well, hair just like Michael Giangrande's.

The attorney took for granted the truth of this evidence, and even if corrected, it "may have caused the jury to give undue weight to the hair evidence" (ibid). Presupposition works in this case as an instrument for manipulating the jury's perception and evaluation of the evidence.

8.3. *Presuppositions as Instruments for Fabricating Evidence*

As mentioned earlier, presuppositions can be used to influence a jury's perception of the evidence. This technique is more effective when used in the closing argument, where counsel and prosecutors are free to argue the evidence and all reasonable inferences from the evidence as it relates to their theory of the case (see, e.g., *Commonwealth v. Andrews*, 427 Mass. 434, 1998). During the closing argument, however, the risk of misconduct is higher, as "improper remarks in closing arguments may be reversible error where they substantially prejudice the defendant or serve no purpose other than to inflame the jury" (*People v. Terry*, 460 N.E.2d 746, 1984).

One of the most powerful tactics is to presuppose evidence not previously supported or proved, or facts rejected or not admitted. For instance, consider the following case (*Ivey v. State*, 113 Ga. 1062, 1901):

CASE 12: CLOSING STATEMENT: PRESUPPOSING DEFENDANT'S CRIMES

[...] he solicitor-general, in his address to the jury, used the following language: "Gentlemen of the jury, I want you to stand by me and help me break up this vile den;" and "Gentlemen of the jury, if you could go over this town and see the good mothers whose pillows have been wet with tears over their boys who have been intoxicated by the acts of this woman."

By using relative clauses, he expands the topic, and therefore the presuppositions of his statement. In this fashion, he presents a supposition as a shared fact (mothers wetting their pillows with tears) in order to arouse emotions that he then directs toward a second presupposition (the sons of the mothers have been intoxicated **by the acts of the defendant**), which is the very controversial point. The speaker takes unsupported evidence for granted in order to arouse emotions and alter the jury's assessment of the implicit facts not in evidence. This type of rhetorical strategy is grounded on a link between emotion and judgment, or rather action. The pity aroused by the speaker leads the hearer to take immediate action to relieve the victim, or the suffering person, from the distressful situation. The crucial move consists in eliciting the feeling of pity to enhance the hearer's need for action, and therefore pushing him to draw a hasty judgment. The scheme can be represented as follows (Walton 1997: 105; Walton, Reed & Macagno 2008: 334):

ARGUMENTATION SCHEME 16: ARGUMENT FROM DISTRESS

Premise 1	Individual x is in distress (is suffering).
Premise 2	If y brings about A, it will relieve or help to relieve this distress.
Conclusion	Therefore, y ought to bring about A.

In this case, the hearer is led to condemn who committed the distressful action, implicitly identified by the speaker as the defendant.

Another strategy of fabrication of evidence consists in presupposing evidence that was not admitted, or even denied or disproven. For instance, in the following concluding statement the speaker attacks the credibility of a crucial witness, taking for granted facts that were actually denied during the trial (*United States v. Beckman*, 222 F.3d 526,527, 2000):

CASE 13: CLOSING STATEMENT: PRESUPPOSING WITNESS'S BAD CHARACTER

Let's talk about the statement he made to Agent Basham that "All my problems started when I met Pat Mitchell." Ladies and gentlemen, his problems, as he describes them, are $400 debt and a guest who had lived in his house for three months who he didn't really want to live there, and the fact that he had used methamphetamine once with Pat Mitchell. All of this, ladies and gentlemen, took place a little over a year, year and a half, shy of a year and a half before Tom Kelly was arrested and interviewed. How would you say, ladies and gentlemen, that this $400 debt was the beginning of all your problems? All my problems started when I met Pat Mitchell. What problems? **It only makes sense, ladies and gentlemen, if your problems that you are referring to are losing your job because you are using meth, not showing up on time when failing your drug test**, of course, he denies. We talk about evaluating credibility.

The force of this strategy lies in using character elements (drug addiction) that can strongly "prejudice the accused in the minds of the jurors" (Ibid.). Even if the implicit allegations had not been proved, the prosecutor took their truth for granted and attacked the witness's credibility by attacking her *ethos*. In this case, the *ad hominem* attack described here is used to undercut the witness's testimony.

8.4. *Presuppositions as Instruments for Jumping to Conclusions*
In closing statements presuppositions also can be used for jumping to a conclusion. Jumping to a conclusion presupposes an argument, which can only provide tentative and defeasible support for a viewpoint. The speaker can disregard the defeasible character of his argument and take the conclusion for granted as if it were accepted as true. The speaker presupposes, as if they were true and shared facts, propositions that cannot be considered

as proven, or propositions that have not been admitted. Instead of communicating inadmissible facts or altering the epistemic weight of some pieces of evidence, the speaker presupposes the very point at stake, or presents his intermediate defeasible or rejected conclusions as admitted proofs. This tactic is obviously not admissible, but it is used to achieve two indirect purposes: altering the jury's perception of evidence and arousing emotions against the defendant (or a crucial witness). Even if the statement is rebutted and withdrawn, the jury's emotions are often aroused.

In law, the domain of inference lies between referring to evidence and introducing new or unproven facts. In law, inferences are admitted. However, an inference is different from evidence. Presuppositions can alter the interlocutor's perception of inferences by transforming them into evidence, thereby enhancing their probative weight, such as in the following case (*Commonwealth v. Rodriguez*, 437 Mass. 554, 565, 2002) (emphasis added):

CASE 14. CLOSING STATEMENT: PRESUPPOSING FACTS AND
RELATIONSHIPS

In his closing argument the prosecutor argued: "[The defendant] entered the store with a knife and **a bag**, and a hat **for a disguise**. ... He took **the baseball hat**. He took the bag, the tools of the trade of a robbery, and he headed out the door. ... I ask you, Ladies and Gentlemen, when an individual walks into a store armed with a knife and **a bag** of sufficient room to carry money, and a hat **to cover a distinctive scar over his eye**, is that consistent with somebody who doesn't know what he is doing...?"

The prosecutor here is not stating facts not in evidence, but simply drawing inferences from pieces of evidence: The bag belonged to the defendant's flat mate; the cap was proven to belong to the defendant, who also had a scar. From such facts the defendant's intent was inferred, and his actions linked to a purpose. However, the prosecutor in this case did not assert such inferences but simply took their conclusions for granted, as if they were evidence. His presupposed viewpoint was grounded on a type of argument that can be described as follows (Walton, Reed & Macagno 2008: 329):

ARGUMENTATION SCHEME 17: ABDUCTIVE ARGUMENT

Premise 1	D is a set of data or supposed facts in a case.
Premise 2	Each one of a set of accounts $A_1, A_2, ..., A_n$ is successful in explaining D.
Premise 4	A_i is the account that explains D most successfully.
Conclusion	Therefore, A_i is the most plausible hypothesis in the case.

This scheme is defeasible, as the conclusion is merely a hypothesis that needs to be supported by other arguments or be evaluated against alternative explanations. Moreover, the explanation, in order to be acceptable, needs to fulfill the requirements of its critical questions:

CQ1	How satisfactory is A_i itself as an explanation of D, apart from the alternative explanations available so far in the dialogue?
CQ$_2$	How much better an explanation is A_i than the alternative explanation so far in the dialogue?
CQ$_3$	How far has the dialogue progressed? If the dialogue is an inquiry, how thorough has the search been in the investigation of the case?
CQ$_4$	Would it be better to continue the dialogue further, instead of drawing a conclusion at this point?

By presupposing a conclusion as a proven fact, the speaker disregards the defeasibility of his inference and presents arguments as if they were facts.

Not only can the speaker take for granted intermediate conclusions as if they were evidence, but he can also presuppose the very point to be proven, the defendant's guilt or innocence. In this case, the presupposed conclusion rests on an implicit alteration of the weight of evidence provided. For instance, in *People v. Dalessandro*, the conclusion that the defendants assaulted the victim was only proved by inconsistent statements given by the witness. The prosecutor's strategy consisted in presupposing the defendants's guilt and taking the inconsistent testimony for granted as if it was substantive evidence. This move, however, was hidden by emotional appeals, in which the hideousness of the crime aroused emotions concealing the lack of proof (*People v. Dalessandro*, 65 Mich. App. 569, 580, 1988) (emphasis added):

CASE 15: CLOSING STATEMENT: PRESUPPOSING DEFENDANT'S GUILT

The intent of Gene Dalessandro and Laurie Cormendy is evidenced by **what they did to him.** ... We've shown injuries in this case that are revolting, that are sickening. They shouldn't happen to a dog, let alone a ten month old baby. They shouldn't happen to anything. No person and no thing should be treated this way.

[...] He was in so much pain, it's a wonder he could eat. William was in so much pain from **what Gene Dalessandro did to him**, it's a wonder he could eat. It's a wonder he lived. It's a wonder he lived. Now, it's important because, in a way, that's this pitiful little ten month old child's only way of telling the world what was being **done to him by this person, Gene Dalessandro**.

The emotions in this case hide the manipulation of the arguments provided, which are presupposed to be evidence.

The final conclusion also can be presupposed to be true based on facts that are taken for granted as true but that are not in evidence. Let's consider case 12, where the prosecutor addressed the jury and took for granted the defendant's guilt. He claims that the gentlemen of the jury can see with their eyes "the good mothers whose pillows have been wet with tears over their boys who have been intoxicated **by the acts of this**

woman. By means of the move just described, the speaker performs a second implicit act and presupposes that the defendant is guilty, which is the very point at stake.

8.5. *The Rhetorical Power of Presuppositions*

Presuppositions are dialectical instruments that can be used strategically. Their role is not simply limited to introducing new commitments without the speaker's taking on the responsibility for doing it. They can also elicit implicit arguments, arouse passions, and lead the interlocutor to the wanted conclusion. Through the act of presupposing, the speaker can alter not only the commitments but principally the interlocutor's (or jury's) perception and evaluation of reality, and therefore his judgment.

9. Conclusion

Presuppositions are a fundamental pragmatic dimension and a crucial dialectical instrument. Hinging on their pragmatic meaning, they can be considered as the preconditions for the felicity of a speech act, the information that the speaker takes for granted and upon which the desired effect of his move depends. From a linguistic point of view, it can occur at different levels of the text: within sentences, inter-sentences and within sequences, or discourse moves.

At each of these levels, the nature of the presuppositions varies. The use of a verb or a predicate imposes certain semantic conditions on its arguments. A connector sets requirements on sentences, while discourse relations frame the characteristics that the moves, the context, and the interlocutors need to have. From a pragmatic perspective, we have shown that presuppositions can be forms of implicit acts. They set conditions that the interlocutor needs to accept to continue the dialogue. They become forms of action, through which the speaker can have a certain proposition accepted without bearing the burden of supporting it or taking on the responsibility of advancing it. This description of presuppositions as implicit and improper speech acts can explain their dialogical effects.

From an epistemic perspective, presuppositions can be conceived as the conclusion of an instance of presumptive reasoning, where the speaker proceeds from rules of presumption and common knowledge about what is ordinarily shared in a specific culture and community to come to a prediction about his interlocutor's particular knowledge. As this prediction is based on a kind of reasoning, it can be assessed as correct or incorrect, or as reasonable or unacceptable. The epistemic and reasoning levels of analysis can explain the dialectical effects of this phenomenon. From a dialectical perspective, presuppositions are instruments for inserting new commitments into the interlocutor's commitment store. Presuppositions shift the burden of proof, in the sense that the hearer needs to interrupt the dialogue and advance a reason to reject the speaker's presupposition. He is held responsible for what has never advanced, and he needs to defend himself against an incorrect presumption. Finally, presuppositions can be rhetorical strategies. They can be used to communicate pieces of information that could not be provided or could not be disproved easily, and that at the same time evoke value judgments and emotions.

This account of presuppositions has been applied in particular to definitions. As noticed in the previous chapter, from a dialectical point of view, there is nothing wrong with redefining a term, as long as it does not introduce dangerous ambiguity and the definition is adequately defended against criticisms. Presupposed redefinitions, or "arguments by redefinition," are extremely powerful because they avoid any burden of proof. From a pragmatic perspective, the speaker sets the acceptance of the redefinition as a condition for the continuation of the dialogue. The hearer needs to perform a meta-dialogical move in order to counter it. He needs to stop the dialogue and start a discussion about its possibile conditions. From an epistemic perspective, presupposed redefinitions are presumptions about the interlocutor's knowledge of the definition concept that is presented as commonly accepted. For this reason, they dialectically shift the burden of proving them. The hearer needs to advance a reason (which can be simply epistemic or needs to be grounded on evidence about the shared meaning) to reject a meaning that he could have never accepted. He needs to refuse what he could never have been committed to. The effectiveness of redefinitions depends on the vagueness, or controversial nature, or the concepts redefined. The absence of a definition, or the existence of several of them, increases the burden of disproof. How is it possible to prove that a definition is not commonly accepted if there is not a commonly accepted meaning?

This account of redefinition can explain a fundamental feature of persuasive definitions and quasi-definitions, which represent the two crucial strategies of emotive language. There is nothing wrong in redefining a word or the values used to evaluate the fragment of reality it refers to. However, the strategic choice of taking redefinitions of meaning and values and new hierarchies of values for granted is based on a fallacious or at best incorrect presumptive reasoning. Fallacious persuasive definitions are strategies consisting in presupposing an unaccepted definition, taking a new unknowable description of meaning as if it were commonly shared. The fallaciousness of quasi-definitions can be described in a similar fashion. The speaker presumes that new hierarchies or definitions of values, or certain commonly unaccepted ones, are commonly shared. This unacceptability premise can be easily detected when it clearly conflicts with common knowledge. However, often values and definitions are controversial, and this lack of consensus makes such moves effective and dangerous. The burden of disproving them is increased, as the hearer cannot oppose an argument that can bar the presumption implicitly introduced by the speaker.

6

Dialogues and Commitments

The previous chapters have given plenty of good reasons to be suspicious about the use of persuasive definitions and emotive language in argumentation, and to often see them, especially when examining discourse from a logical point of view, as suspicious, or even as inherently illegitimate moves. But is it possible that rational persuasion can be shown to be a legitimate aim of argumentation by providing some kind of objective framework in which there are rules for proper persuasion? Is there a procedural setting in which a persuasion attempt could be an appropriate speech act properly employed so that, under the right conditions, it could be a legitimate move in rational argumentation? In this chapter we show how we need to study how definitions and arguments containing loaded terms are put forth as part of a sequence of argumentation in a dialogue exchange. The move made in a dialogue where a party puts forward an argument, or where a party puts forward a definition that she wants the other party to accept, needs to be seen as a kind of speech act that can only be properly understood in a rule-governed dialogue setting, we will argue.

Although there can be different kinds of dialogues, the principal model for evaluating argumentation in cases of the use of emotively loaded language and persuasive definitions is that of the persuasion dialogue, a formal structure with moves and rules, and in which the aim of each participant is rational persuasion based on the values, commitments, and knowledge of the other party. As shown by a thematic example in the chapter, this model enables an analyst to systematically analyze arguments based on persuasive definitions and emotive terms in order to distinguish between cases where such arguments are reasonable and in cases where they are used as fallacious tactics to try to get the best of a speech partner unfairly.

Persuasion dialogues are now widely used in artificial intelligence as normative models that can help an analyst in tasks of identification, analysis, and evaluation of arguments (Greenwood, Bench-Capon & McBurney 2003; Leenes 2001; Lodder 1999; Prakken 2006). A persuasion dialogue, in this sense, refers to a specific type of rule-governed procedure with a specific goal of resolving a difference of opinions by means of arguments put forward and questioned (Prakken 2006). A very simple system based on Common Knowledge (CK) that has formed the basis of many other formal systems of persuasion dialogue is built and applied to illustrative cases that represent interesting problems or phenomena of persuasion arising from the use of emotive language. It is shown that in some instances putting forward a persuasive definition can be quite correct and appropriate as a move in argumentation, especially if the argument is about values, or matters pertaining to values.

1. Persuasion Dialogues

Persuasion dialogue is a term commonly used in argumentation studies (see Walton & Krabbe 1995; Walton 1999), artificial intelligence (see Loui 1998; Brewka 2001), and artificial intelligence in law (see Prakken 2001; Bench-Capon 1998; Gordon 1994). As clearly stated by Prakken (2006: 1), a persuasion dialogue can be broadly defined as a dialogue in which two or more participants try to resolve a difference of opinions by means of arguments, in order for each party to lead the other participants to change their point of view. The historical roots of the notion of persuasion dialogue can be found in the meaning of the word 'persuasion' (Rigotti 1995: 11). This word semantically stems from *pístis*, namely, the credit that a speaker obtains by means of his speech, namely, the recipient's agreement. In Rigotti's view, "the relation constituted by *pístis* is not only cognitive, but goes through the whole area of the human relationships, both institutionalized and personal" (ibid). In persuasion dialogues, the goal is to achieve the interlocutor's agreement with the speaker's viewpoint, respecting his freedom of choice, in order to modify his or her decision making related to a particular judgment on a state of affairs (see Rigotti & Cigada 2004). The purpose is to change some of the interlocutor's commitments (Walton & Krabbe 1995) in order to lead him or her to modify his or her viewpoint. The procedure leading to such a change can be modeled in formal models of dialogue analyzed in the following sections.

1.1. *The Structure of Persuasion Dialogues*

Persuasion dialogues can be seen in online disputes (Godden & Walton 2005b; Atkinson, Bench-Capon & McBurney 2006). In this usage, 'persuasion' refers not to a psychological persuasion of belief-change but to a kind of rational persuasion in which a party who did not previously accept some claim comes in the end to accept it through a process of rational argumentation. In this sense of the term, a proponent in a dialogue persuades a respondent to come to accept her conclusion after she presents an argument containing only premises that the respondent accepts, or is committed to, and uses this argument to get the respondent to come to accept the conclusion. The following example, modified slightly from (Prakken 2005: 3) provides an illustration:

PERSUASION DIALOGUE 1

(P₁) Paul: My car is safe.

(O₁) Olga: Why is your car safe?

(P₂) Paul: Since it has an airbag.

(O₂) Olga: That is true, but this does not make your car safe.

(P₃) Paul: Why does that not make my car safe?

(O₃) Olga: Because the newspapers recently reported on airbags expanding without cause.

(P₄) Paul: Yes, that is what the newspapers say, but that does not prove anything, since newspaper reports are unreliable sources of technical information.

(O₄) Olga: Still, your car is not safe, since its maximum speed is very high.

(P₅) Paul: OK, I was wrong that my car is safe.

In this sample dialogue, the two parties take turns making moves in the dialogue. The moves are indicated by the numbered letters. Paul's moves are P_1, P_2, ..., P_n. Olga's moves are O_1, O_2, ..., O_n.

At P_1 Paul makes the claim that his car is safe. We will treat the speech act of making a claim as equivalent to the speech act of putting forward an assertion. In any given type of dialogue there are rules about what kind of speech acts can be made at any given move. There are also rules about how the respondent is allowed to reply when the proponent makes an assertion. For example, one rule is that when one party makes a claim, the other party is entitled to ask for grounds that support the claim. At her first move, Olga puts forward her speech act of this type. She asks Paul for grounds that support his claim that his car is safe, asking "Why is your car safe?" Here she is asking Paul to present an argument that could be used to prove his claim. The "why" question is not a request for an explanation. It is a request for an argument to prove the claim. In other words, the location "Why is statement S true?" is taken to be equivalent to the command "Prove that S is true."

Providing grounds for support means putting forward an argument that has the claim as its conclusion. At his second move, Paul provides such an argument. It could be put in the following format with a premise and conclusion: My car has an airbag; therefore my car is safe. This argument is an interesting one because, in addition to the explicit premise "My car has an airbag," there is also an implicit premise. This implicit premise can be expressed as a conditional statement, saying that if my car has an airbag, then my car is safe.

Another common dialogue rule is often associated with the concept of burden of proof. In the example dialogue Paul fulfilled his burden of proof at his second move by putting forward an argument that provides grounds for his previous claim that his car is safe. Rules for burden of proof can be formulated in various ways, but the most general way of formulating such a rule is as follows: In a dialogue, if one party makes a claim, and the other party asks for an argument to support the claim, the first party has to either present such an argument or give up the claim. In the example dialogue, Paul has supported his claim, so there is no need for him to give it up.

Another rule relating to claims is that if you make a claim, you become committed to that claim. This means that the claim is inserted as a statement into a database representing all the statements that you have previously committed yourself to in the dialogue. This database also includes a set of statements that both parties are committed to and that neither of them is prepared to dispute. This set of statements is called the Common Knowledge Base. In a dynamic persuasion dialogue, the common knowledge base is continually being updated as new information comes in.

Olga's second move is also interesting for us to comment on, because instead of making a single move, she combines two speech acts, in effect making a double move. It is questionable in some types of dialogue whether this should be allowed, because the basic rule of dialogue is that of turn taking, meaning that each time a party makes a move, she should wait until the other party has an opportunity to make a move before saying anything else. Here it appears then that Olga is cheating, because she first of all makes a concession, a kind of speech act which means that the speaker is making a commitment to something previously claimed, but then in the same move she also makes a counterclaim. She concedes that Paul's car has an airbag, but she claims, contrary to his previous argument, that having an airbag does not make his car safe. There are interesting questions about whether this kind of double move in a dialogue should generally be allowed. In some simple types of dialogue such a double move would not allowed, whereas in the sample dialogue the double move seems reasonable. In a more permissive type of dialogue, as long as the rules are clear, more than one speech act can be made with a single move.

1.2. *Commitments and Persuasion Dialogues*

Persuasion dialogues are grounded on the interlocutors' (or agents') commitments, namely, the speaker's undertaking to a statement he made. The statements of the agents engaged in a persuasion dialogue are not analyzed in terms of belief or knowledge, but rather in terms of interpersonal rules of communication or effects on the dialogical situation. Statements bind the speaker to a certain type of dialogical behavior, obviously relative to the type of communicative setting or type of interaction. For instance, asserting a proposition would reasonably lead the speaker not to deny it in his next move, or to defend it in case it is challenged by the other party. This dialogical perspective was opened by the works of Hamblin (1970, 1971), in which he used the notion of commitment to formalize dialogues and describe fallacies.

Hamblin (1970, 1971) required that the commitment set of each player be a set of public statements, for example, a set of sentences written on a blackboard in view of all the dialogue participants. The rules for a system CBV[1] are given in the following. CBV includes all the rules for CB, along with other rules that allow for implicit commitments as well as explicit commitments. CBV is based on the idea that there is a second set called implicit commitments that are not on public view to the participants. Each party has a commitment set divided into two subsets. One consists of the explicit commitments a party has gone on record as asserting. This set of propositions is on view to both parties. The other consists of a set that neither party can see, or get access to, unless something happens in the dialogue to reveal them. In CBV, implicit commitments of a party are revealed by being transferred from the implicit side to the explicit side, if the party having an implicit commitment tries to avoid acknowledging it. For example, suppose the party denies it is committed to a particular proposition, but it is somehow revealed that it is among its implicit commitments. In such a case, the party has to resolve the apparent inconsistency by either retracting the implicit commitment or going on record as accepting it as an explicit commitment (Walton 1984: 252–254).

In Hamblin's (1971: 148) view, formal dialogues are aimed at exchanging information; however he distinguishes information-oriented dialogues from other systems, in which participants are permitted "to develop an argument by securing assent to individual steps." Those systems are grounded on a rationality principle, meaning that not only is the speaker committed to his statements, but also to their logical consequences. This principle, which seems to be the grounding idea behind the examples of dialogues that Hamblin (1970, 1971) offered, was seen by Walton (1984) as representing something close to the critical discussion type of dialogue that could be generally classified under the category of persuasion dialogue.

In this type of dialogue, the proponent builds up a chain of argumentation using only premises the respondent has become committed to, and her ultimate goal of rational persuasion is only successful when the end point of the chain of argumentation is her thesis in the dialogue (called the ultimate *probandum* in law). In this model there are four basic requirements that determine when the proponent's argumentation in a persuasion dialogue is successful (Walton 1999: 121):

(R1) The respondent is committed to all the premises of the arguments.
(R2) Each single argument in the chain of argumentation is structurally correct.

---

[1] The names of the dialogue systems started with the letters A, AA, AB, B, BA, and so forth. CB was the third of the C systems. V stands for veiled or dark-side (implicit) commitments. The idea was to start with the simplest systems and work up to more complex ones.

(R3) The chain of argumentation has the proponent's thesis as its (ultimate) conclusion.

(R4) Arguments meeting (R1), (R2), and (R3) are the only means that count as fulfilling the proponent's goal in the dialogue.

From this view, persuasion dialogue is taken to represent the motivating idea that enables us to build an abstract normative model of how rational argumentation should ideally proceed when two parties have a difference of opinion and want to try to resolve the issue by bringing forward their strongest arguments, while at the same time criticizing the argument of the other side. Each party has a task to perform in the dialogue, and the successful carrying out of that task by using rational argumentation is the goal of each party. The proponent's task is to rationally persuade the respondent to come to accept her (the proponent's) thesis. The respondent's task is to rationally persuade the proponent to come to accept his (the respondent's) thesis. Of course, how such an abstract model of rational persuasion can be applied to real examples of persuasion attempts in conversational argumentation raises many interesting questions. In this chapter, we build a special abstract model of this sort.

The abstract model of persuasion dialogue set forth in the next section is very simple. There are only two parties, called the proponent and the opponent, and each tries to persuade the other to accept a claim by using arguments to prove it. Persuasion dialogues stem from a conflict of opinion, consisting in the respondent's denial or questioning of the proponent's position, and they presuppose that each party has the capacity and freedom to defend its point of view (see Vanderveken 2001). The commitment to incompatible positions (A: Bob stole the milk; B: Bob did not steal the milk), or the interlocutor's refusal to accept the speaker's viewpoint (A: Bob stole the milk; B: Why do you say that?), is the dialogical situation which the dialogue is aimed at altering. The interlocutor's goal is to change the other party's commitments, and therefore its evaluation of a situation, which can be a description (Bob stole the milk) or a judgment (Bob is a thief). The instrument to lead the interlocutor to change their position is a chain of arguments following from premises belonging to the knowledge shared by the latter. Arguments in persuasion dialogues can be conceived as patterns of reasoning that transfer the strength of the interlocutor's commitment to premises to a conclusion by a chain of inferences.

This account of Hamblin's dialogue systems as being explainable by appeal to an underlying notion of rational persuasion became the foundation of Walton's (1984) formal dialogue games, and the idea of distinguishing different types of dialogues on the grounds of commitment rules and participants' goals was later developed by Walton and Krabbe (1995) in their models of persuasion dialogue.

2. Models of Persuasion Dialogues

In order to analyze the characteristics of a persuasion dialogue, it can be useful to take into consideration two perspectives on it. The first model conceives persuasion dialogues within the framework of different types of dialogues, described using the same dialectical model. The second model, developed by the Pragma-Dialectical school, analyzes it in its internal structure and its components.

2.1. *Persuasion Dialogue as a Type of Dialogue*

The theory of types of dialogues stems from a conception of dialogue games developed by Hamblin (1970), Woods and Walton (1978), Mackenzie (1979), Hintikka (1979), and Barth and Krabbe (1982). Dialogues evolved from the application of logical axioms to propositions that were not considered true or false, but only belonging to the commitment store of the participants. A dialogue is formally defined as an ordered 3-tuple $<O, A, C>$, where O is the opening stage, A is the argumentation stage, and C is the closing stage (Gordon & Walton 2009). Dialogue rules define what types of moves are allowed (Walton & Krabbe 1995). At the opening stage, the participants agree to take part in some type of dialogue that has a collective goal. A global burden of proof is set at the opening stage. In law, this is called the burden of persuasion. During the argumentation stage there is an evidential burden of proof (often called a burden of producing evidence) for each argument that means that the argument will fail to persuade unless sufficient evidence for it is produced. This evidential burden of proof can shift from one side to the other during the argumentation stage as arguments are put forward and critically questioned. Once the argumentation has reached the closing stage, the outcome is determined by the trier, who determines whether one side or the other has met its burden of persuasion, according to the standard of proof set at the opening stage. Dialogues are constituted by a succession of speech acts. Every dialogue has a set of rules, establishing the interlocutors' allowed moves relative to their conversational roles and the types of argument that are to be considered acceptable. These rules depend on the conversational setting (including the interlocutors' common and shared knowledge), framing a meta-dialogical normative level, to which the interlocutors can appeal in case the dialogical procedure has been infringed.

Dialogues were distinguished in Walton and Krabbe (1995: 66), and later in Walton (1998), in basic six types, according to the participants' goal, initial situation, and the goal of dialogue. These are shown with a seventh type of dialogue in Table 6.1.

In Table 6.1 we can notice how the different dialogues are distinguished from the point of view of the type of interpersonal situation (conflict, need to obtain information or proofs) and the goal that interlocutors share.

Table 6.1. Types of Dialogues

Dialogue Type	Initial Situation	Participant's Goal	Communal Goal
Persuasion	Conflict of opinions	Persuade other party	Resolve issue
Inquiry	Need to have proof	Verify evidence	Prove hypothesis
Discovery	Need an explanation	Find a hypothesis	Support hypothesis
Negotiation	Conflict of interests	Get what you want	Settle issue
Information	Need information	Acquire information	Exchange information
Deliberation	Practical choice	Fit goals and actions	Decide what to do
Eristic	Personal conflict	Hit out at opponent	Reveal deep conflict

The identity of the participants' dialogical purpose leads to a dialogical exchange that is characterized by the basic presupposition of their common goal. For instance, in a persuasion dialogue the proponent and the respondent have the common goal of clarifying an issue that is controversial. Each participant has the individual goal of persuading the other party, but not, for instance, by making inappropriate moves, like threatening the other party instead of giving reason to support a claim. The type of goal shared by the interlocutors, along with the initial situation, determines the type of dialogue they are engaged in. The crucial issue in this perspective is to determine what the other party's commitments are in a particular dialogue exchange.

The types of dialogues outlined above are the most basic ones. However, several other mixed types of dialogues can be found in ordinary conversation. In a political debate, the interlocutors try to persuade the public and at the same time to personally attack the other party. Hence this type of dialogue combines eristic and persuasion dialogues (see Walton 2000; Jørgensen 1998). However sometimes the interlocutors apparently are committed to a certain type of dialogue, but in fact one of them is pursuing a goal different from the purpose of the dialogue he is purportedly engaged in. We take up many examples of such interesting phenomena in what follows.

The goal of a persuasion dialogue is to reveal the strongest arguments on both sides by pitting one against the other to resolve the initial conflict posed at the opening stage (Walton 2007b). This burden of persuasion, as it is called (Prakken 2006), is set at the opening stage. In a persuasion dialogue the proponent has a particular thesis to be proved, while the respondent has the role of casting doubt on that thesis or arguing for an opposed thesis. These tasks are set at the opening stage and remain in place until the closing stage, when one party or the other fulfills its burden of persuasion. The proponent has a burden of persuasion to prove (by a set standard of proof) the proposition that is designated in advance as her ultimate thesis. The respondent's role is to cast doubt on the proponent's attempts to succeed in achieving such proof. The crucial aspect of persuasion dialogues, as modeled in recent formal systems, is change of the interlocutor's dialogical situation by means of arguments grounded on propositions already accepted by the other party.

In Walton and Krabbe (1995) some of the formal models of persuasion dialogues studied have precise and simple rules that allow both parties only a limited set of alternatives for putting forward arguments and responding to them. These are called rigorous persuasion dialogues or RPDs. Generally, in an RPD, each participant is allowed to put forward only a single speech act each move, and the respondent will typically have only a limited choice of replies that can be made to that speech act. For example, the proponent may be able to ask whether a particular statement is true or not, and the respondent may have to answer yes or no, possibly with the third option to say "I don't know." The problem is that the RPDs do not model realistic natural language argumentation in a straightforward manner, because natural language persuasion dialogues require more flexibility. In a PPD dialogue, that is, in a permissive persuasive dialogue, instead of merely responding to the other party's arguments, a participant might need the freedom to ask for clarification, to draw a distinction, to go back and question a previous move in the dialogue, or to otherwise make more than one type of move at a given turn.

2.2. *Persuasion Dialogue as a Critical Discussion*

The critical discussion is not itself a formal model of dialogue, but it is a good place to start to show how a list of normative rules can be set up to govern a procedure that can be recognized as containing rational argumentation in a dialogue format. The goal of a critical discussion is to resolve a conflict of opinions by means of rational argumentation. There are two parties, called the proponent and the respondent, and two types of conflicts of opinions that we identified in different types of cases. In the one kind of case, there is another type of conflict of opinions in which only the proponent has a positive thesis to be proved, and all the respondent needs to do in order to be successful in resolving the conflict in his favor is put forward rational arguments that cast doubt on the proponent's attempts to prove her thesis. In the other kind of case, the proponent has the task of proving a designated statement by means of arguments that support it, while the respondent has the task of proving the opposite or negation of that statement. The latter is a symmetrical type of dialog whereas the former is asymmetrical. Thus it is often said that what distinguishes the two types of critical discussions is the difference in the burden of proof. In the latter type of dialogue, sometimes called a dispute, each party has a positive burden of proof to defend its thesis against questioning or attacks by the other party. In the other type of dialogue, sometimes called the dissent, the proponent has a positive burden of proof while the respondent has no positive burden of proof, but only a weaker burden, that might be called a burden of questioning.

According to the Amsterdam model of argumentation (van Eemeren and Grootendorst 1992: 35) a critical discussion has four characteristic stages. In the *confrontation stage*, the two parties agree on the conflict of opinions to be resolved by the discussion. Each party is said to have a viewpoint comprised of an attitude, pro or contra, toward the central statement at issue. The second stage is the *opening stage*, where each party accepts procedural rules to abide by. The third stage is the *argumentation stage*, where each side puts forward arguments to support its claim and raises critical questions about the arguments put forward by the other side. The fourth stage is the *concluding* (*closing*) *stage*, which determines the outcome of the critical discussion by deciding which side had the stronger argument. The participant who was found to have the weaker argument must concede at the closing stage to the party who has the stronger one, and this concession resolves the conflict of opinions. Although the argumentation stage is highly adversarial, because the winner or loser is determined by who put forward the most convincing argumentation, the outcome is objectively determined by whether the participants followed the rules and how strong their arguments were. Of course, any real instance of the temporal order of how the arguments were put forward does not need to correspond to the ordering of the normative structure of the four stages.

The argumentation stage of the critical discussion is governed by ten rules (van Eemeren and Grootendorst 1987: 184–293) that can be explained in a simplified form as follows. (1) Parties must not prevent each other from advancing arguments, for example, by using threats or force. (2) An arguer must respond to critical questions and must defend her argument if asked to do so. (3) An attack on an arguer's viewpoint must relate to that viewpoint. (4) More generally, a claim can only be defended by giving relevant arguments for it. (5) An arguer can be held to his implicit or unstated premises. (6) A party may not falsely present a premise as an accepted starting point nor deny a premise representing an accepted starting point. (7) An argument must be regarded as conclusively defended if its conclusion has been inferred by a structurally correct form of inference from premises that have been accepted by both parties at the outset of the discussion. (8) Arguments must be valid, or be capable of being made valid by the addition of implicit premises. (9) A party must retract his standpoint if he failed to defend it; a conclusive defense of the standpoint must result in the other party retracting its doubt about the standpoint. (10) Formulations must not be unduly vague or ambiguous. These rules are general in nature, and there could be many ways to implement them more precisely when precision is needed, but they do give the reader some idea of how a set of dialogue rules could function as a normative model representing how a productive discussion should ideally go if it is to be useful to resolve a conflict of opinions by rational argumentation. The parties are bound by their agreement to the rules through all four stages of the critical discussion, and hence it is easy to see how popular kinds of deviations from such rules, for example, using quarrelsome attacks, could violate one or more of these rules.

One problem is that many real dialogues seem to be quite successful even though the original conflict of opinions was not resolved by conclusively showing that the argument of the one side is stronger than that of the other. An example would be a philosophical discussion like one of the early Platonic dialogues, where two opposing viewpoints are put forward and at the closing stage there is no clear winner or loser. For these reasons, a distinction was drawn in Walton and Krabbe (1995) between persuasion dialogues generally and a critical discussion, which can be classified as a particular type of persuasion dialogue.

3. Dark-Side Commitments

When we think about dialogues and dialogue moves, we often think about what is said, and not to what is *not* said. There is a hidden dimension of dialogue games consisting of the premises on which the arguments or the explicit moves are based. In order to account for this dark side of the dialogues, it is necessary to inquire into the structure of arguments and common knowledge.

3.1. *Dark-Side Moves*

In persuasion dialogue 1, Olga's second move (O_2) is especially interesting because it presents a counterclaim that that goes against Paul's implicit premise that "having an airbag makes a car safe." We see here how one party's implicit premise in his previous argument can be attacked by the other party using a counterargument directed to that premise. There are different kinds of counterarguments, and this is an especially interesting one.

At his third move, Paul responds to Olga's counterclaim by asking for proof of it. Olga replies with an argument having the premise that the newspapers recently reported on airbags expanding without cause. This argument has some implicit premises. One is that if airbags are expanding without cause, cars containing those airbags are not safe. Another is that if the newspapers recently reported that airbags are expanding without cause, airbags are expanding without cause. Another is that newspapers are reliable sources of this kind of information. These implicit premises, taken together with Olga's explicit premises, imply the statement that Paul's car is not safe by a sequence of reasonable argumentation.

At his fourth move, Paul concedes this claim that the newspapers recently reported on airbags expanding without cause. But then he, as Olga did before at her second move, makes a double move by adding a counterargument. He replies that newspaper reports are unreliable sources of technical information. His argument is a counterattack to one of Olga's implicit premises, namely her assumption that newspapers are reliable sources of information.

At her fourth move, Olga, instead of continuing the thread of argumentation about airbags, moves to a different topic by claiming that Paul's car is not safe because its maximum speed is very high. Paul is persuaded by this argument, and retracts his original claim that his car is safe. This move represents the closing of the persuasion dialogue, since Paul has now conceded that his original claim has been disproved and is not acceptable.

In addition to the usual accoutrements of formal dialogue systems, including speech acts, commitment stores, commitment rules, and other kinds of rules governing the moves that can be made by one party, and how these moves must be responded to by the other party, another component needs to be added. It is a database representing the common knowledge shared by both parties. At the opening stage of the dialogue, both parties must agree to abide by the dialogue rules, and each must also have a commitment set and a specific statement identified as his or her global conclusion or thesis to be argued for or against during the whole sequence of the dialogue. This pair of global conclusions makes up the issue of the dialogue. In addition, both parties may agree to take on as commitments a set of statements that neither of them is inclined to dispute. These commitments represent statements that are not directly related to the issue under dispute and represent background assumptions of a kind that can be broadly classified under the heading of common knowledge. The term 'knowledge,' used in this way, is something of a misnomer, because the statements do not represent knowledge of the kind that might, for example, be restricted to scientific knowledge, or to propositions that are known to be true beyond reasonable doubt. They are merely propositions that are generally accepted, both by a majority and the wise (*endoxa*), or at any rate would not be likely to be disputed in the context of the particular argumentation under discussion. Such acceptance is a matter of degree, because a proposition that would not normally be disputed in an everyday conversation might be disputed in a philosophical discussion, for example. Thus, whether something can rightly be classified as common knowledge or not depends very much on the issue that is being discussed and the type of dialogue that the participants are engaged in.

In this theory, it is important to make a distinction between commitments based on common knowledge and those not based on common knowledge. In some cases an arguer may be taken to be committed to a proposition because it is an item of common knowledge that nobody would be likely to dispute in everyday conversational practices and that is not directly related to the issue being disputed in any obvious way. For example, if you and

I are having a dispute on the abortion issue, it is not likely that either of us would dispute the proposition that snow is white. It could be taken for granted as an implicit commitment of both parties, unless either party gave some reason to seriously dispute it, or lead us to believe that he or she had doubts about it. In contrast, however, there will be many other cases where it is clear that a participant can be taken to be committed to a particular proposition, based on how he or she has argued so far in the dialogue and has strongly advocated a particular position, even where this proposition couldn't reasonably be placed in the category of common knowledge. For example, in a case of an argument about abortion, one party who has adopted a pro-life view and argued that abortion is murder may be committed to the proposition that the fetus should be classified as a person. But this proposition could not reasonably be classified under the heading of common knowledge, and indeed it may be that the opposed party in the abortion dispute would strongly contest its truth. And it may well be, as in this case, that many people in the general population would contest such a proposition, and therefore that it would be inappropriate to categorize it under the heading of common knowledge.

3.2. *Enthymemes and Common Knowledge*

An example of an argument (Walton 2008: 365) may be used to illustrate an enthymeme: "Animals in captivity are freer than in nature because there are no natural predators to kill them." The conclusion is the statement that animals in captivity are freer than in nature. The explicit premise is that there are no natural predators to kill animals in captivity. The first implicit premise is the statement that there are natural predators to kill animals in nature. It can be classified as common knowledge. The second implicit premise is the statement that if animals are in a place where there are no natural predators to kill them, they are freer than if they are in a place where there are natural predators to kill them. It is not based on common knowledge. It is based on a persuasive definition of the word 'free' that would very likely be disputed by those who are opposed to the argument. It is not classifiable as common knowledge because it goes against the commonly accepted assumption that animals in the wild are freer than animals in captivity.

In the argument diagram shown in Figure 6.1, the explicit premise is shown on the left in the text box with no background. The two implicit premises are shown on the right in the darkened boxes.

The implicit premise in the middle, containing the statement that there are natural predators that kill animals in nature, is based on common knowledge. The implicit premise on the right represents a dark-side commitment of the arguer. It is a statement he is clearly committed to as part of his position in the argument he is advocating, but once we have articulated it as a

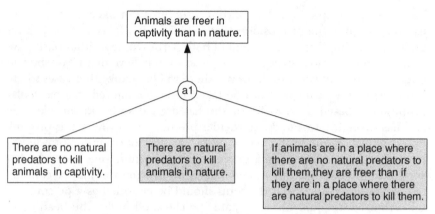

FIGURE 6.1. Argument diagram of the free animals example

premise, it might well be a statement that anyone who is skeptical about his argument, or opposes it, would be inclined to question or dispute.

4. Use of Defeasible Reasoning in Persuasion Dialogues

The dialogue system described in the following is meant to model argumentation that contains emotive language and persuasive definitions. The origins of this way of building a dialogue system are based on the four simple formal persuasion dialogue systems in Walton (1984). The four systems start from a minimal one called CB, mentioned above, that is similar to the system H of Hamblin (1970) and the system DC of Mackenzie (1981). In the formal theory of Hamblin (1971: 130) a move in a dialogue is defined as a triple $\{n, p, l\}$, where n is the length of the dialogue, defined as the number of moves made; p is a participant; and l is a locution (nowadays called a speech act). At the first move, the proponent begins the dialogue by making a move of some designated type allowed by the rules of the dialogue. At the next, the respondent replies by making a move. Thus in Hamblin's model, a dialogue is a sequence of single moves of this sort. One important type of move is the speech act consisting of putting forward an argument.

In the Hamblin-style system, there are only two parties, called the proponent and the respondent. Hamblin only considered simple two-party models of this sort. Each party has a thesis (proposition) to be proved that is designated at the opening stage, and each party puts forward arguments to try to persuade the other party to accept this proposition using as premises only propositions that are commitments of this other party. Hence, although Hamblin did not clearly distinguish between different types of dialogue, nowadays we would classify this type as being a persuasion dialogue.

For its rules of inference CB used only classical propositional calculus, but to bring the system up to date we also need defeasible rules of inference of the kind now called argumentation schemes. In this new system, instead of having a set of rules for propositional calculus, we just have two rules of inference. One rule, which might be called deductive *modus ponens*, is now also sometimes called strict *modus ponens*. It is the rule: If *A*, then *B*; *A*; therefore *B*, where the if–then is a strict (material) conditional, meaning that it is false that *A* is true and *B* is false. Let's let the symbol → stand for this familiar type of strict conditional of the kind used in deductive propositional logic. A strict *modus ponens* has the following form as a rule of inference that enables a conclusion to be drawn from a set of premises: $A \rightarrow B$; *A*; therefore *B*. Next we extend that very simple system by having a rule of inference for a defeasible *modus ponens* as well: If *A*, then defeasibly *B*; *A*; therefore (defeasibly) *B*. A familiar example is the canonical illustration of defeasible reasoning often used in computing: If Tweety is a bird, Tweety flies; Tweety is a bird; therefore Tweety flies. This inference is defeasible, meaning that even though the premises are true, and the conclusion will also be true in a typical normal case, in an exceptional case the conclusion may be false. In such a case we say that the inference *defaults*. For example, let's suppose that Tweety is a penguin. In such a case, the premises may be true, and the defeasible *modus ponens* form of inference may hold generally, but even so the conclusion may be false. We let the symbol => stand for a defeasible conditional. Then the defeasible *modus ponens* has the form: $A \Rightarrow B$; *A*; therefore *B*. A defeasible *modus ponens* will be called DMP, while a strict *modus ponens* will be called SMP. This system will also have classical negation, but we will not have rules of inference like *modus tollens* and contraposition that are familiar from deductive logic.

In general, the inference system fits defeasible logic (Nute 1994), used to model reasoning from partial and sometimes conflicting information. The basic units of defeasible logic are called *facts* and rules. Facts are statements that are accepted as true within the confines of a discussion. Here we use the terms proposition, fact, and statement interchangeably. They are denoted by the letters *S*, *T*, *U* ... and so forth, using subscripts if we run out of letters. What are called rules in defeasible logic are conditionals with a conjunctive antecedent of the following form. A strict rule has the form *S*, *T*, *U* ..., → *V*, where each of the statements *S*, *T*, *U* ... is called a prerequisite. With this kind of rule, it is not possible for all the prerequisites to be true and the consequent *V* false. A defeasible rule has the form *S*, *T*, *U* ..., => *V*, and it is possible for all the prerequisites to be true and the consequent false. In a system of defeasible logic rules can conflict, but the conflict can sometimes be resolved by using a priority relation on the rules. In addition, defeasible logic is able to tell whether a conclusion is or is not provable (Governatori et al. 2004). To prove a conclusion you have to look at the

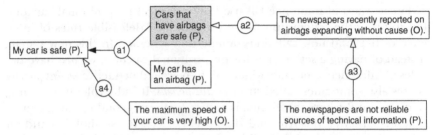

FIGURE 6.2. Pro and con argumentation in the airbag example

arguments both for and against the conclusion by carrying out three steps (Governatori 2008):

1. Give an argument for the conclusion to be proved
2. Consider the possible counterarguments for the conclusion that can be given.
3. Defeat each counterargument by showing that some premise does not hold or by producing a stronger counterargument for the original argument.

A conclusion is proved as the outcome if there is at least one argument supporting it and all the arguments against it are defeated. This is shown by examining all the arguments pro and contra deployed during the argumentation stage of a dialogue.

In Figure 6.2, representing the argumentation in the airbag example (persuasion dialogue 1), pro arguments are represented by an inference arrow with the closed arrowhead, and con arguments are represented by an inference arrow with an open arrowhead. The letters P and O indicate the arguers, Paul and Olga. Where the box has been darkened, it means that the statement in the box is an implicit premise. The arguments are numbered a1, a2, a3, and a4.

Paul's claim, represented at the left, is the statement that his car is safe. His pro argument has two premises, that his car has an airbag, and the implicit generalization that cars that have airbags are safe. Olga then attacks the implicit premise of his argument by stating that the newspapers recently reported on airbags expanding without cause. But then Paul attacks this statement by asserting that the newspapers are not reliable sources of technical information. So far we seem to have a standoff. From the viewpoint of defeasible logic, Olga has attacked Paul's argument, but then in turn Paul has attacked Olga's argument, since there is at least one argument supporting Paul's ultimate claim, but there is an argument attacking that argument, then another argument attacking an argument, and finally yet another argument attacking that argument. We still haven't considered the final argument, an additional argument supporting Paul's claim that his car is safe.

This is the argument a4, seen on the left in Figure 6.2, that the maximum speed of Paul's car is very high. Now Olga has two arguments, and the latest one about the maximum speed of Paul's car has not yet been attacked by any other argument. It would seem, then, from the point of view of defeasible logic, that Olga has won the argument. But is that all we need to know about this argument? We will go on to show that there are other aspects of the argument that need to be examined in more detail before we can do a deeper evaluation of a kind that will be more useful for our purposes.

We draw a distinction following Mackenzie (1981): A statement T is said to be an immediate consequence of a set of statements S_0, S_1, ..., S_n if and only if "S_0, S_1, ..., S_n, therefore T" is a substitution instance of an inference rule in the dialogue system. A statement T is said to be a consequence of a set of statements S_0, S_1, ..., S_n if and only if T is derived by a finite number of immediate-consequence steps from immediate consequences of S_0, S_1, ..., S_n. The question now to be decided is how the respondent can react in a dialogue where, at the previous move, the proponent has shown that statement S can be derived, either by a Defeasible *Modus Ponens* (DMP) or a Strict *Modus Ponens* (SMP), from a set of premises the respondent is committed to. It would seem that if the inference has the form of an SMP, the respondent can only retract a commitment from the conclusion if he retracts a commitment to one of the premises as well. The situation is different, however, if the inference has the form of a DMP. If this is the case, there may be an exception to the rule, and therefore the respondent should have the right to ask a critical question about whether the rule properly applies in the given case.

5. Defeasible Reasoning in the Airbag Example

We can recall in the airbag discussion between Paul and Olga that Paul provided the following argument to prove his claim that his car is safe: My car has an airbag, therefore my car is safe. As noted in the first section, there is an implicit premise of this argument which can be represented as a conditional statement saying that if a car has an airbag, the car is safe. This statement can be taken in two ways – as expressing a strict conditional or a defeasible conditional.

My car has an airbag → my car is safe.
My car has an airbag => my car is safe.

Representing this conditional statement in the first way as expressing a strict conditional does not seem to be right because my car having an airbag is not a sufficient condition of its being safe. For example, it might have an airbag but also have defective brakes. The second way is better. It expresses the statement that if my car has an airbag, then, all else being equal and subject to exceptions, it is safe.

Once the conditional premise is expressed in this way, we can see that the argument can be shown to fit the DMP form as follows.

Implicit Premise	My car has an airbag => my car is safe.
Explicit Premise	My car has an airbag.
Conclusion	My car is safe.

This argument can be attacked in three different ways. For the explicit premise, for example, Olga might say, "I looked at your car and I didn't see any airbag." Or for the implicit premise, for example, Olga might say, "Yes, your car as an airbag, but I also noticed that it has defective brakes." Or a counterargument having the opposite conclusion can be put forward; for example, consider Olga's argument that the newspapers recently reported on airbags expanding without cause, put forward at her third move in the example dialogue.

At his third move, Paul responded to Olga's counterclaim by asking for proof of it. Olga replied with an argument having the premise that the newspapers recently reported on airbags expanding without cause. As noted previously, this argument has three implicit premises. One is that if airbags are expanding without cause, cars containing those airbags are not safe. The other is that if the newspapers recently reported that airbags are expanding without cause, airbags are expanding without cause. Another is that newspapers are reliable sources of this kind of information. Her ultimate conclusion in the dialogue, which we claimed in Section 4 is based on logical reasoning, is that Paul's car is not safe.

This argumentation can be analyzed in more depth than the reconstruction shown in Figure 6.1 by adding the following implicit assumptions:

ARGUMENT 1

Explicit Premise	Paul's car has an airbag (A).
Implicit Premise	If Paul's car has an airbag (A), his car is safe (B).
Explicit Conclusion	Pauls' car is safe (B).

ARGUMENT 2

Explicit Premise	The newspapers recently reported on airbags expanding without cause (C).
Implicit Premise	If the newspapers recently reported that airbags are expanding without cause (C), airbags are expanding without cause (D).
Implicit Conclusion	Airbags are expanding without cause (D).
Implicit Premise	If airbags are expanding without cause (D), cars having airbags are not safe (E).

Implicit Conclusion	Cars having airbags are not safe (E).
Explicit Premise	Paul's car has an airbag (A).
Conclusion	Paul's car is not safe (not-B).

ARGUMENT 3

Explicit Premise	Newspapers are not reliable sources of technical information (F).
Implicit Premise	A report on airbags expanding without cause is technical information (G).
Implicit Premise	If newspapers are not reliable sources of technical information (F) and the report on airbags expanding without cause is technical information (G), then the newspaper report on airbags expanding without cause is not reliable (H).
Implicit Conclusion	The newspaper report on airbags expanding without cause is not reliable (H).
Implicit Premise	If the newspaper report on airbags expanding without cause is not reliable (H), then it is not the case that if the newspapers recently reported that airbags are expanding without cause (C), airbags are expanding without cause (D).
Implicit Conclusion	It is not the case that if the newspapers recently reported that airbags are expanding without cause (C), airbags are expanding without cause (D).

ARGUMENT 4

Explicit Premise	The maximum speed of Pauls' car is very high (I).
Implicit Premise	If the maximum speed of Paul's car is very high (I), his car is not safe (not-B).
Conclusion	Paul's car is not safe (not-B).

The first argument has this structure:

1. A; premise
2. A => B; premise
3. B; from 1 and 2 by DMP

The second argument has this structure:

1. C; premise
2. C => D; premise
3. D => E; premise
4. A; premise
5. D; from 1 and 2 by DMP
6. E; from 6 and 9 by DMP

The third argument has this structure:

1. C; premise
2. C => D; premise
3. D => E); premise
4. A; premise
5. D; from 2 and 1 by DMP
6. E; from 3 and 5 by DMP

The fourth argument has this structure:

1. I; premise
2. I => not-B; premise
3. Not-B; from 1 and 2 by DMP

This deeper analysis has brought out more implicit premises, and has made the inferential network of the argumentation tighter. Next we need to see how this inferential network fits into a larger structure by drilling down to an even deeper analysis.

6. The Formal Dialogue System CK

In order to describe the dialogical moves of definition, we need to formalize the dialogical structure in which they are performed. To this purpose we will build on the existing formal dialogue systems developed by Hamblin and outline a model that can solve the fundamental problems that definitional moves raise.

6.1. *Limits of the Existing Models*

The problem of retraction is the main difficulty in developing a useful system of persuasion dialogue that can be applied to realistic argumentation in a helpful way by dealing with phenomena like emotive language and persuasive definitions (Walton & Krabbe 1995). It will often happen in problematic cases of the kind associated with fallacies or other questionable dialogue moves that a party will often retract a commitment as soon as he realizes that the other party might use it to defeat his argument. This difficulty was even more prominent in the persuasion dialogue system, because it recognized implicit commitments as well as explicit commitments of the arguer. The CBV was based on the idea that there is an additional set of implicit commitments that are called dark-side commitments because they are not on view to either party. The regular or explicit (light-side) commitments, the only kind recognized by Hamblin, represent statements in the commitment sets that are visible to all parties in a dialogue, and perhaps even to an audience, if there is one. Hamblin (1970, 1971) required that the commitment set of each player be a set of public statements, for example, a set of sentences written on a blackboard, readable by all the dialogue participants.

Here we can have another kind of problem arise. Hamblin made no general requirement that the statements in the party's commitment had to be set up to be consistent with each other. But there is a certain kind of more limited type of consistency of commitments that could arguably be an important requirement in persuasion dialogue. Suppose that at a particular point in the dialogue one party denies that he is committed to a particular proposition, but then the same proposition is found in his set of implicit commitments. This kind of situation could certainly be significant with respect to certain kinds of informal fallacies. For example, suppose a proponent goes on record as being explicitly committed to being opposed to a certain proposition, but then suppose that the respondent finds out that this proposition can be shown to be contained in his dark-side commitment set. This could be a problem for the proponent, and the respondent could use the implicit inconsistency to attack the proponent's credibility. Suppose the respondent does so. Should it be a rule of persuasion dialogue that the respondent must immediately resolve the inconsistency by retracting either the implicit commitment or the explicit commitment? For extensive discussions of the problem and how to solve the problem of retraction in different types of persuasion dialogues the reader is referred to Walton and Krabbe (1995).

6.2. *Developing Formal Dialogue Models*

The aforementioned CBV system is a simple system of persuasion dialogue, like the systems of Hamblin and Mackenzie and many other familiar systems, in that it did not include a representation of the knowledge that the participants have access to, nor did it include any facility for updating knowledge. In the system called CKP (Common Knowledge Persuasion), which will be presented in the following, there is a special set of propositions designated at the opening stage of the dialogue called the "Common Knowledge Base." This knowledge base is shared by both parties to the dialogue, meaning that they both have access to it and they both agree on the propositions that it contains or does not contain. The argumentation used by either party, in order to be rationally persuasive, must rest only on premises drawn from common knowledge or from premises that are commitments of the other party, even if they are not accepted as knowledge by both parties. The commitment structure of a persuasion dialogue can be represented as shown in Figure 6.3.

The common knowledge base represents a set of propositions that neither party in the dialogue is inclined to question or dispute. Generally, it represents a set of propositions that are widely accepted as being true, or at any rate are not widely subject to doubt or disputation in relation to the topic currently being discussed in the persuasion dialogue. Without some

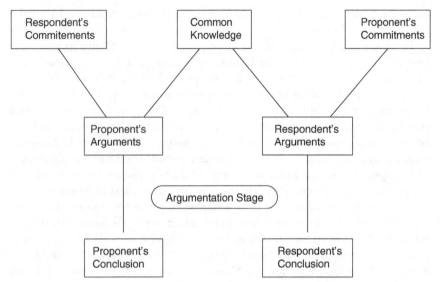

FIGURE 6.3. Commitment structure of persuasion dialogue

basis of agreement of this sort, deep disagreements cannot be resolved by a critical discussion. For example, both parties to the dialogue might agree to include all the statements made in an encyclopedia in the common knowledge base.

A second feature that is included in CKP is that this knowledge base can be updated. As new knowledge comes in each participant may have to add new statements to his commitments or retract some of the statements that were previously in his commitment set. For example, if it is shown that there is an exception to a rule, and this exception is widely accepted, it can be included in the common knowledge base. This inclusion may affect whether certain arguments are acceptable or not. We also need to add to CK the possibility of shifting to a higher level of dialogue. There is also a third feature that needs to be included. In addition to the primary level of dialogue, there also needs to be a meta-dialogue level in which a third party critically analyzes a given argument in CKPor any other speech act put forth by either of the two parties in the CKP dialogue at the primary level.

So far everything that has been described occurs at a primary level in which the two parties, the proponent and the respondent, take turns putting forward arguments or making other moves directed to each other. In some cases, analysis at this level will enable us to offer a dialectical theory of enthymemes, because there are cases where the respondent to an argument needs to identify implicit assumptions in it before he can respond to it appropriately. However, there are other cases where it is the function of a third party to clarify arguments by bringing out implicit premises or conclusions in them. In these cases, we must move to the secondary level, or the meta-dialogue level (Krabbe 2003), in which a third party critically analyzes the argumentation put forward by the other two parties at the primary level. This third party uses the evidence of the text of discourse of the dialogue known at the point where the dialogue has proceeded so far. It is important that there be a specific text of discourse that has been tracked and recorded. In law, this third party is the trier, the judge, or the jury that decides the outcome of the trial. In everyday conversational argumentation, this third party may be an argument analyst of the kind found in a critical thinking course or an applied logic course, where real examples of arguments are being analyzed and evaluated in a university classroom. In order to analyze a given argument, here we first have to identify the argument, meaning that we have to identify its premises and conclusion. This task, of course, takes us right into the problem of enthymemes, because typical real arguments of the kind studied in such an environment tend to have premises and conclusions that may not be explicitly stated but need to be taken into account in order to give a fair analysis and evaluation of the argument.

6.3. *Rules of the CKP Dialogue System*
The following set of rules for CKP follow the original Hamblin (1970, 1971) format used in the system CB in Walton (1984: 132–135)[2] and extend some of the conventions used in the system CBVK (an extended dialogue system including not only the commitment stores, but also the common knowledge base) used to model argumentation about implicit commitments in the study of enthymemes in Walton (2007c). There are two participants, α and β, and each take turns moving according to the following set of rules. As indicated previously, the speech act of putting forward a statement in this type of persuasion dialogue is taken to be equivalent to the speech act of making a claim.

PERMITTED SPEECH ACTS

(i) *Statement:* Statement letters, S, T, U, ... are permissible speech acts, and compounds of statement letters made up from negation, the strict conditional, and the defeasible conditional are as well.

(ii) *Withdrawal:* "No commitment S" is the speech act for withdrawing (retraction) a statement.

(iii) *Question:* The question "S?" asks "Is it the case that S is true?"

(iv) *Challenge:* The challenge "Why S?" requests some statement that can serve as an argument for S.

(v) *Argument:* A participant can put forward a set of statements $\{S_1, S_2, \dots S_n\}$ that are to be taken as premises that offer evidential support for T.

---

[2] An example dialogue called Republic of Taronga is given in Walton (1984:120–127).

(vi) *Definition*: A participant can put forward a statement of the form, "X is defined as S," where X is some word, phrase, or other linguistic expression to be defined (called the *definiendum*) and S is a statement (the *definiens*) that purports to give a set of necessary and/or sufficient conditions that enable the hearer to determine whether something can be classified as an X or not.

(vii) *Accept Definition*: A participant can put forward a statement of the form "I accept that X is defined as S."

(viii) *Reject Definition*: A participant can put forward a statement of the form "I do not accept that X should be defined as S."

COMMITMENT RULES

(i) After a participant makes a statement, S, it is included in his commitment store.

(ii) After the withdrawal of S, the statement S is deleted from the speaker's commitment store.

(iii) All statements in the common knowledge set are included in the commitment sets of both parties from the opening stage onward.

(iv) A statement from the common knowledge base can only be retracted if new information comes into that set that is now shown to be inconsistent with a previously accepted statement.

(v) "Why S?" can only be asked by a speaker if the hearer is committed to S, but cannot be asked if S is in the common knowledge set.

(vi) Every statement shown by the speaker to be an immediate consequence of statements that are commitments of the hearer becomes a commitment of the hearer.

(vii) If a participant states "No commitment S" and S is in the dark side of his commitment store, then S is immediately transferred into the light side of his commitment set.

(viii) When a participant puts forward a statement of the form, "X is defined as S" by making a definition speech act, that statement is immediately put into the light side of his commitment set.

(ix) When a participant puts forward a statement of the form, "I accept that X is defined as S," the statement "X is defined as S" is immediately put into the light side of his commitment set.

DIALOGUE RULES

(i) Each speaker takes his turn to move by making a single speech act at each move (with one exception, namely, R2).

(ii) A no-commitment speech act may accompany a why speech act within one move.

(iii) A question "*S*?" must be followed by (i) a statement "*S*," (ii) a statement "Not-*S*," or (iii) "No commitment *S*."

(iv) "Why *S*?" must be followed by (i) "No commitment *S*" or (ii) showing that *T* is in the common knowledge base, or (iii) offering some statement *T*, where *S* is a strict or defeasible consequence of *T*.

(v) "*X* is defined as *S*" must be followed by (i) the statement "I accept that *X* is defined as *S*" or (ii) "I do not accept that *X* should be defined as *S*" for the following reason [accompanied by an argument].

WIN-LOSS RULES

(i) Both players agree at the opening stage that the argumentation stage of their dialogue will reach the closing stage after some finite number of moves.

(ii) At the opening stage, a standard of proof has to be agreed upon by both parties. Typically, in a persuasion dialogue, the standard of proof is that of preponderance of the evidence, meaning that if one argument is stronger than the other, the stronger argument wins.

(iii) At the closing stage, the argumentation on both sides is evaluated to see if either side has met its required standard of proof.

(iv) The side judged to have met its standard of proof at the closing stage wins the dialogue.

In the simplest case, both parties have to agree on the question of whether either of them has met its required burden of proof. In some instances, however, this two-participant model will be insufficient for our purposes, because in some cases in which enthymemes conceal implicit premises about values and what is implied by an argumentative term, the dialectical context is more complex than a two-party framework. In such cases the dialogue needs to allow for the activity of an argument analyst who reconstructs the argument based on the textual evidence indicating the commitment of the primary participants. The third party judges which statements can or cannot be reasonably inserted as missing premises or conclusions (commitments) using the text of discourse, based on the explicit wording of the text and on common knowledge. Hence we need to allow for three-party CK dialogues in which a third party who plays the role of audience or judge evaluates the argumentation on each side of the issue to determine not only which one had the stronger arguments but also what the implicit commitments of each party can rightly be taken to be, based on the evidence.

6.4. *Argumentation in CKP*

We can see that persuasion dialogues of this type are partly adversarial, in that each party is trying to win out over his adversary. However, in this model, persuasion dialogues are also partly collaborative, because each party needs to follow the rules and cannot use all kinds of aggressive tactics, for example, tactics to prevent the other party from speaking or using irrelevant arguments that do not really prove anything in relation to the issue being discussed. Generally, in order to succeed in his goal of persuading β to accept his or her ultimate thesis T to be proved, α needs to find premises that β is committed to but that imply α's thesis by a valid chain of reasoning. β will try to avoid making commitments that could be used as premises in any chain of argumentation that proves T, and will mainly take on commitments that support his own thesis. During a successful CKP dialogue, more dark-side commitment sets of both parties will be revealed. This progress through the dialogue allows each party to understand the position of the other party more deeply, and it also allows each party to gain insight into the reasons behind his own views. This side benefit of persuasion dialogues has been called the maieutic effect, meaning that it assists in giving birth to new ideas.

To illustrate what typical sequences of argumentation CKP look like, we present a sample dialogue in Table 6.2. R stands for a round, a pair of moves, the first by α and the second by β. Implicit commitments are shown in bold print. Before the dialogue in Table 6.2 begins, **U => V** is a dark-side commitment of β. α's thesis to be proved in the dialogue is V.

At the first move, α asks β whether he accepts S. β replies that he does. Then she asks him whether he accepts $S => T$. He replies that he does. Already at move two, then, it is clear that α successfully persuades β to accept U if he can be persuaded to accept T. It is easy to see that α does this, and thereby proves U. Commitment rule (v) applies at move seven, now making his former implicit commitment **U => V** an explicit commitment of β. U implies V; V is the missing component needed to prove V by DMP. B resists commitment to V at move nine, but it is no good. His previous moves have now committed him to V, and so V goes into his commitment set. So this dialogue illustrates a winning strategy for α.

7. Dialogues Containing Arguments about Definitions

In this section we examine two examples of dialogues that contain arguments about definitions. The first example is a comparatively simple one where an ordinary definition is put forward and responded to by arguments that cast doubt on it. The second example is a persuasive definition.

7.1. *Persuasion Dialogues and Definitions*

Martha begins the following dialogue in the first example by making a claim. She states that current research in e-humanities is putting an increasing emphasis on multimedia. There is no information given about the opening stage of the dialogue, but since Martha has made a factual claim she is

Table 6.2. A Sample Dialogue in CKP

R	Move of α	Move of β	Commitments α	Commitments β
1	*S?*	*S*		S
2	*(S => T)?*	*S=>T*		S=>T
3	*T?*	No commitment *T*		
4	*(S; S => T) => T*	*T*		T
5	*U?*	No commitment *U*		
6	*T=>U?*	*T=>U*		T=>U
7	*U?*	*U*		U
8	*U=>V?*	No commitment *U => V*		U => V
9	*(U; U=>V) => V*	No commitment *V*		V

obliged to defend it, and from what we see from the remaining moves in the dialogue, where Edward challenges Martha to defend her viewpoint, it is reasonable to classify it as a persuasion dialogue. The interesting thing about it, however, is that it is a persuasion dialogue about the meaning of a word.

PERSUASION DIALOGUE 2

(M₁) Martha: Current research in e-humanities is putting an increasing emphasis on multimedia.

(E₁) Edward: What do you mean by 'multimedia'?

(M₂) Martha: The term 'multimedia' is used to contrast with media which only use traditional forms of printed or hand-produced material. Multimedia includes a combination of text, audio, still images, animation, video, and interactivity content forms.

(E₂) Edward: Are you sure that definition is accurate?

(M₃) Martha: Well yes, I think so, I took it from Wikipedia.

(E₃) Edward: Wikipedia is not a reliable source.

(M₄) Martha: How do you know that?

(E₄) Edward: Wikipedia's openness makes it subject to errors.

(M₅) Martha: Why should that be?

(E₅) Edward: Anyone can edit a wiki. Wikipedia cannot be reliable if anyone can edit a wiki.

At his first move, Edward asks Martha what she means by the term 'multimedia.' It is reasonable to view this move as a request for a definition of a word. At her second move, Martha offers a definition that has two parts. The first part is a contrastive statement that sets up the second part, which is a list of several other terms that Martha can expect Edward to be familiar with. These terms are classified under the general heading of multimedia. It is important for us to note that Martha's move is not an argument. It is an explanation, an attempt to explain to Edward the meaning of the word 'multimedia,' a term that is current in everyday usage, even though it is a recent term that Edward may not be familiar with or know the precise meaning of. Thus it is important to be aware that Martha is offering a lexical definition, meaning a definition of a word that has an established meaning in natural language.

Next we need to observe that Edward and Martha engage in a sequence of argumentation that identifies the example as an instance of persuasion dialogue. In the second move, Edward asks whether she is sure that the definition is accurate. In other words, he is being skeptical about the definition she has offered. He is not making the stronger claim that the definition is wrong. He is only making the weaker claim that there is doubt about whether this definition is accurate. The normal explanatory move in such a case would be to cite a dictionary entry, or perhaps several of them. Instead, however, Martha cites Wikipedia as her source. Edward then makes the claim that Wikipedia is not a reliable source, thereby challenging Martha's definition. He then backs up this challenge with some arguments.

The structure of the entire chain of argumentation is represented in Figure 6.4. The text box at the far left contains Martha's statement made at her first move in the dialogue sequence, where she put forward her definition of the term 'multimedia.' She supports this statement by claiming that her definition comes from Wikipedia. The inference from this premise to her conclusion about the meaning of the term 'multimedia' is represented as argument a1 on the diagram. The arrow leading from argument a1 to its conclusion has a closed arrowhead, indicating it is a pro argument. In contrast, the next argument, a2, has an open arrowhead, indicating it is a con argument. Edward states that Wikipedia is not a reliable source, revealing his opposition to Martha's implicit assumption that Wikipedia is reliable. Her implicit premise, shown in the darkened box, is the assumption that Wikipedia is a reliable source. The argument continues as Edward attacks Martha's assumption claim that Wikipedia is a reliable source. This example has been relatively unproblematic as far as understanding the argumentation in it is concerned, but grasping the structure of the argumentation in the second example is more problematic.

7.2. *Persuasion Dialogues and Persuasive Definitions*

As a thought experiment let's extend the dialogue between Paul and Olga in the airbag example. Let's say that they continue the dialogue as follows.

PERSUASION DIALOGUE 3

(O5) Olga: Would you care to respond?

(P6) Paul: Yes, my car has a very high maximum speed, but that does not mean it is unsafe. Your argument wrongly assumes that if a car has a very high maximum speed, the car is not safe.

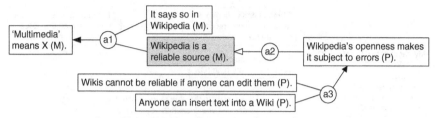

FIGURE 6.4. Chain of argumentation in the multimedia dialogue

(O6) Olga: Many people get killed on the roads because cars are going too fast, and that is not safe. Young drivers like to drive too fast, and this is responsible for many road fatalities.

(P7) Paul: The solution to this problem is better training and supervision for young drivers, not introducing bureaucratic regulation by the government requiring speed control devices on cars.

(O7) Olga: I was not talking about requiring speed control devices on cars.

(P8) Paul: Lessening a car's capability for maneuvering to avoid accidents is not safe either. Safety is maximizing the freedom of choice to avoid bad outcomes. If you reduce the maximum speed that a car has, you also lessen its capability for maneuvering to avoid accidents.

Paul's argument begins with a concession, and then follows (at the same move) with a new argument. His new argument is relevant because it attacks Olga's previous argument claiming that his car is not safe. He attacks it by finding an implicit premise that her argument depends on, the conditional statement that if a car has a very high maximum speed, the car is not safe. Next, at her move six, Olga makes some statements about the causes of vehicle accidents. At their seventh moves, they exchange some arguments about the solution to the problem. Paul argues against installing speed control devices on cars as a solution, claiming that this would be a bad solution because it would introduce what he calls "bureaucratic regulation by the government." Olga replies, quite correctly, that she was not talking about requiring speed control devices on cars.

At his seventh move, it is interesting to observe that Paul has moved significantly into the arena of emotive language, especially by his use of the word 'bureaucratic,' a term with highly negative emotive connotations. This can emphatically be described as an unfair move on his part, and Olga should both observe that and object to it. However, instead of that, she makes the equally important point that it was Paul, not her, who had introduced the talk about requiring speed control devices on cars.

At Paul's eighth and final move, he moves more deeply into the arena of emotive language by putting forward a persuasive definition to support his argument. We recall that at his move six, Paul had attacked by claiming that

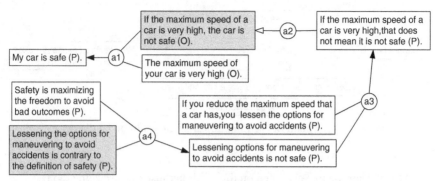

FIGURE 6.5. Paul's new argument

Olga wrongly assumes that if a car has a very high maximum speed, the car is not safe. This attack is based on the following three statements:

1. If you reduce the maximum speed the car has, you also lessen its capability for maneuvering to avoid accidents.
2. Lessening a car's capability for maneuvering to avoid accidents is not safe.
3. Safety is maximizing the freedom of choice to avoid bad outcomes.

The question is how these three explicit assertions go together to make up the argument that Paul uses to attack Olga's argument. An outline of the structure of Paul's argument is shown in Figure 6.5.

Olga's original argument against Paul's claim that his car is safe is presented at the top left of Figure 6.5. The rest of the argumentation shown in Figure 6.5 represents Paul's attack on Olga's argument. This attack was based on Paul's explicit statement, "If the maximum speed of the car is very high, that does not mean it is not safe," shown at the top right of Figure 6.5. But what does this statement mean? How are we to interpret it? One way we might interpret it is as making a claim to the effect that the maximum speed of a car should not be a criterion, or at least a decisive criterion, for the safety of the car. To support this claim, Paul presents an argument based on a definition. This part of the argument does not appear until Paul's eighth move in the dialogue, where he defines safety as maximizing the freedom of choice to avoid bad outcomes. According to the rules of CKP, Olga has the right to not accept this definition, but as far as we are told in the example, she does not exercise this right. The question is how she might go about this. According to the rules of CKP, she will have to present an argument against Paul's proposed definition. How might she do that? Before Paul's move eight, neither party had tried to define the notion of safety, so until Paul's move the way to define it was up for grabs. Maybe Olga could put forward an opposed definition, or at least a different one. But first, according to CKP, she has to put forward an argument against Paul's proposed definition.

Paul's definition uses the expression "freedom of choice," which in the current climate of word usage is loaded in a highly positive emotive way. Maximizing freedom of choice is taken to be a positive value for the audience to which Paul's argument is directed. We recall that among the triad of Paul's explicit statements is the sentence that lessening the car's capability for maneuvering to avoid accidents is not safe. Given this much of Paul's argument put in place, provided we have the implicit premise that lessening the options for maneuvering to avoid accidents is contrary to the definition of safety, argument a4 can easily be put in place to prove Paul's statement. As far as the argumentation has gone to this point, then, Paul is winning. There is no rule in CKP against putting forward a persuasive definition. And in general there should not be, since, as we now show, Paul's general line of argumentation to the end of the dialogue is based on forms of argument that are reasonable.

8. Applying Argumentation Schemes to Persuasive Definitions in CKP

To grasp the argumentation structure of Paul's argument, we have to review some of the defeasible argumentation schemes of the kind that are used to in the CKP system. The CKP dialogue system requires all parties to have the capability to reason with each other using defeasible argumentation schemes, especially ones for arguments from values. Just such a framework has been proposed by Bench-Capon (2002). In attempting to resolve disagreements of the kind that arise in ethics and law, according to Bench-Capon, it may be impossible to provide conclusive proof of a claim, but it may be possible to provide persuasion based on the values of the intended audience, after the manner of Perelman and Olbrechts-Tyteca (1969). To model such argumentation, Bench-Capon has introduced value-based argumentation frameworks (VAFs) in which arguments are assessed relative to the strengths of the values involved. For example (Bench-Capon 2002: 231), universities may put forward the argument that more money should be spent on universities on the grounds that standards need to be maintained. Government may resist this argument by arguing that increased funding would require raising taxes. Even though both parties to the dispute may agree on the facts, there is a need to try to resolve the disagreement based on rational persuasion rather than coercion.

8.1. *Definitional Moves and Argumentation Schemes*

To analyze how arguments based on (1) values underlying emotive language and (2) classifications based on persuasive definitions work, we need to apply the argumentation schemes from definitions (argumentation scheme 3) and from values (argumentation scheme 1). Paul's attack on Olga's argument starts with argument a2, where Paul makes the statement that if the maximum speed of the car is very high, that does not mean the car is not safe. Here

Paul has put forward an argument from verbal classification, only it is in the negative form. The argumentation scheme for this negative form of argument from a verbal classification (argumentation scheme 2) can be expressed as follows:

NEGATIVE ARGUMENT FROM VERBAL CLASSIFICATION

Major Premise	For all x, even if x has property F, x cannot properly be classified as having property G.
Minor Premise	a has property F.
Conclusion	a has property G.

What he can be taken as saying is that classifying the car as being safe or not should not be done on the basis of the maximum speed that the car has. At this point, he has not yet given any alternative way of classifying cars that could be used to infer conclusions about their safety. Paul's argument can be criticized at this point on the basis that it does not answer the second critical question matching the scheme for argument from classification, because he has not yet given us a reason to think that classifying a car is unsafe based on the criterion of its maximum speed is subject to doubt. However, we know from looking forward in the dialogue that he will come up with an argument that will address this question.

Paul's argument a4 begins to address this issue by using an argument from definition to verbal classification. This argument has two premises. The premise that safety is maximizing the freedom to avoid bad outcomes is the definition premise. The premise that lessening the options for maneuvering to avoid accidents is contrary to the definition of safety fits the classification premise. This argument is a negative form of argument from definition to verbal classification that has the conclusion that lessening options for maneuvering to avoid accidents is not safe. If we look at the critical questions corresponding to the scheme for argument from definition to verbal classification, we see that Paul has not answered the question of what evidence there is that his definition of safety is an adequate definition in light of other possible alternative definitions that might be applied. This is the key weakness in Paul's argument. It doesn't mean that Paul couldn't give some evidence to support the conclusion that safety may properly be defined as maximizing the freedom to avoid bad outcomes. It just means that he hasn't done so yet. Still, it is important for us to note that this failure represents a gap in his argument that needs to be addressed before his argument can reasonably be judged to be acceptable. Finally, we need to note that Paul's definition is based on values. As noted previously, his argument defines safety as a form of maximizing freedom to avoid bad outcomes, like accidents. Once again, there is nothing inherently wrong with this aspect of it because it **is** a rational argument. Nevertheless, it will turn out to be an important factor to be aware of.

8.2. *Countermoves and Critical Questions*

How could Olga respond to Paul's new argument? It would not be easy. The most natural strategy, given what we've seen of Olga's sixth move in the dialogue, would be to bring forward more positive arguments to support her basic argument that Paul's car is not safe because it has a very high maximum speed. At her sixth move, she cited positive arguments to show that cars having a very high speed are not safe. She claimed that many people get killed on the roads because cars are going fast, and it is not safe. She supported this claim with evidence. She made further claims that young drivers like to drive too fast, and that this is responsible for many road fatalities. Olga does not support these claims with empirical evidence, but we need to recall that CKP is a knowledge-based type of persuasion dialogue that allows searching through the knowledge base to find evidence to support claims. But even though, in this respect, her argument is on a sound basis and could be further supported, even if she did go in this direction by trying to support it with further evidence, from the audience's point of view, it might still seem that she is not getting anywhere. The reason is essentially that after Paul used his emotively loaded argument from a persuasive definition, it seems like her argument is doomed to failure because she cannot get over the obstacle that he has put in place. Once Paul has redefined safety, all of Olga's positive arguments, even though they may be based on good evidence, cannot prove that Paul's car is unsafe. So we need to ask the question, how could Olga respond to Paul's new argument so that it could get around this obstacle?

Ideally she should know about both persuasive definitions and emotive language, be able to employ these concepts to analyze the argument, find the weak points in it, and mount an effective criticism or counterargument by putting all these things together. What Olga needs to do is to critically question Paul's argument a4 by asking the first critical question corresponding to the argumentation schemes for argument from definition to verbal classification:

CQ$_1$ What evidence is there that D is an adequate definition, in light of other possible alternative definitions that might exclude a's having G?

CQ$_2$ Is the verbal classification in the classification premise based merely on a stipulative or biased definition that is subject to doubt?

These questions ask what evidence there is for thinking that Paul's definition is an adequate definition of safety in light of other possible alternative definitions that might exclude his classification of his car being safe on this basis. Also, she might concede that while freedom is an important value, there are questions to be raised about defining safety in terms of freedom. Carrying out all these moves into a coherent strategy in a manner that is both systematic and effective is difficult for three reasons. The first one is that, as we showed in detail, Paul's argumentation, once analyzed carefully, fits together well and is reasonable as an orderly sequence of reasoning that leads toward its conclusion based on defeasible logic. The second one is that there is a danger that the audience might dismiss all discussion of definitions as being a trivial kind of "mere semantics," given that Paul's argument does seem reasonable by current standards of logic. The only way to overcome this problem is to educate about the importance of definitions and values in argumentation. The third difficulty is that Olga will have to be highly skilled to use the tools of CK in a way to identify the structure of Paul's argumentation, as well as to analyze and evaluate it by showing its weak points that are subject to doubts and critical questions.

9. Conclusions

We can summarize the CKP model of dialogue put forward here briefly as follows. CKP is meant to model a procedure whereby two parties can engage in rational argumentation with each other and each party has the individual goal of persuading the other party to adopt its viewpoint on the issue being discussed. The model allows for the possibility that the dialogue might occasionally shift to a negotiation or an information-seeking type of dialogue where this kind of shift is helpful to move the persuasion dialogue along toward achieving its goal. Each type of dialogue has three stages: an opening stage, an argumentation stage, and a closing stage. Each party takes turns making moves by putting forward speech acts like the speech act of asking a question or the speech act of making an assertion. The speech acts allowed in CKP are summarized in Table 6.3.

There are procedural rules called dialogue protocols that determine when a particular speech act can be put forward as a move and how the other party may or must reply to that move. These protocols include rules for putting forward definitions as well as rules for responding to them.

As each party makes a move, the commitment rules insert a statement or a set of statements into the commitment set of the participant who made the move. These commitments are visible to all parties in CKP, and it is assumed that statements can also be retracted from a party's commitment set. CKP can also contain a party's implicit commitments. These are the so-called dark-side commitments that are not known to the participants at the opening stage and only become known to them gradually as they put forward arguments and respond to them during the argumentation stage. These commitments become visible in arguments as implicit premises and conclusions that are needed to fill out the argument so that it meets the requirements of its argumentation scheme and it can be taken to fit in with an arguer's light-side commitments so far as these have been determined in the dialogue preceding the argument. CKP can accommodate

Table 6.3. Summary of Speech Acts Allowed in CKP Dialogues

SPEECH ACT	DIALOGUE FORM	FUNCTION
Question (yes-no type)	*S?*	Speaker asks whether *S* is the case.
Assertion (claim)	Assert *S*	Speaker asserts that *S* is the case.
Concession (acceptance)	Accept *S*	Speaker incurs commitment to *S*.
Retraction (withdrawal)	No commitment *S*	Speaker removes commitment to *S*.
Challenge (demand for proof of claim)	Why *S?*	Speaker requests that hearer give an argument to support *S*.
Put Argument Forward	$P_1, P_2, \ldots, P_n$ therefore *S*.	$P_1, P_2, \ldots, P_n$ is a set of premises that give a reason to support *S*.
Put Definition Forward	*X* is defined as *S*.	*S* is a statement that gives a set of conditions so the hearer can tell whether something is an *X* or not.
Accept Definition	I accept that *X* is defined as *S*.	Speaker indicates he is committed to definition of *X* as *S*.
Reject Definition	I do not accept that *X* should be defined as *S*.	Speaker indicates he is not committed to definition of *X* as *S*.

argumentation schemes as defeasible forms of inference leading from a set of premises to a conclusion. CKP has rules for commitment to definitions.

In addition to the dark- and light-side commitment stores there is a special set of propositions designated at the opening stage of the dialogue called the common knowledge base. The common knowledge base is shared by both parties to the dialogue, and it represents propositions that neither party would dispute, or has any interest in disputing, and are widely accepted as being true, or at any rate are not widely subject to doubt or disputation. In special instances, specific sources could be cited for common knowledge. For example, both parties to the dialogue might agree to include all of the statements made in an encyclopedia in the common knowledge base. We also added to CK the possibility of shifting to a higher level of dialogue. In addition to the primary level of dialogue, there also needs to be a meta-dialogue level in which a third-party audience, critic, or judge critically analyzes a given argument or other speech act put forth by either of the two parties in the CKP dialogue at the primary level. This third party can make rulings on whether the moves made by the two primary parties have followed the rules or may have used some kind of unfair tactics, and this third party should have the capability to resolve disputes on such matters in an orderly way.

Both the pragma-dialectical model and the CKP model are grounded on a similar notion of persuasion as a change of attitude stemming from a shared or common ground. The interlocutors can persuade each other because they proceed from a set of shared propositions; the problem is how the speaker may know the hearer's beliefs or commitments. In pragma-dialectics, such propositions are agreed upon in the opening stage; however, there might be an indefinite number of propositions to be agreed on. In Krabbe's view, one solution to these problems arising from a dialectical level aimed at solving commitment problems can be found in assigning a separate status to this type of discussion (Krabbe 2007: 240–241). From this perspective, some crucial questions that are tackled in the opening stage can be shifted to a meta-dialogical level, namely a dialogue on the conditions of the dialogue (Krabbe 2003: 641; Finocchiaro 2007). In CKP dialogues, the persuasion process is based not only on the explicit commitments of the parties, but also on the arguers' dark-side or implicit commitments. These commitments are not revealed, but are used during a dialogue in order to build up persuasive arguments. For instance, it will be unsuccessful to argue that "Bob stole public money; therefore he is a thief" if our interlocutor does not hold that stealing public money is a crime. This proposition is not made explicit in the argument, but it is the grounds of its persuasiveness. During a dialogue, more dark-side commitment sets of both parties are revealed. The hearer can come to know the implicit foundations of the other's position by understanding the grounds of his or her arguments, and the speaker can explain the success or failure of a piece of reasoning by analyzing the propositions taken for granted that the other party has not accepted (Walton 1984: 252–254). In such cases, implicit commitments can be brought to the light side, discussed, and negotiated or corrected. By revealing, defending, and retracting inconsistent implicit commitments, the parties discover the real deep disagreements underlying their differences of opinion. For instance, different values may be the unexpressed reason of different choices or judgments; unless such a conflict of values is resolved, the process of persuasion is unlikely to proceed further. Therefore, the analysis of what lies beneath a persuasion dialogue leads the interlocutors to understand the other party's position more deeply, and to analyze the implicit grounds of their own viewpoints. From this perspective, investigating the implicit commitments is a dialogical process that results in a redefinition of the problem at issue to make it more understandable or acceptable to the other party.

7

Metadialogues and Redefinitions

Dialogue games provide rules to establish the relationship between a move and a possible effect on commitments. However, such games are highly abstract, and the moves are reduced to logical operations between symbols indicating sentences. The type of speech act performed is not considered, nor is the kind of relation between the predicates in the sentence taken into account. However, a statement affects the commitment store differently from an order or a reminder, and a relation of classification leaves to the interlocutor a range of possible rebuttals different from an analogical relation. In order to apply such games to actual dialogues, we need to go a step further and analyze the nature of the moves and the structure of the sentences. In this chapter we will apply dialogue games to a particular type of move, the act of defining or redefining. As seen in Chapters 3, 4, and 5, definitions can be distinguished according to their pragmatic nature and their propositional structure. In our dialectical approach, definitions can be thought of as moves in a dialogue game, which open different possibilities of continuation of the dialogue and refutation according to the definitional act performed and the type of definitional sentence. For this reason, we will examine the dialectical structures of the different types of definitional sentences and combine them with the commitment effects of the different acts of defining.

1. Types of Definitions and Dialogue Moves

As seen in Chapter 3, there can be different types of definitional sentences. Each of these definitions is characterized by different logical properties, which affect both its effects on the interlocutor and the possible refutation strategies. On the one hand, every definition can be used for arguments characterized by specific rules, or axioms, of reasoning. For instance, a genus-difference definition can be used to support the attribution of the genus to the species by *modus ponens*, a definition by parts can trigger arguments proceeding from disjunctive syllogism, and a definition by negation can be grounded on arguments characterized by the axiom of *modus tollens*. Moreover, the structure of the definition affects the force of the arguments based on it. For instance, the same reasoning from verbal classification proceeding from a definition to an entity will be much weaker in the case of definitions by metaphor or by example, as in these cases it is grounded on implicit reasoning from analogy or from example. On the other hand, every definition opens a range of possible strategies of refutations in addition to the simple attack on the factual premise (*x* is not *S*, therefore it cannot be classified as the definition of *S*). For instance, one of the strongest refutations for a genus-difference definition consists in showing that one of the defined concepts cannot fall within the genus, while definitions by essential parts can be rebutted easily by pointing out the existence of a species not included in the definition. Moreover, every definition different from genus-difference can be rejected by claiming that it does not explain what the concept is, but only provides a criterion for classification or a description. For this reason, all the other definitions can be attacked by opposing a genus-difference one.

1.1. *Genus-Difference Definition*

This definition is characterized by singling out a more generic predicate, the genus, and a characteristic that distinguishes the definiendum, or species, from the other concepts falling under the same genus. For this reason, it explains the meaning of the concept by providing simpler and more generic predicates. The force of this definition is grounded on the dialectical topics of the genus, rules commonly considered as irrefutable. For this reason, if the interlocutor grants the definition, he also needs to grant the conclusion following from it. The only refutations possible are the factual premise (*x* is *S*) or the definition itself, and in particular the rightful attribution of the genus or difference. We can represent the dialectical structure of this definition as follows:

<table>
<tr><td colspan="4" align="center">I.   **Genus (*G*) – Difference (*D*) Definition**
S (Species) is *GD*
Ex: *Peace is freedom from want.*</td></tr>
<tr><td colspan="2" align="center">**Effects**</td><td colspan="2" align="center">**Possible Refutations of the Definition**</td></tr>
<tr>
<td>1. If *x* is *S*, then *x* is *GD* (MP; MT).
2. If *x* is *GD*, then *x* is *S* (MP; MT).
3. If *x* is *S*, then *x* is *G* (MP; MT).</td>
<td>1. In Libya people are not free from want. Therefore they are not at peace.
2. We free people from want. Therefore our actions are peaceful.
3. They are not free. Therefore there cannot be peace there.</td>
<td>1. S_1 is not a *G*.
2. *G* is *Cat* (Category). But *S* is not *Cat*.
3. *x* is *S* but not *G*.</td>
<td>1. Cold peace is not freedom.
2. Freedom is affection, but peace is a quality.
3. Russia is at peace, but it is not free.</td>
</tr>
</table>

4. If *x* is G, then it can be *S*. 5. If *x* is *S*, then it cannot be *non-G*. 6. If *x* is not *D*, then *x* is not *S*. *G* is *Q* (Qualification). Therefore *S* is *Q*. 7. *G* is *Q* (Qualification). Therefore *S* is *Q*	4. There is freedom in Russia. Therefore there may be peace there. 5. In the U.S. there is peace. Therefore there are no restrictions of human rights. 6. In Libya people desire human rights. Therefore there cannot be peace there. 7. Freedom is something worth fighting for. Therefore it is worth fighting for peace.	4. *S* is not the definition of the Genus *(Def.G)*.	4. Freedom is an exemption from an onerous condition. But peace is not an exemption from an onerous condition (there can be peace without war).

1.2. *Definite Description*

As mentioned in Chapter 3, definite descriptions consist in the attribution of a genus and a property, a predicate that distinguishes the *definiendum* from any other concept, either absolutely or relatively. For instance, the definition of man as the animal able to laugh was considered the typical definition by property. However, this concept can be extended to attributes that simply describe the *definiendum*, without any claim to distinguish it from other concepts. For this reason, the strength of this definition lies in the properties of the genus, but its weak point is the property. The definite description does not explain the meaning of the concept; it is only useful to classify entities, and therefore a genus-difference definition can be opposed. Moreover, the property can be attacked.

II. Definite description – Genus and Property (*P*)			
S is *GP*.			
Ex: *Terrorists are bandits who hide behind political, religious or nationalist slogans to try to resolve questions that have nothing to do with what they publicly state.*			
Effects		**Possible Refutations of the Definition**	
1. If *x* is *S*, then *x* is *P*. 2. If *x* is *GP*, then *x* is *S* (MP; MT).	1. Chechens are terrorists. Therefore, they try to achieve something that has nothing to do with what they state. 2. Chechens are bandits that hide... Therefore, they are terrorists.	1. *S* is *GD*. 2. *x* is *S* but not *P*.	1. A terrorist is one who systematicaly uses violence and intimidation to achieve some goal. 2. Anarchists are terrorists, but they do pursue what they state.

3. If *x* is *S*, then *x* is *GP* (MP; MT). 4. If *x* is *S*, then *x* is *G* (MP; MT). 5. If *x* is *G*, then *x* can be *S*. 6. If *x* is *S*, then *x* cannot be *non-G*.	3. Chechens are terrorists. Therefore they are bandits who hide behind political, religious or nationalist slogans. 4. Chechens are terrorists. Therefore, they are bandits. 5. Chechens are bandits. Therefore, they can be terrorists. 6. Chechens are terrorists. Therefore, they cannot be lawful combatants.	3. *x* is *P* but not *S*. 4. *S* is not *G*. 5. *G* is *Cat* (Category). But *S* is not *Cat*. 6. *x* is *S* but not *G*. 7. *S* is not *Def.G*.	3. Mafia bosses are outlaws hiding behind the slogan of honor to gain money, but they are not terrorists. 4. A terrorist is not a bandit. 5. A bandit is an outlaw, but terrorists are not outlaws. 6. The Contras were terrorists but not bandits. 7. A terrorist is not an outlaw that lives by plunder.

1.3. *Definition by Etymology*

Definition by etymology is defining a term by reference to its origin and historical development, or even by finding its origins in other languages. For instance, a classical example is the definition of trust (*fides*) as "when what is said is also carried out (*fit*)" (Victorini, *Liber de Definitionibus*, 15, 14–15). Etymology establishes equivalence, but only between names. It can only support a classification, as the origin can explain the meaning of a word. For this reason, the classificatory conclusion is only plausible, given the hearer's acceptance of the definition. It can be rejected by advancing a stronger definition or criterion of classification, or by attacking the actual word origin or interpretation.

III. Etymology – Interpretation (*Int.*) of the Old Noun (*N_{old}*) *S* means *$IntN_{old}$*			
Ex: Maiestas minuta *means diminishing (minuere) the amplitude of a state.*			
Effects		**Possible Refutations of the Definition**	
1. If *x* falls within *$IntN_{old}$*, then *x* can fall within *S*.	1. Saturninus diminished the treasury of the state. Therefore he is guilty of *maieslas minuta*.	1. *S* is *GD*.	1. *Maiestas minuta* is the damage to the sovereignty of the Roman people or the tribunate.
2. If *x* is *S*, then *x* can fall within *$IntN_{old}$*.	2. Caepio is guilty of *maiestas minuta*.	2. *S* does not derive from *N_{old}*.	2. *Maiestas* is not the simple nominalization of *maius* (great, ample).

Therefore he diminished the state instead of making it richer,	3. N_{old} does not mean $IntN_{old}$. 4. S means $IntN_{old}$, but it does not follow that if an x is $IntN_{old}$, then it is S.	3. *Maiestas minuta* does not mean make something. 4. A crime of *maiestas minuta* does not necessarily affect the amplitude of a state.

1.4. *Definition by Essential Parts*

Definition by essential parts consists in a list of the possible specific instances of the concept to be defined. This definition allows a form of *modus tollens* reasoning, in which the negation of the *definiendum* follows from the negation of all its possible more specific concepts (species). Such a definition by essential parts does not explain the meaning of the concept, nor does it contain a genus that can support other forms of reasoning. It can be defeated by pointing out the existence of a further specific case.

<table>
<tr><td colspan="4" align="center">IV. Definition by Essential Parts
S is either S_i, or S₂, or S_{3...} or S_n
Ex: If someone has not been freed by either having his name entered in the census-roll or by being touched with the rod or by a provision in a will, then he is not free.</td></tr>
<tr><td colspan="2" align="center">Effects</td><td colspan="2" align="center">Possible Refutations of the Definition</td></tr>
<tr>
<td>1. If x is S_1, then x is S.
2. If x is not S_1, nor S_2, nor S_1...nor S_n, then x is not S.</td>
<td>1. Socrates was freed by provision in a will. Therefore he is free.
2. Socrates has not had his name in the census-roll, nor has he been touched with the rod, nor has he been freed by a provision in a will. Therefore he is not free.</td>
<td>1. S can be also S_{n+1}.
2. S is GD, and x is GD but not S_1, nor S_2, nor S_3...nor S_n.</td>
<td>1. A man can be freed also by decision of the consul, or when his master dies.
2. To free a man means to set him at liberty. Socrates was set at liberty, but in none of the aforementioned ways.</td>
</tr>
</table>

1.5. *Definition by Material Parts*

Definition by material parts depends on the relation between them. If the parts constituting the whole are simply listed, the definition is not convertible, as the simple gathering of the parts cannot make a whole (a motor, four wheels, a body, and four seats do not make a car, unless they are all joined somehow). Even if the conjunction is specified, the predication of a property to a part does not imply its predication to the whole, and vice versa. This definition can be easily rejected by contesting the essentiality of a part, or the incompleteness of the list provided, or the nature of the conjunction (Tarello 1980: 213).

V. Definition by Material Parts (P)

S is P_1, P_2, $P_{3...}$ and P_n

Ex: *For "Tuscan flask" is meant a glass recipient made up of a body approximately the shape of a rotated ellipse, joined along its longest axes to a tapered neck, the total height of which is not less than half and not three times bigger the diameter of the body, covered in part in reed, straw or other natural vegetable plaiting material. The base can be with flat or slightly concave (Decreto Ministero della Salute no. 299, 22 December 2005).*

Effects		Possible Refutations of the Definition	
1. *If x is P_1, P_2, $P_{3...}$ and P_n then x is S.* 2. If x is not characterized by P_1 (or P_2, or P_3...or P_n), then x is not S.	1. This bottle is shaped as a rotated ellipse, it has a tapered neck, it is a bit higher than the diameter of the body, and it is covered in reed. 2. This bottle is not covered in reed or other materials. Therefore it is not a Tuscan flask.	1. S can be also P_{n+1}. 2. x can be S even if x does not P_1. 3. If P_1 is destructed, x is still S. 4. The addition of P_1, P_2, $P_{3...}$ and P_n does not result in a Tuscan flask.	1. The cork is a fundamental part of the Tuscan flask. 2. A flask without the reed cover can be still a Tuscan flask. 3. If we take the cover off, it is still a Tuscan flask. 4. If we put a flask under a heap of reed, is it still a Tuscan flask?

1.6. *Definition by Operation*

Operational definitions consist in describing not the concept but the fragment of reality it refers to, and are therefore strategies of classification more than definitions. They provide the efficient or final cause of the thing the *definiendum* refers to, and are useful especially in science, where the cause is often known and can be reduced to an operation. When the cause is only plausible the conclusion can only be presumptive.

VI. Definitions by Operation
S is *Function(x)* (*Fx* = efficient/final cause)
Ex: *Democracy is the form of government which gives, or tries to give, the people the illusion of their own sovereignty.*

Effects		Possible Refutations of the Definition	
1. If *Fx* is the case, then *x* is S.	1. The Italian government gives the people the illusion of their own sovereignty. Therefore Italy is a democracy.	1. S is *GD*.	1. Democracy is a form of government in which all the people have an equal say in the decisions that affect their lives.
2. If *x* is S, then *F* applies to X.	2. Italy is a democracy. Therefore it gives the people the illusion of their own sovereignty.	2. *F* is not the final/ efficient cause of S.	2. Giving the people the illusion of their sovereignty is not the effect or purpose of democracy.
3. *Fx* is Q. Therefore S is also Q.	3. Pretenses are bad. Therefore democracy is bad.	3. Not all *Fx's* are S. 4. *F* can be the result/ cause of many other things.	3. Only degenerate democracies are based on illusion and falsity. 4. Tyranny and dictatorships give the people the illusion of their sovereignty.

1.7. *Definition by Negation*

A definition by negation consists in the negation of the other member of a binary paradigm. For instance, the paradigm of 'work' can be divided into two species: administrative and productive work. One of the opposites is defined through the negation of the other. This definition does not explain what the concept means or is. It allows a form of defaultive reasoning, subject to the condition that the opposites exhaust the paradigm and that the denied concept has been defined somewhere else. If these conditions apply, the reasoning based on a definition by negation can support a classificatory conclusion, but not the attribution of a property; otherwise it is simply a strategy of shifting the burden of proof onto the interlocutor, providing a solely presumptive classification. In both cases it can be rejected by a definition by providing a positive description of the *definiendum*. In its weaker formulation, the paradigm can be attacked, or the contrary concept defined, by negating the original *definiendum* and shifting the burden of proof back to the speaker.

VII. Definition by Negation				
S_1 is what is not S_2 (x can be only either S_1 or S_2)				
Ex: *Administrative work is what is not productive work.*				

Effects			Possible Refutations of the Definition	
1. If x is not S_2, then x is S_1. 2. If x is S_1, then x is not S_2. 3. If S_1 is P, then S_2 is *non-P* (*P* and *non-P* characterize the genus of S).	1. The defendant performed criminal investigations, which cannot be production work. Therefore he performed an administrative work. 2. The defendant produced goods, which are part of production work. Therefore he was not performing an administrative work. 3. Administrative work involves management. Therefore production work does not involve management.	1. S_1 is *GD*. 2. x can be also S_3. 3. S_2 is what is not S_1.	1. Administrative work provides support to the operational or production employees. 2. An employee can also perform an operational work. 3. Productive work is what is not administrative work (The defendant was not a manager, therefore he performed production work).	

1.8. *Inductive Definition*

Inductive definitions consist in a list of the possible instances of a concept and do not explain the meaning of the *definiendum*. Their force lies in the completeness of knowledge, which rarely can be presupposed. In the contrary case, they are incomplete, as new instances can be found. They are powerful strategies for shifting the burden of proving the contrary, advancing a presumptive classification.

VIII. Inductive definition			
S is either x_1 or x_2, or x_3... or x_n,			
Ex: *For the purpose of this section, no consent is obtained where the complainant submits or does not resist by reason of:* *1. the application of force to the complainant or to a person other than the complainant;* *2. threats or fear of the application of force to the complainant or to a person other than the complainant;* *3. fraud;* *4. the exercise of authority.*			

Effects		Possible Refutations of the Definition	
1. If x is x_1, or x_2, or x_3,... or x_n, then x is (can be) S.	1. The defendant was the complainant's boss and threatened her. Therefore there was no consent.	1. S is *GD*. 2. x is x_1, but x is not S (because of argument A).	1. Consent is possession and exercise of sufficient mental capacity to make an intelligent decision.

2. If x is not x_1, nor x_2, nor x_3,…nor x_n, then x is (may be) not S.	2. The defendant was not in a position of authority, nor did he use fraud, threats or fear against the complainant, nor did he use force against her.	3. Also x_{n+1} can be S (because of GD)	2. The defendant exercised his authority and complainant did not resist, but she was consentient (she stated so). 3. A person can also be not consentient when she is under the effect of substances.

1.9. *Definition by Example*

Definitions by example are only presumptive criteria of classification relying on reasoning from example. They provide the most prototypical (or strategically significant) cases in order to elicit a classification or judgment. From a dialectical point of view they cannot be considered as instruments of classification, but from a rhetorical perspective they are effective because they can be used to trigger a value judgment or provide a criterion of classification in the absence of a definition.

IX. Definitions by Example			
S is what is similar to x_1.			
Ex: '*Peacekeeping missions' as 'missions such as Operation Restoring Hope in Somalia.'*			
Ex: *My living will states that if I would not recover from a disability I "not be kept alive by artificial means or 'heroic measures', including, but not limited to, any resuscitation efforts, the transplant of any vital organ, or the use of a respirator."*			
Effects		**Possible Refutations of the Definition**	
1. If x is (not) similar to x_1, then x can be presumed (not) to be S. 2. x_1 is Q (Qualification), therefore also S can be Q. 3. x_1 falls within G; therefore $S(x)$ also can fall within G.	1. This mission is (not) similar to Operation Restoring Hope. Therefore, it is (not) a peacekeeping mission. 2. Operation Restoring Hope was good (bad). Therefore also peacekeeping missions are good (bad). 3. Operation Restoring Hope was an act of war. Therefore, peacekeeping missions (this mission) are (is) acts (an act) of war.	1. S is GD. 2. x_1 is not a prototypical S. 3. x is (not) similar to x_1, but it is not S.	1. Peacekeeping is the process of maintaining peace by the use of neutral troops to enforce a truce or separate hostile groups. 2. Operation Restoring Hope actually involved large-scale operations, which is not usual of peacekeeping. 3. The mission in Libya is similar to Operation Restoring Hope, but it is an actual invasion.

| | | 4. x_1 is P, but x is not P.
5. x_1 falls within G, but $S(x)$ is not a G | 4. Operation Restoring Hope tried to save lives, but the operation in Libya does not.
5. Operation Restoring Hope was a peaceful operation, but the operation in Libya is not. |

1.10. *Definition by Metaphor*

Comparable to a definition by example, definition by metaphor can be considered as a definition only *latu sensu*. The classificatory conclusion relies on a pattern of reasoning from analogy and can provide only a tentative conclusion, useful when associated with other arguments. This definition is useful for drawing value judgments.

X. Definitions by Metaphor S is M. Ex: *Terrorism is Nazism of the 21st century.*			
Effects		**Possible Refutations of the Definition**	
1. If x is S, then x is presumptively like M.	1. Chechens are terrorists. Therefore, they are like Nazis.	1. S is GD.	1. Terrorism is the use of violence and threats to intimidate or coerce, especially for political purposes.
2. M is Q. Therefore S is presumptively also Q.	2. Nazism is horrible. Therefore terrorism is horrible.	2. S has nothing essential in common with M.	2. Terrorism and Nazism are completely different.
3. M is Q. Therefore what is S can be also Q.	3. Nazism is horrible. Therefore Chechens are horrible.	3. S cannot be compared to M because of A.	3. Nazism was a totalitarian regime. Terrorism is the use of violence for a specific purpose.

The different types of definitions are characterized by the different types of inferences, or effects, that they allow. Such effects can be dialectical or rhetorical, or rather conclusive or simply presumptive. For instance, the inferences that can be drawn from a genus-difference definition are much stronger than the ones of a definition by example or metaphor, whose conclusions are only presumptive or rhetorical. In other cases, further assumptions need to be made in order for inferences to be dialectical. For instance, in cases of definitions by negation it is necessary to presuppose that the paradigm is binary. All definitions can be rejected by stronger ones, as a criterion providing a stronger and better grounded classificatory inference can defeat a presumptive or defeasible one. Moreover, definitions have internal critical points toward which the attacks can be directed.

2. Acts of Defining and Dialogue Commitment Structure

The structure of definitional sentences opens possible strategies of attack. However, the possibility and reasonableness of carrying out such attacks depends on how the definitional move affects the commitment structure. Taking for granted an unshared definition alters the hearer's commitment store differently from advancing it as a standpoint or stipulating it. Building on the pragmatic analysis of the acts of defining of Chapter 4, we can provide sets of possibilities of reply opened by each definitional move.

2.1. A. *Advancing a Definition*
The act of advancing a definition is the most similar to the typical move of a dialogue game. The speaker advances a standpoint and is committed to defending it. The interlocutor can accept it, reject it, question it, or advance a contrary standpoint. He can also accept it tentatively (in the following table, indicated in parentheses). However, the speaker can also anticipate the possible rejections and counterarguments, increasing the acceptability of the argument and preventing the hearer from advancing a possible dangerous move that has already been rejected.

R	Move of the Speaker (α)	Commitments α	Commitments β	Possible Moves of the Hearer (β)	Possible Moves of the Speaker (α)
1.	$F_{adv}Def(S)$	1. $Def(S)$. 2. $Def(S)$ is not accepted by β.			Prolepsis (anticipation): 1. Rejection X is not acceptable because of argument A. 2. No $Def_2(S)$ (because of argument β).
2			1. $Def(S), \{Def(S)\}$. 2. $[]$ 3. $[]$ 4. $Def_2(S)$.	1. Accept $Def(S)$. 2. Question $Def(S)$. 3. Reject $Def(S)$. 4. Advance $Def_2(S)$.	

3			*Def(S)*,			Defense:
						1. Argument *C*,
						   therefore no
						   rejection *X*/ no
						   Def₂(S)

Obama provides a clear case of advancing a definition as a standpoint when he redefines peace as "freedom from want." He takes for granted that this definition conflicts with the ordinary one, which he rejects in his argument. He provides reasons for supporting his view, showing how stability is the foundation of peace. The interlocutors could have attacked his argument, or the structure of his definition. Since the definition provides a generic property and a specification, it could fall within the category of genus-difference definition, leaving open the possible attacks analyzed in Subsection 1:

REJECT *Def(S)*:

1. S_1 is not a *G*.
2. *G* is *Cat* (Category). But *S* is not *Cat*.
3. *x* is *S* but not *G*.
4. *S* is not the definition of the genus (*Def.G.*)

This analysis of the prototypical case of advancing a definition combines the two dimensions of definition. If we consider other acts of defining, the structure of the commitments change and the possibilities of reply are restricted.

2.2. B. *Defining for Informing*

As seen in Chapter 4, definitions can be advanced to inform the interlocutors of a commonly accepted meaning. The act of informing presupposes that the definition is shared, and that the interlocutor may not be committed to it yet. This act is an implicit argument: as the definition is commonly known, it should be accepted by the hearer too. The effect is that the definition becomes part of the commitment store of both the participants unless the presuppositions of the act of informing are contested. The speaker can support his move by providing reasons to believe the common acceptance of such a meaning, but he does not have to provide an argument for its correctness. On the contrary, the hearer needs to reject the common acceptance of such a proposition in order to delete it from its commitment store. We can represent the illocutionary force as *F*, specifying the specific type of act (informing, reminding, etc.) and the propositional content, in this case the definition, as *Def(S)*.

R	Move of the Speaker (α)	Commitments α	Commitments β	Possible Moves of the Hearer (β)	Possible Moves of the Speaker (α)
1	$F_{inf}Def(S)$	1. *Def(S)*. 2. *Def(S)* is commonly accepted. 3. β may not know *Def(S)*.			Prolepsis (anticipation): *Def(S)* is shared because of Arguments.
2			1A. *[]* 1B. *[]* 2. *Def(S)*, *{Def(S)}* 3. *[]*	1. Attack (F_{inf}): A) *Def(S)* is not commonly known. B) *Def(S)* is different from the commonly known definition. 2. Accept *Def(S)*. 3. Provide reasons for not commitment.	
3			Def(S),		Defense: *Def(S)* is shared because of Argument *A*

In order to explain the structure of this move, we can consider the example of Obama's act of informing his audience of the meaning of 'just war.' He takes for granted that such a meaning is not a stipulated one, but it is and shall be commonly shared. However, he prevents possible objections to the possibility of such an act by providing the authorities on which the sharedness of the concept lies. He mentions legal and philosophical sources, so that the audience cannot claim that the act is not allowed.

2.3. C. *Defining for Reminding*

The act of reminding presupposes that the reminded proposition is already a commitment of the interlocutor. It is a form of dark-side commitment, based not only on a presumption grounded on common knowledge but also on shared knowledge. The effect is shifting the burden of proof. The hearer needs to retract a commitment or prove that the conditions of the act of reminding are not met. While the act of informing is the advancing of a proposition on the basis of an implicit appeal to common ground, the act of reminding brings a dark-side commitment to the light side, or rather inserts a commitment in the hearer's commitment store.

R	Move of the speaker (α)	Commitments α	Commitments β	Possible Moves of the Hearer (β)	Possible Moves of the Speaker (α)
1	$F_{rem}Def(S)$	*1. Def(S)* is / shall be known by the hearer.	1. *Def(S)*		Prolepsis (anticipation): *1. Def(S)* is /shall be shared because of a previous commitment.
2			1 A. Delete *Def(S)* 1B. Delete *Def(S)* 2. *Def(S)*	1. Attack (F_{rem}): A) No previous commitment to *Def(S)*. B) *Def(S)* is different from the accepted definition. 2. Acknowledge *Def(S)*.	
3					Defense: 1. *Def(S)* is shared because of a previous commitment.

The definition as a reminder changes the object of retraction. The hearer needs to reject the move (F_{rem}), not simply the definition. He needs to start a meta-dialogue, or a dialogue on the conditions of a move in which he brings forward arguments against its presuppositions. For instance, the hearer can deny his previous commitment and provide reasons for it, if needed. Or he can claim that his commitment was different.

2.4. D. *Declaring a Definition*

The act of declaring a definition imposes a commitment onto the hearer and the speaker, and presupposes that the definition is a new one, or is not the only one, and that the speaker holds the authority to do it. The definition does not need to be grounded on reasons, and in order to refuse his commitment the hearer needs to reject the possibility of the act, or attack the reasonableness of the act of imposing such a definition.

R	Move of the Speaker (α)	Commitments α	Commitments β	Possible Moves of the hearer (β)	Possible moves of the speaker (α)
1	$F_{dec}Def(S).$	1. $β$ is not committed to (only to) *Def(S)*. 2. $α$ is in position of performing F_{dec}. 3. *Def(S)*.	1. *Def(S)*.		

| 2 | | | 1. Delete $Def(S)$. | 1. Attack (F_{dec}):
 A) α is not in position of performing F_{dec}.
 B) $Def(S)$ can have bad consequences. | |
| 3 | | | | | Defense: $Def(S)$ is good because of argument A |

The imposition of a definition leaves open to the interlocutor only the possibility of attacking the decision or rejecting the move. For instance, the criticisms against the redefinitions of 'wetland' could point out the unreasonableness of having different successive definitions for the same concept, but could not delete the audience's commitments.

2.5. E. *Defining for Committing*

The act of committing the speaker to a definition is the most usual strategy to impose a criterion of interpretation. The speaker commits himself to use a word with a specific meaning, which can be shared, even if not unique, or new. The speaker imposes a commitment only on himself. However, such a move also implicitly alters the hearer's commitment store, as the hearer becomes bound to the speaker's intended meaning. The hearer's commitment can be regarded as a limit to the freedom of the speaker's self-committing, as the chosen meaning can introduce ambiguity and therefore have negative consequences on the dialogue. The hearer can attack the move, and the definition, based on its negative consequences.

R	Move of the Speaker (α)	Commitments α	Commitments β	Possible Moves of the Hearer (β)	Possible Moves of the Speaker (α)
1	$F_{com}Def(S)$	1. $Def(S)$.	1. When used by α, S means $Def(S)$. 2. β shall interpret S as $Def(S)$, when used by α.		
2			1. Delete commitment β 1,2.	1. Attack (F_{com}): A) E_{com} hinders the dialogue (introduces ambiguity) because of $Def_2(S)$.	
3					Defense: $Def(S)$ specifies the meaning of S $(Def(S)$ is shared).

The act of committing to a definition can be an instrument to avoid or introduce ambiguity. In the first case, the speaker chooses one of the possible meanings ('we' shall also include the audience, which is not a *pluralis maiestatis*), so that the hearer does not have interpretative doubts. In the second case, the speaker stipulates a new meaning and imposes on the hearer an interpretative rule. In this case, the hearer can reject the move based on its consequences on the dialogue.

2.6. F. *Implicit Definition*

An implicit definition can be considered an act when the speaker is not simply using a dark-side commitment, but also when he is treating a new commitment as a dark-side one, when he is presupposing it (F_{pp}). He commits the hearer to a proposition that he never accepted and places on him the burden of disproving it. The shifting of the burden makes this move extremely powerful, as the hearer needs to provide arguments in order not to be committed. The speaker can increase the burden by redefining vague words or omitting the definitions of crucial concepts in order to take their definitions for granted later.

R	Move of the Speaker(α)	Commitments α	Commitments β	Possible Moves of the Hearer (β)	Possible Moves of the Speaker(α)
1	$F_{pp}Def(S)$	1. $Def(S)$. 2. β is committed to $Def(S)$.	1. $Def(S)$.		
2			1. Delete $Def(S)$.	1. Attack (F_{pp}) No previous commitment to $Def(S)$ because of argument A (S means Def_2S).	
3		1. $Def(S)$ 2. $Def(S)$ 3. $Def(S)$ 4. $Def_3(S)$			Defense: 1. $Def(S)$ *is* commonly known. 2. No alternative definitions of S. 3. Def_2S is not shared. 4. β misinterpreted $Def(S)$; S means $Def_3(S)$.

The dialogue game opened by an implicit redefinition is a meta-dialogue attacking the conditions of the move. The hearer needs to reject the move by showing that he cannot be presumed to be committed to the presupposed definition. In this meta-dialogue game, the speaker is playing with the interlocutor's commitments. He can reject his arguments, and the effect of his defenses consists in preventing the hearer from deleting a commitment that should remain in place. The strength of this move lies in the nature and number of possible defenses of the speaker, which make any meta-attacks of the hearer more difficult and less effective.

3. Conclusion

Dialogue theory provides an abstract framework in which the participants perform certain moves and follow specific rules. One of its crucial limits is applicability. How is it possible to determine which moves shall be made? If we move from formal dialogue models to actual speech acts, we notice that formal dialogue structures are of little use, as they cannot predict the possible future moves. However, if we describe dialogical moves in terms of the moves that they allow the interlocutor to perform, we can build a potentially predictive system. In this chapter we have shown how the act of defining and the structures of definitional sentences can outline the possible reasonable replies and exclude other possible moves. The force of a definition can be described in terms of its dialectical effects on the hearer, or rather the moves that it allows the hearer to perform and the arguments that he can use to reject them. Obviously, the dialogue sequence in which a definition is left open can be conceived as the most complex scenario, where strict rules define the boundaries of reasonableness. This dialectically worst case scenario can become much less complicated in contexts where the hearer can simply refuse a standpoint without providing any argument, or retract a commitment without any reason or counter-reaction by the speaker. The dialectical structures of the moves of defining provided here are aimed at showing how a definition can potentially affect the dialectical setting.

The framework provided describes definitions according to two dimensions: their pragmatic nature (listed in letters) and their sentential structure (in numbers). The combination of the two dimensions can be used to provide a means to reveal the structure of the possible rejections of a definition (and the effects thereof), based on its limits. We have shown in the case of the act of advancing a definition how this mechanism works for the genus-difference definition mentioned in the example. Other definitional acts allow only meta-dialogical rejections, aimed at undermining the reasonableness or acceptability of the speech act.

Conclusion

When we think about words we only consider what they express, what they are used for "saying." We often may not realize that words have a silent side. Their use can hide implicit moves and complex arguments based on propositions that are left unsaid. Nobody would be moved by the description of a battlefield as a place of war, or by the claim that missionaries acted in peace. However, these words become emotive when we speak of the war on terror or missions of peace. Something unsaid hides behind them and justifies their use or appears to justify it, leading us to certain conclusions. They do more than express a categorization of reality. They are silent emotional persuaders.

Some words have the power to influence our judgments and our decisions. We approve of an action when brought about for the purpose of 'peace.' We are horrified when a nation allows practices such as 'torture.' The use of these words can influence our emotions and our evaluation of reality, and at the same time their deceptive use can distort our perceptions of the world and lead an audience toward accepting conclusions that are not supported by evidence-based reality.

The problem that has been solved in the investigation through the chapters of this book is to get some theoretical grasp of how this effect is created and how it influences the hearer. Emotive words have two dimensions. On the one hand, they are mere words. They have a meaning, which can be described in a more or less specific fashion, which can be defined even if vaguely, provisionally, or incompletely. On the other hand, they are emotive. They generate immediate and powerful evaluative responses that can affect our assessment of the fragment of reality described, and in some cases justify a certain course of action. The distinction between these two dimensions, pointed out by Stevenson (1944), reveals the dialectical and rhetorical structure of emotive words. From the perspective advanced in this book, their force lies in the arguments that they hide. Emotive terms are forms of implicit arguments, and therefore they need to be inquired into by considering the reasoning patterns they trigger, the possible moves that they allow an interlocutor to perform, and the missing, or hidden propositions that are taken for granted when they are used. The reasoning is embedded in a dialectical and pragmatic framework that is interwoven and needs to be disentangled in order to provide an instrument for describing and evaluating them.

The most evident feature of emotive words is their effect. Their emotive meaning, or rather the evaluative dimension of their structure, can elicit an immediate response, a swift judgment that can be followed by an appropriate decision to act. However, the same emotive force can lure the interlocutor into evaluating a word, instead of the reality referred to. For this reason, these words can become instruments for hiding reality, instead of tools for communicating it. In order to understand how these words can trigger judgments, and why and when they can be used to get the best of a speech partner unfairly, we analyzed the reasoning mechanism leading to evaluating a state of affairs. The same word, the same description, can affect interlocutors differently. Depending on values and knowledge, concepts such as 'culture,' 'honesty,' or 'money' can be regarded more or less positively. In order to account for the potential different evaluative effects, we uncovered an evaluative (or emotive) dimension that rests on implicit arguments from values and patterns of reasoning grounded on what it is normally regarded as desirable or objectionable. From this view, the vivid representation of a situation triggers a particular type of argument, in which the conclusion is the classification of the represented fragment of reality as, for instance, 'good' or 'bad.' Often such a value judgment can be a premise for a further reasoning step, leading from a desired state of affairs to a decision to bring about the means to reach it.

This argumentation-theoretic explanation of the emotive dimension of meaning needs to be related to an account of its counterpart, its descriptive meaning, representing the conceptual dimensions of a word. As mentioned previously, emotive words are first merely words, which need to be "said of" (using an Aristotelian expression), or rather used to refer to a fragment of reality characterized by certain features. From this perspective, using a word amounts to a form of reasoning, where the generic properties of a word meaning are applied to a specific instance. This reasoning hinges on a fundamental premise, constituted by the definition of the term. In order to describe reality differently from what it appears to be, it is sufficient to alter the reasoning from classification, either by distorting reality, by concealing or manipulating the characteristics of a state of affairs, or by modifying the definition of the predicate that we want to use.

This account is based on an extremely problematic notion: definition. The same concept can be defined in many different ways, and all the different definitional sentences are apparently equally valid. This relativistic aspect can be dealt with by analyzing definitions from an argumentation perspective. Definitions are not all the same; they differ in their structure, their logical properties, and their possible weak points where they can be attacked and rejected. Every definitional sentence (genus-difference, definition by parts, by etymology, etc.) has its own distinctive argumentative force and can be attacked only in certain ways. Every definition, in this view, leaves the interlocutor a wider or narrower field of refutation, a limited range of possible countermoves. Therefore, even if it is not possible to state that a definition is 'true' or 'false,' it is still possible to assess it, accept it, and hold it as a proposed hypothesis until the contrary is proven. The mechanism of the inappropriate use of emotive words depends on the way a concept is implicitly redefined in order to be predicated of a certain state of affairs. The speaker presupposes a redefinition that can be easily countered or rejected and uses it to trigger a value judgment.

This analysis of the mechanisms of definition and redefinition leads us from the realm of reasoning patterns into the fields of pragmatics and dialectics. Having looked at some famous speeches, we observed how the speaker often advances new definitions, reminds the audience of accepted ones, informs the interlocutors of the meanings of crucial concepts, or commits himself to using a word with a specific meaning. If he is in a position of authority, he can actually impose a new meaning that the listeners will have to accept. We call all these moves definitions; however, we have shown that they are more carefully analyzed as definitional *moves* in a dialogue framework, acts aimed to fulfill a specific purpose. By advancing, imposing, reminding, or informing the audience of a definition, the speaker alters the dialogical situation and the dialectical relationship with the listener.

When we remind the hearer of a definition, we take for granted that the definition has already been accepted. When we advance one, we presuppose that it is not shared and can be attacked, and that we are committed to having proposed it. As in a chess game, we can perform a definitional move only on certain conditions. However, the situation is different from that of a game, where there is an umpire present to call the moves. We can remind the audience of a definition that is actually controversial, or impose a new meaning without being entitled to do so. As on a chessboard, the speaker can alter the dialogical situation by inserting new commitments into his own and the interlocutor's commitment stores, which can be used for further moves.

The aforementioned acts are only the light side of what defining amounts to. Crucial words such as 'enemy,' 'terrorist,' 'torture,' or 'peace' are often not defined. They are redefined, but no act is performed explicitly. They are left without a definition, but this choice does not amount to a *speech* act. These non-acts constitute the dark side of defining, because they are hidden moves. They are intended and have specific purposes. They modify the interlocutors' dialogical situations. Implicit redefinitions and omissions of definition are the most powerful and deceitful of definitional moves. The speaker can omit a definition, so that he can use the undefined term with any possible definition he wishes. For instance, in countries where 'torture' is not defined, this crime, even though clearly and openly practiced, is often left unpunished. The speaker can also engage in subterfuge by implicitly redefining a word. He changes the commitments of the interlocutor and grounds his further moves on a proposition that has never been accepted. But he is not committed to any action.

The dark side of definitions, and emotive words, can be analyzed as an improper act, the act of presupposing. With this concept we refer to the act of taking for granted a proposition and grounding the felicity of our moves upon it. When the speaker takes for granted what is not shared, a simple mechanism of linguistic economy becomes a powerful move that brings about dialogical, dialectical, and rhetorical effects. The crucial problem with presupposition and implicit redefinitions is drawing the line between proper uses and deceptive manipulation. It makes little sense to judge a speaker's beliefs about his interlocutor's knowledge. Presupposing for him amounts to taking for granted what he believed to be known, and such a mental state cannot be accessed, let alone objectively judged. The problem of presupposition can be analyzed from a reasoning perspective. Presupposition can be thought of as the conclusion of presumptive reasoning, or rather a pattern of reasoning proceeding from what is usually accepted, or from the usual co-occurrences or relationships between events. When a speaker presupposes a proposition, he is implicitly engaging in a form of argumentation that can be reasonable or unreasonable. It would be unreasonable to ground an argument on the premise that usually ordinary people drive Bentleys, or that the shared definition of 'hostilities' excludes bombings. A presupposition can therefore be evaluated, and emotive language and implicit redefinitions assessed according to the standards applied to shared definitions based on common knowledge.

Our analysis of emotive force, definitions, acts of defining, and presupposition provides the instruments for describing the dialogical and dialectical effects of redefinitions. From this perspective, an implicit redefinition has a dialogical role when it is used to trigger a certain implicit message, leading the interlocutor to draw a specific conclusion. In this sense, an implicit redefinition becomes a dialogical move when it is aimed at persuading the hearer. What Stevenson called a 'persuasive definition' can be understood as a use of emotive or rather argumentatively pivotal words based on their implicit redefinitions. In earlier paragraphs we described speech acts using the metaphor of a chessboard. The same metaphor reveals another crucial aspect of redefinitions. Chess moves have two sides. They perform an explicit action, consisting in occupying a square or removing an opponent's piece from play. However, the explicit move has a hidden counterpart, which is often the most important one. Every move opens or blocks certain possible moves that the other player can perform. In this sense, a move can be described as a strategy, as a maneuver to force the other party to carry out only specific actions and not others. This same idea can be applied to the dialectical analysis of definitions and implicit redefinitions.

The theory of formal dialogue systems, representing a conversation as a set of moves and commitments of the two participants, becomes the chessboard and sets the rules of a game that is played every day in politics, law, and ordinary conversation. Every act of defining and every definitional sentence allows the hearer to perform certain countermoves. He can attack a definition if advanced, but he may need to attack the authority of the speaker if he wants to reject a definition that has been imposed.

Moreover, every definitional sentence can be successfully refused only in certain fashions. Certain definitions are always incomplete, while others are always not convertible and only presumptive. The stronger the structures of the definition, the more restricted are the possible refutations allowed. Implicit redefinitions are the dialectically most powerful strategies, as they shift the burden of proof onto the interlocutor, who actually needs to prove that the presupposed meaning is not the one shared by providing supporting arguments. For this reason, presupposing a redefinition amounts to reversing the dialectical roles.

Words can be powerful instruments of persuasion. They can hide, modify, and manipulate the way we perceive and evaluate a situation, an action, or an event. Words can hide implicit arguments and fundamental premises, values, and definitions. The use of a redefined word can conceal dialectical strategies aimed at shifting the burden of proof. In this sense words can be silent. Their persuasive force can be found not in what they say, but in the silent message conveyed without words by what is not explicitly said.

References

Aakhus, Mark (2005). The Act and Activity of Proposing in Deliberation. In P. Ridley (ed.), *Engaging Argument: Selected Papers from the 2005 National Communication Association/American Forensic Association Summer Conference on Argumentation* (pp. 402–408). Washington, DC: National Communication Association.

Aarnio, Aulis (1977). *On Legal Reasoning.* Turku: Turun Yliopisto.

Aarnio, Aulis (1987). *The Rational as Reasonable.* Dordrecht: Reidel.

Abaelardus, Petrus (1970). *Dialectica.* L. M. De Rijk (ed.). Assen: Van Gorcum.

Aberdein, Andrew (2000). Persuasive Definition. In C. W. Tindale, H. V. Hansen, & E. Sveda (eds.), *Argumentation at the Century's Turn, OSSA (Ontario Society for the Study of Argumentation) Proceedings,* Windsor 2000.

Anscombe, G. E. M. (1998). Practical Inference. In R. Hursthouse, G. Lawrence, & W. Quinn (eds.), *Virtues and Reasons: Philippa Foot and Moral Theory: Essays in Honour of Philippa Foot* (pp. 1–34), Oxford: Clarendon Press.

Anscombre, Jean-Claude & Ducrot, Oswald (1978). Lois logiques et lois argumentatives. *Le Français Moderne* 46(4): 347–357.

Anscombre, Jean-Claude & Ducrot, Oswald (1983). *L'Argumentation dans la langue.* Bruxelles: Mardaga.

Anscombre, Jean-Claude & Ducrot, Oswald (1986). Argumentativité et informativité. In M. Meyer (ed.), *De la métaphysique à la rhétorique* (pp. 79.94), Bruxelles: Université de Bruxelles.

Antley, Kenneth (1974). McCawley's Theory of Selectional Restriction. *Foundations of Language* 11(2): 257–272.

Aqvist, Lennart (1974). A New Approach to the Logical Theory of Actions and Causality. In S. Stenlund (ed.), *Logical Theory and Semantics* (pp. 73–91), Dordrecht: D. Reidel.

Aristotle (1969). Topica. In W. D. Ross (ed.), *The Works of Aristotle.* Oxford: Oxford University Press.

Aristotle (2007). *On Rhetoric. A Theory of Civic Discourse.* Translated by G. Kennedy. Oxford University Press.

Aristotle (1995). Nicomachean Ethics. In J. Barnes (ed.), *The Complete Works of Aristotle,* vol. II, Princeton, NJ: Princeton University Press.

Artsybashev, Michael (1915). *Sanine.* New York: Huebsch.

Asher, Nichoals & Lascarides, Alex (1998). The Semantics and Pragmatics of Presupposition. *Journal of Semantics* 15(3): 239–300.

Asher, Nichoals & Lascarides, Alex (2003). *Logics of Conversation*. Cambridge: Cambridge University Press.

Atkinson, Katie, Bench-Capon, Trevor, & McBurney, Peter (2005): Generating Intentions through Argumentation. In F. Dignum, V. Dignum, S. Koenig, S. Kraus, M. Singh, & M. Wooldridge (eds.), *Proceedings of the Fourth International Joint Conference on Autonomous Agents and Multi-Agent Systems* (AAMAS 2005) (pp. 1261–1262), Utrecht, The Netherlands: ACM Press.

Atkinson, Katie, Bench-Capon, Trevor, & McBurney, Peter (2006). PARMENIDES: Facilitating Deliberation in Democracies. *Artificial Intelligence and Law* 14(4): 261–275.

Atlas, Jay (2004). Presupposition. In L. R. Horn & G. Ward (eds.), *The Handbook of Pragmatics* (pp. 29–52), Malden, MA: Blackwell Publishers.

Austin, John (1962). *How to Do Things with Words: The William James Lectures delivered at Harvard University in 1955*. (ed. J. O. Urmson) Oxford: Clarendon Press.

Bach, Kent (1999). The Myth of Conventional Implicature. *Linguistics and Philosophy* 22(4): 237–366.

Bach, Kent (2006). Speech acts and pragmatics. In M. Devitt & R. Hanley (eds.), *The Blackwell Guide to the Philosophy of Language* (pp. 147–167). Oxford: Blackwell.

Baker, Michael. (2003). Computer-Mediated Argumentative Interactions for the Co-Elaboration of Scientific Notions. In J. Andriessen, M. Baker, & D. Suthers (eds.), *Arguing to Learn: Confronting Cognitions in Computer-Supported Collaborative Learning Environments* (pp. 47–78), Dordrecht: Kluwer.

Ballard Lee, Conrad, Robert. & Longacre, Robert (1971). The Deep and Surface Grammar of Interclausal Relations. *Foundations of Language* 7(1): 70–118.

Barth, Else & Krabbe, Erik (1982). *From Axiom to Dialogue*. Berlin: de Gruyter.

Barwick, Karl (1965). Zur Rekonstruktion der Rhetorik des Hermagoras von Temnos. *Philologus* 109(3/4): 186–218.

Basler, Roy (ed.) (1946). *Abraham Lincoln. His Speeches and Writings*. Cleveland: World Publishing Company.

Bayles, Michael (1991). Definitions in Law. In J. Fetzer, D. Shatz, & G. Schlesinger (eds.), *Definitions and Definability: Philosophical Perspectives* (pp. 253–267), Dordrecht: Kluwer.

Bellavita, Christopher (2008). Changing Homeland Security: What is Homeland Security? *Homeland Security Affairs* 4(2).

Bench-Capon, Trevor (1998). Specification and Implementation of Toulmin Dialogue Game. In *Legal Knowledge-Based Systems. JURIX: The Eleventh Conference* (pp. 5–19), Nijmegen: Gerard Noodt Instituut.

Bench-Capon, Trevor (2002). Agreeing to Differ: Modelling Persuasive Dialogue between Parties with Different Values. *Informal Logic* 22(3): 231–245.

Bench-Capon, Trevor (2003). Persuasion in Practical Argument Using Value-Based Argumentation Frameworks. *Journal of Logic and Computation* 13(3): 429–448.

Bench-Capon, Trevor & Atkinson, Katie (2009). Abstract Argumentation and Values. In Iyad Rahwan & Guillermo Simari (eds.), *Argumentation in Artificial Intelligence* (pp. 45–64), Berlin: Springer.

Bentham, Jeremy (1952). *Bentham's Handbook of Political Fallacies*. H. A. Larrabee (ed.), Baltimore, MD: Johns Hopkins Press.

Ben-Ze'ev, Aaron (2000). *The Subtlety of Emotions*. Cambridge, MA: MIT Press.

Bierwisch, Manfred (1969). On Certain Problems of Semantic Representation. *Foundations of Language* 5(2): 153–184.

Blackstone, William (1769). *Commentaries on the Laws of England. Vol. IV*. Oxford: Clarendon Press.

Blakey, Robert (1982). The RICO Civil Fraud Action in Context: Reflections on Bennett v. Berg. *Notre Dame Law Review* 58(2): 237–349.

Blokker, Niels (2000). Is the Authorization Authorized? Powers and Practice of the UN Security Council to Authorize the Use of Force by 'Coalitions of the Able and Willing.' *European Journal of International Law* 11(3): 541–568.

Bocchino, Anthony & Sonenshein, David (2006). *A Practical Guide to Federal Evidence*. Louisville, CO: NITA.

Boethius, Anicius Manlius Severinus (1891). *Liber de Diffinitione*. In J.-P. Migne (ed.), *Patrologia Latina*, vol. 64, Paris.

Boethius, Anicius Manlius Severinus (1966). *Porphyrii Isagoge, Translatio Boethii*. In L. Minio-Paluello (ed.). Bruges: Desclée De Brouwer.

Boethius's De Topicis Differentiis. Translated by E. Stump. Ithaca, NY: Cornell University Press.

Boethius's In Ciceronis topica (1988). Translated, with notes and Introduction by Eleanore Stump. Ithaca, NY: Cornell University Press.

Braet, Antoine (1987). The Classical Doctrine of Status and the Rhetorical Theory of Argumentation. *Philosophy & Rhetoric* 20(2): 79–93.

Brewer, Scott (1996). Exemplary Reasoning: Semantics, Pragmatics and the Rational Force of Legal Argument by Analogy. *Harvard Law Review* 109(5): 923–1028.

Brewka, Gerhard (2001). Dynamic Argument Systems: A Formal Model of Argumentation Processes Based on Situation Calculus. *Journal of Logic and Computation* 11(2): 257–282.

Broda-Bahm, Kenneth (1999). Finding Protection in Definitions: The Quest for Environmental Security. *Argumentation & Advocacy* 35(4): 159–170.

Brown, Donald (1955). Evaluative Inference. *Philosophy* 30(114): 214–228.

Brown, Lester (1977). Redefining National Security. *Worldwatch Paper 14*. Washington DC: Worldwatch Institute.

Buchanan, Bruce, Carenini, Giuseppe, Mittal, Vibhu, & Moore, Johanna (1998). Designing Computer-Based Frameworks that Facilitate Doctor–Patient Collaboration. *Artificial Intelligence in Medicine* 12(2): 169–191.

Burgess-Jackson, Keith (1995). Rape and Persuasive Definition. *Canadian Journal of Philosophy* 25(3) appeared in issue 3: 415–454.

Burnyeat, Myles (1980). Aristotle on Learning to be Good. In A. Rorty (ed.), *Essays on Aristotle's Ethics* (pp. 69–92), Berkeley: University of California Press.

Burton-Roberts, Noel (1989). *The Limits to Debate: A Revised Theory of Semantic Presupposition*. Cambridge: Cambridge University Press.

Calboli Montefusco, Lucia (2004). Stylistic and Argumentative Function of Rhetorical "Amplificatio". *Hermes* 132(1) appeared in issue 1: 69–81.

Carston, Robyn (2002). *Thoughts and Utterances*. Malden, MA: Blackwell.

Chesterton, Gilbert (2009). *Heretics*. Rockville, MD: Serenity.

Chi, Michelene & Roscoe, Rod (2002). The Process and Challenges of Conceptual Change. In M. Limon & L. Mason (eds.), *Reconsidering Conceptual Change: Issues in Theory and Practice* (pp. 3–27). Dordrecht: Kluwer.

Chisholm, Roderick (1976). *Person and Object: A Metaphysical Study*. London: Routledge.

Chomsky, Noam (1971). Deep Structure, Surface Structure and Semantic Interpretation. In D. Steinberg & L. Jakobovits (eds.), *Semantics, an Interdisciplinary Reader in Linguistics, Philosophy and Psychology* (pp. 183–216), Cambridge: Cambridge University Press.

Chomsky, Noam (1972). Some Empirical Issues in the Theory of Transformational Grammar. In Stanley Peters (ed.), *Goals of Linguistic Theory* (pp. 63–130). Englewood Cliffs, NJ: Prentice-Hall.

Cicero, Marcus Tullius (1916). *The Orations of Marcus Tullius Cicero. vol. 1. The First Oration Against Verres*. Translated by C. D. Yonge. London: G. Bell and Sons.

Cicero, Marcus Tullius (1965). *Rhetorica ad Herennium*. Translated by Harry Caplan. Cambridge, MA: Harvard University Press.

Cicero, Marcus Tullius (1988). *De Inventione*. In *The Orations of Marcus Tullius Cicero*. Translated by C. D. Yonge. London: George Bell & Sons.

Cicero, Marcus Tullius (2003). *Cicero's Topica*. Edited and translated by Tobias Reinhardt. Oxford: Oxford University Press.

Cigada, Sara (2006). Connectif et relation entre locuteurs. In Giovanni Gobber, Maria Cristina Gatti, & Sara Cigada (eds.), *Sýndesmoi* (pp. 97–173), Milano: Vita e Pensiero.

Clark, Herbert (1993). *Arenas of Language Use*. Chicago: University of Chicago Press.

Connor-Linton, Jeff (1991). A Sociolinguistic Model of Successful Speech Act Construction. In Jef Verschueren (ed.), *Pragmatics at Issue* (pp. 93–112). Amsterdam: John Benjamins.

Corblin, Francis (2003). Presuppositions and Commitment Stores. In *Proceedings Diabruck, 7th Workshop on the Semantics and the Pragmatics of Dialogue*. Wallerfangen, Germany.

Crothers, Edward (1979). *Pragmatic Structure Inference*. Norwood: Ablex.

Crowley, Sharon & Hawhee, Debra (1999). *Ancient Rhetorics for Contemporary Students*. Boston: Allyn and Bacon.

Damascenus, Johannes (1953). *Dialectica*. O. Colligan (ed.), St. Bonaventure: The Franciscan Institute.

Damasio, Antonio (1994). *Descartes' Error: Emotion, Reason, and the Human Brain*. New York: G. P. Putnam's Sons.

Damasio, Antonio (2000). *The Feeling of What Happens: Body, Emotion and the Making of Consciousness*. London: Vintage.

Dascal, Marcelo (2001). Nihil sine ratione → Blandior ratio ('Nothing without a reason → A softer reason'). In H. Poser (ed.), *Nihil sine ratione – Proceedings of the VII. Internationaler Leibniz-Kongress* (pp. 276–280). Berlin: Gottfried-Wilhelm-Leibniz Gesellschaft.

De Bessé, Bruno (1990). La définition terminologique. In J. Chaurand & F. Mazière (eds.), *La définition, Actes du Colloque organisé par CELEX* (pp. 252–261). Paris: Larousse.

De Sousa, Ronald (1987). *The Rationality of Emotion*. Cambridge, MA: MIT Press.

Doyle, Michael & Sambanis, Nicholas (2006). *Making War and Building Peace: United Nations Peace Operations*. Princeotn, NJ: Princeton University Press.

Ducrot, Oswald (1966). "Le roi de France est sage". Implication logique et Présupposition linguistique. *Etudes de linguistique appliquée* 4: 39–47.

Ducrot, Oswald (1968). Le structuralisme en linguistique. In O. Ducrot, T. Todorov, et al. (eds.), *Qu'est-ce que le structuralisme?* (pp. 13–96). Paris: Seuil.

Ducrot, Oswald (1972a). *Dire et ne pas dire*. Paris: Hermann

Ducrot, Oswald (1972b). De Saussure à la philosophie du langage. Preface to John Searle, *Les actes de langage* (pp. 7–34). Paris: Hermann

Ducrot, Oswald (1978). Deux mais. *Cahier de linguistique* 8: 109–120.

Dummett, Michael (1973). *Frege: Philosophy of Language*. Cambridge, MA: Harvard University Press.

Eco, Umberto (1976). *A theory of semiotics*. Bloomington, IN: Indiana University Press.

Engel, Morris (1980). *Analyzing Informal Fallacies*. Englewood Cliffs, NJ: Prentice-Hall.

Engel, Morris (1994). *Fallacies and Pitfalls of Language: The Language Trap*. New York: Dover Publications.

Ephratt, Michal (2008). The functions of Silence. *Journal of Pragmatics* 40 (11) appeared in issue 11: 1909–1938.

Fillmore, Charles (1982). Towards a Descriptive Framework for Spatial Deixis. In R. Jarvella & W. Klein (eds.), *Speech, Place, and Action* (pp. 31–59), London: Wiley.

Fillmore, Charles (2003). Double-Decker Definitions: The Role of Frames in Meaning Explanations. *Sign Language Studies* 3 (3): 263–295.

Finocchiaro, Maurice (2007). Arguments, Meta-arguments, and Metadialogues: A Reconstruction of Krabbe, Govier, and Woods. *Argumentation* 2(3): 253–268.

Fisher, Nick (1992). *Hybris: A Study in the Values of Honour and Shame in Ancient Greece*. Warminster, UK: Aris & Phillips.

Forcellini, Egidio (1831). *Totius latinitatis lexicon, Vol. 2*. Schneeberg: Schumann.

Freeman, James (2005). *Acceptable Premises: An Epistemic Approach to an Informal Logic Problem*. Cambridge: Cambridge University Press.

Frege, Gottlob (1897). Logic. In H. Hermes, F. Kambartel, & F. Kaulbach (eds.), *Posthumous Writings: Gottlob Frege*, translated by P. Long and R. White (pp. 126–151). Oxford: Blackwell, 1979.

Frege, Gottlob (1948). Sense and Reference. *The Philosophical Review* 57(3): 209–230.

Frijda, Nico (1998). The Laws of Emotion. In J. Jenkins, K. Oatley, & N. Stein (eds.), *Human Emotions: A Reader* (pp. 271–287). Malden, MA: Blackwell.

Frijda, Nico & Mesquita, Batja (1998). The Analysis of Emotions: Dimensions of Variation. In M. Mascolo & S. Griffin. (eds.), *What Develops in Emotional Development?* (pp. 273–295). New York: Plenum Press.

Frijda, Nico & Mesquita, Batja (2000). Beliefs through Emotions. In N. Frijda, A. Mansteade, & S. Bem (eds.), *Emotions and Beliefs: How Feelings Influence Thoughts* (pp. 45–77). Cambridge: Cambridge University Press.

Fusco, Federico (2008). Commencement of the Prescription Period in Case of Damage Due to Omissions. In Helmut Koziol & Barbara Steininger (eds.), Tort and Insurance Law Yearbook. European Tort Law. volume 2007(pp. 79–93). New York: Springer.

Gallie, Walter (1956). Essentially Contested Concepts. *Proceedings of the Aristotelian Society* 56: 167–198.

Gano, Darwin Curtis & Williams, Samuel C. (2008). *Teacher's Handbook to Accompany Gano's Commercial Law.* Charleston, SC: BiblioLife

Gildenhard, Ingo (2011). *Creative Eloquence: The Construction of Reality in Cicero's Speeches.* Oxford: Oxford University Press.

Giuliani, Alessandro (1972). The Aristotelian Theory of the Dialectical Definition. *Philosophy & Rhetoric* 5(3) appeared in issue 3: 129–142.

Glanville, Williams (1983). *Textbook of Criminal Law.* London: Steven & Sons.

Gobber, Giovanni (2007). Some Remarks on Interrogativity and Argumentation. In F. H. van Eemeren, A. Blair, C. Willard, & B. Garssen (eds.), *Proceedings of the Sixth Conference of the International Society for the Study of Argumentation* (pp. 461–464). Amsterdam: SicSat.

Gordon, Thomas (1994). The Pleadings Game: An Exercise in Computational Dialectics. *Artificial Intelligence and Law* 2(4) appeared in issue 4: 239–292.

Gordon, Thomas & Walton, Douglas (2009). Proof Burdens and Standards. In Iyad Rahwan & Guillermo Simari (ed.), *Argumentation in Artificial Intelligence* (pp. 239–260). Berlin: Springer.

Gorsky, D.P. (1981). *Definition.* Moscow: Progress Publishers.

Governatori, Guido (2008). Labelled modal tableaux. In Carlos Areces and R. Goldblatt (eds.), *Advances in Modal Logic,* volume 7: 87–110.

Governatori, Guido, Maher, Michael, Billington, David, & Antoniou, Grigoris (2004). Argumentation Semantics for Defeasible Logic. *Journal of Logic and Computation* 14(5): 675–702.

Green, Georgia (1996). *Pragmatics and Natural language understanding.* Mahwah, NJ: Erlbaum.

Green, Keith & Kortum, Richard (2007). Can Frege's Farbung Help Explain the Meaning of Ethical Terms? *Essays in Philosophy* 8(1): Article 10. Available at: http://commons.pacificu.edu/eip/vol8/iss1/10 (retrieved on 16 June 2011).

Green-Pedersen, Niels (1984). *The Tradition of the Topics in the Middle Ages: The Commentaries on Aristotle's and Boethius' Topics.* Munich: Philosophia Verlag.

Greenwood, Katie, Bench-Capon, Trevor, & McBurney, Peter (2003). Structuring Dialogue between the People and Their Representatives. In R. Traunmuller (ed.), *Electronic Government, Lecture Notes in Computer Science* vol. 2739 (pp. 55–62). Berlin: Springer.

Grice, Paul (1975). Logic and Conversation. In P. Cole & J. Morgan (eds.), *Syntax and Semantics 3: Speech Acts* (pp. 41–58). New York: Academic Press.

Grice, Paul (1989). *Studies in the Way of Words.* Cambridge, MA: Harvard University Press.

Grimaldi, William (1988). *Aristotle, Rhetoric II. A Commentary.* New York: Fordham University Press.

Grimes, Joseph (1975). *The Thread of Discourse.* The Hague: Mouton.

Groarke, Leo & Tindale, Christopher (2004). *Good Reasoning Matters!* Oxford: Oxford University Press.

Gundel, Jeanette & Fretheim, Thorstein (2004). Topic and Focus. In L. Horn & G. Ward (eds.), *The Handbook of Pragmatic Theory* (174–196). Oxford: Blackwell.

Hahn, Ulrike, & Oaksford, Mike (2006). A Normative Theory of Argument Strength. *Informal Logic* 26(1): 1–24.

Halldén, Sören (1960). *True Love, True Humour and True Religion: A Semantic Study.* Lund: Gleerup.

Hamblin, Charles (1970). *Fallacies.* London: Methuen.

Hamblin, Charles (1971). Mathematical Models of Dialogue. *Theoria* 37(2) appeared in issue 2: 130–155.

Hammond, Scott, Hardwick, Kevin, & Lubert, Howard (2007). *Classics of American Political and Constitutional Thought. Volume 1: Origins through the Civil War.* Indianapolis, IN: Hackett.

Hare, Richard (1952). *The Language of Morals.* Oxford: Oxford University Press.

Hare, Richard (1963). *Freedom and Reason.* Oxford: Oxford University Press.

Hart, Herbert (1948–1949; 1951). The Ascription of Responsibility and Rights. *Proceedings of the Aristotelian Society* 49: 171–194. Reprinted in *Logic and Language,* ed. A. Flew, Oxford: Blackwell, 1951, 145–166.

Hart, Herbert (1961). *The Concept of Law.* Oxford: Oxford University Press.

Hastings, Arthur (1963). *A Reformulation of the Modes of Reasoning in Argumentation.* Ph.D. Dissertation, Northwestern University, Evanston, IL.

Heath, Malcolm (1994). The Substructure of Stasis-Theory from Hermagoras to Hermogenes. *The Classical Quarterly, New Series* 44(1): 114–129.

Hickey, Leo (1993). Presupposition under Cross-Examination. *International Journal for the Semiotics of Law* 6(1): 89–109.

Hintikka, Jaakko (1979). Information-Seeking Dialogues: A Model. *Studia Logica* 38(4): 355–368.

Hjelmslev, Louis (1961). *Prolegomena to a theory of language.* Madison: University of Wisconsin Press.

Hobbs, Jerry (1979). Coherence and Coreference. *Cognitive Science* 3(1) appeared in issue 1: 67–90.

Hobbs, Jerry (1985). *On the Coherence and Structure of Discourse.* Report No. CSLI-85-37, Center for the Study of Language and Information, Stanford University.

Hockett, Charles (1950). Peiping Morphophonemics. *Language* 26(1): 63–85.

Holtgraves, Thomas (2002). *Language as Social Action.* Mahwah, NJ: Erlbaum.

Honigsberg, Peter Jan (2007). Chasing 'Enemy Combatants' and Circumventing International Law: A License for Sanctioned Abuse. *UCLA Journal of International Law and Foreign Affairs* 12(1): 1–74.

Hopper, Robert (1981a). The Taken-for-Granted. *Human Communication Research* 7(3): 195–211.

Hopper, Robert (1981b) How to Do Things without Words: The Taken-for-Granted as Speech-Action. *Communication Quarterly* 29(3): 228–236.

Horn, Laurence & Ward, Gregory (2004). *The handbook of pragmatics.* Oxford: Blackwell.

Houtlosser, Peter (2001). Points of View. In F. H. van Eemeren (ed.), *Crucial Concepts in Argumentation Theory* (pp. 27–50). Amsterdam: SicSat.

Huxley, Aldous (1955) *Eyeless in Gaza.* London: Chatto & Windus.

Huxley, Aldous (1998). *Brave New World.* New York: Harper Perennial.

Isidore of Seville (2005). *Isidore of Seville 's Etymologies: Complete English Translation, Volume 1.* Translated by Priscilla Throop. Charlotte, VT: MedievalMS.

Isidorus Hispalensis (1966). *Etymologiarum libri XX.* W. M. Linsday (ed.). Oxford: Clarendon Press.

Jackendoff, Ray (1972). *Semantic Interpretation in Generative Grammar.* Cambridge, MA: MIT Press.

Jørgensen, Charlotte (1998). Public Debate – An Act of Hostility? *Argumentation* 12(4): 431–443.

Kamp, Hans & Reyle, Uwe. (1993). *From Discourse to Logic.* Dordrecht: Kluwer.

Karimi, Simin (2003). *Word Order and Scrambling.* Malden, MA: Blackwell.

Karttunen, Lauri (1973). Presuppositions of Compound Sentences. *Linguistic Inquiry* 4(2): 169–193.

Katz, Jerrold (1973). On Defining "Presupposition." *Linguistic Inquiry* 4(2): 256–260.

Katz, Jerrold & Fodor, Jerry (1963). The Structure of a Semantic Theory. *Language* 39(2): 170–210.

Kauffeld, Fred (1995a). The Persuasive Force of Arguments on Behalf of Proposals. In In F. H. van Eemeren, R. Grootendorst, J. A. Blair & C. A. Willard (Eds.), *Analysis and evaluation: Proceedings of the third ISSA conference on argumentation.* (Vol. II, pp. 79–90). Amsterdam: International Centre for the Study of Argumentation.

Kauffeld, Fred (1995b). On the Difference between Assumptions and Presumptions. In S. Jackson (ed.), *Argumentation and Values: Proceedings of the Ninth SCA/AFA Conference on Argumentation* (pp. 509–514). Annandale, VA: Speech Communication Association.

Kauffeld, Fred (1998). Presumptions and the Distribution of Argumentative Burdens in Acts of Proposing and Accusing. *Argumentation* 12(2): 245–266.

Kauffeld, Fred (2003). The Ordinary Practice of Presuming and Presumption with Special Attention to Veracity and the Burden of Proof. In F. H. van Eemeren et al. (eds.), *Anyone Who Has a View: Theoretical Contributions to the Study of Argumentation* (pp. 136–146). Dordrecht: Kluwer.

Kauffman, Charles. (1989). Names and Weapons. *Communication Monographs* 56(3): 273–285.

Keenan, Edward (1971). Two Types Of Presupposition in Natural Language. In C. J. Filmore & D. T. Langendoen (eds.), *Studies in Linguistic Semantics* (pp. 45–54). New York: Holt.

Kelly, Gregory & Bazerman, Charles (2003). How Students Argue Scientific Claims: A Rhetorical-Semantic Analysis. *Applied Linguistics* 24(1): 28–55.

Kempson, Ruth (1975). *Presupposition and the Delimitation of Semantics.* Cambridge: Cambridge University Press.

Kerbrat-Orecchioni, Catherine (1977). *La connotation.* Lyon: Presses Universitaires de Lyon.

Kienpointner, Manfred (1992). *Alltagslogik: Struktur und Funktion von Argumentationsmustern.* Stuttgart: Fromman-Holzboog.

Kiewe, Amos & Houck, Davis (1991). *A Shining City on a Hill: Ronald Reagan's Economic Rhetoric, 1951–1989.* New York: Praeger.

Krabbe, Erik (2003). Metadialogues. In F. H. van Eemeren, J. A. Blair, C. A. Willard, & A. F. Snoeck Henkemans (eds.), *Proceedings of the Fifth Conference of the International Society for the Study of Argumentation* (pp. 641–644). Amsterdam: Sic Sat.

Krabbe, Erik (2007). On How to Get Beyond the Opening Stage. *Argumentation* 21(3) appeared in issue 3: 233–242.

Kramer, Adam (2003). Common Sense Principles of Contract Interpretation. *Oxford Journal of Legal Studies* 23(2): 173–196.

Kupperman, Joel (2002). *Ethical Knowledge*. London: Routledge.

Lakoff, George (1971). On Generative Semantics. In D. Steinberg & L. Jakobovits (eds.), *Semantics: An Interdisciplinary Reader in Philosophy, Linguistics and Psychology* (pp. 232–296). Cambridge: Cambridge University Press.

Lakoff, George (1999). Cognitive Models and Prototype Theory. In E. Margolis & S. Laurence (eds.), *Concepts* (pp. 391–421). Cambridge, MA: MIT Press.

Lakoff, George (2004). *Don't Think of an Elephant! Know Your Values and Frame the Debate*. White River Junction: Chelsea Green Publishing.

Lakoff, George (2006). *Thinking Points: Communicating Our American Values and Vision*, available at: http://www.cognitivepolicyworks.com/resource-center/ thinking-points/ (URL accessed on 11 October 2011).

Lakoff, Robin (1971). If's, and's, and but's about conjunction. In C. Fillmore & D. Langendoen (eds.), *Studies in Linguistic Semantics* (pp. 115–150). New York: Holt.

Lascarides, Alex & Asher, Nicholas (1993). Temporal Interpretation, Discourse Relations and Commonsense Entailment. *Linguistics and Philosophy* 16(5): 437–493.

Leech, Geoffrey (1974). *Semantics*. Harmondsworth, UK: Penguin.

Leenes, Ronald (2001). Burden of Proof in Dialogue Games and Dutch Civil Procedure. In *Proceedings of the Eighth International Conference on Artificial Intelligence and Law* (pp. 109–118). New York: ACM Press.

Leigh, Matthew (2004). Quintilian on the Emotions (Institutio Oratoria 6 Preface and 1–2). *The Journal of Roman Studies* 94: 122–140.

Leighton, Stephen (1984). Feelings and Emotion. *The Review of Metaphysics* 38(2): 303–320.

Leighton, Stephen (1988). Modern Theories of Emotion. *The Journal of Speculative Philosophy* 2(3): 206–224.

Leonard, Henry (1967). *Principles of Reasoning*. New York: Dover Publications.

Levinson, Stephen (1983). *Pragmatics*. Cambridge: Cambridge University Press.

Lewis, David (1979). Scorekeeping in a Language Game. *Journal of Philosophical Logic* 8(1): 339–359.

Lifton, Robert (1986) *The Nazi Doctors: Medical Killing and the Psychology of Genocide*. New York: Basic Books.

Lodder, Arno (1999). *DiaLaw. On Legal Justification and Dialogical Models of Argumentation*. Dordrecht: Kluwer.

Loui, Ronald (1998). Process and Policy: Resource-Bounded Non-Demonstrative Reasoning. *Computational Intelligence* 14(1) appeared in issue 1: 1–38.

Louisell, David (1977). Construing Rule 301: Instructing the Jury on Presumptions in Civil Actions and Proceedings. *Virginia Law Review* 63(2): 281–321.

Macagno, Fabrizio & Walton, Douglas (2009a). Reasoning from Classifications and Definitions. *Argumentation* 23(1): 81–107.

Macagno, Fabrizio & Walton, Douglas (2009b). Argument from Analogy in Law, the Classical Tradition, and Recent Theories. *Philosophy and Rhetoric* 42(2): 154–182.

Mackenzie, Jim (1979). Question-Begging in Non-Cumulative Systems. *Journal of Philosophical Logic* 8(1): 117–133.

Mackenzie, Jim (1981). The Dialectics of Logic. *Logique et Analyse* 94: 159–177.

Mahadevan, Swaminatha & Garmel, Gus (2005). *An Introduction to Clinical Emergency Medicine*. Cambridge: Cambridge University Press.

Manicas, Peter & Kruger, Arthur (1968). *Essentials of Logic.* New York: American Book Company.

Marsh Charles (2005). The Syllogism of Apologia: Rhetorical Stasis Theory and Crisis Communication. Paper presented at the Association for Education in Journalism and Mass Communication in San Antonio, Texas August 2005.

Martins, Isabel, Mortimer, Eduardo, Osborne, Jonathan, Tsatsarelis, Charalampos, & Jiménez Aleixandre, Maria Pilar (2001). Rhetoric and Science Education. In H. Behrendt et al. (eds.), *Research in Science Education – Past, Present, and Future* (pp. 189–198). Amsterdam: Kluwer.

Max, Ingolf (2008). Dimensions of Discourse: Presuppositions of (German) Connectors. In A. Steube (ed.), *The Discourse Potential of Underspecified Structures* (pp. 551–580). Berlin: Walter de Gruyter.

Mayall, James (1996). *The New Interventionism 1991–1994: United Nations Experience in Cambodia, Former Yugoslavia and Somalia.* Cambridge: Cambridge University Press.

Mazilu, Simona (2011). Persuasive Definitions in Ethical Argumentation on Abortion. In F. H. van Eemeren (ed.), *Proceedings of the 7th ISSA Conference* (pp. 1208–1220). Amsterdam: SicSat.

McCawley, James (1971). Interpretative semantics meets Frankenstein. *Foundations of Language* 7(2): 285–296.

Mel'cuk, Igor (1997). *Vers une linguistique Sens-Texte. Leçon inaugurale.* Paris: Collège de France.

Mill, James (1869). *Analysis of the Phenomena of the Human Mind.* London: Longmans, Green, Reader, and Dyer.

Molière, Jean-Baptiste (2000). Don Juan. In J. Wood & D. Coward (trans.), *Molière. The Miser and other plays.* Toronto: Penguin Books.

Mostovaia, Anna (2009). Color Words in Literary Russian: Connotations and Gender Differences in Use. *Journal of Literary Semantics* 38(1): 1–37.

Mousourakis, George (2003). *The Historical and Institutional Context of Roman Law.* Aldershot: Ashgate.

Myers, Norman (2004). Environmental Security: What's New and Different? *Background paper for the Hague Conference on Environment, Security, and Sustainable Development, 9–12 May, 2004,* The Hague, The Netherlands.

Naess, Arne (1966). *Communication and Argument.* London: Allen & Unwin LTD.

Naess, Arne (2005). *Interpretation and Preciseness.* In A. Drengson (ed.), *The Selected Works of Arne Naess,* vol. I. Dordrecht: Springer (Original edition: Dybway 1953).

Nakhnikian, George (1959). An Examination of Toulmin's Analytical Ethics. *The Philosophical Quarterly* 9(34): 59–79.

Nute, Donald (1994). Defeasible Logic. In *Handbook of Logic in Artificial Intelligence and Logic Programming, Volume 3: Nonmonotonic Reasoning and Uncertain Reasoning* (pp. 353–395). Oxford: Oxford University Press.

O'Connell, Mary Ellen (2002). The Myth of Preemptive Self-Defense. The American Society of International Law. Available at http://www.asil.org/taskforce/oconnell.pdf.

Olscamp, Paul (1970). Hare's Failure to Define Good Reasons. *Mind* 79(314): 241–244.

Orwell, George (1946). Politics and the English Language. *Horizon.* April.

Orwell, George (1949). *Nineteen Eighty-Four.* London: Martin Secker & Warburg.

Page, Herbert (1919). *The Law Of Contracts.* Cincinnati, OH: W. H. Anderson.

Partee, Barbara (1992). Syntactic Categories and Semantic Type. In M. Rosner & R. Johnson (eds.), *Computational Linguistics and Formal Semantics* (pp. 97–126), Cambridge: Cambridge University Press.

Perelman, Chaim & Olbrechts-Tyteca, Lucie (1951). Act and Person in Argument. *Ethics* 61(4): 251–269.

Perelman, Chaim & Olbrechts-Tyteca, Lucie (1969). *The New Rhetoric: A Treatise on Argumentation*. Notre Dame, IN: University of Notre Dame Press.

Petrus Hispanus (1947). *Petri Hispani Summulae Logicales* (ed. I. M. Bochenski). Torino: Marietti.

Phillipps, Samuel (1815). *A Treatise on the Law of Evidence*. London: Strahan.

Plantin, Christian (2004). On the Inseparability of Reason and Emotion in Argumentation. In E. Weigand (ed.), *Emotion in Dialogic Interaction* (pp. 269–280). Amsterdam: John Benjamins.

Polanyi, Livia (1985). A theory of discourse structure and discourse coherence, In: *Proceedings of the 21st Annual Meeting of the Chicago Linguistics Society*. Chicago: University of Chicago, Dept. of Linguistics.

Prakken, Henry (2001). Modelling Reasoning about Evidence in Legal Procedure. In *Proceedings of the Eighth International Conference on Artificial Intelligence and Law* (pp. 119–128). New York: ACM Press.

Prakken, Henry (2005). Coherence and Flexibility in Dialogue Games for Argumentation. *Journal of Logic and Computation* 15(6): 1009–1040.

Prakken, Henry (2006). Formal Systems for Persuasion Dialogue. *The Knowledge Engineering Review* 21(2): 163–188.

Pugmire, David (1998). *Rediscovering Emotion*. Edinburgh: Edinburgh University Press.

Pugmire, David (2005). *Sound Sentiments. Integrity in the Emotions*. Oxford: Clarendon Press.

Pustejovsky, James (1991). The Generative Lexicon. *Computational Linguistics* 17(4): 409–441.

Pustejovsky, James (1998). The Semantics of Lexical Underspecification. *Folia Linguistica* 32 (3–4): 323–347.

Quintilian, Maximus Fabius (1996). *Institutio Oratoria*. Translated by H. E. Butler. Cambridge, MA: Harvard University Press.

Ranney, Frances (2005). *Aristotle's Ethics and Legal Rhetoric: An Analysis of Language Beliefs and the Law*. Farnham, UK: Ashgate Publishing.

Rebuschi, Georges & Tuller, Laurice (eds.) (1999). *The Grammar of Focus*. Amsterdam and Philadelphia: John Benjamins.

Rescher, Nicholas (1977). *Dialectics: A Controversy-Oriented Approach to the Theory of Knowledge*. Albany: State University of New York Press.

Rescher, Nicholas (2006). *Presumption and the Practices of Tentative Cognition*. Cambridge: Cambridge University Press.

Rigotti, Eddo (1993). La sequenza testuale. *L'analisi linguistica e letteraria* 1: 43–148.

Rigotti, Eddo (1995). Verità e Persuasione. *Il nuovo areopago* 14(1): 3–14.

Rigotti, Eddo (1997). *Lezioni di Linguistica Generale*. Milano: CUSL.

Rigotti, Eddo (2005). Towards a Typology of Manipulative Processes. In Louis de Saussure & Peter Schulz (eds.), *Manipulation and Ideologies in the Twentieth Century: Discourse, Language, Mind* (pp. 61–83), Amsterdam: John Benjamins.

Rigotti, Eddo & Cigada, Sara (2004). *La comunicazione verbale*. Milano: Apogeo.

Rigotti, Eddo & Greco, Sara (2006). *Topics: The Argument Generator, Argumentum eLearning Module.* Available at www.argumentum.ch (accessed on 14 September 2011).

Rigotti, Eddo & Rocci, Andrea (2006). Denotation vs. Connotation. In K. Brown (ed.), *Encyclopedia of Language and Linguistics*, 2nd Edition (pp. 1–9), Oxford: Elsevier.

Robinson, Daniel (1947). *The Principles of Reasoning: An Introduction to Logic and Scientific Method.* New York: D. Appleton – Century.

Robinson, Richard (1950). *Definition.* Oxford: Clarendon Press.

Ruiter, Dick (1993). *Institutional Legal Facts: Legal Powers and Their Effects.* Dordrecht: Kluwer.

Russell, Bertrand (1905). On Denoting. *Mind* 14(4): 479–493.

Sager, Juan (2000). *Essays on Definition.* Amsterdam: John Benjamins.

Sandulescu, George (1975). Presupposition, Assertion, and Discourse Structure. In N. E. Enkvist and V. Kohonen (eds.), *Reports on Text Linguistics: Approaches to Word Order* (pp. 197–214.). Åbo: Åbo Akademi, No. 8.

Schaff, Philip (1894). *A Religious Encyclopaedia or Dictionary of Biblical, Historical, Doctrinal, and Practical Theology*, 3rd ed., Vol. 1. New York: Funk & Wagnalls.

Schiappa, Edward (1989). The Rhetoric of Nukespeak. *Communication Monographs* 56(3): 253–272.

Schiappa, Edward (1993). Arguing about Definitions. *Argumentation* 7(4) appeared in issue 4: 403–417.

Schiappa, Edward (1996). Towards a Pragmatic Approach to Definition: 'Wetlands' and the Politics of Meaning. In A. Light & E. Katz (eds.), *Environmental Pragmatism* (pp. 209–230). New York: Routledge.

Schiappa, Edward (1998). Constructing Reality Through Definitions: The Politics of Meaning. A lecture presented for the Center for Interdisciplinary Studies of Writing and the Composition, Literacy, and Rhetorical Studies Minor, Speakers Series 11.

Schiappa, Edward (2003). *Defining Reality. Definitions and the Politics of Meaning.* Carbondale and Edwardsville: Southern Illinois University Press.

Schwarz, David (1977). On Pragmatic Presupposition. *Linguistics and Philosophy* 1(2): 247–257.

Seager, Robin (2001). Maiestas in the Late Republic: Some Observations. In John Cairns and Olivia Robinson (eds.), *Critical Studies in Ancient Law, Comparative Law and Legal History* (pp. 143–153). Oxford and Portland, OR: Hart Publishing.

Searle, John (1969). *Speech Acts: An Essay in the Philosophy of Language.* London: Cambridge University Press.

Searle, John (1979). *Expression and Meaning: Studies in the Theory of Speech Acts.* Cambridge: Cambridge University Press.

Searle, John, & Vanderveken, Daniel (1985). *Foundations of Illocutionary Logic.* Cambridge: Cambridge University Press.

Searle, John, & Vanderveken, Daniel (2005). Speech Acts and Illocutionary Logic. In Daniel Vanderveken (ed.), *Logic, Thought and Action* (pp. 109–132). Dordrecht: Springer.

Seuren, Peter (2000). Presupposition, Negation and Trivalence. *Journal of Linguistics* 36(2): 261–297.

Seuren, Peter (2010). *The Logic of Language: Language from Within (vol. 2).* Oxford: Oxford University Press.

Simons, Greg (2006). The Use of Rhetoric and the Mass Media in Russia's War on Terror. *Demokratizatsiya* 14(4): 579–600.

Simons, Herbert, Morreale, Joanne, & Gronbeck, Bruce (2001). *Persuasion in Society.* Thousand Oaks, CA: Sage.

Sinclair, John (2004). *Trust the Text: Language, Corpus and Discourse.* London and New York: Routledge.

Sini, Francesco (1991). *Bellum Nefandum. Virgilio e il problema del "diritto internazionale antico."* Sassari: Libreria Dessì Editrice.

Soames, Scott (1982). How Presuppositions Are Inherited: A Solution to the Projection Problem. *Linguistic Inquiry* 13(3): 483–545.

Soboleva, Anita (2007). *Topical Jurisprudence: Reconciliation of Law and Rhetoric.* In A. Wagner, W. Werner, & D. Cao (eds.), *Interpretation, Law and the Construction of Meaning* (pp. 49–63). Amsterdam: Springer.

Solomon, Robert (2003). *Not Passion's Slave: Emotions and choice.* New York: Oxford University Press.

Soter, Steven (2007). What is a Planet? *Scientific American*, 296(1): 34–41.

Stalnaker, Robert (1970). Pragmatics. *Synthese* 22(1–2): 272–289.

Stalnaker, Robert (1974). Pragmatic Presuppositions. In M. Munitz & P. Unger (eds.), *Semantics und Philosophy* (pp. 197–214). New York: New York University Press.

Stalnaker, Robert (1998). On the Representation of Context. *Journal of Logic, Language, and Information* 7(1): 3–19.

Stalnaker, Robert (2002). Common Ground. *Linguistics and Philosophy* 255–6: 701–721.

Stati, Sorin (1990). *La Transphrastique.* Paris: PUF.

Stebbing, Susan (1933). *A Modern Introduction to Logic.* New York: Humanities Press.

Stevenson, Charles Leslie (1937). The Emotive Meaning of Ethical Terms. *Mind* 46(181): 14–31.

Stevenson, Charles Leslie (1938a). Persuasive Definitions. *Mind* 47(187): 331–350.

Stevenson, Charles Leslie (1938b). Ethical Judgments and Avoidability. *Mind* 47 (185): 45–57.

Stevenson, Charles Leslie (1944). *Ethics and Language.* New Haven, CT: Yale University Press.

Strawson, Peter (1950). On referring. *Mind* 59(235): 320–344.

Strawson, Peter (1952). *Introduction to logical theory.* London: Methuen.

Strawson, Peter (1971). Identifying Reference and Truth-Values. In *Logico-Linguistic Papers* (pp. 75–95). London: Methuen.

Stump, Eleonore (1989). *Dialectic and Its Place in the Development of Medieval Logic.* Ithaca, NY: Cornell University Press.

Sutton, Clive (1996). The Scientific Model as a Form of Speech. In G. Welford, J. Osborne, & P. Scott (eds.), *Research in Science Education in Europe* (pp. 143–152). London: Falmer Press.

Sweitzer, Brett G. (1997). Implicit Redefinitions, Evidentiary Proscriptions, and Guilty Minds: Intoxicated Wrongdoers after *Montana v. Egelhoff. University of Pennsylvania Law Review* 146(1): 269–321.

Szwedek, Aleksander (1980). Lexical Cohesion in Text Analysis. *Papers and Studies in Contrastive Linguistics* 11: 95–100.

Tadros, Victor (2006). Rape Without Consent. *Oxford Journal of Legal Studies* 26(3): 515–543.

Tannen, Deborah (1985). Silence: Anything but. In D. Tannen & M. Saville-Troike (eds.), *Perspectives on Silence* (pp. 93–111). Norwood, NJ: Ablex.

Tarello, Giovanni (1980). *L'interpretazione della legge*. Milano: Giuffrè.

Taylor, Bryan (1998). Nuclear Weapons and Communication Studies: A Review Essay. *Western Journal of Communication* 62(3): 300–315.

Tellegen-Couperus, Olga (2003). *Quintilian and the Law: The Art of Persuasion in Law and Politics*. Leuven: Leuven University Press.

Temkin, Jennifer (2002). *Rape and the Legal Process*. Oxford: Oxford University Press.

Thayer, James (1898). *A Preliminary Treatise on Evidence at the Common Law*. Boston: Little Brown.

Tiersma, Peter (1999). *Legal Language*. Chicago: University of Chicago Press.

Toulmin, Stephen (1950). *An Examination of the Place of Reason in Ethics*. Cambridge: Cambridge University Press.

Toulmin, Stephen (1958). *The Uses of Argument*. Cambridge: Cambridge University Press.

Ullman-Margalit, Edna (1983). On Presumption. *The Journal of Philosophy* 80(3): 143–163.

Van Dijk, Teun (1977). *Text and Context: Explorations in the Semantics and Pragmatics of Discourse*. New York: Longman.

Van Eemeren, Frans & Grootendorst, Rob (1984). *Speech Acts in Argumentative Discussions*. Dordrecht: Foris.

Van Eemeren, Frans & Grootendorst, Rob (1987). Fallacies in Pragma-Dialectical Perspective. *Argumentation* 1(3) appeared in issue 3: 283–301.

Van Eemeren, Frans & Grootendorst, Rob (1992). *Argumentation, Communication, and Fallacies. A Pragma-Dialectical Perspective*. Hillsdale, NJ: Erlbaum.

Van Eemeren, Frans & Grootendorst, Rob (2004). *A Systematic Theory of Argumentation: The Pragma-Dialectical Approach*. Cambridge: Cambridge University Press.

Vanderveken, Daniel (1990). *Meaning and Speech Acts: Principles of Language Use*. Cambridge: Cambridge University Press.

Vanderveken, Daniel (2001). Illocutionary Logic and Discourse Typology. *Revue internationale de philosophie* 216(2) appeared in issue 2: 243–255.

Vanderveken, Daniel (2002). Universal Grammar and Speech Act Theory. In D. Vanderveken & S. Kubo (eds.), *Essays in Speech Act Theory* (pp. 25–62). Amsterdam: John Benjamins.

Vendler, Zeno (1964). The Grammar of Goodness. *The Philosophical Review* 72(4): 446–465.

Verheij, Bart (2003). Dialectical Argumentation with Argumentation Schemes: An Approach to Legal Logic. *Artificial Intelligence and Law* 11(2–3): 167–195.

Victorini, Caius Marius (1997). *Liber de definitionibus: eine spätantike Theorie der Definition und des Definierens* (mit Einleitung, Übersetzung und Kommentar von A. Pronay). Frankfurt: Peter Lang.

Viskil, Erick (1994). *Definieren – Een bijdrage tot de theorievorming over het Opstellen Van Definities*. Amsterdam: IFOTT.

Von Fintel, Kai (2008), What is Presupposition Accommodation, Again? *Philosophical Perspectives* 22(1): 137–170.

Von Wright, Georg (1972). On So-Called Practical Inference. *Acta Sociologica* 15(1): 39–53.

Walton, Douglas (1980). Omissions and other negative actions. *Metamedicine* 1(3): 305–324.

Walton, Douglas (1984). *Logical dialogue-games and fallacies*. Lanham, MD: University Press of America.

Walton, Douglas (1993). The Speech Act of Presumption. *Pragmatics & Cognition* 1(1): 125–148.

Walton, Douglas (1996). *Argumentation Schemes for Presumptive Reasoning*. Mahwah, NJ: Erlbaum.

Walton, Douglas (1997). *Appeal to Pity*. Albany: State University of New York Press.

Walton, Douglas (1998). *The New Dialectic. Conversational Contexts of Argument*. Toronto: University of Toronto Press.

Walton, Douglas (1999). Dialectical Relevance in Persuasion Dialogue. *Informal Logic* 19(2): 119–143.

Walton, Douglas (2000). *Scare Tactics: Arguments that Appeal to Fear and Threats*. Dordrecht: Kluwer.

Walton, Douglas (2002). *Legal Argumentation and Evidence*. University Park: Pennsylvania State University Press.

Walton, Douglas (2004). *Abductive Reasoning*. Tuscaloosa: University of Alabama Press.

Walton, Douglas (2005a). Deceptive Arguments Containing Persuasive Language and Persuasive Definitions. *Argumentation* 19(2): 159–186.

Walton, Douglas (2005b). *Argumentation Methods for Artificial Intelligence in Law*. Berlin: Springer.

Walton, Douglas (2006). How to Make and Defend a Proposal in Deliberation Dialogue. *Artificial Intelligence and Law* 14(3): 177–239.

Walton, Douglas (2007a). *Media Argumentation*: Dialectic, Persuasion, and Rhetoric. Cambridge: Cambridge University Press.

Walton, Douglas (2007b). The Speech Act of Clarification in a Dialogue Model. *Studies in Communication Sciences* 7(2): 165–197.

Walton, Douglas (2007c). The Three Bases for the Enthymeme: A Dialogical Theory. *Journal of Applied Logic* 6(3): 361–379.

Walton, Douglas & Godden, David (2005). Persuasion Dialogue in Online Dispute Resolution. *Artificial Intelligence and Law* 13(2) appeared in issue 2: 273–295.

Walton, Douglas & Krabbe, Erik (1995). *Commitment in Dialogue. Basic Concepts of Interpersonal Reasoning*. Albany: State University of New York Press.

Walton, Douglas & Macagno, Fabrizio (2005a). Common Knowledge and Argumentation Schemes. *Studies in Communication Sciences* 5(2): 1–22.

Walton, Douglas & Macagno, Fabrizio (2005b). Common Knowledge in Legal Reasoning about Evidence. *International Commentary on Evidence* 3(1): 1–42.

Walton, Douglas, Reed, Chris, & Macagno, Fabrizio (2008). *Argumentation Schemes*. New York: Cambridge University Press.

Weaver, Richard (1953). *The Ethics of Rhetoric*. Chicago: Henry Regnery.

Weiler, Michael (1992). The Reagan Attack on Welfare. In Michael Weiler & Pearce W. Barnett (eds.), *Reagan and Public Discourse in America* (pp. 227–250). Tuscaloosa: University of Alabama Press.

Weiler, Michael & Barnett, Pearce (1992). *Reagan and Public Discourse in America*. Tuscaloosa: University of Alabama Press.

Weinreb, Lloyd. (2005). *Legal Reason: The Use of Analogy in Legal Argument*. Cambridge: Cambridge University Press.

Welsh, Paul (1957). On the Nature of Inference. *The Philosophical Review* 66(4): 509–524.

Whitehead, Alfred & Russell, Bertand (1927). *Principia Mathematica* (3rd ed.). Cambridge: Cambridge University Press.

Wigmore, John (1940). *A Treatise on the Anglo-American System of Evidence in Trials at Common Law: Including the Statutes and Judicial Decisions of all Jurisdictions of the United States and Canada* (2nd ed.). Boston: Little Brown.

Williams, Glanville (1983). *Textbook of Criminal Law*. London: Stevens.

Wilson, Deidre (1975). *Presupposition and Non-Truth-Conditional Semantics*. London: Academic Press.

Windes, Russell & Hastings, Arthur (1965). *Argumentation and Advocacy*. New York: Random House.

Woods, John & Walton, Douglas (1978). Arresting Circles in Formal Dialogues, *Journal of Philosophical Logic* 7(1): 73–90.

Woolf, Amy (2004). Nonstrategic Nuclear Weapons. Washington, DC: CRS Report for Congress, RL32572. Retrieved from www.digital.library.unt.edu/govdocs/crs/data/2004/upl-meta-crs-6104/meta-crs-6104.ocr (accessed on 11 October 2011).

World Commission on Environment and Development (1987). *Our Common Future*. New York: Oxford University Press.

Wüest, Jakob (2001). La gerarchia degli atti linguistici nel testo. *Studies in Communication Sciences* 1(1): 195–211.

Zarefsky, David (1998). Definitions. In J. F. Klumpp (ed.), *Argument in a Time of Change: Definitions, Frameworks, and Critiques* (pp. 1–11). Annandale, VA: National Communication Association.

Zarefsky, David (2004). Presidential Rhetoric and the Power of Definition. *Presidential Studies Quarterly* 34(3): 607–619.

Zarefsky, David (2006). Strategic Maneuvering through Persuasive Definitions: Implications for Dialectic and Rhetoric. *Argumentation* 20(4): 399–416.

Zarefsky, David, Miller-Tutzaur, Carol, & Titzuar, Frank E. (1984). Reagan's Safety Net for the Truly Needy: The Rhetorical Uses of Definition. *Communication Studies* 35(2): 113–119.

Zeevat, Henk (1992). Presupposition and Accommodation in Update Semantics. *Journal of Semantics* 9(4): 379–412.

Index

Aarnio, Aulis, 118
Abductive argumentation
  argumentation scheme for
    (AS 17), 202
  critical questions for, 203
Abortion dispute, 2–3, 219
Acceptability, 156
Accident, 89–90
  defined, 92
Accommodation, 176
  boundaries of, 176
  conditions of, 176–78
  dimensions of, 178–79
Ad hominem argument, 124
  argumentation scheme for
    (AS15), 198
Ad hominem attack, 201
Ad misericordiam argument, 14
Adams et al. v. United States, 101
Administrative work, definition of, 101
Advancing a definition, 253–54
Adversary exaggeration (case 12), 15
Airbag safety (persuasion dialogue 1
  & 3), 209–10, 217–18, 222–26,
  234–40
Allegation, implicit, 201
Ambiguity, 115, 119, 193
  avoidance, 140
  definitional, 145, 150
  dialectical, 146, 150, 153
  fallacy of, 16
  interpretive, 123
  introducing, 149, 185, 258

pragmatic, 126, 139, 145, 149,
  152, 154
semantic, 154
word, 185
Amplificatio, 6
Amplification, 6–7, 9, 13, 66–67,
  69, 96
Amplitude, redefined, 151
Amsterdam mode of
  argumentation, 216
Anscombre, Jean-Claude, 45–46
Appeal to the definition, 73
Argument, 131, 212
  emotionally loaded, 239
  weaker, 216
Argument by definition, 17–19,
  110, 154
Argument by redefinition, 205
Argument from analogy, 94
Argument from authority, 95, 123
Argument from classification, 87,
  106, 126
Argument from consequences, 135
  from negative consequences,
    argumentation scheme for
    (AS 6), 56
  from positive consequences,
    argumentation scheme for
    (AS 5), 56
Argument from criteria to verbal
  classification, 76, 81
  argumentation scheme for, 75
  critical questions for, 76

Argument from definition,
  argumentation scheme for, 80
Argument from definition to
    characteristics, 77
  critical questions for, 76
Argument from definition to verbal
    classification, 238, 244
  critical questions for, 239
  negative form, 238
  premises, 230
Argument from distress
  argumentation scheme for
    (AS16), 201
Argument from values, 51
  complex, 54
  controversial decisions in, 57
  from negative value, 57
    argumentation scheme for
      (AS 2), 52
  from positive values, 57
    argumentation scheme for
      (AS 1), 52
Argument from verbal
    classification, 238
  argumentation scheme for (AS 3), 54
  critical questions for, 54, 84
  negative form, argumentation
    scheme for, 238
Argument proceeding from disjunctive
    syllogism, 243
Argumentation,
  chain of, 234
  ulterior moves, 74
Argumentation frameworks
  value-based, 237
Argumentation schemes, 51, 221
Argumentative bridge, 182–83
Argumentative structuralism, 45
Aristotle, 47
  assessment of a definition, 93
  concept of good, 48
  conflicting values, 50
  definition advancement, 96
  definition by contrary, 100–02
  definitory, 88
  naming, 7
  on classification, 55, 89–92

  on emotions, 64–65
  words, use of, 8
Armed conflict, definition of, 114–15
Artificial intelligence, 208
Artificial means, definition of, 99
Asher, Nicholas, 177
Assumptions, implicit, 224
Attack, 185, 257
Austin, John, 130–31, 157, 163, 179

Backup evidence question, 95
Bag, definition of, 85–86
Baker, Michael, 71
Begging the question, 19
Belligerent, omitted definition of, 115
Bench-Capon, Trevor, frameworks, 237
Binding, 142
Bird, definition of, 120
Blackguard, quasi-definition of, 26–27,
    62, 194–95
Body, definition of, 73
Brave New World example, 30–31
Burden of disproving, 258
Burden of persuasion, 213–15
Burden of producing evidence, 182
Burden of proof, 209
  global, 213
  increasing, 150
  positive, 215
  requirement met, 231
  rules for, 210
  shifting, 149, 151, 205, 249, 250,
    255, 264
Burden of questioning, 216
Burden of rejection, 189, 192
Bureaucratization, concealment in, 20
Burgess-Jackson, Keith, 44
Buridan's ass dilemma, 57
Bush, George, President 41, 43–44, 113,
    127, 145, 151, 190

Caepio, Quintus, 149–51
Calboli Montefusco, Lucia, 7
Carter, President (case 19), 20
Character attack, 197–98
Chesterton, Gilbert, 1
Cicero, Marcus Tullius, 8, 13

on redefinitions, 10–11, 147–48
Circular reasoning, 77
Circumstances, 50
Claims, descriptive, 34
Clarification, 126
　imposing, 120
　usage, 132
Classification,
　definition requirement of, 80
　principle of, 74–75, 78
Closing statement: presupposing
　　defendant's crimes (case
　　28), 200
Closing statement: presupposing
　　defendant's guilt (case 31), 203
Closing statement: presupposing facts
　　and relationships (case 30), 202
Closing statement: presupposing
　　witness's bad character (case
　　29), 201
Cmi Corp. v. Gurries, 119
Coherence relation, 161, 165
Cohesion relation, 158, 171
Commitment, 55, 72, 81
　consistency of, 227
　dark-side, 188, 217, 219, 226, 232,
　　240, 242, 255, 258
　explicit, 211, 242
　implicit, 211
　　brought to light, 242
　inserting, 204, 262
　light-side, 226, 240
　new object of, 122
　retraction of, 211
　rules, 230
　set by redefinition, 144
　structures of, 131
Commitment store
　alteration of, 187
　hearer's, 253
　interlocutor, 191
　new commitments inserted, 205
Common ground, 34, 39, 72, 121, 154
　proposition as part, 173
Common knowledge, 35, 41, 172
　commitment based on, 218
　questioned, 183

Common Knowledge Base, 210,
　227–28, 241
Commonwealth v. Andrews, 200
Commonwealth v. Rodriguez, 202
Communicative rule, 140–41, 210
Concealing words (case 15), 18
Conclusion
　ethical, 34
　global, 218
　implicit, 190
　intermediate, 203
　provisional, 181
Conditions
　preparatory, 129, 132
　propositional, 129, 179
　sincerity, 129, 144, 179
Congruity theory, 39
Conjugations, 159, 169
　emotive, 2
Conjectura, 9
Connective, 160, 161
　logical–semantic, 165
Connector, 169–70, 204
　explicit, 170
　implicit, 170
　unexpressed, 170
Connotation, 38–39, 45, 179, 235
Connotative semiotic code, 39
Consequence, 170
Consumption, definition of, 102
Contrariness, 184
Cornificius, 9
Critical discussion
　goal of, 215
　stages of, 72, 216
　　argumentation stage, 72, 216
　　concluding stage, 72, 216
　　confrontation stage, 72, 216
　　opening stage, 72, 216
　　rules, 216–17
　theoretical model of, 72
Cross-examination
　enhancing evidential weight
　　(case 27), 199
　presupposing facts not in evidence
　　(case 26), 199
Culture redefinition, 22–23, 49, 109

Damasio, Antonio, 65
Decision making, 47, 51, 56, 63, 65,
    68, 124
Declaration, 55
Declaring a definition, 256–57
Defeasible, 82
Definiendum, 43, 119, 137, 146, 245, 249
    negation of, 247
Definiens, 105
Defining
    act of, 129
    dark side of, 262
Defining for committing, 257
Defining for informing, 254–55
Defining for reminding, 255–56
Definite description, 87, 245
Definition, 44, 89–90
    abandoned, 121
    absence of, 116
    acceptability of, 78, 108
    arbitrary, 73
    argumentative effectiveness of, 87
    argumentative instruments, 74
    as a commitment, 113
    as a standpoint, 112, 121, 122, 134,
        145, 254
    circularity in, 97
    classifying, 110
    commissive, 139
    commitment based, 81
    communicative goal basis, 9
    correctness of, 93
    described, 69–71
    essence expression of, 93
    essential, 94, 107
    goal supported, 44
    implicit, 76, 125, 152, 154
    imposing, 118–20, 137, 256–57
    logical properties of, 86–87
    new, 11
    obscure, 94
    omitted, 124–25, 140, 258, 262
    persuasive, 22, 113
        analyzed, 194
        fallacious, 205
        historical origins, 71
        purpose, 23, 71
    purpose of, 70, 121
    reminding of a, 134
    requirements for advancing, 96
    rules for assessment of, 93
    shared, 111
        qualified, 146–47
    stipulative, 118
    to elicit a value judgment, 11
    types of, 85–86, 131
    unshared, 20, 253
Definitions by contrary, 100
Definition by entomology, 87, 246
Definition by enumeration, 99
Definition by essential parts, 247
Definition by example, 251–52
Definition by exclusion, 99
Definition by genus and difference,
    105
Definition by illustration, 99
Definition by integral parts, 104
Definition by material parts, 105, 248
Definition by metaphor, 244, 252–53
Definition by negation, 249–50, 253
Definition by negation of the contrary,
    97, 101–02
Definition by operation, 248–49
Definition by parts, 87, 243
Definition by property, 245
Definition by species, 97
Deliberate homicide, 144
Democracy, 21
    emotively loaded, 32
    redefinition of, 16
    quasi–definition, 27
Desire, 65
Dialogical presuppositions–explicit
        connectors (case 7), 170
Dialogue,
    basic types of, 213
    implicit grounds of, 155
    Platonic, 217
    rules, 209, 210, 230
        defining moves, 213
        commitment rules, 230
        speech act rules, 229
        win–loss rules, 231
Dialogue game, 212

conditions set, 173
continuation of, 175
limits of, 259
rules, 243
system DC, 220–21, 223
system H, 220–21, 226, 229
Difference, concept of, 104
Disputable definition (case 13), 15
Dispute, 215–16
Distorting reality (case 16), 18
Double direction of fit, 130
Douglas–Lincoln debate, 58–60
Ducrot, Oswald, 45–47, 163–64, 172–73, 175, 179, 191

E-humanities (persuasion dialogue 2), 232–34
Eco, Umberto, 39
Embezzlement defined, 87–88
Emotion, 66
aroused, 200
conceal effect of, 7
motivational, 64
reaction to appraisals, 63
triggers, 15
types
anger, 65
fear, 64–65
Emotive words,
amplification aspect of, 15
deceptive, 8
dimensions of, 32, 260
directing attitudes, 31
dynamic, 32
effect of, 261
illicit use of, 12
reasoning dimension of, 8
Emotive language, 235
error of, 56
reality distortion, 16, 261
triggers, 56, 260
Emotive meaning, 22
Enemy combatant redefinition, 25, 74, 127, 140, 145
Endoxa, 57, 81
semantics, 105
unaccepted, 195

Enthymeme, 219
Epistemic weight
altered, 202
Essential definition, 89
Essex v. Millikan, 197
Ethical judgment (*see also* Value judgment), 32–35
twofold dimension, 31
Ethical words (*see also* Emotive words), 31–32, 56
influential force, 35
prescriptive effect, 38
Ethotic argument
argumentation scheme for (AS 14), 198
Eugenics, definition of, 186
Euphemism, 16–17, 88
reality concealing, 18
Euthanasia, definition of, 185–86
Evidence,
lack of, 181–82
weight of, 203
Exclusion, 152
Explanation, 170, 233–34
Exploitation of definitions, 16
Expressive dimension of language, 38

Facts, unwarranted, 14
Faithful, 195–96
Fascism (case 18), 19
Fillmore, 41
Finis, 9
Focus (*see also* Rheme), 160, 166, 168
Fodor, Jerry, 40
Folly (case 7), 12
Frames, Charles, 41–43
reshaped, 44
Framing, 19
Framing events (case 17), 19
Free (animals), persuasive definition of, 219
Freedom (from fear), 193
redefinition of, 24–25, 147
Freeman, James, 183
Frege, Gottlob, 39, 156, 159
Full employment, definition of, 80

Generalization,
  qualified, 81
  universal, 81
Generic terms (case 14), 17
Genus, 89–90, 96, 243
  clarified, 102
  of actions, 147
Genus difference definition, 243,
      244, 245
  dialectical structure of, 244
Goal, 51, 212
  of life, 50
  rhetorical, 197
  ultimate, 211
Good
  semantic analysis of, 31, 37
  uses of, 55–59
Grice, Paul, 164
  maxims, 46
Grimaldi, William, 7
Grimes, Joseh, 165
Grootendorst, Rob, 72

Habitudo, 79
Halldén, Sören, 63
Hamblin, Charles, 156, 210–11
  system H, 220–21, 226, 229
Hamdi v. Rumsfeld, 127–28
Hare, Richard, 34–35, 47, 63
Hart, Herbert, defeasible reasoning, 82
Hastings, Arthur, 74–78, 81
Hasty judgment, 200
Hjelmslev, Louis, 39
Homeland security
  definition of, 114
  redefinition of, 114
Hostilities,
  implicit redefinition of, 116, 142
  omitted definition of, 115, 140, 145
  presupposed definition of, 192–93
Huxley, Aldous, 30–31, 109
Hybris (case 2), 7–8

Illocutionary force, 129
Implicit acts, 128, 142
Implicit criteria of classification, 54
Implicit definition, 258–59
Implicit reasoning from analogy, 244

Inappropriate words (case 20), 21
Indignant language, 6, 7, 14, 15
Inductive definition, 250–51
Inference, 181
  based on the genus, 105
  defaults, 221
  evaluative, 33–34
  principle of, 46, 178, 181
  semantic connection, 79
  structure of, 83
Inferences based on analogy, 94
Informer citizen (case 6), 12
Informing, act of, 132
Innuendo, 171
Insurance example, 75–76
Interlocutor
  experiences of, 67
  presuppositions of, 131
  shared definitions of, 111
Interpretation, 257
Inter-sentence presuppositions–implicit
      connectors (case 8), 171
Inter-sequences presuppositions–
      connectors (case 5), 169
Inter-sequences presuppositions–
      disjunctive questions
      (case 6), 169
Introducing manipulation
      (manipulation case 1), 182–83
Invitation to respond, 130
Ivey v. State (Case 1), 6, 200

Jackendoff, Ray, 160
John's children are all bald
      example, 157
Judgment, 204
Jumping to conclusion,
      201
Just war, defined, 111, 132–33

Katz, Jerrold, 40
Kauffeld, Fred, 188
Kempson, Ruth, 172
Kennedy, John F., President
      quarantine, 17, 20
Kienpointner, Manfred 79–80, 82
King of France is bald example,
      155–56, 158, 160, 164

Knowledge
  gap of, 180
  presumption of, 180
Krabbe, Erik 215, 242
  dialectical model, 187
  dialogue games, 212

Lakoff, George, 161
Language, 44
  connotative, 39
  denotative, 39
  emotively loaded, 207
  indignant, 6–7, 14
  loaded, 6
Lascarides, Alex, 177
Legal definitions,
  dangerous, 98
  dimension (narrow), 10
  implicit redefinition, 126
  statutory, 118–20, 122–23, 137, 142, 193
  unexpressed, 125
Legal dialogues, 118
  burden of persuasion (*see also* Burden
    of persuasion), 213
  evidential burden of proof, 213
  shifting evidential burdens, 99
Legal institution, 128–29
  artificial intelligence in law, 208
  character evidence, 176
  contracts, 42, 120
  crimes, definitions of, 9
  cross-examination, 196–97, 199
  definitions in, 133, 137
  discourse, 167
    not allowed, 196
  drawing inferences, 168
  evidence, 202
    altered, 199
  inference, 202
  language in, 123
  lawyers, purpose of, 66
  legal framework, 182
  natural, 156
  omissions in, 123
  testimony, inconsistent, 203
  ultimate *probandum*, 211
  witness commitment, 197
  witness examination, 197

Lewis, David, 176
Lincoln/Douglas debate, 58–60
Linguistic code, 30
Linguistic structure, 39
Loaded question, 197
  as an attack, 197–98
Loaded words, 13, 16, 169, 237

Macagno, Fabrizio, 83
Mackenzie, Jim, DC system, 220–21, 223
Man, definition of, 85–86, 90, 92–93
Man who was beaten (case 10), 14
Manipulation, 144
Manipulation (case 1), 185
Manipulation (case 2), 186
Manzoni's I *promessi sposi*, 188–89
Marriage
  quasi–definition of, 60–61
  redefinition of, 43–44
Marrying Sean example, 52–53
Maxim , 84
Meaning, 44
  emotive, 45
Meta-dialogue, 205, 241–42, 258–59
Metaphor, 20, 67, 94
Mill, James, 73
Modus ponens, 243–44
  deductive, 79, 221
  defeasible (DMP), 81–82, 221, 223
  strict (SMP), 221, 223
Modus tollens, 27, 97
Monopoly
  classification of, 74–75
  definition of, 85
Montana v. Egelhoff, 126
Moral judgments, 55
Motor Grader, definition of, 119
Muscarello v. United States, 122
Myers, Norman, 23

Naming, 7, 28–29
Natural man, redefinition of, 38
Nature of man, redefinition of, 194
Needy, defined, 116, 140, 151–53
Nicomachean Ethics, 36, 47–48
No consent, definition of, 98
Nouns, 40
Null or empty direction of fit, 130

Obama, Barack, President, 132, 134–35,
137, 142, 147, 175, 191–93, 254
Administration letter to Congress,
116, 194
commitment to Geneva Conventions,
190–91
In a Dark Valley, 113
Nobel Peace Prize Address, 94,
111–12, 132, 174, 189, 193–94
quasi-definition of war, 62
Olbrechts-Tyteca, Lucie, 57, 74, 237
Old maid example, 22
Omission, 117
described, 123
Omission of a definition, 123
Opponent, 212
Organized criminal group, definition
of, 121, 135
Orwell, George, 6, 16, 18, 19, 21
Oxymoron, 43

Padilla v. Bush, 128
Padilla v. Rumsfeld, 25
Paris (case 3), 8
Peace, 193
definition of, 94, 111
implicit redefinition of, 112
meaning attacked, 146
redefinition of, 134, 254
Peacekeeping missions, definition of,
99–100
People v. Aguirre, 169
People v. Dalessandro, 203
People v. Enis, 197
People v. Giangrande, 199
People v. Terry, 200
Perelman, Chaim, 57, 74, 237
Persecution, redefinition of, 127, 144
Personal enemy, redefinition of, 11
Persuasion, 152
act of, 21
Persuasion dialogue
arguments in, 72
basic requirements, 211–12
basis of, 212
collaborative, 232
common goals in, 214

described, 207, 208
dynamic, 210
goal of, 208
historical origins, 208
rules of, 230–31
speech acts in, 229–30
stages of, 213–15
systems, 220
Persuasion dialogue, types
CB, 211, 220–21, 229
CBV, 211, 226, 227
CBVK, 229
Common Knowledge Persuasion
(CKP), 208, 227–28, 239
adversarial, 231
rules for, 229, 236, 237
shifting from, 241
speech acts allowed, 210, 240–41
successful, 232
summarized, 240
permissive persuasion dialogue
(PPD), 215
rigorous persuasion dialogues
(RPD), 215
Persuasive tactic, 25
Plantin, Christian, 65
Pleading a cause, 21
Political realm
definitions in, 135, 153
persuasion in, 117
Practical reasoning, 55
argumentation scheme for
(AS 4), 55–56
Pragma-dialectical model, 242
Pragma-dialectical school, 213
Prakken, Henry 208
Predicate,
abstract structure of, 39
contrary, 101
functional, 160
limits of, 166
motivational, 161
presupposing function, 174
rhetorical, 165
semantic, 158–59, 163, 166, 178
Premises, 51
definitional, 55

endoxical, 55, 82, 84
factual, 244
false, 178
Presumption
    described, 182
    epistemic rules of, 183
    of meaning, failure of, 192
    pragmatic, 181
    principle of, 185
    rhetorical effect of, 190
    rules, 181
Presumptive reasoning,
    conclusion of, 187
    described, 181
    fallacious, 186, 187
    unacceptable, 194, 195
Presupposing new definitions
        (manipulation case 2), 186–87
Presupposition, 156, 263
    act of, 155
    breadth of, 164
    commitment, 189
    controversial, 190, 191
    described, 172, 180
    dialogical modification by, 175
    explanation of, 172
    evaluated, 183–84
    failure of, 156, 157, 183–84
    foundations of discourse, 166
    historical origins of, 155
    logical, 157
    manipulation by, 200
    possibility of, 178
    pragmatic function of, 157,
        166, 196
    presumptive reasoning
        conclusion, 204
    reasonableness, 179
    rhetorically bound, 177
    semantic, 159
    speaker's intentions and, 172
    strategies of, 169
    triggers, 167
    two-fold effect of, 191
    utterance, 176
    weak, 190
Private enemy, redefinition of, 11

Property, 89–90
Proponent, 212
Proposition, acceptability of, 178, 227
Prosecutor v. Al Bashir, 21

Qualification, 14
Quantification, 159
    universal, 78, 79, 83
Qualitas, 9
Quasi-definition, 26, 194
    explicit, 62
    subtlety of, 27
Question, 131
    answered, 130
Quintilian, Maximus Fabius, 10, 13, 66–67
    on definitions, 9

R. v. Buzzanga and Durocher, 9
R. v. Robertson, 99
Rape, definition of, 44
Reagan, Ronald, President, 116, 140,
        151–52
Reality,
    altered, 204
    defined, 9, 70
    distortion, 69
    hiding, 185
Reason, 34
Reasoning,
    defeasible, 82
    default, 29
    implicit patterns of, 47
    rhetorical, 10
Reasoning from authority
    argumentation scheme for
        (AS 9), 95
    critical questions for, 95
Reasoning from classification, 57,
        78–79, 108
    argumentation scheme for
        (AS 10), 97–98
Reasoning from/to classification of a
        definition
    altered, 261
    argumentation scheme for
        (AS 13) 106
    critical questions for, 107

Reasoning from classification of an entity, argumentation scheme for (AS 12), 106

Reasoning by definition, indefeasible, 73

Reasoning from defeasible classification, argumentation scheme for (AS 7), 83

Reasoning from example, argumentation scheme for (AS 11), 100

Reasoning from metaphysical definitions, argumentation scheme for (AS 8), 94

Reasoning from values, 44

Reasoning in ignorance, 182

Rebuttal, 185, 190, 243
 burden of, 188

Redefinition, 262
 advancing, 126
 controversial, 109
 described, 44
 effectiveness of, 205
 effects on interlocutors, 44
 ethical terms, 22, 24
 implicit, 25, 115, 144, 147, 150, 192, 264
  power of, 26, 128, 153, 192, 262–63
 imposing, 126
 of values, 194
 political, 1
 presuppose, 171, 185, 205
 redirection of, 31
 reminding effect of, 147
 strategies of, 13

Reed, Chris, 83

Refutation, 262
 strategies of, 244

Regina v Ojibway, 120, 132–33

Reminding, 146

Request, 130

Rescher, Nicholas, 181–82

Rescission of a contract (case 22), 77

Retraction, problem of, 226

Rheme, 160
 opposed to theme, 167

Rhetoric, 6, 7, 50, 55, 64

Robinson, Richard, 76

Russell, Bertrand, 2

Sacrilege, definition of, 10

Sahi v. Gonzales, 126

Sanine, 194–95

Schiappa, Edward, 21, 44, 113, 154

School City of Gary v. Claudio, 199

Searle, John, 142, 179

Securities, definition of, 98

Security, redefinition of, 23

Seditious citizen (case 5), 10–11, 149

Semantic structure of predicates values, 41

Sentence presupposition–infra-sentence syntactic predicates (case 4), 168

Sentence presupposition–predicates (case 2), 167

Sentence presupposition–predicates (verbs and nouns) (case 1), 167

Sentence presupposition–theme (case 3), 168

Sentences
 content, 45
 reasonableness, 184
 unsound, 162

Seventh commonplace (case 11), 14, 203

Silence, 140
 as a speech act, 117

Slavery, definition of, 95

Soames, Scott, 176

Socrates is a man syllogism 1, 2, 3, 78–79

Socrates is wise (case 4), 10

Speech acts
 binding, 139
 conditional failure of, 163
 conditions, 179
  felicity, 179
 context, 165
 cooperative, 164
 directions of fit, 130
 failure of, 175
 fundamental types, 129
 implicit, 142, 173

presuppositions of, 163
void, 172
Speaker, goal of, 13
Stalnaker, Robert, 171, 180
Stasis, 9
State v. Childs, 167
State v. Fisher, 118–19
State v. Frank, 168
Stevenson, Charles Leslie, 30–33, 49,
    107, 109
  descriptive meaning, 69
  dimension of meaning, 22, 34, 260
  emotive meanings, 38, 46–47, 63
  persuasive definitions, 22, 70, 263
  quasi-definition, 26
Strawson, Peter, 156, 160, 180
Sudan example, 21

Tactics, aggressive, 232
Taking for granted
  (*see also* Presupposition), 142
Teleological interpretation of action, 48
Term, redefining a, 205
Terrorism, quasi-definition of, 28
Terrorist, quasi-definition of, 27–28
Theme, opposed to rheme of, 168
To free, definition of, 97
Tolerance (case 21), 76–77
Topic, 160, 162, 166, 168, 172, 174,
    189–90, 200
Topics, 47, 50, 81, 89, 92, 94
Topoi, 46
Torture
  non-definition of, 124
  omitted definition of, 124–25, 140
Toulmin, Stephen, 33–34, 81
Translatio, 9
Treason, redefinition of, 150–51
Triggers, 177
  emotional, 13, 15, 56, 67, 69
  emotive language, 56
  value judgment, 14, 94
Trust, definition of, 246
Turn taking, 210
Tweety is a bird, 221

Undercut, witness testimony, 201
United States v. Beckman, 201

United States v. Dixon, 170
United States v. Stockdale, 167, 197
Universe of discourse (*see also* Common
  knowledge), 172

Vagueness, 25, 36, 77, 94, 116, 152, 193,
    205, 258
  historical origins, 150–51
Values, 64
  attack on, 62
  conflict of, 57–58
  conflicting negative and positive, 62
  controversial, 57
  disagreeing about, 54
  hierarchy of, 194
    alteration of, 63, 195
    conflict of, 59
  redefinition of, 194–196
  shared, 55
  system of, 41, 44, 60, 62, 64–65
  understanding, 54
Value-based practical reasoning,
  scheme for, 51
Value judgment, 33, 53, 55, 64, 66, 94,
    252, 262
  condition of hope, 63
  cultural basis of, 66
Van Eemeren, Frans, 72
Vanderveken, Daniel, 142, 179
Vehicles in the park example, 82
Vendler, Zeno, semantic analysis of
  good, 37
Verbs, 40
Verification, 156, 157, 158
Victorinus, Caius Marius, 84–85, 95, 99
Viskil, Erick, 110, 131
Void example, 73

Walton, Douglas, 81, 83, 211, 215
  commitment, 72
  dialectical models, 187
  dialogue games, 212
  omission, 123
  persuasion dialogue systems, 220
War, quasi-definition of, 61–62
Warrant, 81
  commonly shared, 34
We, definition of, 113

West v. Seabold, 170
Wetland, redefinition of, 257
Widow living freely (case 9). 13, 14
Wigmore, John, 182
Wisdom (case 8), 12
Wisdom, redefined, 12
Word-to-world direction of fit, 130
Words
  defined, 46
  descriptive meanings of, 36
  emotive
    force of, 107
    predicative dimension, 8–9
  ethical, 50
  inappropriate use of, 21

  loaded, 169
  persuasive aspect of, 16
  pivotal, 263
  reality describing, 28
  scene depiction ability of, 67
  semantic structure of, 42
  silent side of, 260, 264
  vague, 45
World of discourse, 174
  shared world, 174
  unknown world, 174
Written, definition of, 118

Zarefsky, David, 16–17, 20,
  26, 154